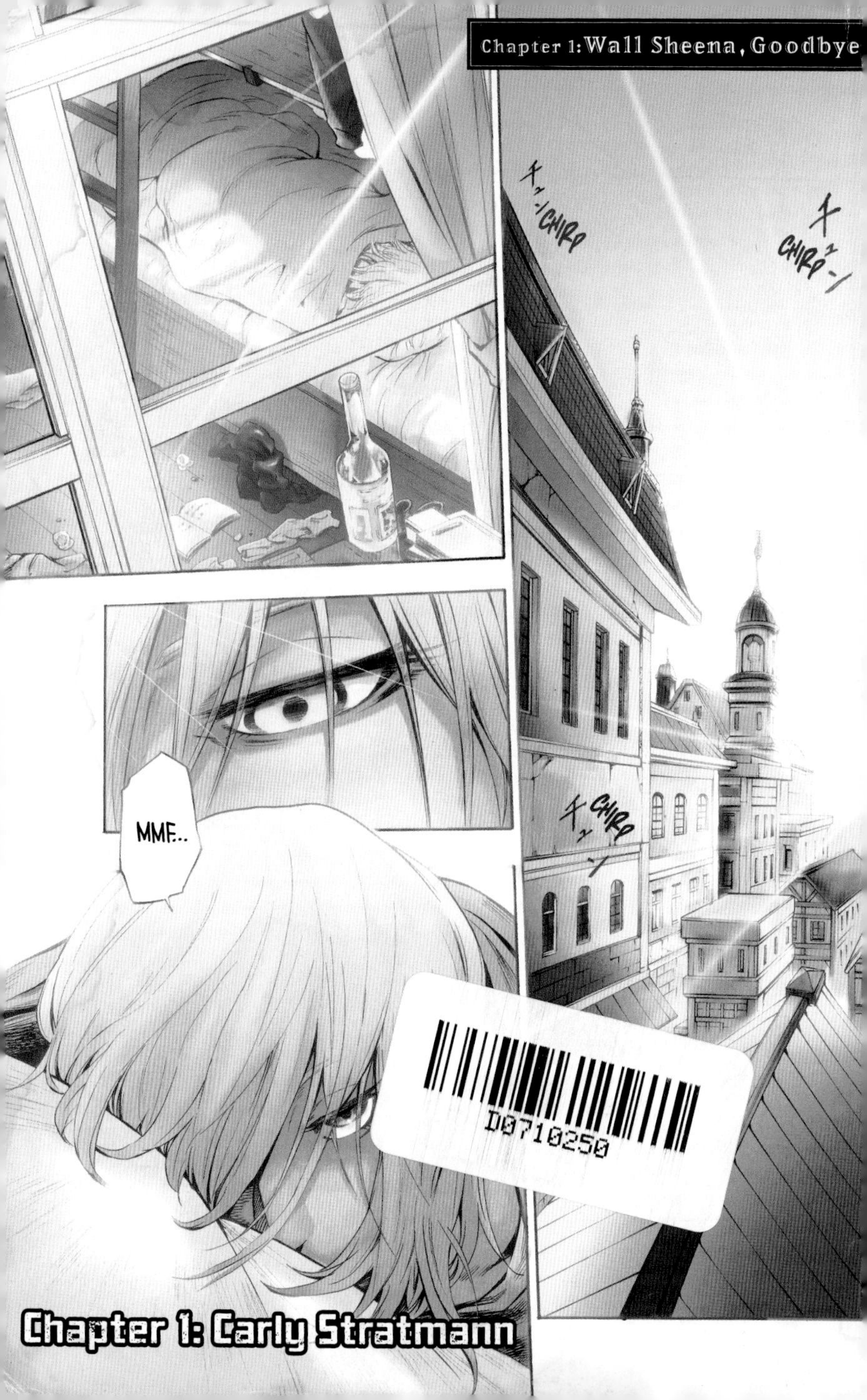
Chapter 1: Wall Sheena, Goodbye
CHIRP
CHIRP
MMF...
CHIRP
Chapter 1: Carly Stratmann

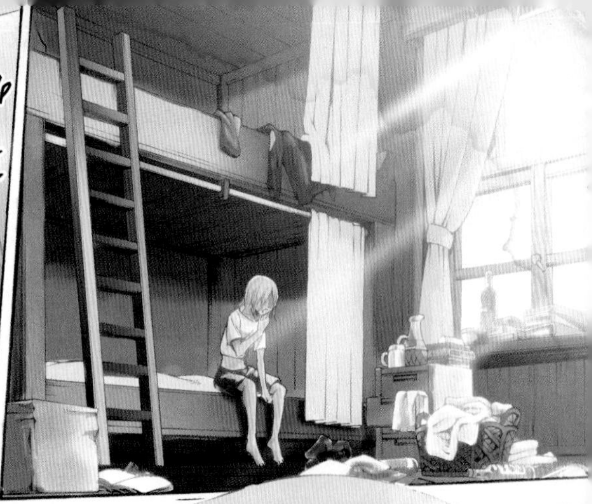
CHIRP
チュン

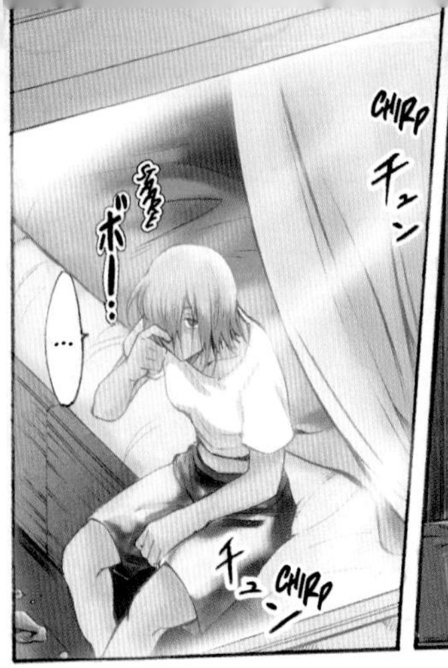
ボー…!!
...
チュン
CHIRP

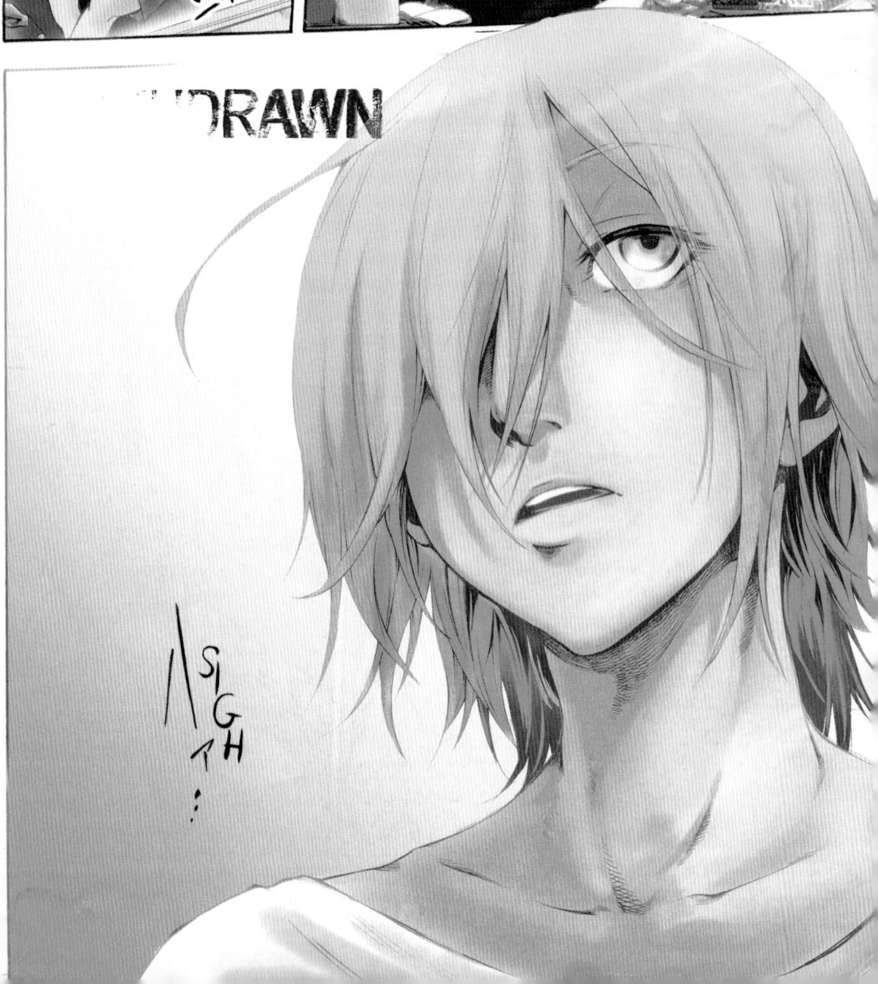
DRAWN
SIGH
ハア…

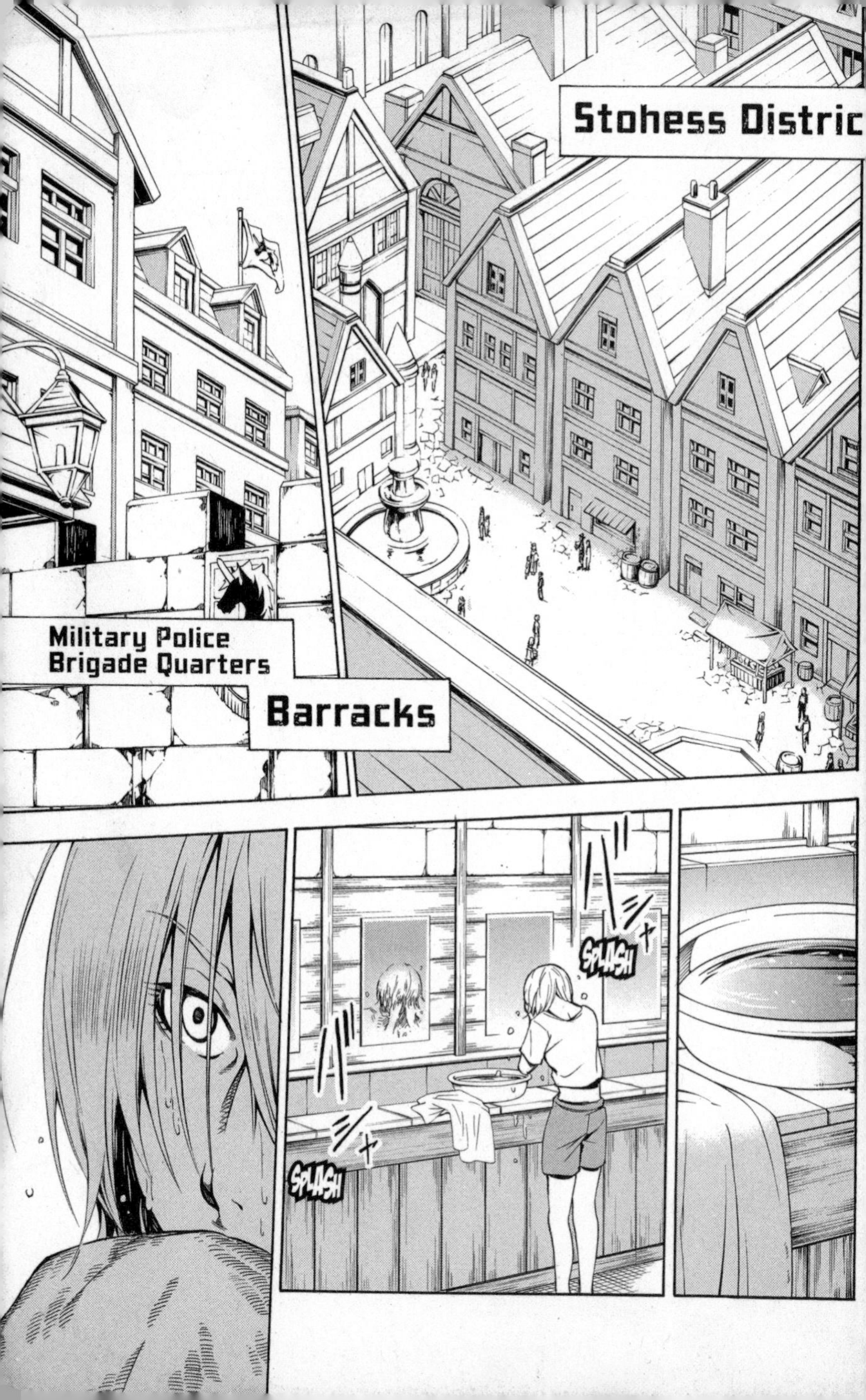
Stohess Distric
Military Police
Brigade Quarters
Barracks
SPLASH
SPLASH

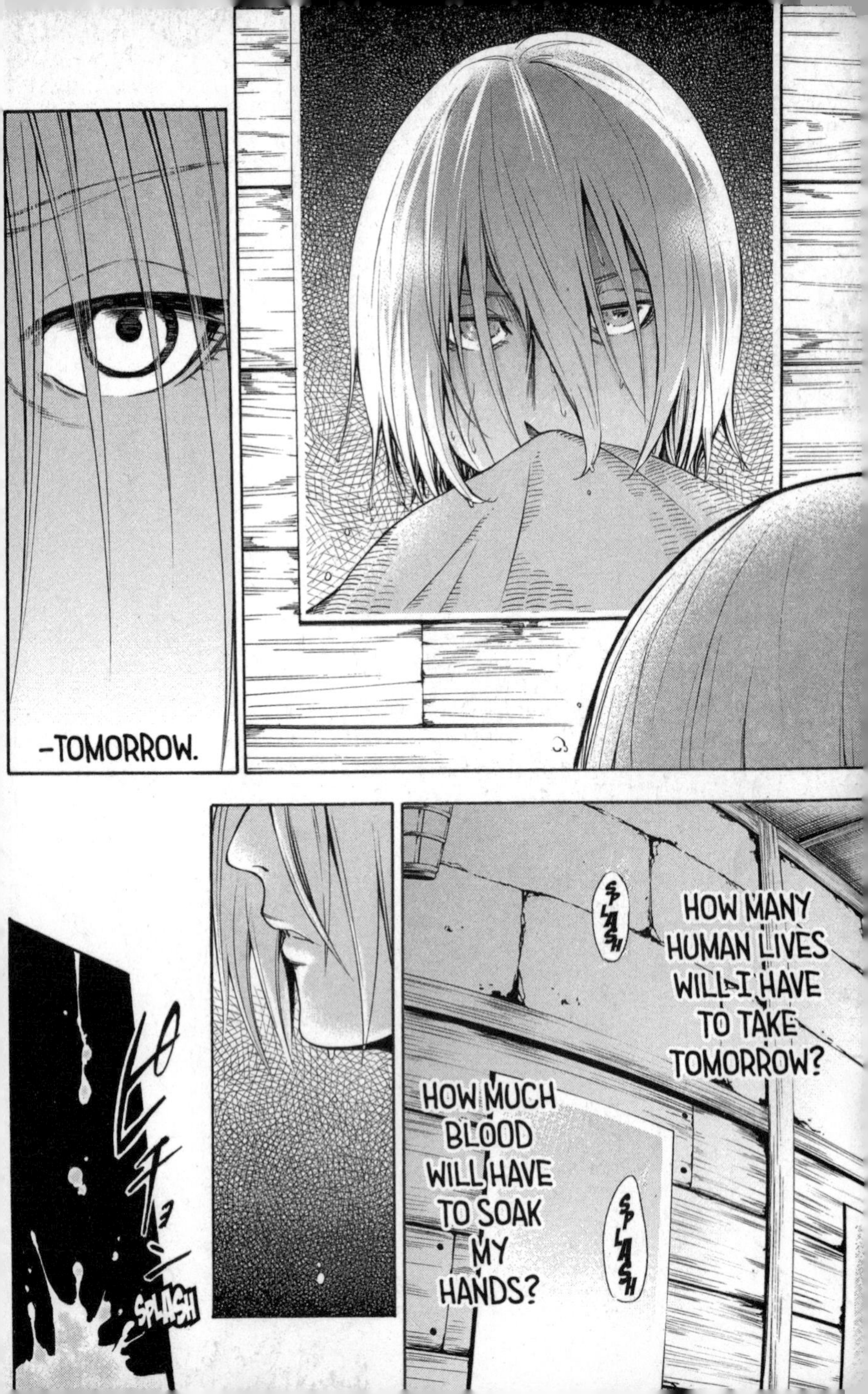
-TOMORROW.
SPLASH
HOW MANY HUMAN LIVES WILL I HAVE TO TAKE TOMORROW?
HOW MUCH BLOOD WILL HAVE TO SOAK MY HANDS?
SPLASH
SPLASH

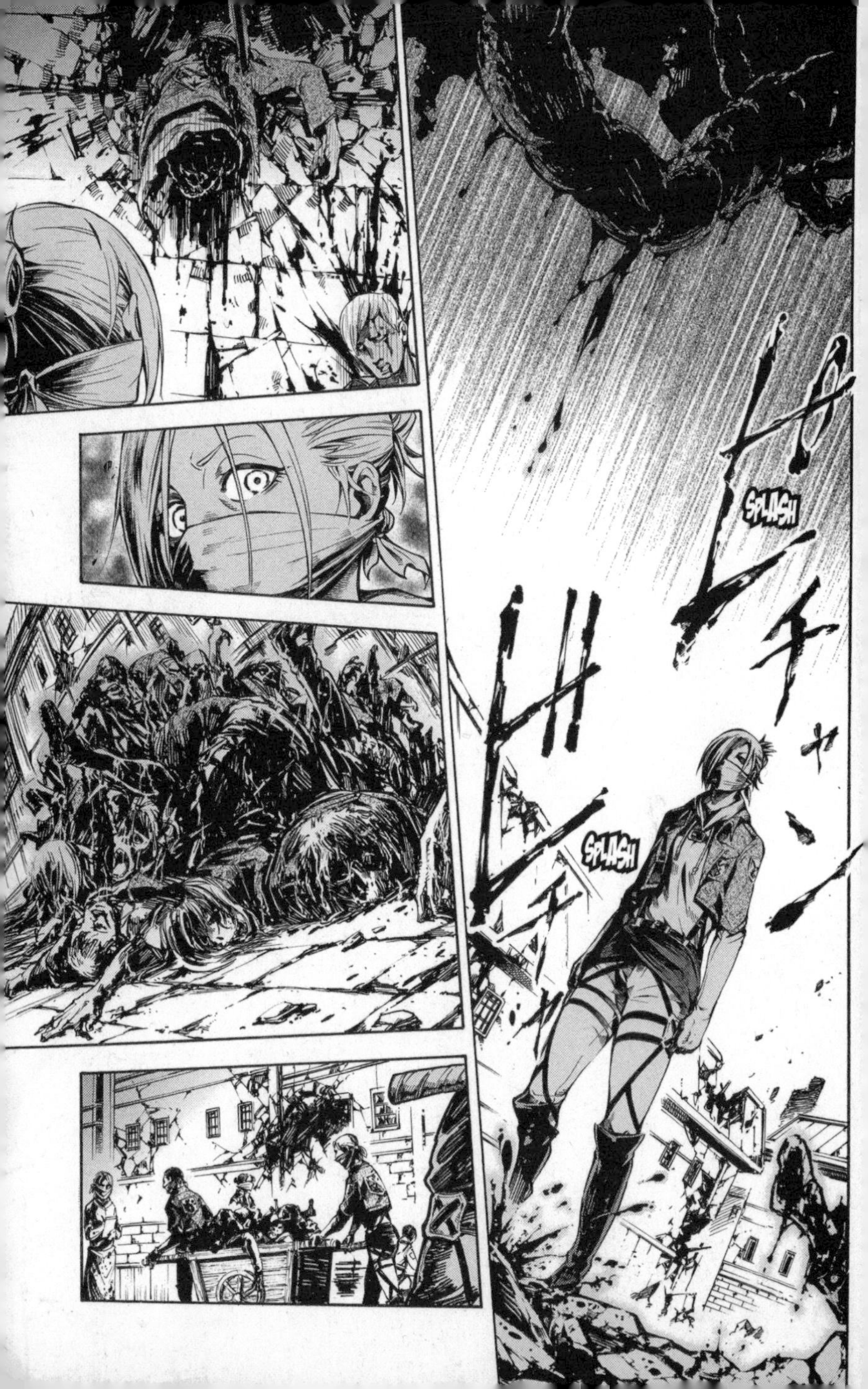
SPLASH
SPLASH

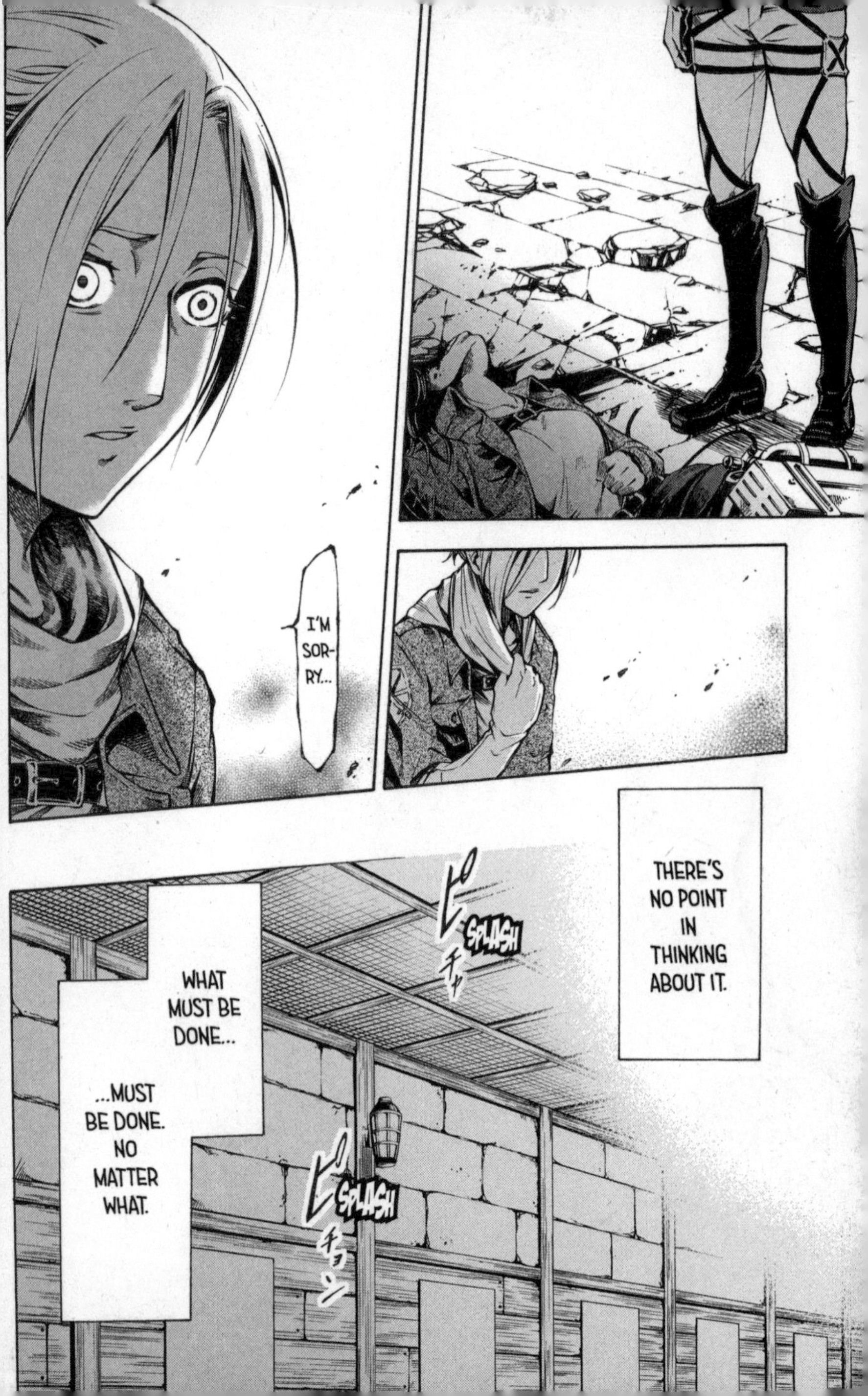
I'M SORRY...
THERE'S NO POINT IN THINKING ABOUT IT.
SPLASH
SPLASH
WHAT MUST BE DONE...
...MUST BE DONE. NO MATTER WHAT.

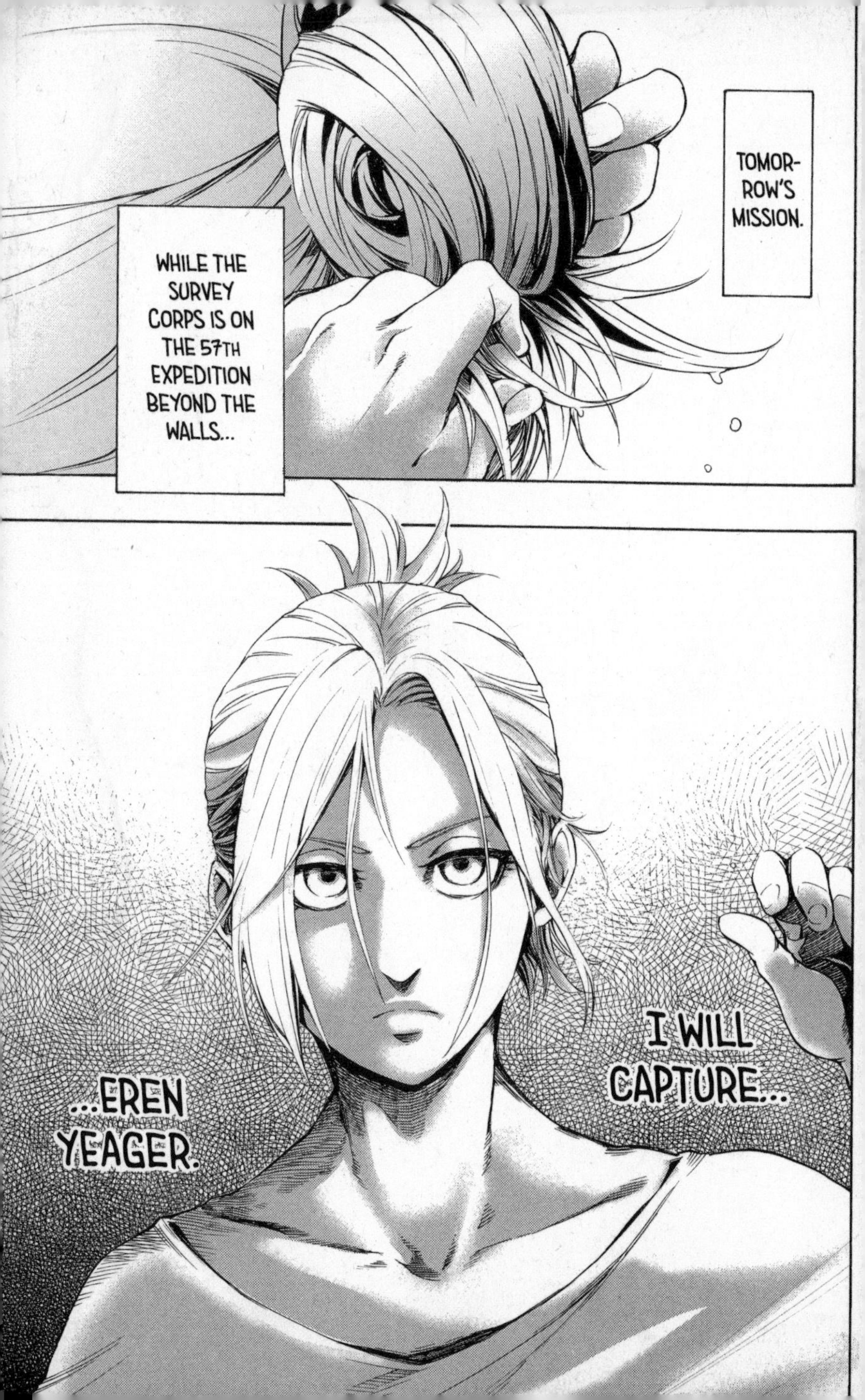
TOMOR-ROW'S MISSION.
WHILE THE SURVEY CORPS IS ON THE 57TH EXPEDITION BEYOND THE WALLS...
I WILL CAPTURE...
...EREN YEAGER.

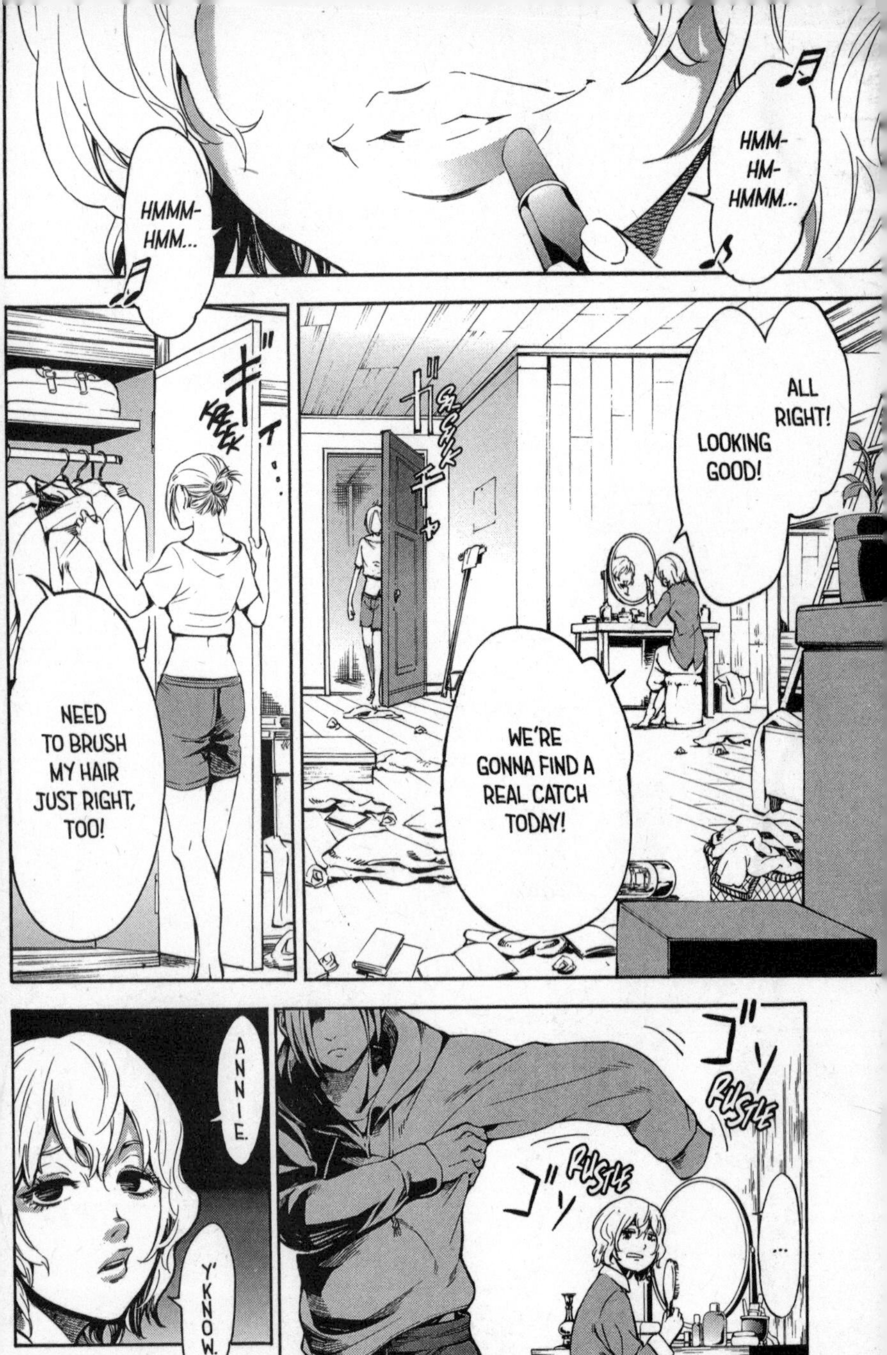
HMM-HM-HMMM...
HMMM-HMM...
ALL RIGHT! LOOKING GOOD!
GACHIK
WE'RE GONNA FIND A REAL CATCH TODAY!
KREEK
...
NEED TO BRUSH MY HAIR JUST RIGHT, TOO!
RUSTLE
RUSTLE
...
ANNIE.
Y'KNOW.

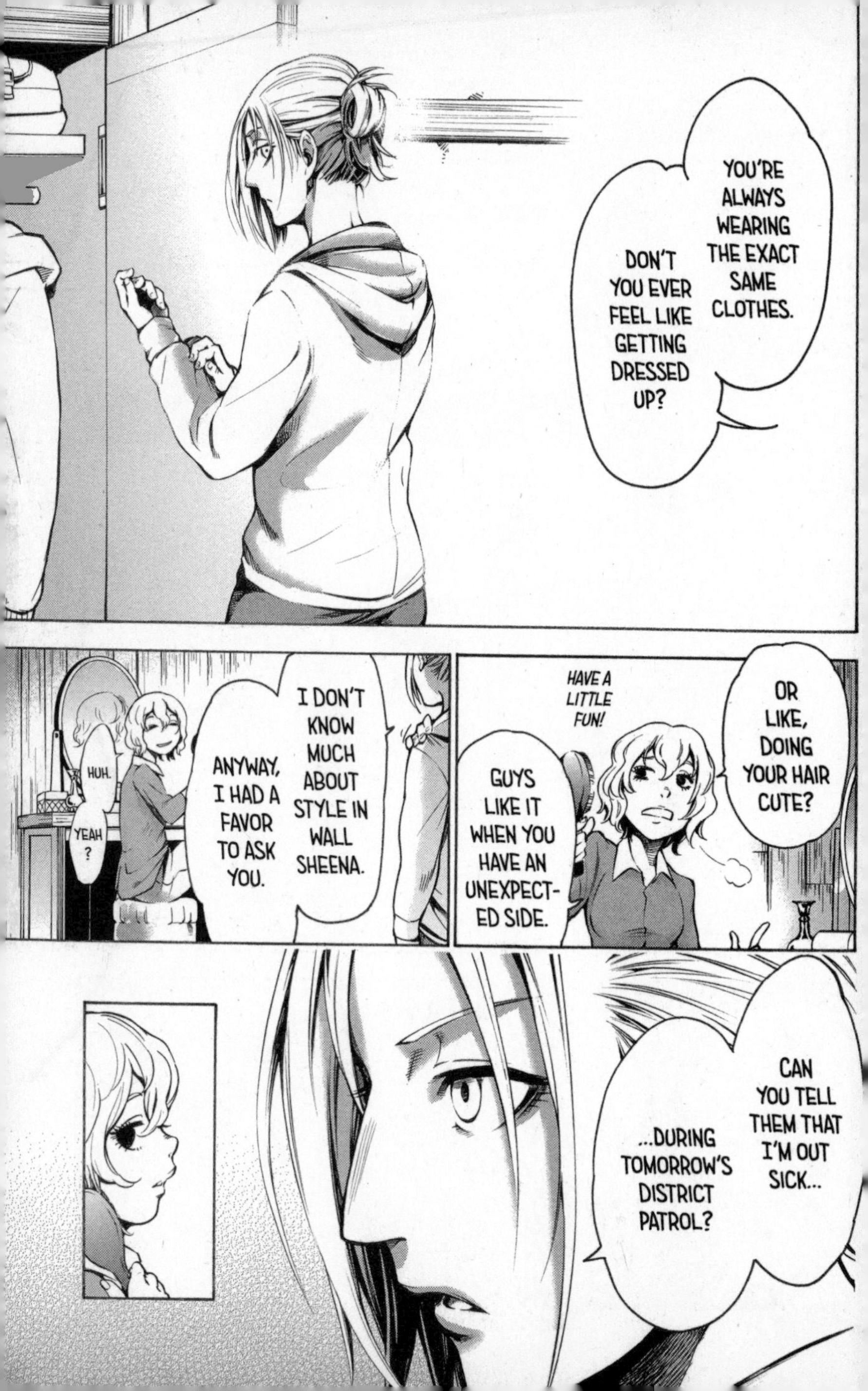
YOU'RE ALWAYS WEARING THE EXACT SAME CLOTHES. DON'T YOU EVER FEEL LIKE GETTING DRESSED UP?
OR LIKE, DOING YOUR HAIR CUTE?
HAVE A LITTLE FUN!
GUYS LIKE IT WHEN YOU HAVE AN UNEXPECT-ED SIDE.
I DON'T KNOW MUCH ABOUT STYLE IN WALL SHEENA.
ANYWAY, I HAD A FAVOR TO ASK YOU.
HUH.
YEAH?
CAN YOU TELL THEM THAT I'M OUT SICK... ...DURING TOMORROW'S DISTRICT PATROL?

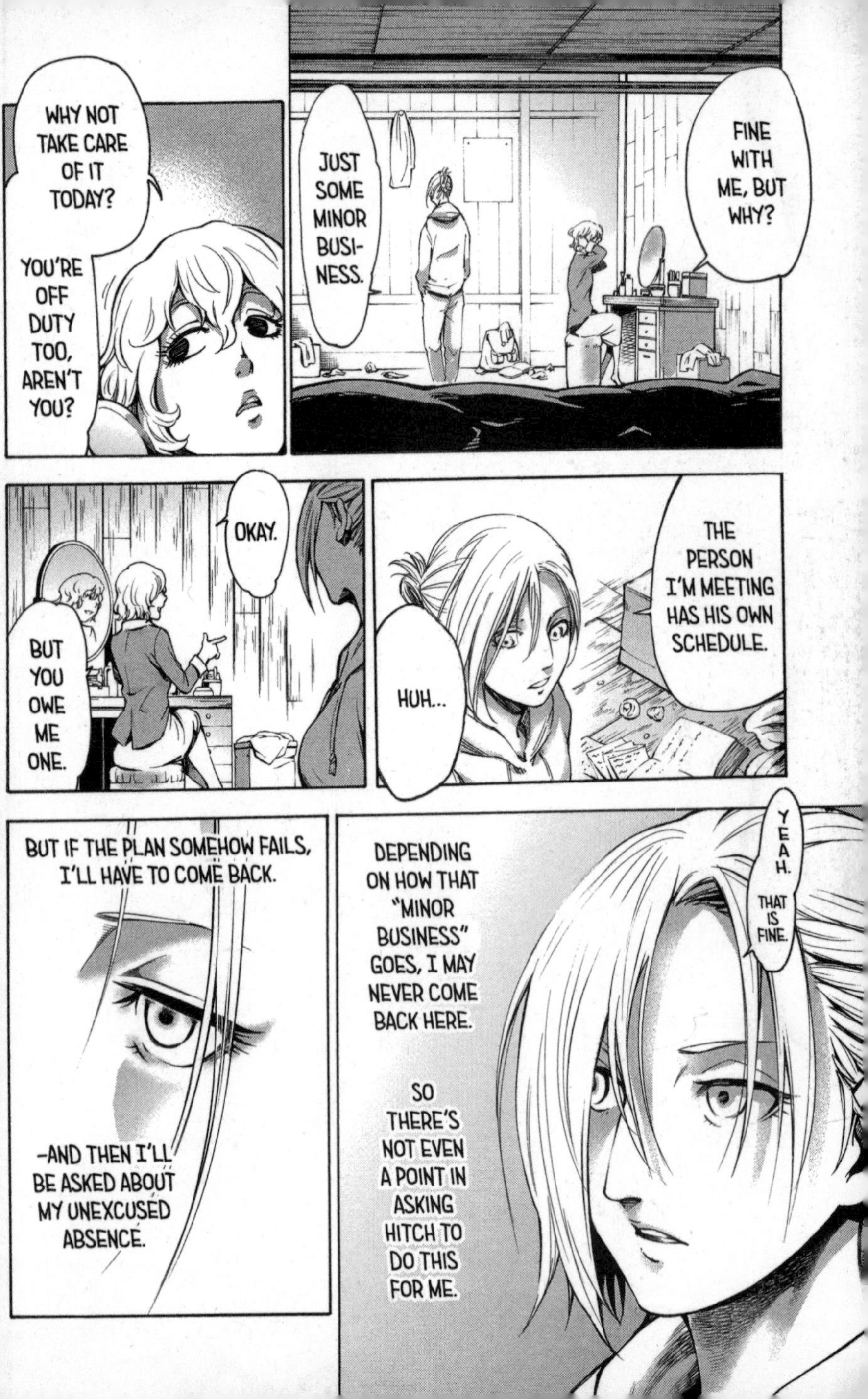
FINE WITH ME, BUT WHY?
JUST SOME MINOR BUSINESS.
WHY NOT TAKE CARE OF IT TODAY?
YOU'RE OFF DUTY TOO, AREN'T YOU?
THE PERSON I'M MEETING HAS HIS OWN SCHEDULE.
HUH...
OKAY.
BUT YOU OWE ME ONE.
YEAH.
THAT IS FINE.
DEPENDING ON HOW THAT "MINOR BUSINESS" GOES, I MAY NEVER COME BACK HERE.
SO THERE'S NOT EVEN A POINT IN ASKING HITCH TO DO THIS FOR ME.
BUT IF THE PLAN SOMEHOW FAILS, I'LL HAVE TO COME BACK.
-AND THEN I'LL BE ASKED ABOUT MY UNEXCUSED ABSENCE.

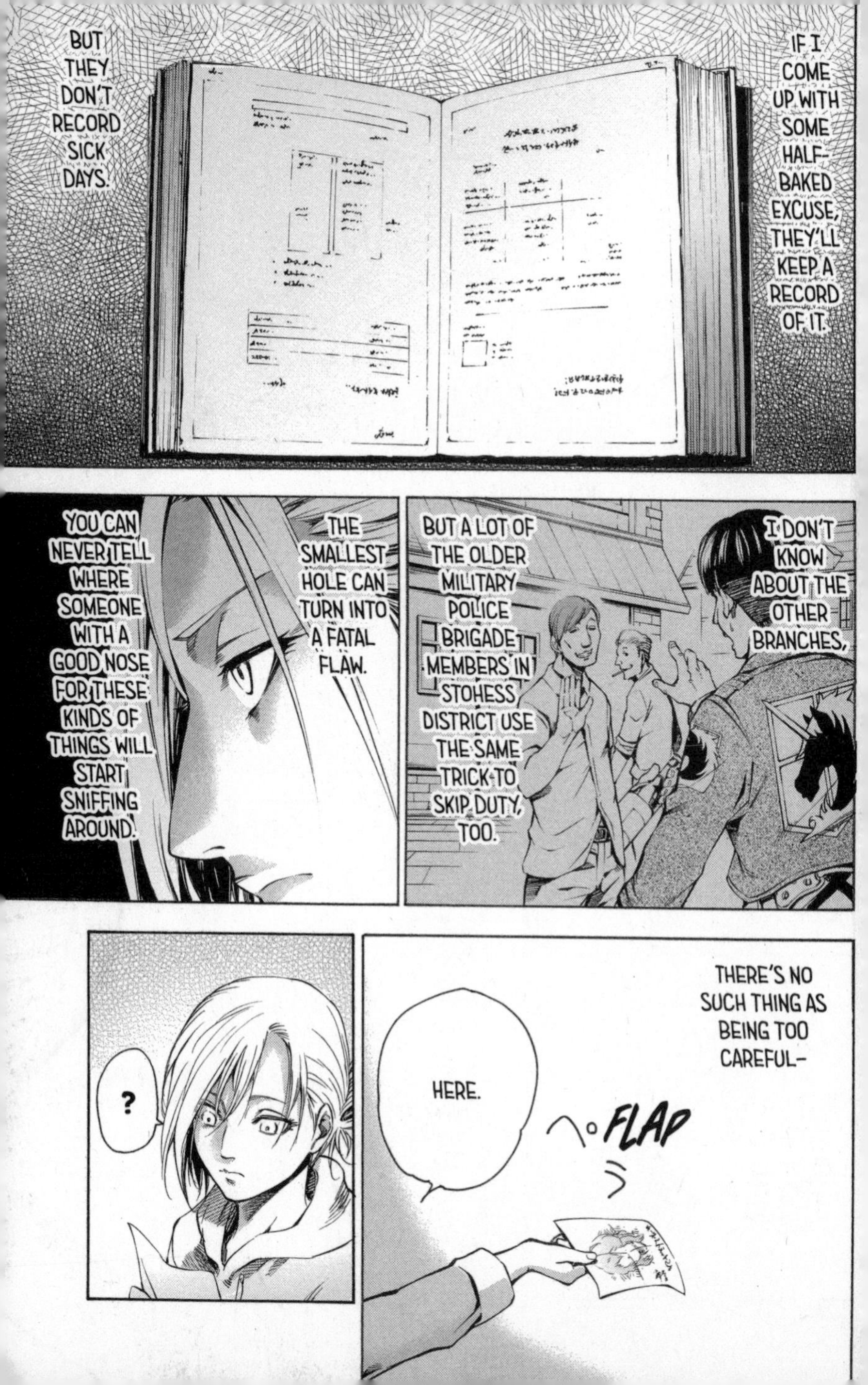
IF I COME UP WITH SOME HALF-BAKED EXCUSE, THEY'LL KEEP A RECORD OF IT.
BUT THEY DON'T RECORD SICK DAYS.
I DON'T KNOW ABOUT THE OTHER BRANCHES,
BUT A LOT OF THE OLDER MILITARY POLICE BRIGADE MEMBERS IN STOHESS DISTRICT USE THE SAME TRICK TO SKIP DUTY, TOO.
THE SMALLEST HOLE CAN TURN INTO A FATAL FLAW.
YOU CAN NEVER TELL WHERE SOMEONE WITH A GOOD NOSE FOR THESE KINDS OF THINGS WILL START SNIFFING AROUND.
THERE'S NO SUCH THING AS BEING TOO CAREFUL–
FLAP
HERE.
?

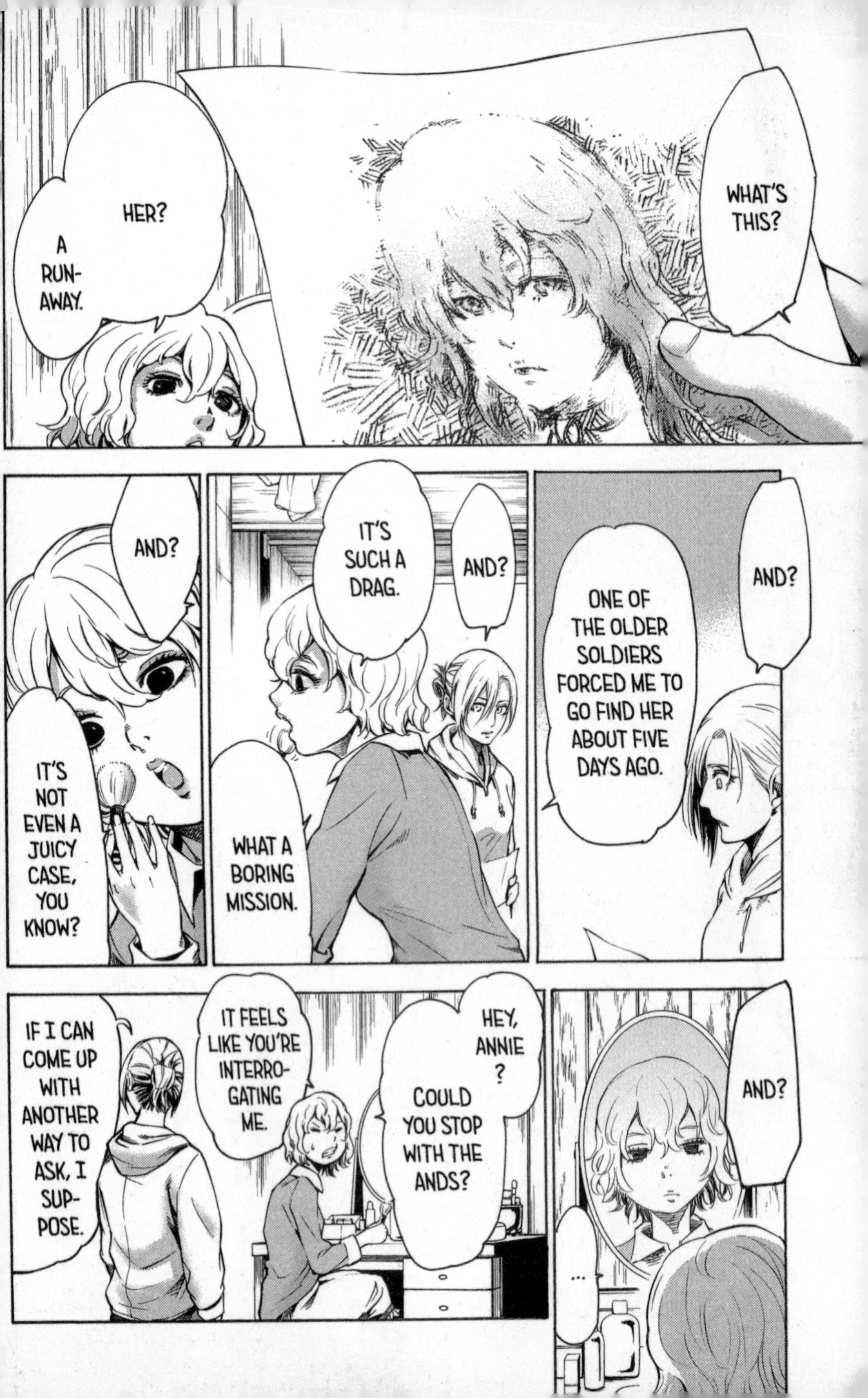
WHAT'S THIS?
HER?
A RUN-AWAY.
AND?
ONE OF THE OLDER SOLDIERS FORCED ME TO GO FIND HER ABOUT FIVE DAYS AGO.
AND?
IT'S SUCH A DRAG.
WHAT A BORING MISSION.
AND?
IT'S NOT EVEN A JUICY CASE, YOU KNOW?
AND?
...
HEY, ANNIE?
COULD YOU STOP WITH THE ANDS?
IT FEELS LIKE YOU'RE INTERROGATING ME.
IF I CAN COME UP WITH ANOTHER WAY TO ASK, I SUPPOSE.

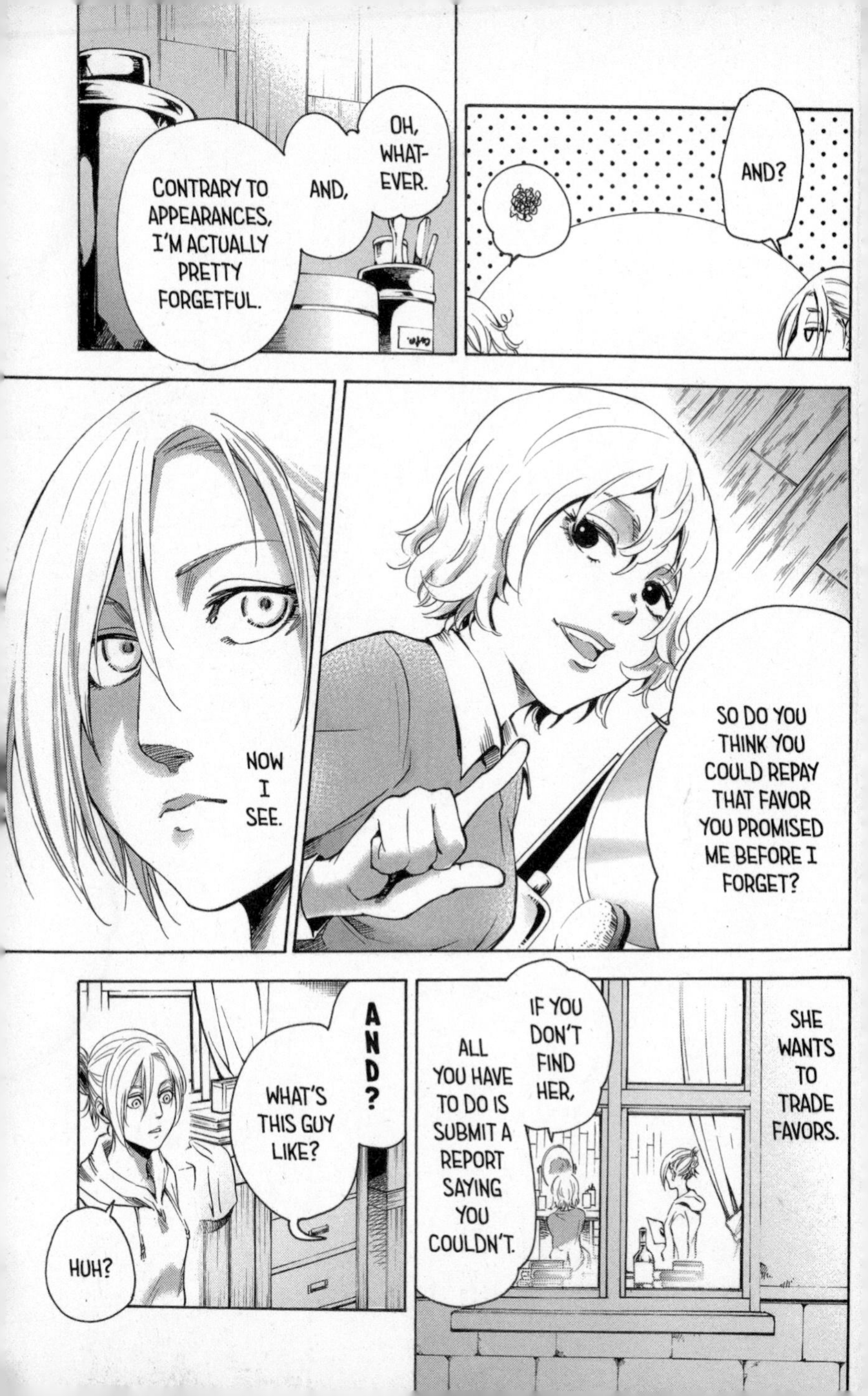
AND?
OH, WHATEVER.
AND,
CONTRARY TO APPEARANCES, I'M ACTUALLY PRETTY FORGETFUL.
SO DO YOU THINK YOU COULD REPAY THAT FAVOR YOU PROMISED ME BEFORE I FORGET?
NOW I SEE.
SHE WANTS TO TRADE FAVORS.
IF YOU DON'T FIND HER,
ALL YOU HAVE TO DO IS SUBMIT A REPORT SAYING YOU COULDN'T.
AND?
WHAT'S THIS GUY LIKE?
HUH?

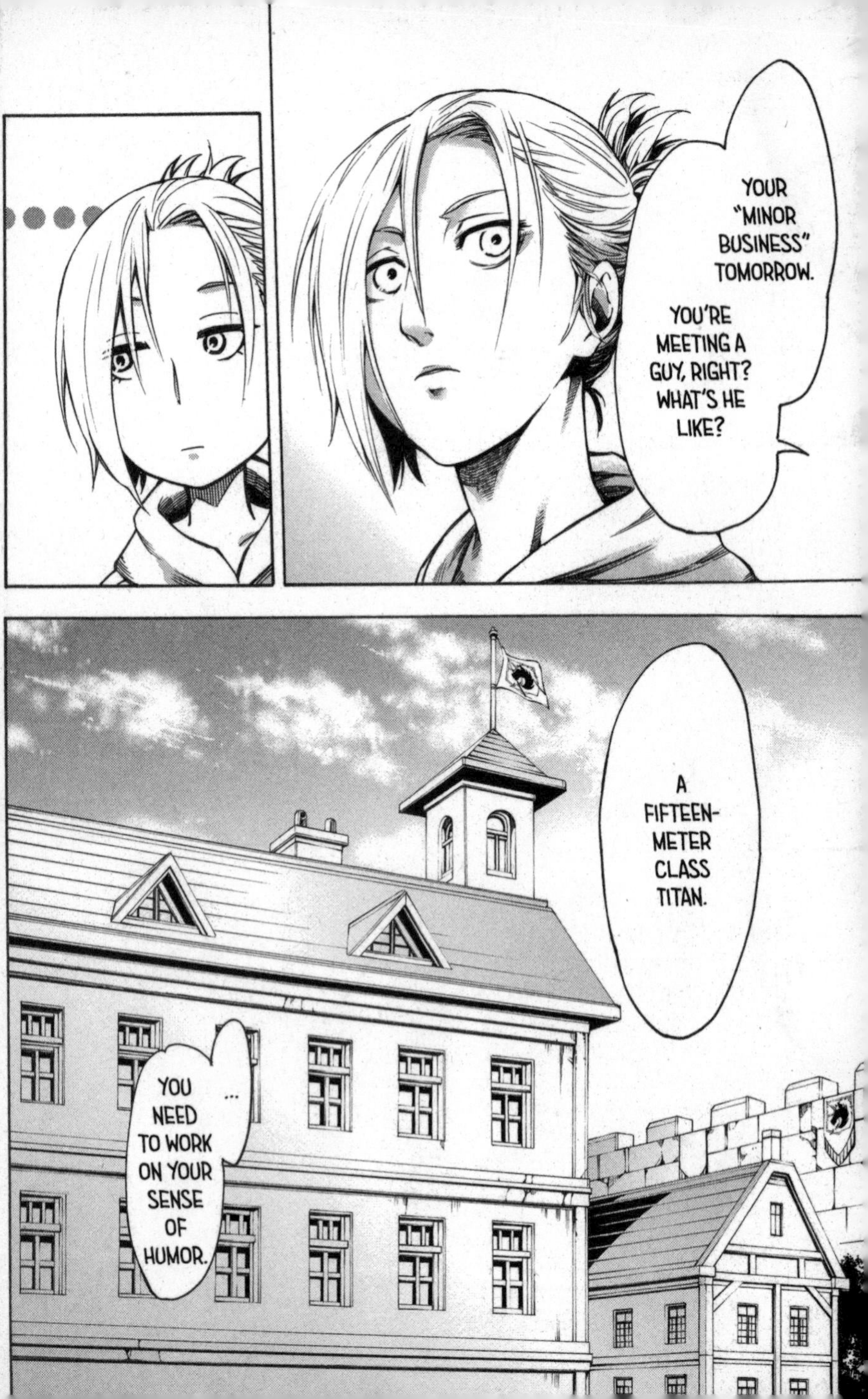
YOUR "MINOR BUSINESS" TOMORROW.
YOU'RE MEETING A GUY, RIGHT? WHAT'S HE LIKE?
......
A FIFTEEN-METER CLASS TITAN.
...
YOU NEED TO WORK ON YOUR SENSE OF HUMOR.

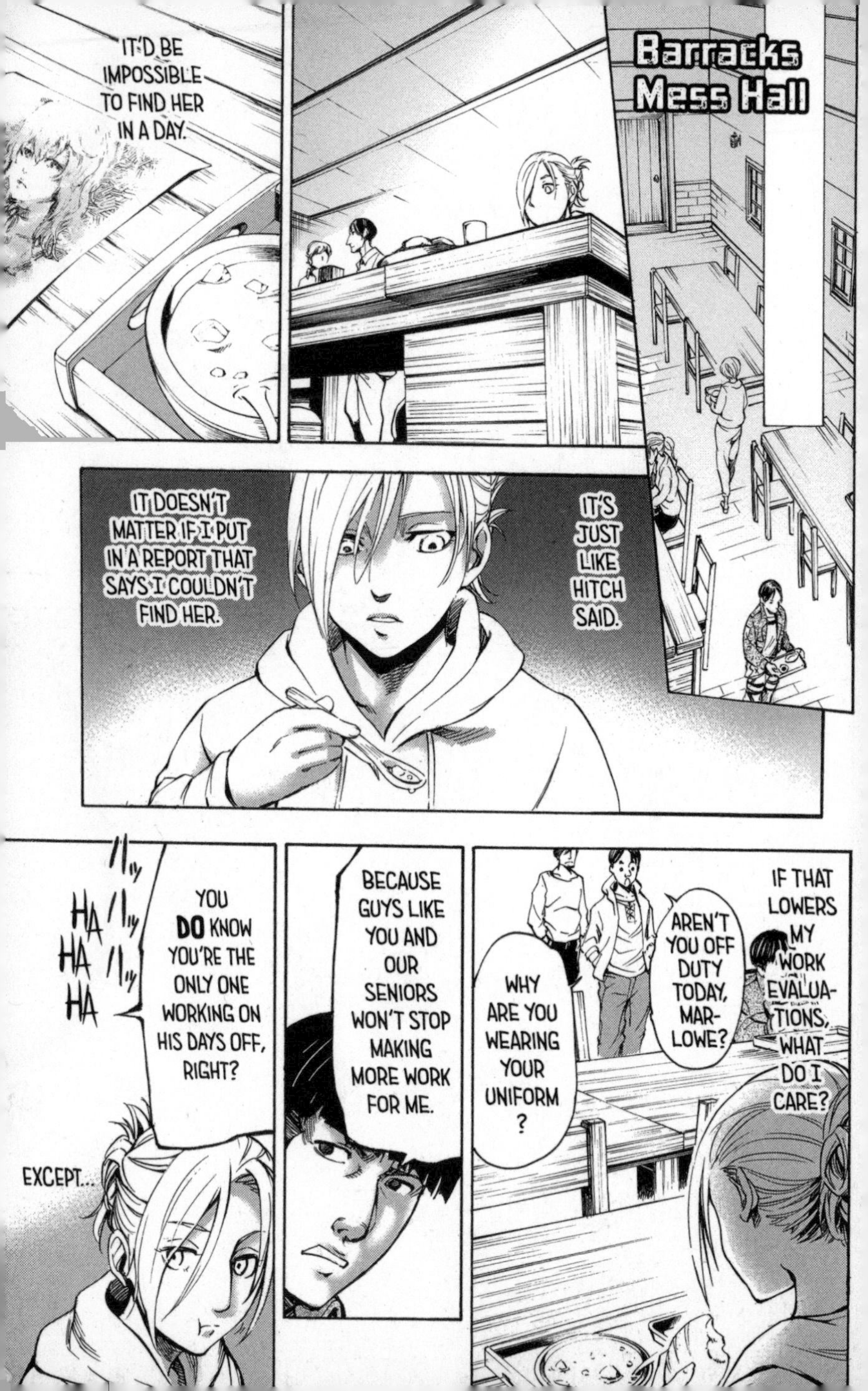
Barracks Mess Hall
IT'D BE IMPOSSIBLE TO FIND HER IN A DAY.
IT'S JUST LIKE HITCH SAID.
IT DOESN'T MATTER IF I PUT IN A REPORT THAT SAYS I COULDN'T FIND HER.
IF THAT LOWERS MY WORK EVALUA-TIONS, WHAT DO I CARE?
AREN'T YOU OFF DUTY TODAY, MAR-LOWE?
WHY ARE YOU WEARING YOUR UNIFORM?
BECAUSE GUYS LIKE YOU AND OUR SENIORS WON'T STOP MAKING MORE WORK FOR ME.
YOU DO KNOW YOU'RE THE ONLY ONE WORKING ON HIS DAYS OFF, RIGHT?
HA HA HA
EXCEPT...

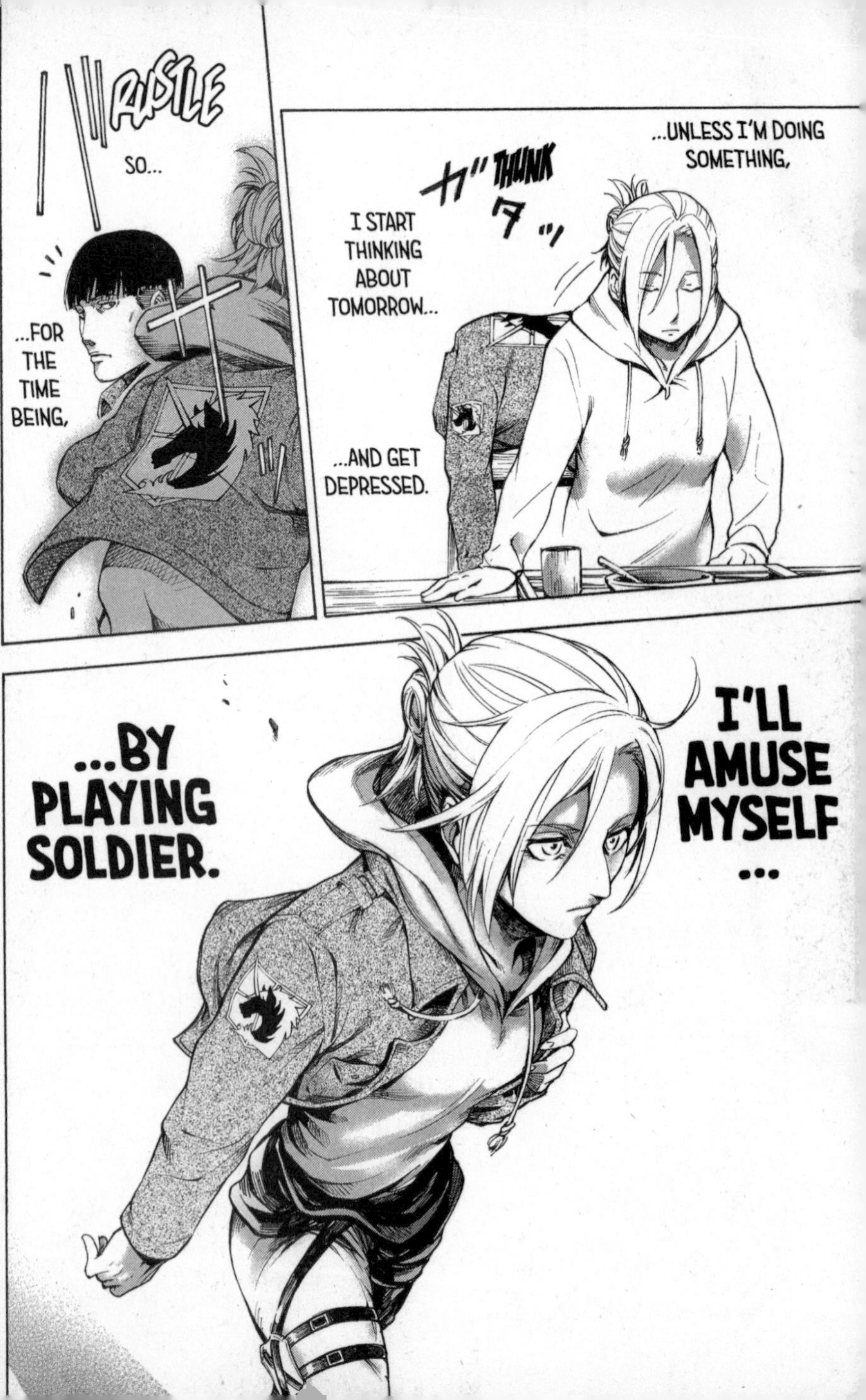

...UNLESS I'M DOING SOMETHING,
THUNK
I START THINKING ABOUT TOMORROW...
...AND GET DEPRESSED.
RUSTLE
SO...
...FOR THE TIME BEING,
I'LL AMUSE MYSELF...
...BY PLAYING SOLDIER.

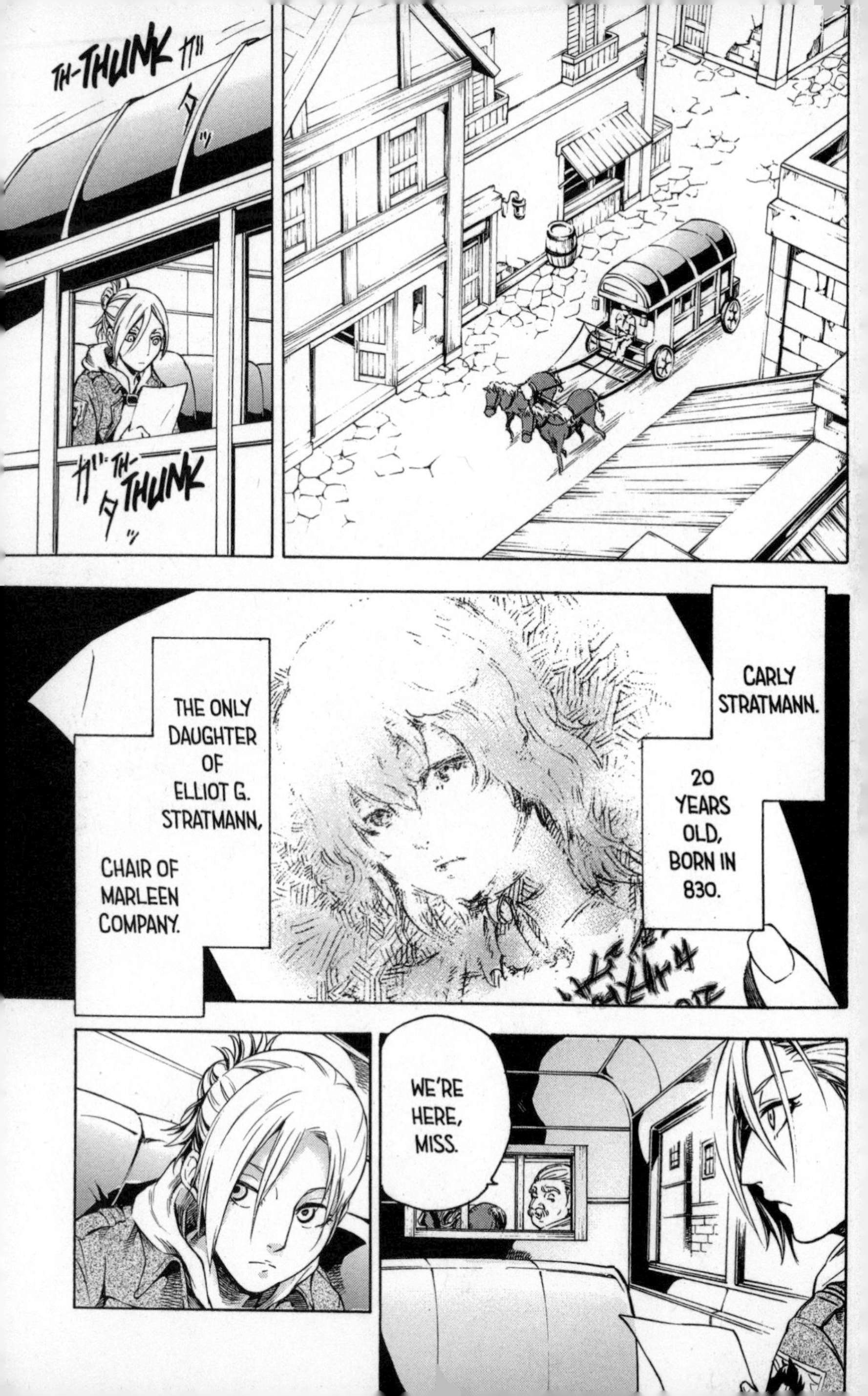
TH-THUNK
ガタッ
TH-THUNK
ガタッ
CARLY STRATMANN.
20 YEARS OLD, BORN IN 830.
THE ONLY DAUGHTER OF ELLIOT G. STRATMANN,
CHAIR OF MARLEEN COMPANY.
WE'RE HERE, MISS.

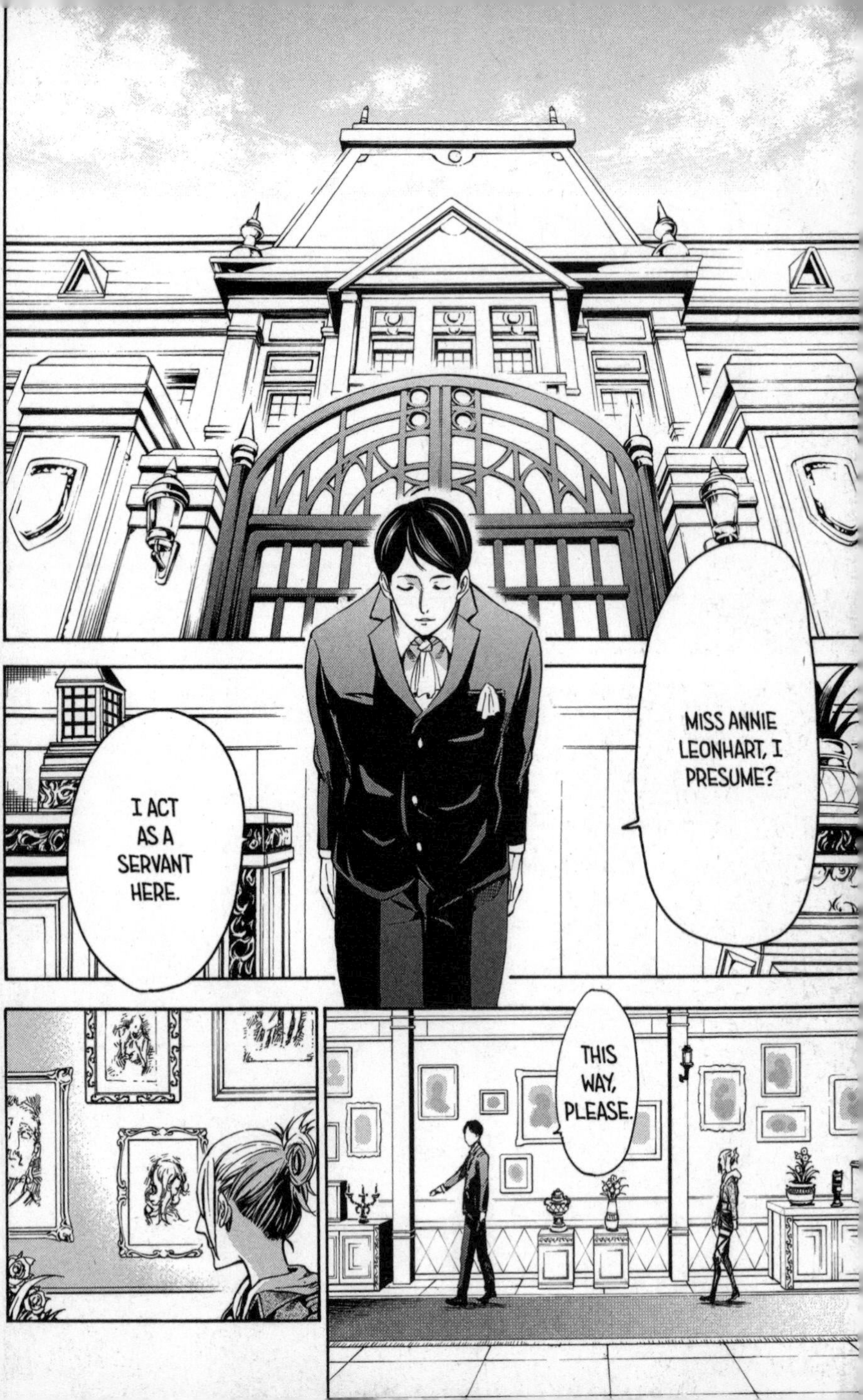

MISS ANNIE LEONHART, I PRESUME?
I ACT AS A SERVANT HERE.
THIS WAY, PLEASE.

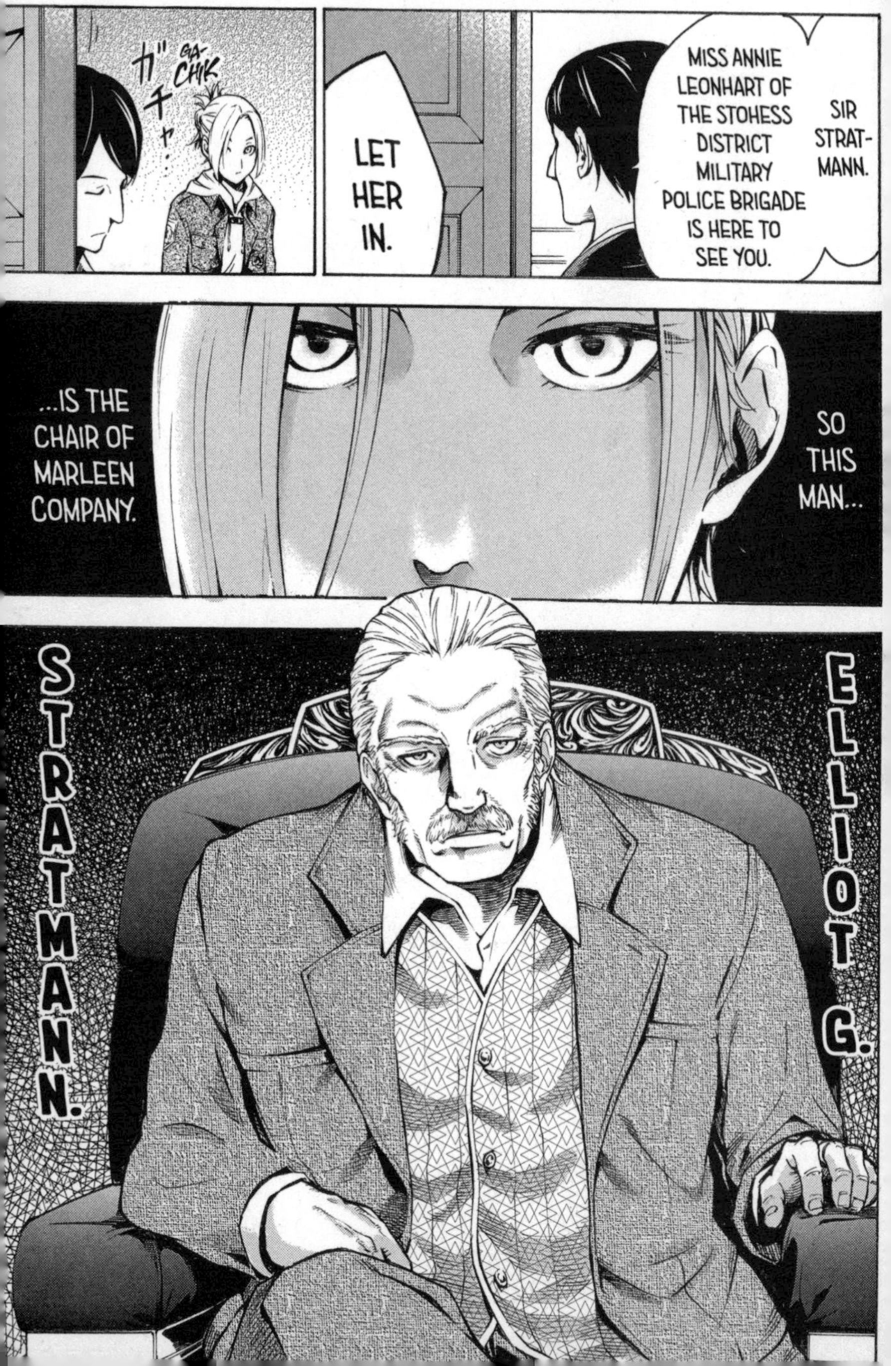
SIR STRAT-MANN.
MISS ANNIE LEONHART OF THE STOHESS DISTRICT MILITARY POLICE BRIGADE IS HERE TO SEE YOU.
LET HER IN.
GA-CHIK
ガチャ
SO THIS MAN...
...IS THE CHAIR OF MARLEEN COMPANY.
ELLIOT G.
STRATMANN.

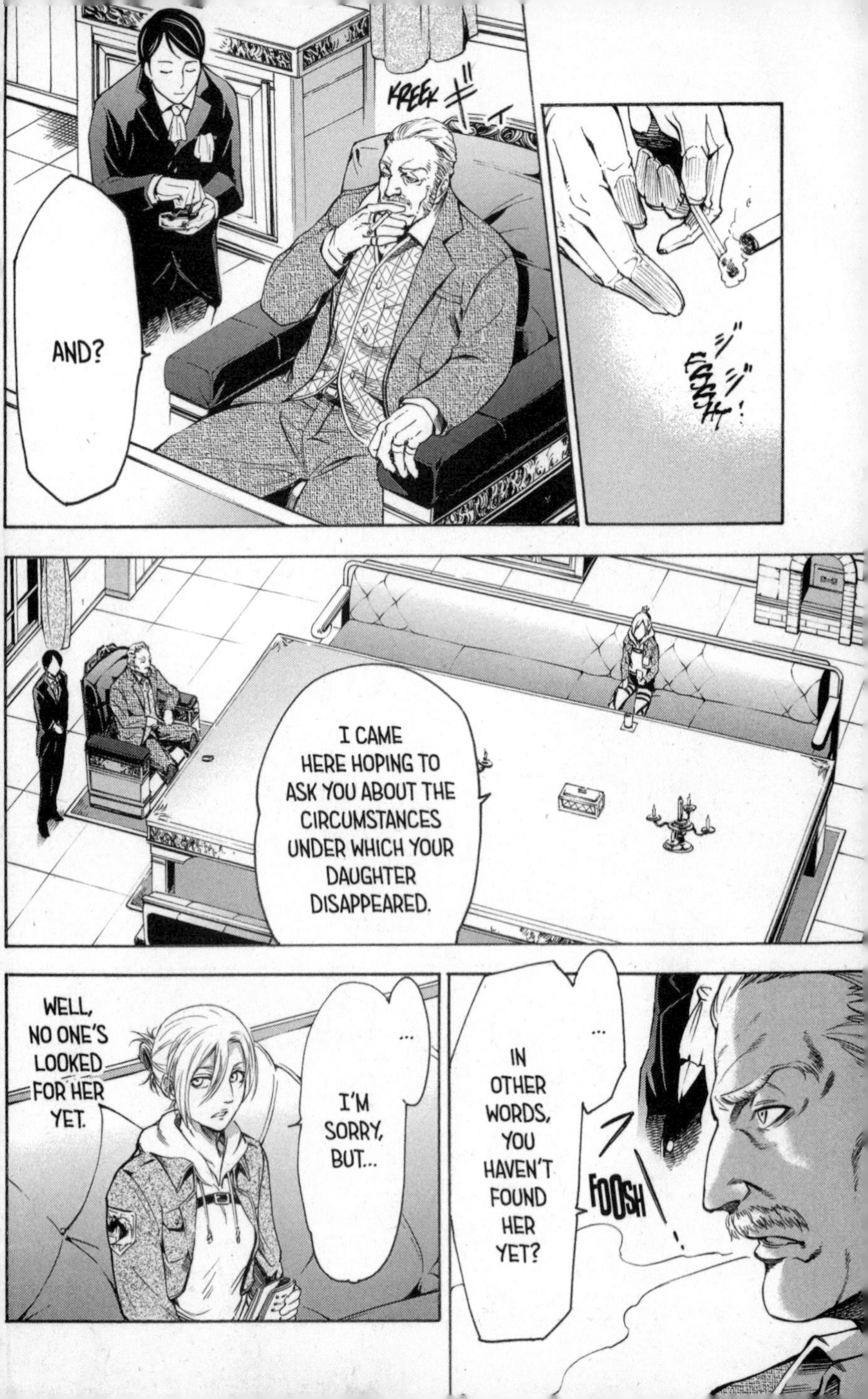

ジジ
FSSSH!
KREEK
AND?
I CAME HERE HOPING TO ASK YOU ABOUT THE CIRCUMSTANCES UNDER WHICH YOUR DAUGHTER DISAPPEARED.
...
IN OTHER WORDS, YOU HAVEN'T FOUND HER YET?
FOOSH
...
I'M SORRY, BUT...
WELL, NO ONE'S LOOKED FOR HER YET.

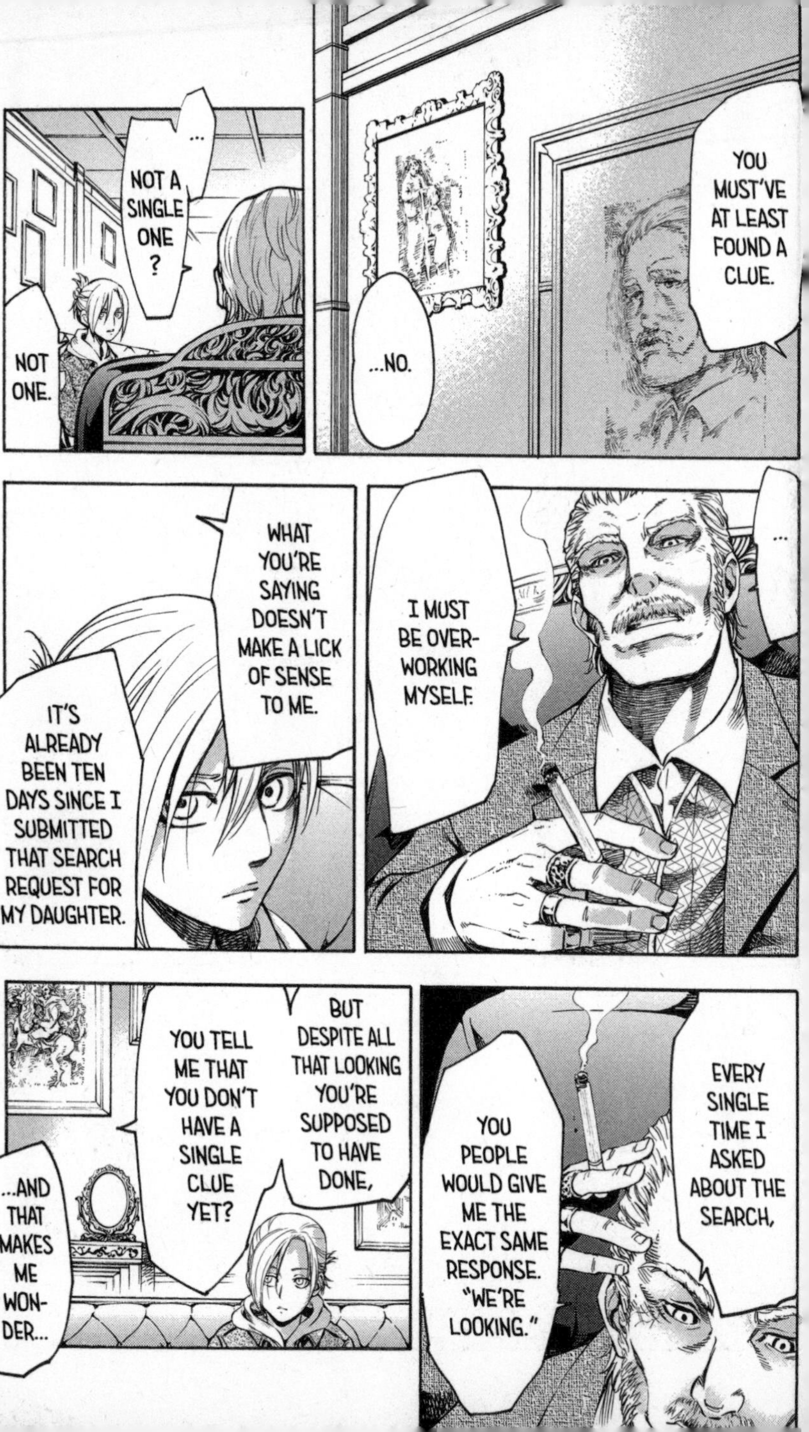
YOU MUST'VE AT LEAST FOUND A CLUE.
...NO.
...
NOT A SINGLE ONE?
NOT ONE.
...
I MUST BE OVER-WORKING MYSELF.
WHAT YOU'RE SAYING DOESN'T MAKE A LICK OF SENSE TO ME.
IT'S ALREADY BEEN TEN DAYS SINCE I SUBMITTED THAT SEARCH REQUEST FOR MY DAUGHTER.
EVERY SINGLE TIME I ASKED ABOUT THE SEARCH,
YOU PEOPLE WOULD GIVE ME THE EXACT SAME RESPONSE. "WE'RE LOOKING."
BUT DESPITE ALL THAT LOOKING YOU'RE SUPPOSED TO HAVE DONE,
YOU TELL ME THAT YOU DON'T HAVE A SINGLE CLUE YET?
...AND THAT MAKES ME WONDER...

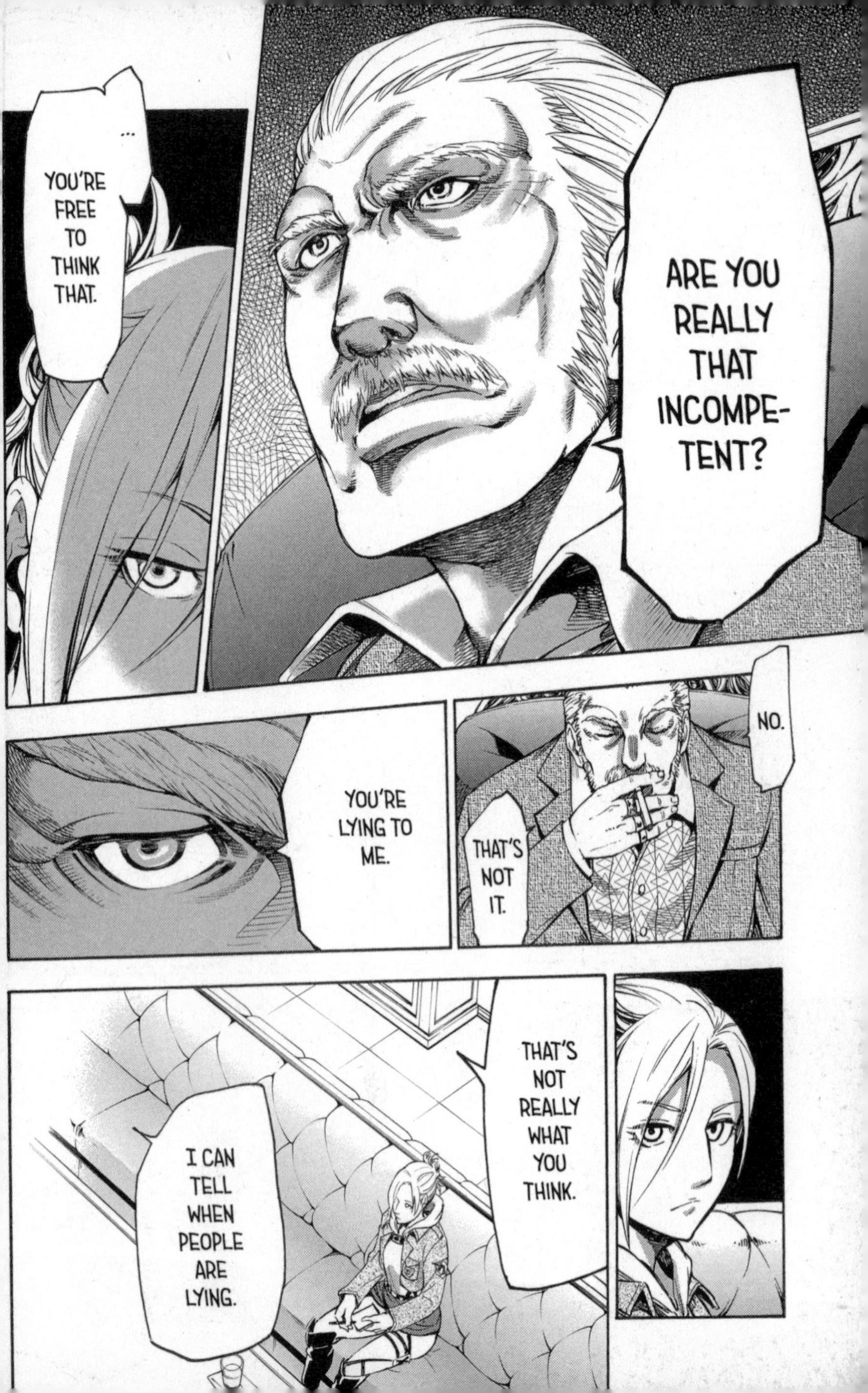
ARE YOU REALLY THAT INCOMPETENT?
... YOU'RE FREE TO THINK THAT.
NO.
THAT'S NOT IT.
YOU'RE LYING TO ME.
THAT'S NOT REALLY WHAT YOU THINK.
I CAN TELL WHEN PEOPLE ARE LYING.

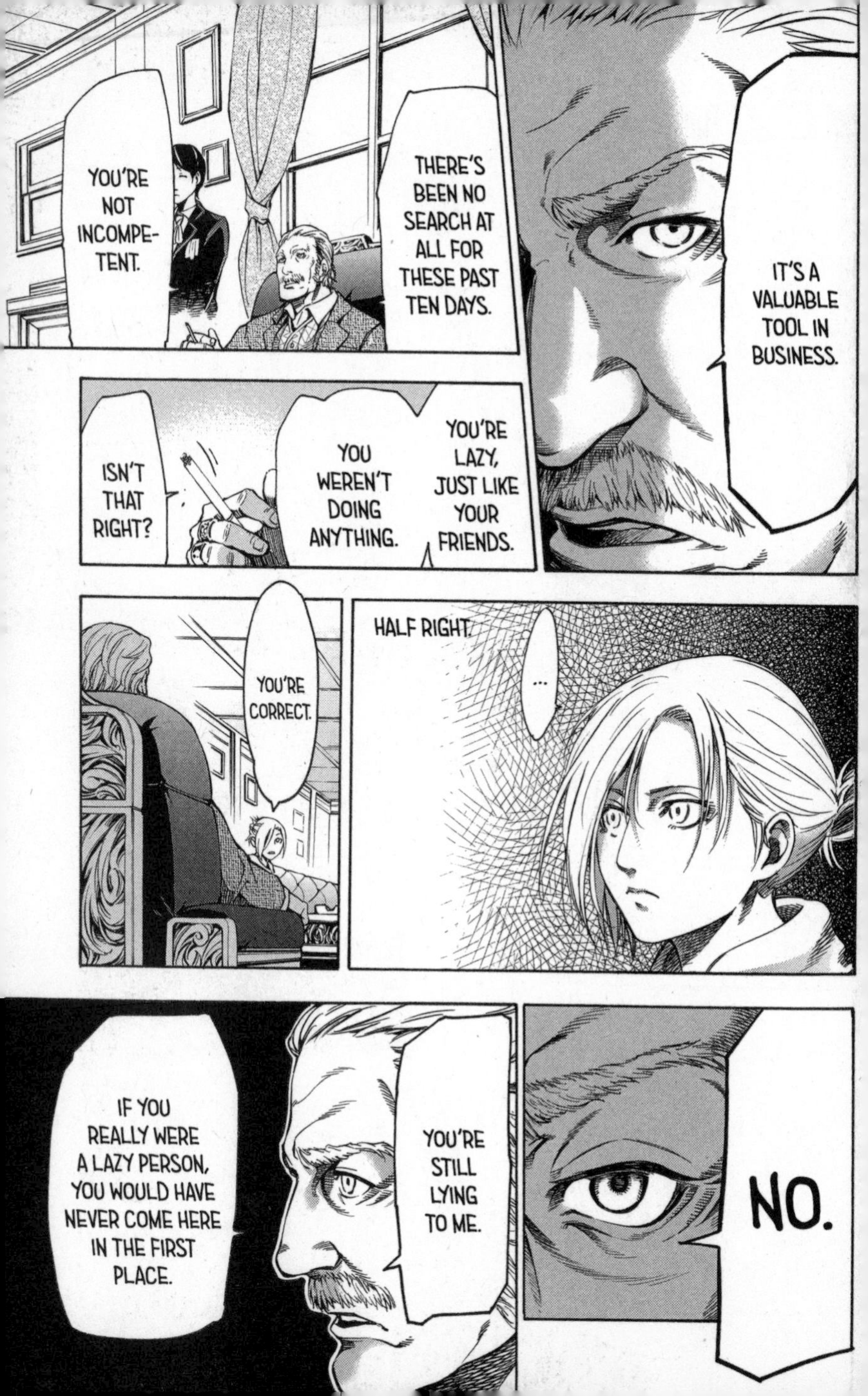

IT'S A VALUABLE TOOL IN BUSINESS.
THERE'S BEEN NO SEARCH AT ALL FOR THESE PAST TEN DAYS.
YOU'RE NOT INCOMPETENT.
YOU'RE LAZY, JUST LIKE YOUR FRIENDS.
YOU WEREN'T DOING ANYTHING.
ISN'T THAT RIGHT?
...
HALF RIGHT.
YOU'RE CORRECT.
NO.
YOU'RE STILL LYING TO ME.
IF YOU REALLY WERE A LAZY PERSON, YOU WOULD HAVE NEVER COME HERE IN THE FIRST PLACE.

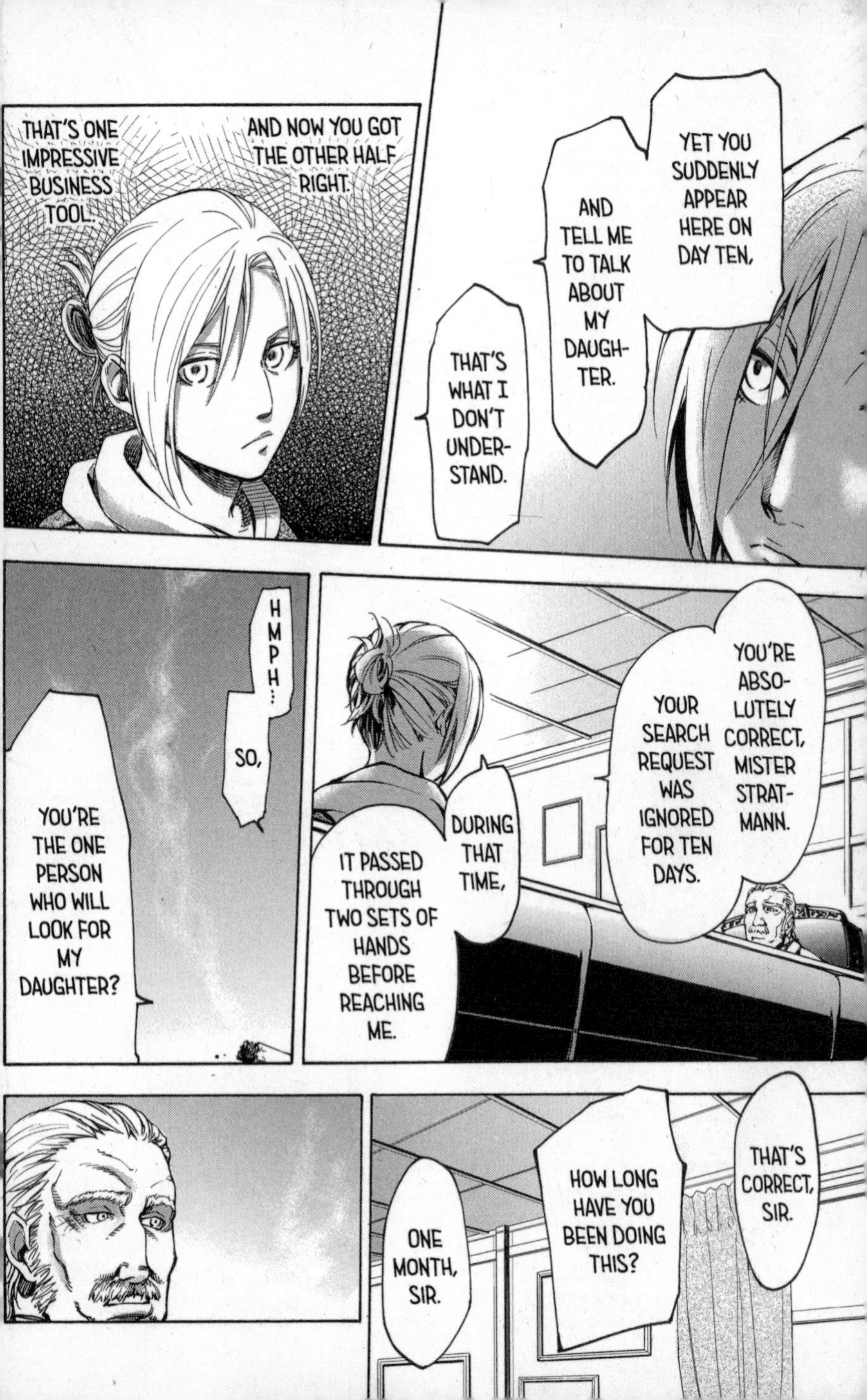
YET YOU SUDDENLY APPEAR HERE ON DAY TEN,
AND TELL ME TO TALK ABOUT MY DAUGHTER.
THAT'S WHAT I DON'T UNDERSTAND.
AND NOW YOU GOT THE OTHER HALF RIGHT.
THAT'S ONE IMPRESSIVE BUSINESS TOOL.
YOU'RE ABSOLUTELY CORRECT, MISTER STRATMANN.
YOUR SEARCH REQUEST WAS IGNORED FOR TEN DAYS.
DURING THAT TIME,
IT PASSED THROUGH TWO SETS OF HANDS BEFORE REACHING ME.
HMPH...
SO,
YOU'RE THE ONE PERSON WHO WILL LOOK FOR MY DAUGHTER?
THAT'S CORRECT, SIR.
HOW LONG HAVE YOU BEEN DOING THIS?
ONE MONTH, SIR.

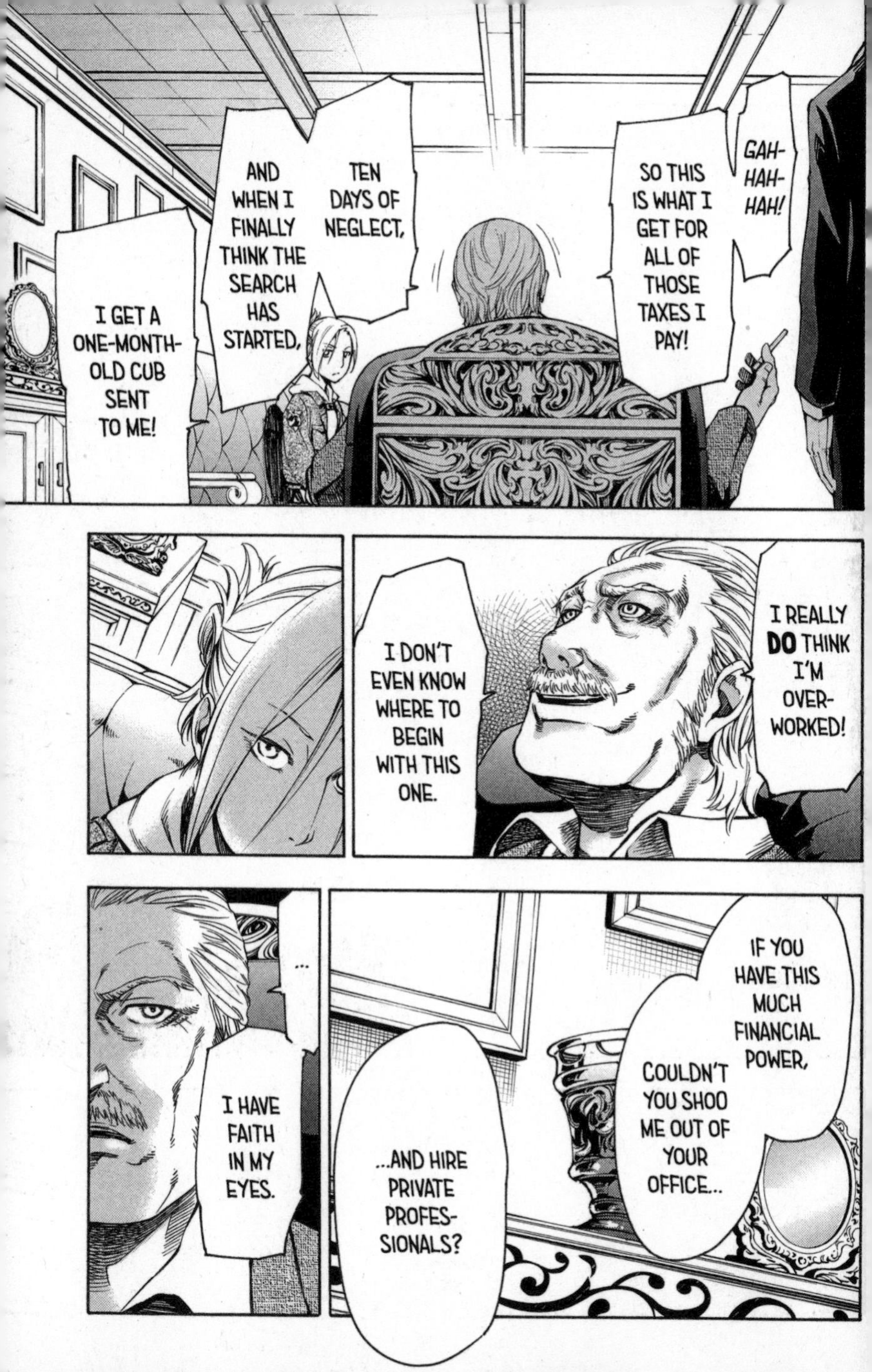
GAH-HAH-HAH!
SO THIS IS WHAT I GET FOR ALL OF THOSE TAXES I PAY!
TEN DAYS OF NEGLECT,
AND WHEN I FINALLY THINK THE SEARCH HAS STARTED,
I GET A ONE-MONTH-OLD CUB SENT TO ME!
I REALLY **DO** THINK I'M OVERWORKED!
I DON'T EVEN KNOW WHERE TO BEGIN WITH THIS ONE.
IF YOU HAVE THIS MUCH FINANCIAL POWER,
COULDN'T YOU SHOO ME OUT OF YOUR OFFICE...
...AND HIRE PRIVATE PROFESSIONALS?
...
I HAVE FAITH IN MY EYES.

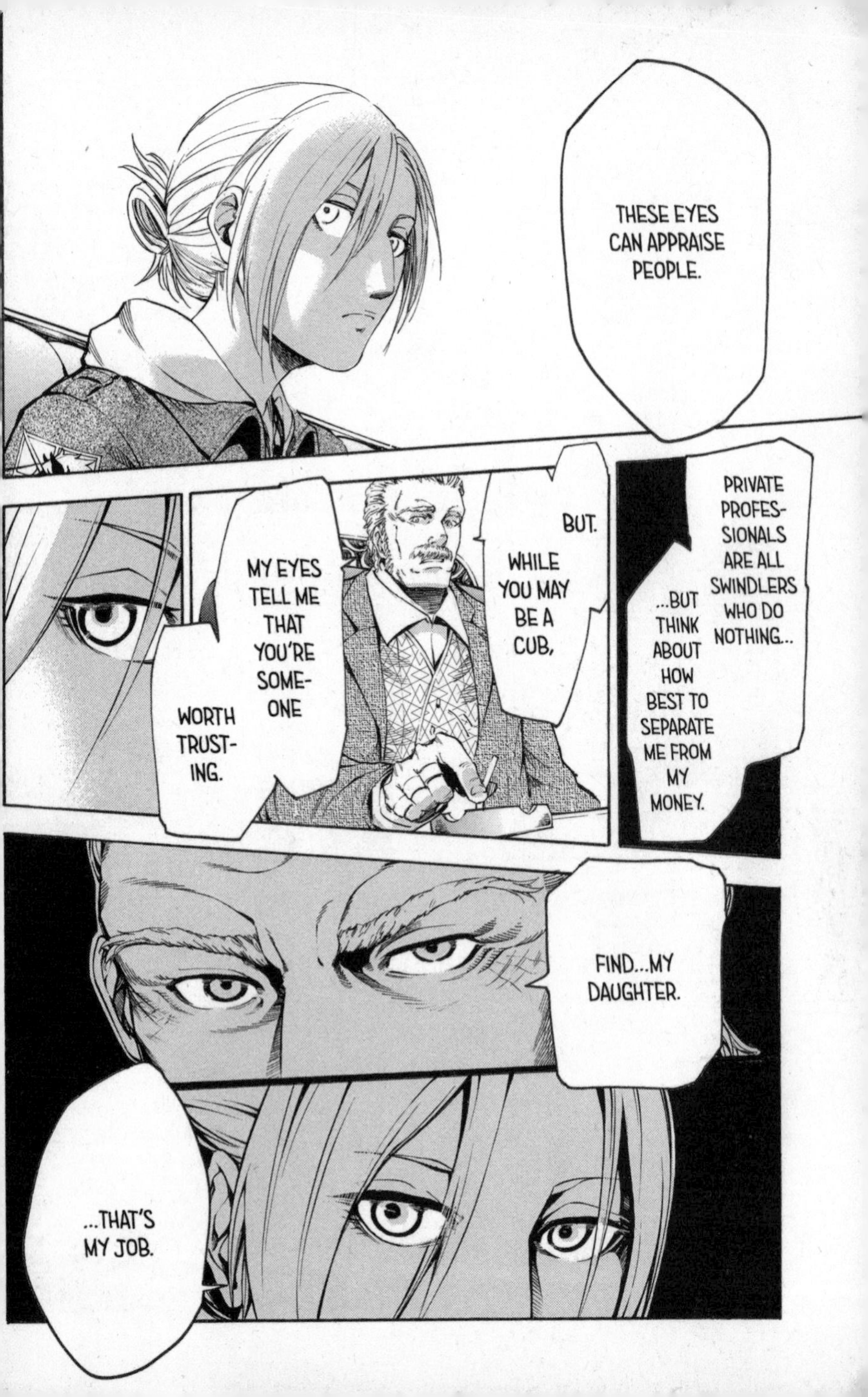
THESE EYES CAN APPRAISE PEOPLE.
PRIVATE PROFESSIONALS ARE ALL SWINDLERS WHO DO NOTHING...
...BUT THINK ABOUT HOW BEST TO SEPARATE ME FROM MY MONEY.
BUT.
WHILE YOU MAY BE A CUB,
MY EYES TELL ME THAT YOU'RE SOMEONE
WORTH TRUSTING.
FIND...MY DAUGHTER.
...THAT'S MY JOB.

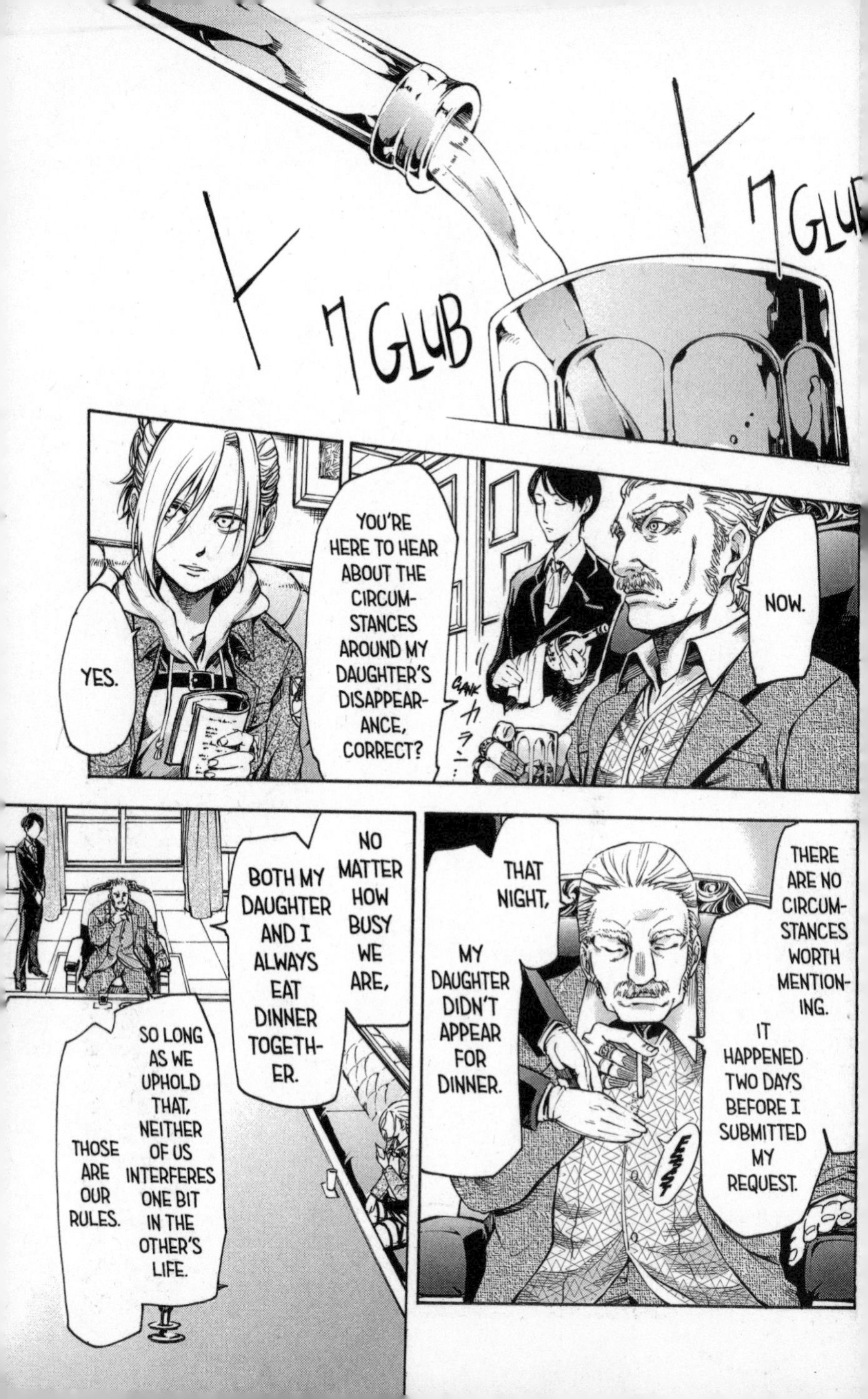
GLU
GLUB
NOW.
YOU'RE HERE TO HEAR ABOUT THE CIRCUMSTANCES AROUND MY DAUGHTER'S DISAPPEARANCE, CORRECT?
CLANK
YES.
THERE ARE NO CIRCUMSTANCES WORTH MENTIONING.
IT HAPPENED TWO DAYS BEFORE I SUBMITTED MY REQUEST.
THAT NIGHT,
MY DAUGHTER DIDN'T APPEAR FOR DINNER.
NO MATTER HOW BUSY WE ARE,
BOTH MY DAUGHTER AND I ALWAYS EAT DINNER TOGETHER.
SO LONG AS WE UPHOLD THAT, NEITHER OF US INTERFERES ONE BIT IN THE OTHER'S LIFE.
THOSE ARE OUR RULES.

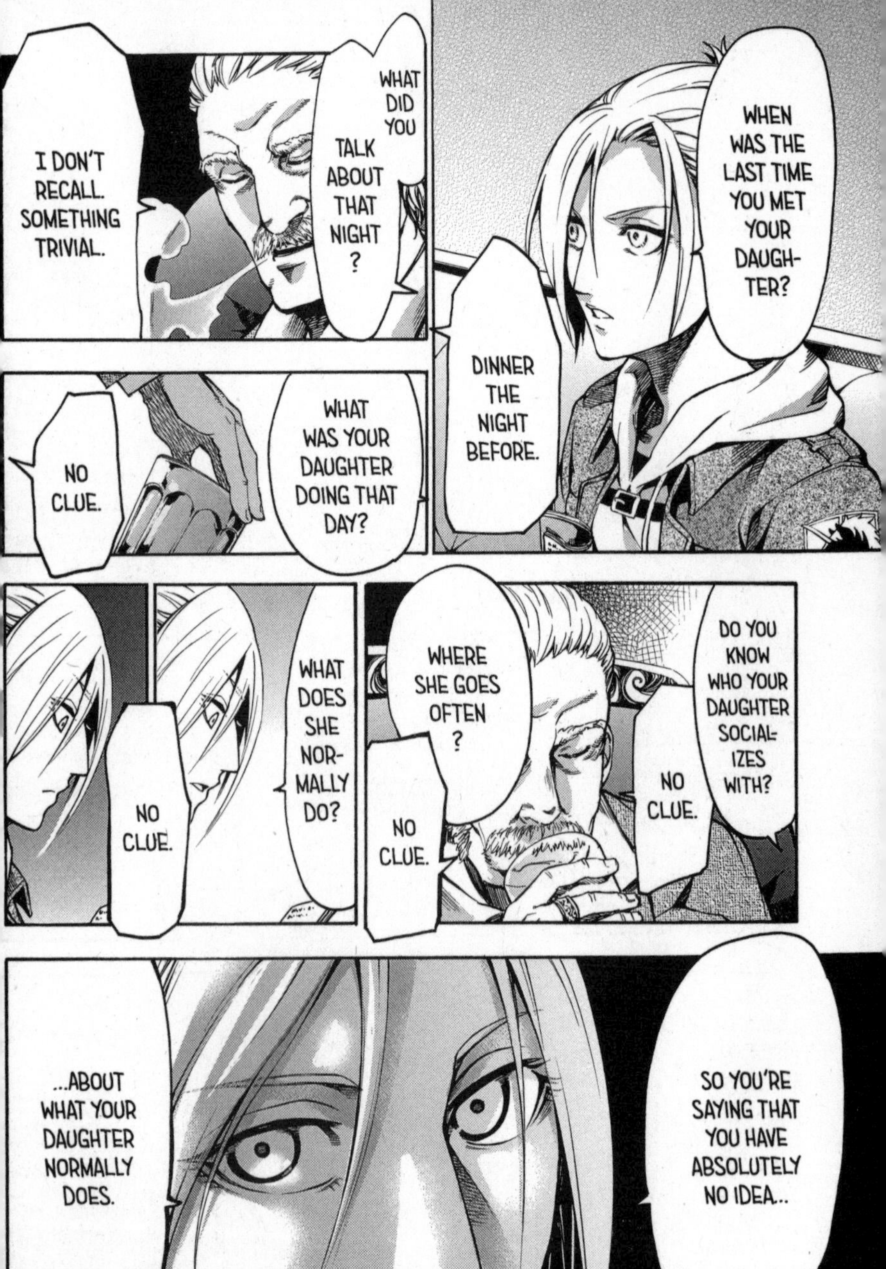
WHEN WAS THE LAST TIME YOU MET YOUR DAUGHTER?
DINNER THE NIGHT BEFORE.
WHAT DID YOU TALK ABOUT THAT NIGHT?
I DON'T RECALL. SOMETHING TRIVIAL.
WHAT WAS YOUR DAUGHTER DOING THAT DAY?
NO CLUE.
DO YOU KNOW WHO YOUR DAUGHTER SOCIALIZES WITH?
NO CLUE.
WHERE SHE GOES OFTEN?
NO CLUE.
WHAT DOES SHE NORMALLY DO?
NO CLUE.
SO YOU'RE SAYING THAT YOU HAVE ABSOLUTELY NO IDEA...
...ABOUT WHAT YOUR DAUGHTER NORMALLY DOES.

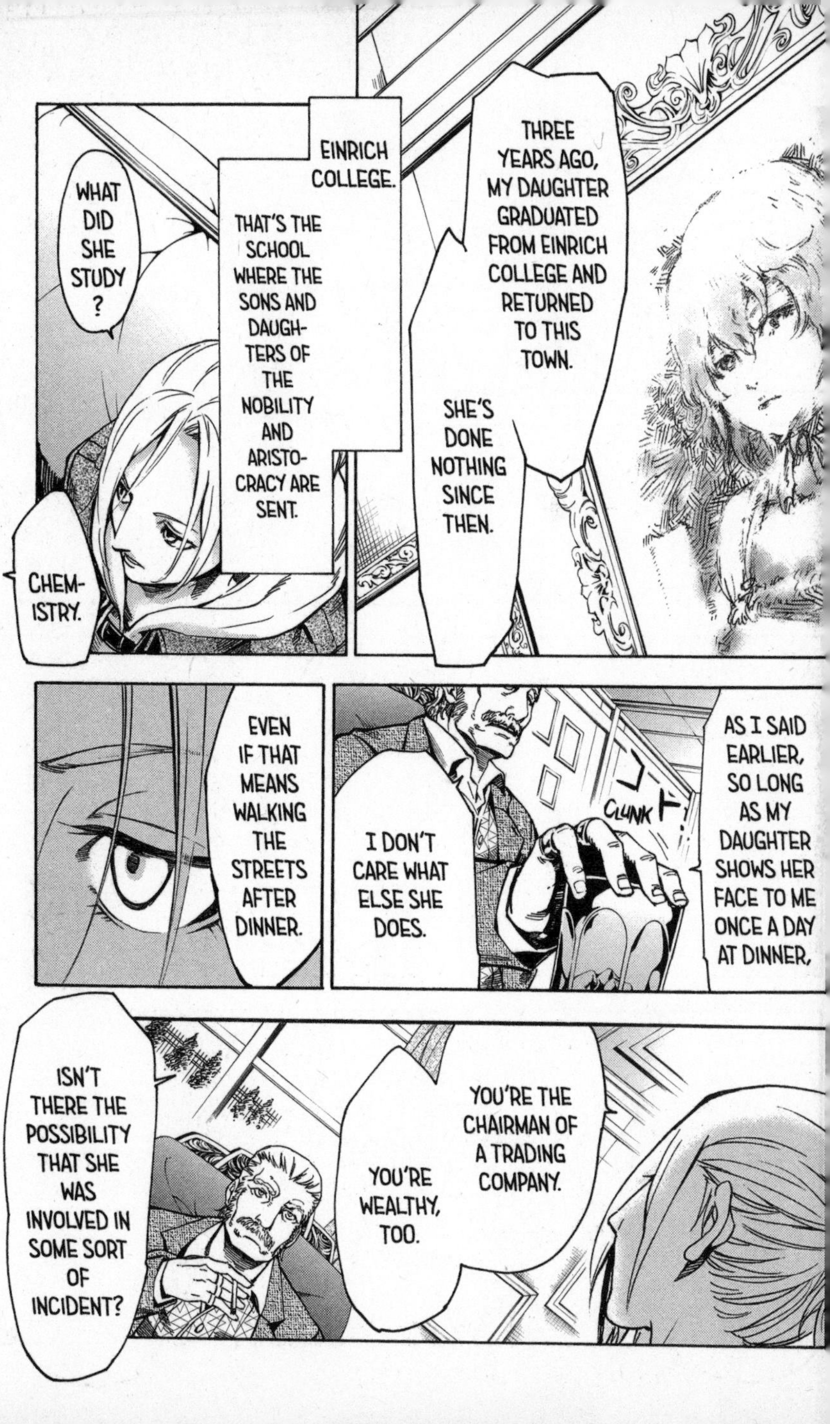
THREE YEARS AGO, MY DAUGHTER GRADUATED FROM EINRICH COLLEGE AND RETURNED TO THIS TOWN.
SHE'S DONE NOTHING SINCE THEN.
EINRICH COLLEGE.
THAT'S THE SCHOOL WHERE THE SONS AND DAUGHTERS OF THE NOBILITY AND ARISTOCRACY ARE SENT.
WHAT DID SHE STUDY?
CHEMISTRY.
AS I SAID EARLIER, SO LONG AS MY DAUGHTER SHOWS HER FACE TO ME ONCE A DAY AT DINNER,
CLUNK
I DON'T CARE WHAT ELSE SHE DOES.
EVEN IF THAT MEANS WALKING THE STREETS AFTER DINNER.
YOU'RE THE CHAIRMAN OF A TRADING COMPANY.
YOU'RE WEALTHY, TOO.
ISN'T THERE THE POSSIBILITY THAT SHE WAS INVOLVED IN SOME SORT OF INCIDENT?

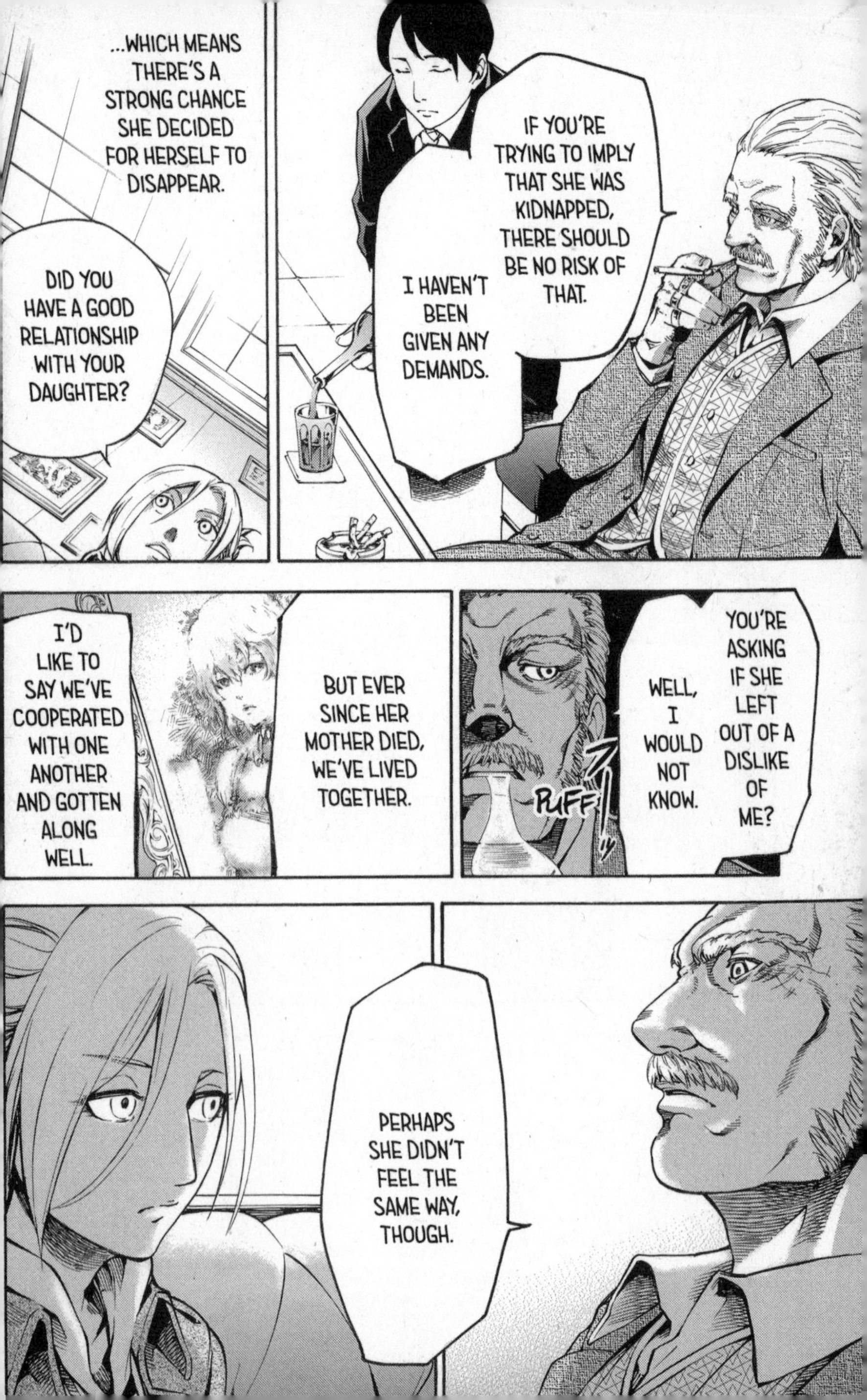
IF YOU'RE TRYING TO IMPLY THAT SHE WAS KIDNAPPED, THERE SHOULD BE NO RISK OF THAT.
I HAVEN'T BEEN GIVEN ANY DEMANDS.
...WHICH MEANS THERE'S A STRONG CHANCE SHE DECIDED FOR HERSELF TO DISAPPEAR.
DID YOU HAVE A GOOD RELATIONSHIP WITH YOUR DAUGHTER?
YOU'RE ASKING IF SHE LEFT OUT OF A DISLIKE OF ME?
WELL, I WOULD NOT KNOW.
PUFF
BUT EVER SINCE HER MOTHER DIED, WE'VE LIVED TOGETHER.
I'D LIKE TO SAY WE'VE COOPERATED WITH ONE ANOTHER AND GOTTEN ALONG WELL.
PERHAPS SHE DIDN'T FEEL THE SAME WAY, THOUGH.

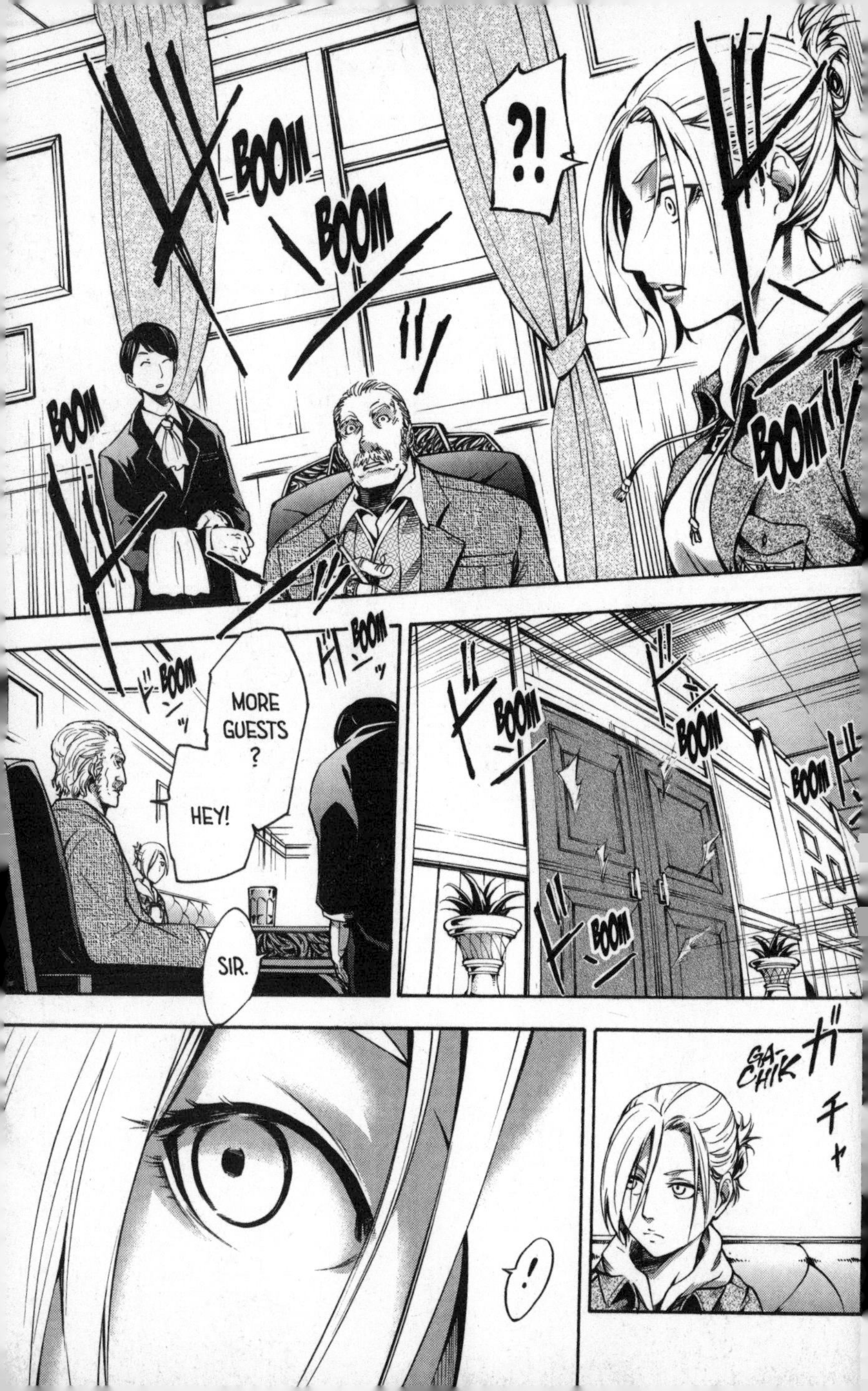

?!
BOOM
BOOM
BOOM
BOOM
BOOM
BOOM
BOOM
BOOM
BOOM
BOOM
MORE GUESTS?
HEY!
SIR.
GA-CHIK
ガチャ
!

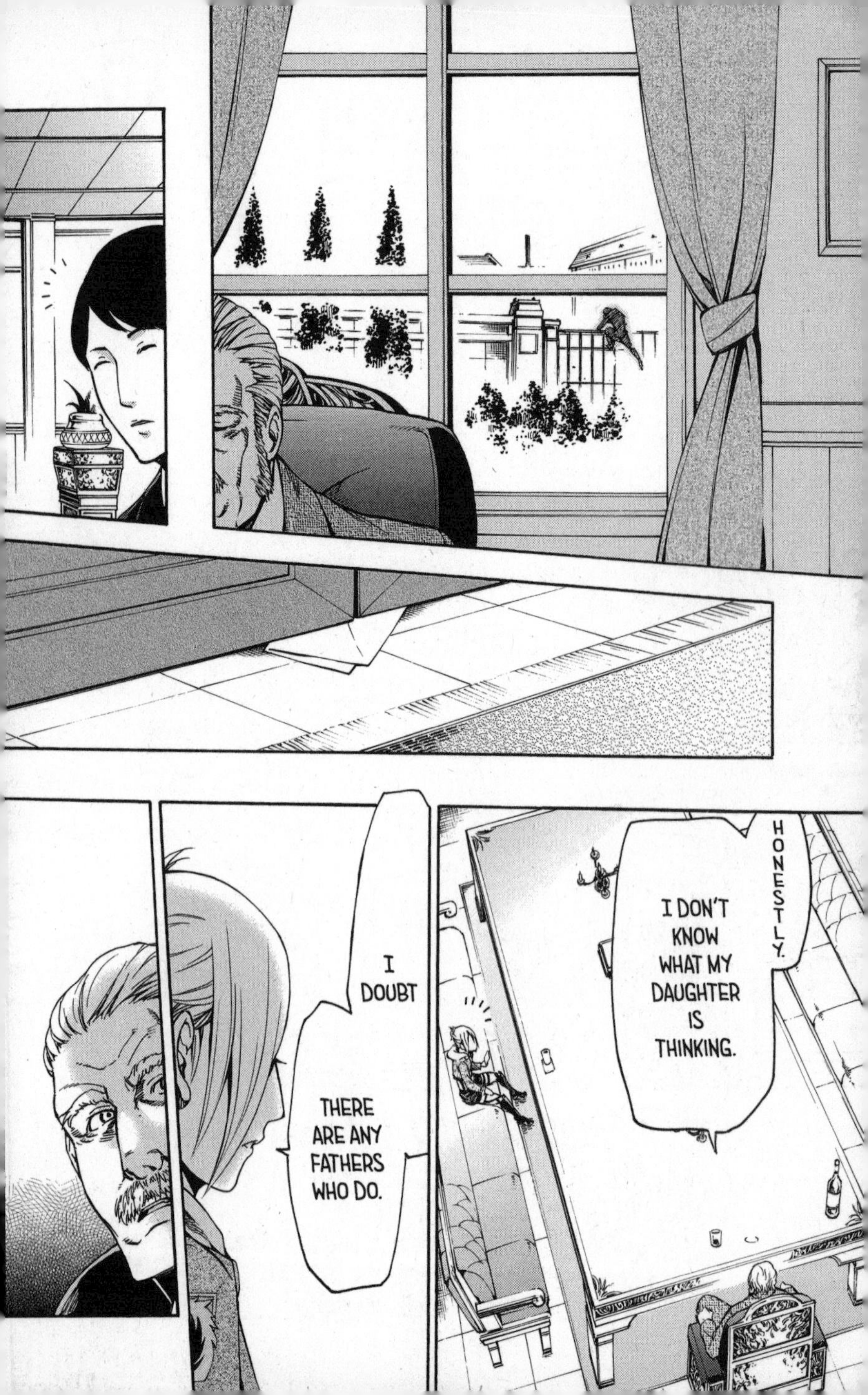
HONESTLY.
I DON'T KNOW WHAT MY DAUGHTER IS THINKING.
I DOUBT
THERE ARE ANY FATHERS WHO DO.

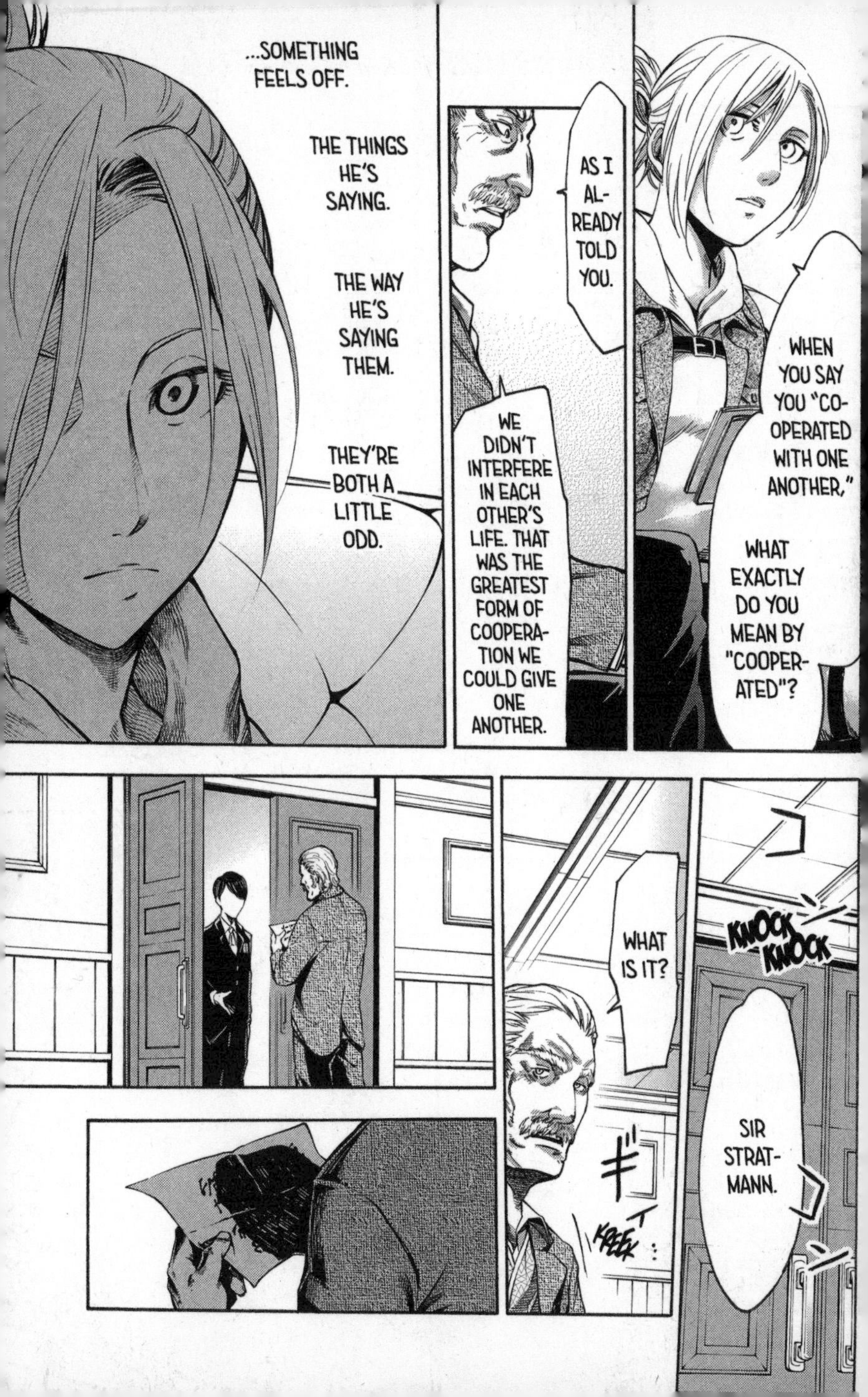
WHEN YOU SAY YOU "CO-OPERATED WITH ONE ANOTHER,"
WHAT EXACTLY DO YOU MEAN BY "COOPERATED"?
AS I ALREADY TOLD YOU.
WE DIDN'T INTERFERE IN EACH OTHER'S LIFE. THAT WAS THE GREATEST FORM OF COOPERATION WE COULD GIVE ONE ANOTHER.
...SOMETHING FEELS OFF.
THE THINGS HE'S SAYING.
THE WAY HE'S SAYING THEM.
THEY'RE BOTH A LITTLE ODD.
KNOCK KNOCK
SIR STRATMANN.
WHAT IS IT?
KREEK

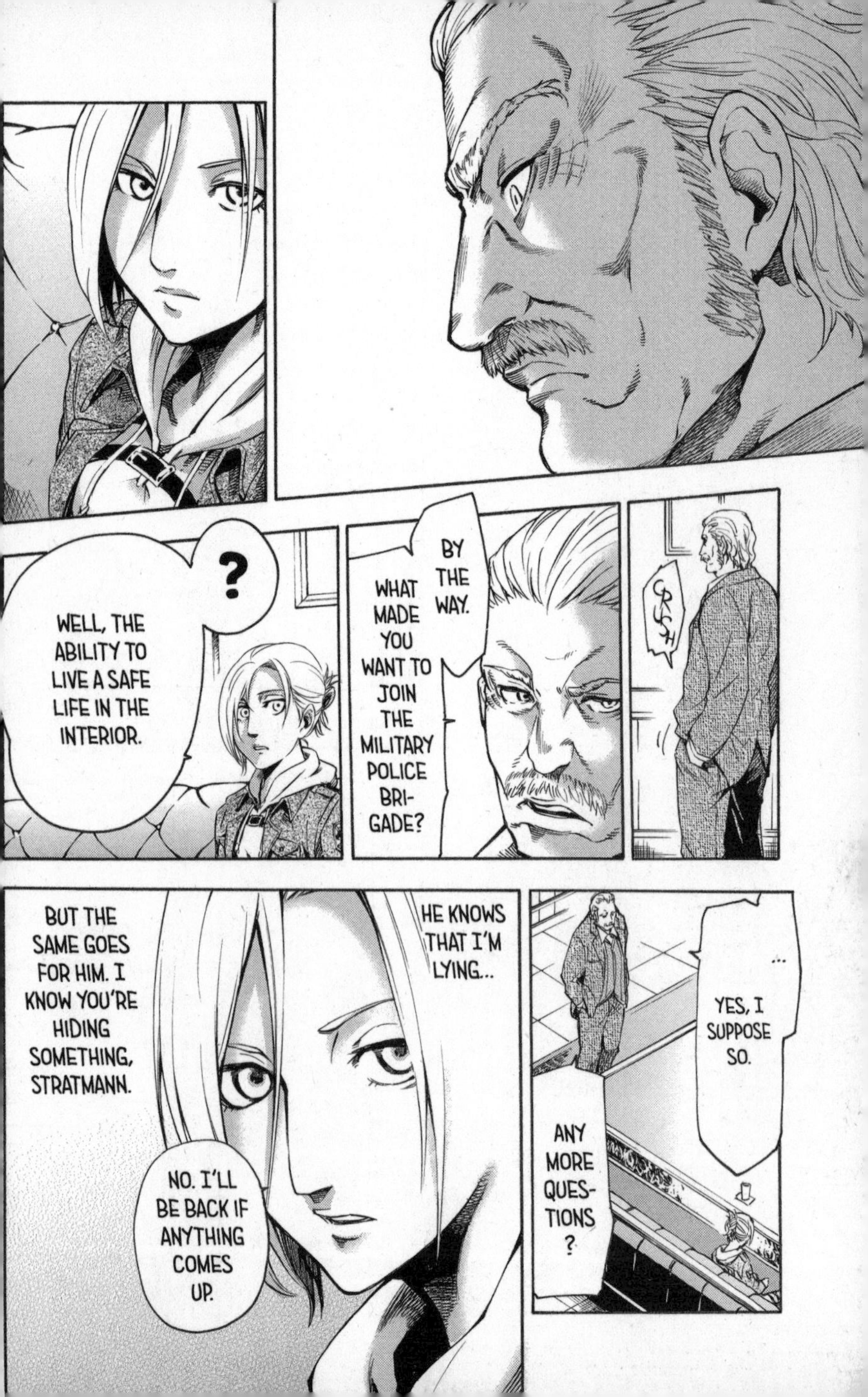
CRUSH
BY THE WAY.
WHAT MADE YOU WANT TO JOIN THE MILITARY POLICE BRIGADE?
?
WELL, THE ABILITY TO LIVE A SAFE LIFE IN THE INTERIOR.
...
YES, I SUPPOSE SO.
ANY MORE QUESTIONS?
HE KNOWS THAT I'M LYING...
BUT THE SAME GOES FOR HIM. I KNOW YOU'RE HIDING SOMETHING, STRATMANN.
NO. I'LL BE BACK IF ANYTHING COMES UP.

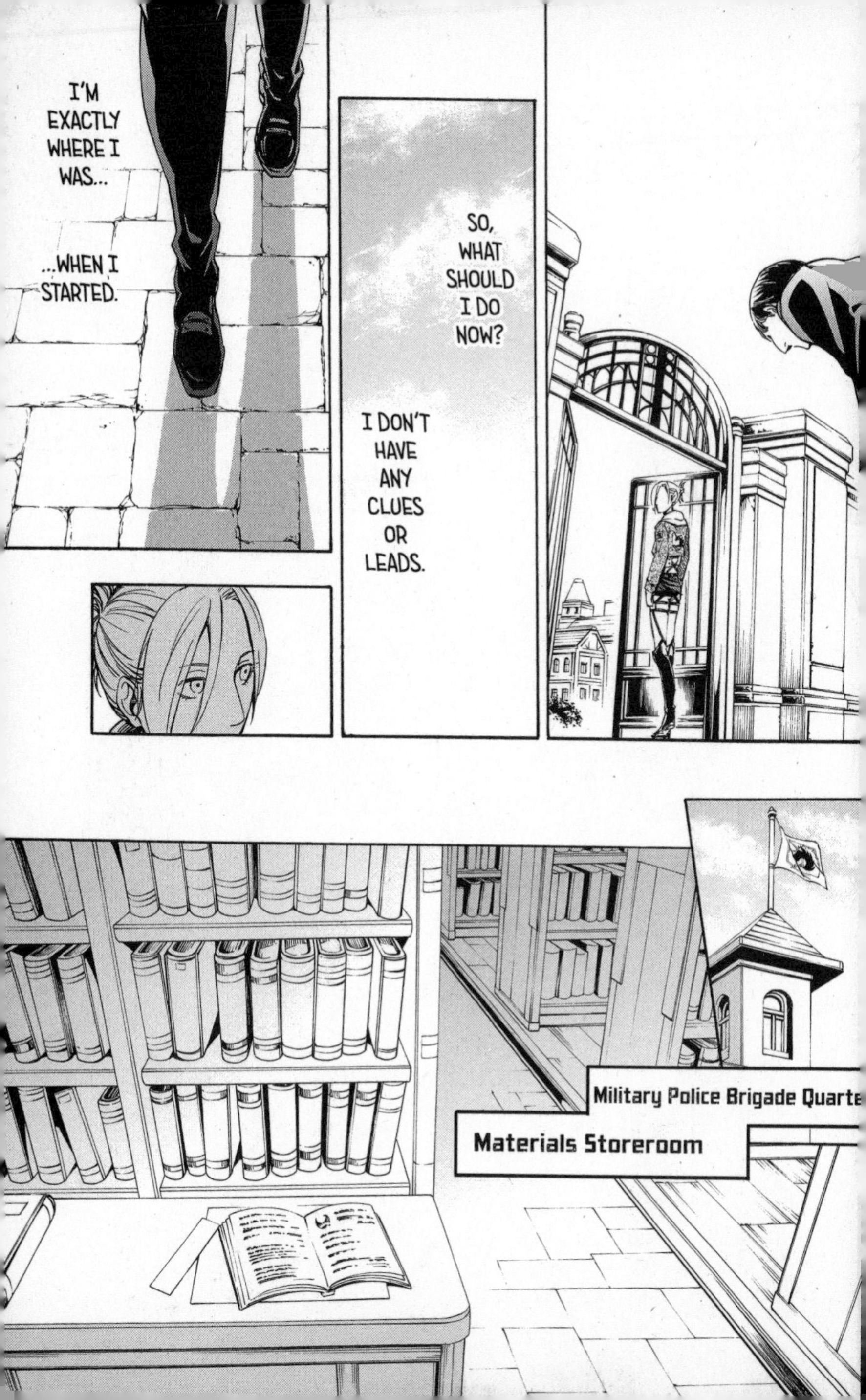
SO, WHAT SHOULD I DO NOW?
I DON'T HAVE ANY CLUES OR LEADS.
I'M EXACTLY WHERE I WAS...
...WHEN I STARTED.
Military Police Brigade Quarte
Materials Storeroom

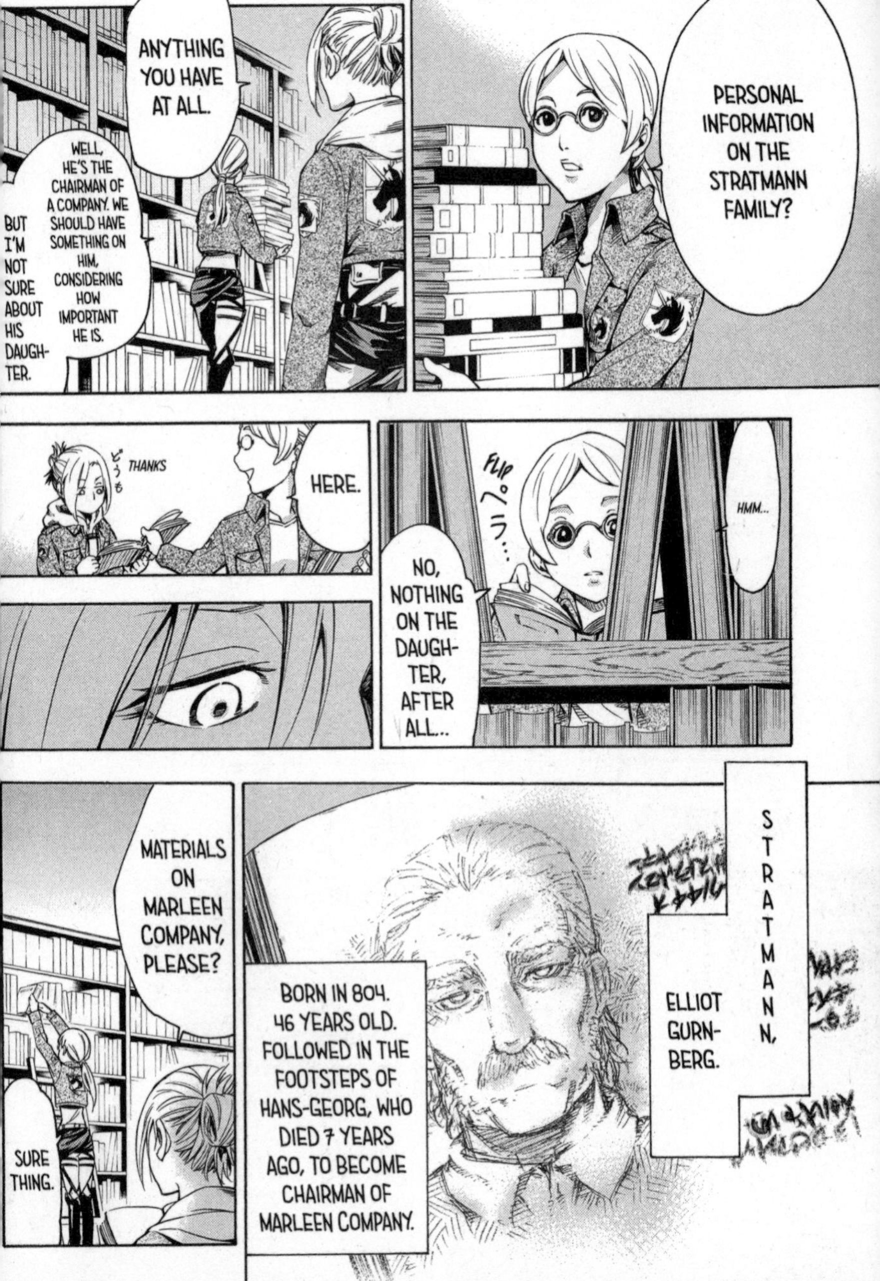
PERSONAL INFORMATION ON THE STRATMANN FAMILY?
ANYTHING YOU HAVE AT ALL.
WELL, HE'S THE CHAIRMAN OF A COMPANY. WE SHOULD HAVE SOMETHING ON HIM, CONSIDERING HOW IMPORTANT HE IS.
BUT I'M NOT SURE ABOUT HIS DAUGHTER.
HMM...
FLIP ペラ…
NO, NOTHING ON THE DAUGHTER, AFTER ALL...
HERE.
どうも THANKS
STRATMANN,
ELLIOT GURNBERG.
BORN IN 804. 46 YEARS OLD. FOLLOWED IN THE FOOTSTEPS OF HANS-GEORG, WHO DIED 7 YEARS AGO, TO BECOME CHAIRMAN OF MARLEEN COMPANY.
MATERIALS ON MARLEEN COMPANY, PLEASE?
SURE THING.

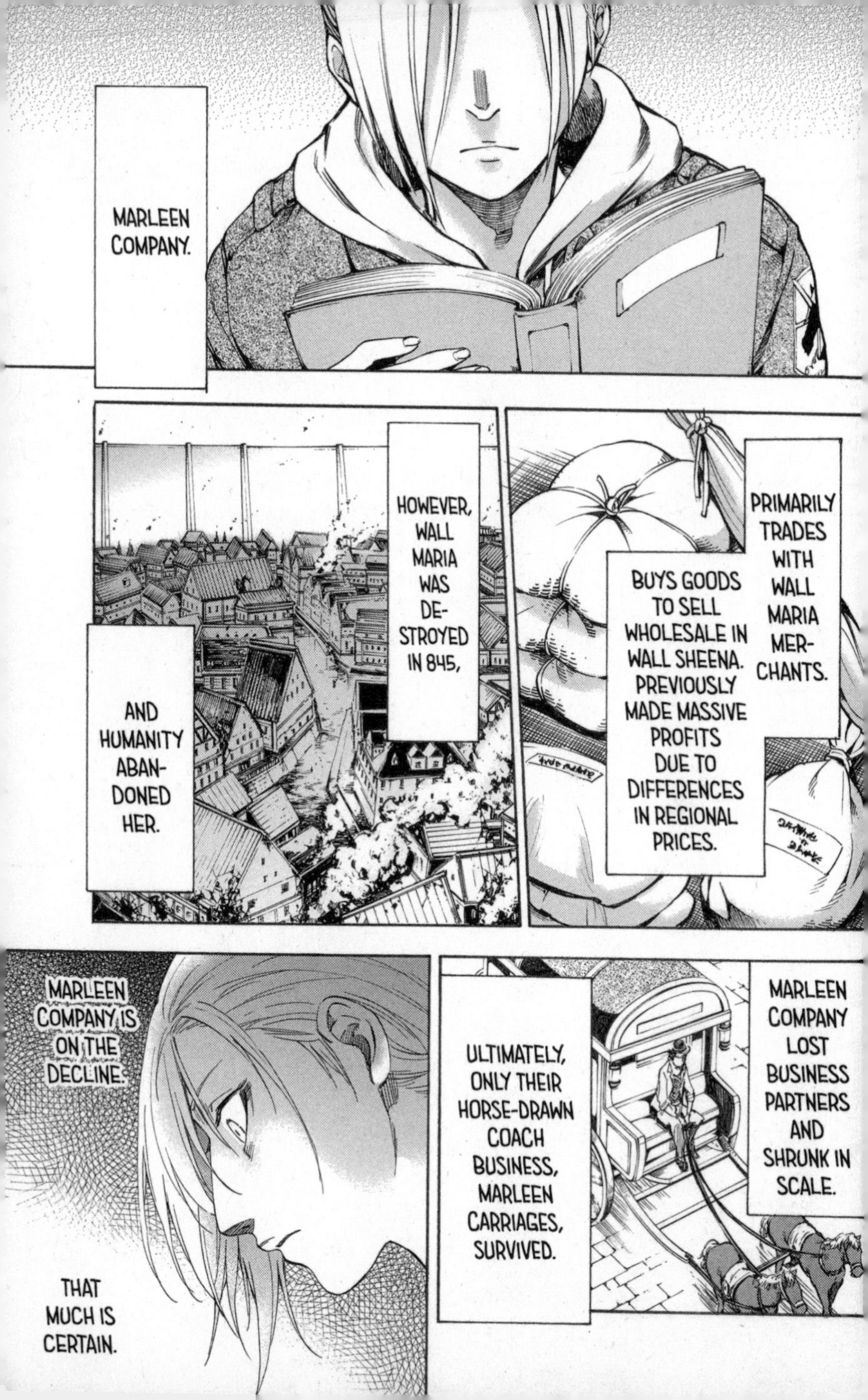
MARLEEN COMPANY.
PRIMARILY TRADES WITH WALL MARIA MERCHANTS.
BUYS GOODS TO SELL WHOLESALE IN WALL SHEENA. PREVIOUSLY MADE MASSIVE PROFITS DUE TO DIFFERENCES IN REGIONAL PRICES.
HOWEVER, WALL MARIA WAS DESTROYED IN 845,
AND HUMANITY ABANDONED HER.
MARLEEN COMPANY LOST BUSINESS PARTNERS AND SHRUNK IN SCALE.
ULTIMATELY, ONLY THEIR HORSE-DRAWN COACH BUSINESS, MARLEEN CARRIAGES, SURVIVED.
MARLEEN COMPANY IS ON THE DECLINE.
THAT MUCH IS CERTAIN.

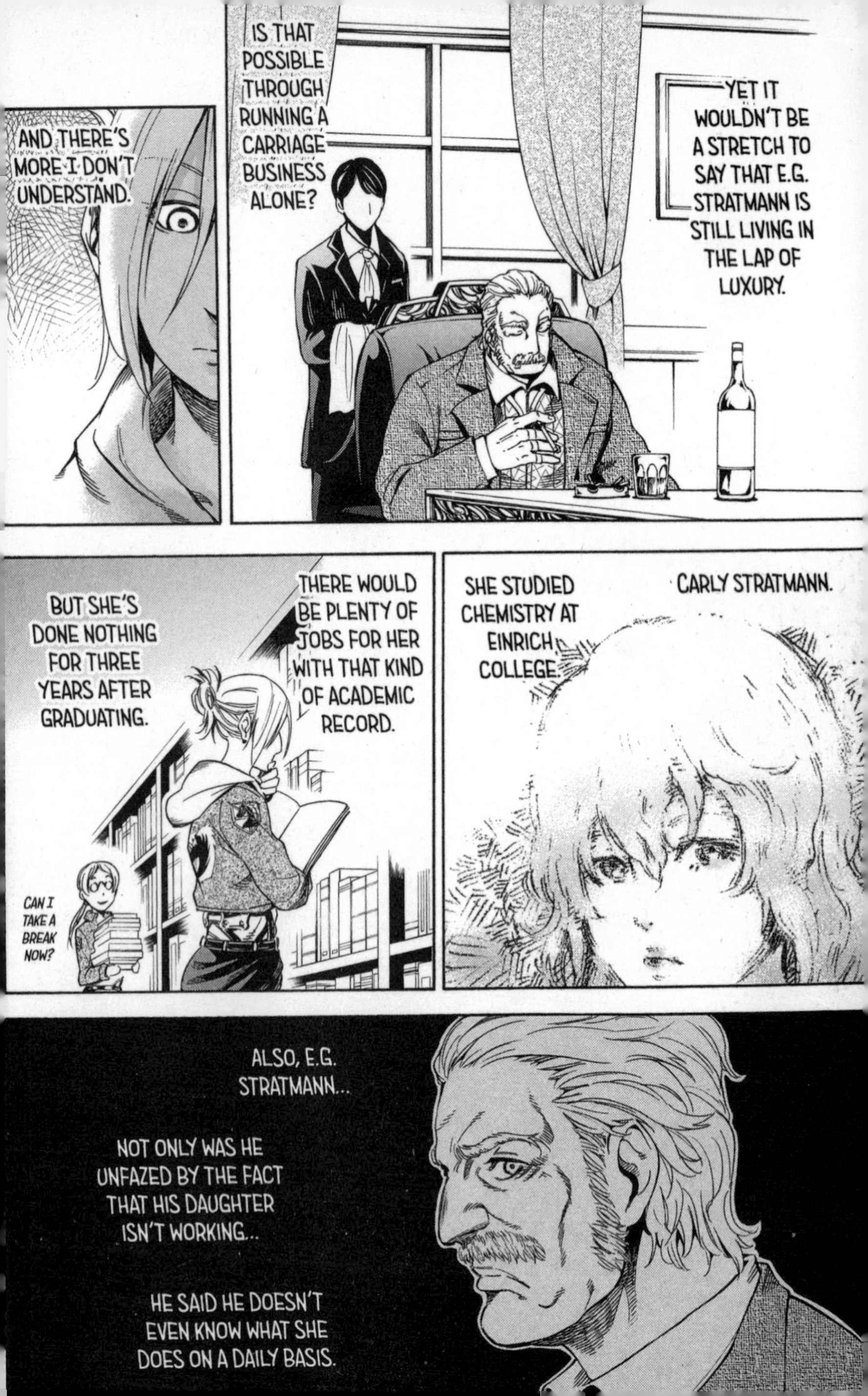
YET IT WOULDN'T BE A STRETCH TO SAY THAT E.G. STRATMANN IS STILL LIVING IN THE LAP OF LUXURY.
IS THAT POSSIBLE THROUGH RUNNING A CARRIAGE BUSINESS ALONE?
AND THERE'S MORE I DON'T UNDERSTAND.
CARLY STRATMANN.
SHE STUDIED CHEMISTRY AT EINRICH COLLEGE.
THERE WOULD BE PLENTY OF JOBS FOR HER WITH THAT KIND OF ACADEMIC RECORD.
BUT SHE'S DONE NOTHING FOR THREE YEARS AFTER GRADUATING.
CAN I TAKE A BREAK NOW?
ALSO, E.G. STRATMANN...
NOT ONLY WAS HE UNFAZED BY THE FACT THAT HIS DAUGHTER ISN'T WORKING...
HE SAID HE DOESN'T EVEN KNOW WHAT SHE DOES ON A DAILY BASIS.

AND ON TOP OF THAT,

THEY HAVE ACTUAL RULES ABOUT NOT INTERFERING IN EACH OTHER'S LIFE.

WHAT A STRANGE FAMILY.

WELL,

IF I'M GOING TO CALL THAT STRANGE...

THAT WOULD MAKE...

...ME AND MY FATHER PRETTY STRANGE, TOO.

HE TRAINED ME IN MARTIAL ARTS FROM SUNRISE TO SUNSET.

DAY AFTER DAY AFTER DAY.

I KEPT ON KICKING, EVEN WHEN MY LEGS WERE SWOLLEN.

I WASN'T ALLOWED ANY TIME OFF.

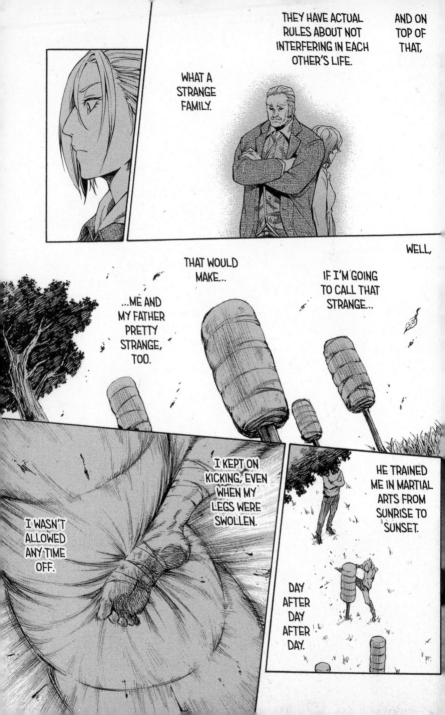

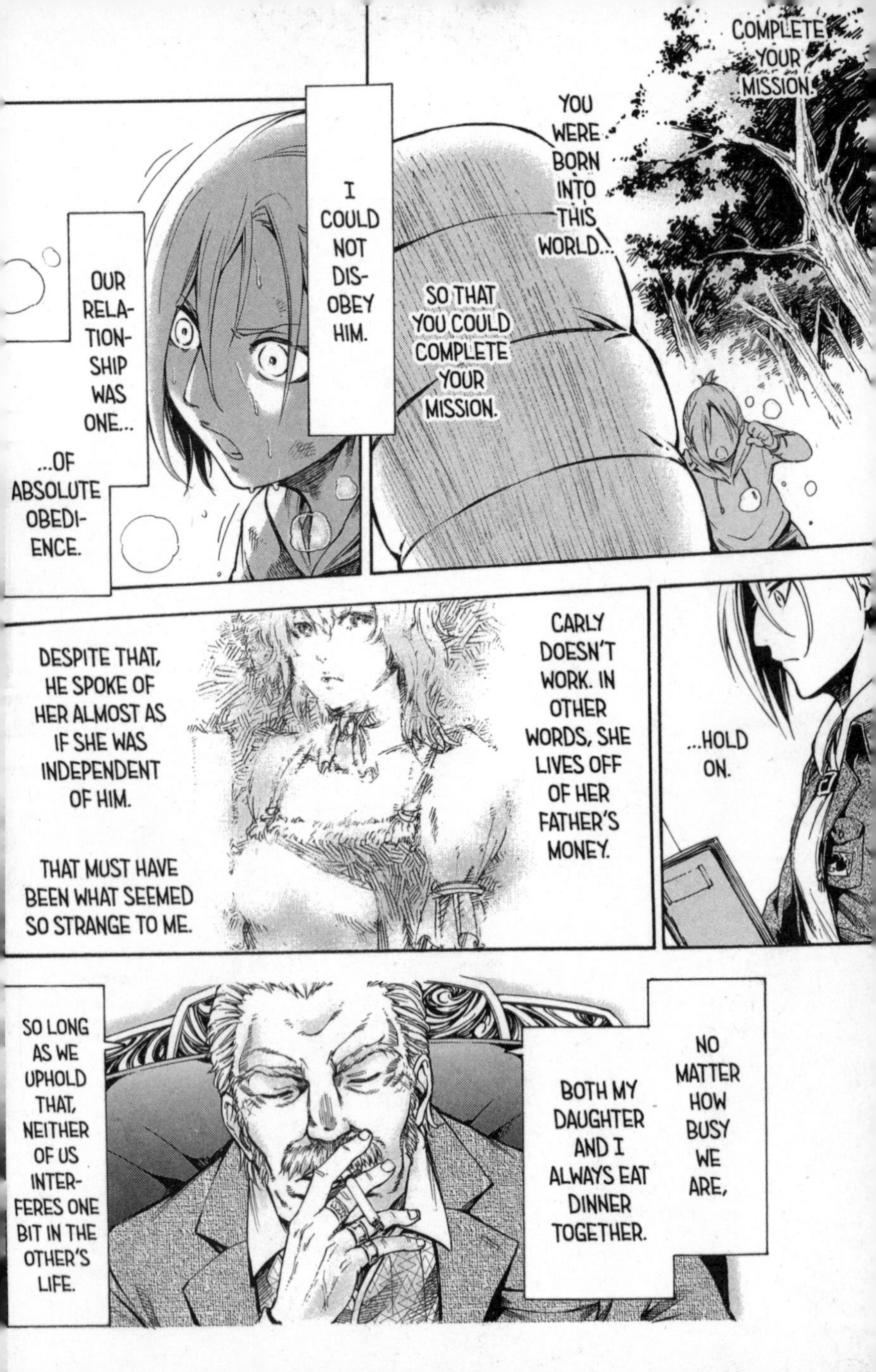
COMPLETE YOUR MISSION.
YOU WERE BORN INTO THIS WORLD...
SO THAT YOU COULD COMPLETE YOUR MISSION.
I COULD NOT DIS-OBEY HIM.
OUR RELA-TION-SHIP WAS ONE...
...OF ABSOLUTE OBEDI-ENCE.
...HOLD ON.
CARLY DOESN'T WORK. IN OTHER WORDS, SHE LIVES OFF OF HER FATHER'S MONEY.
DESPITE THAT, HE SPOKE OF HER ALMOST AS IF SHE WAS INDEPENDENT OF HIM.
THAT MUST HAVE BEEN WHAT SEEMED SO STRANGE TO ME.
NO MATTER HOW BUSY WE ARE,
BOTH MY DAUGHTER AND I ALWAYS EAT DINNER TOGETHER.
SO LONG AS WE UPHOLD THAT, NEITHER OF US INTER-FERES ONE BIT IN THE OTHER'S LIFE.

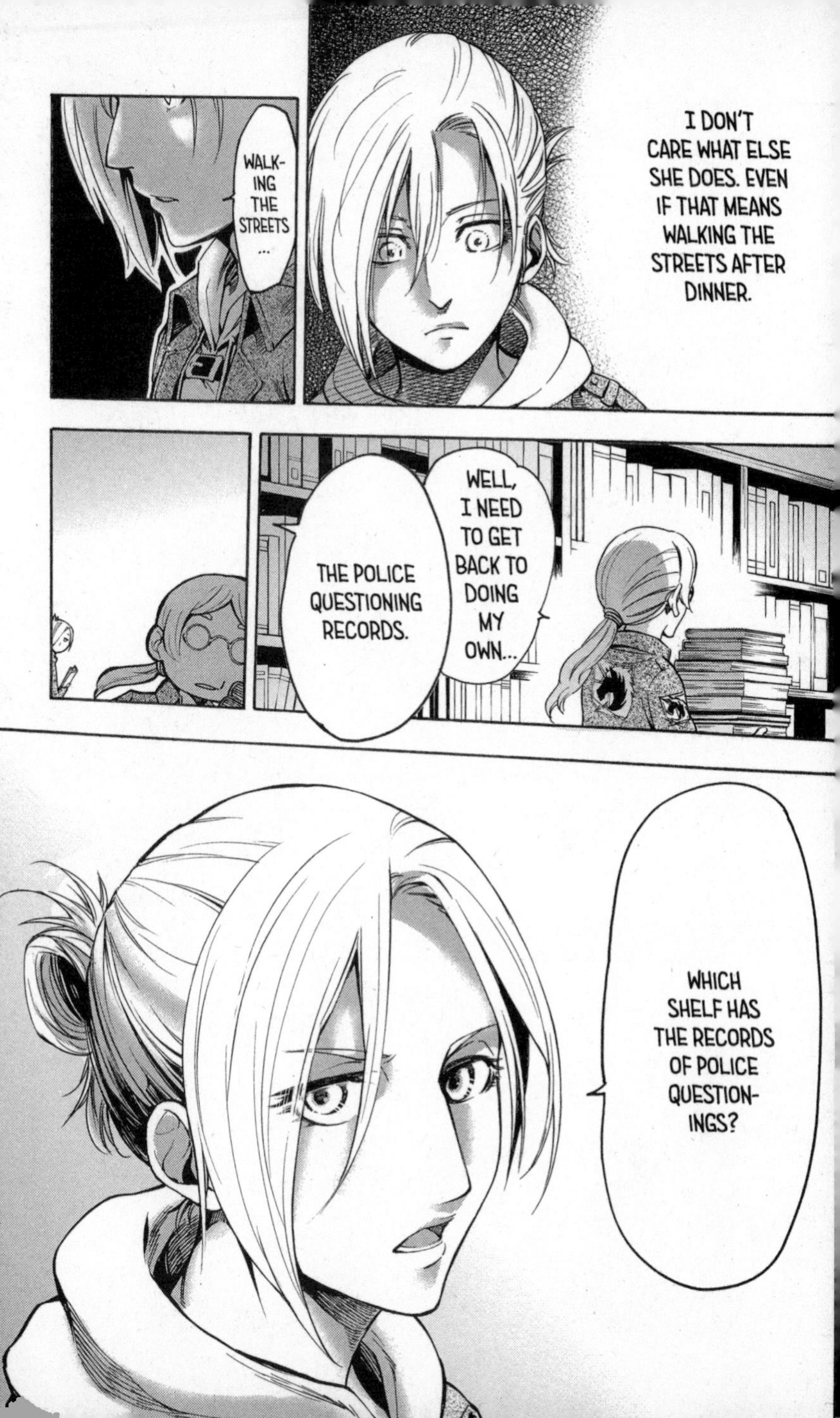
I DON'T CARE WHAT ELSE SHE DOES. EVEN IF THAT MEANS WALKING THE STREETS AFTER DINNER.
WALK-ING THE STREETS ...
WELL, I NEED TO GET BACK TO DOING MY OWN...
THE POLICE QUESTIONING RECORDS.
WHICH SHELF HAS THE RECORDS OF POLICE QUESTION-INGS?

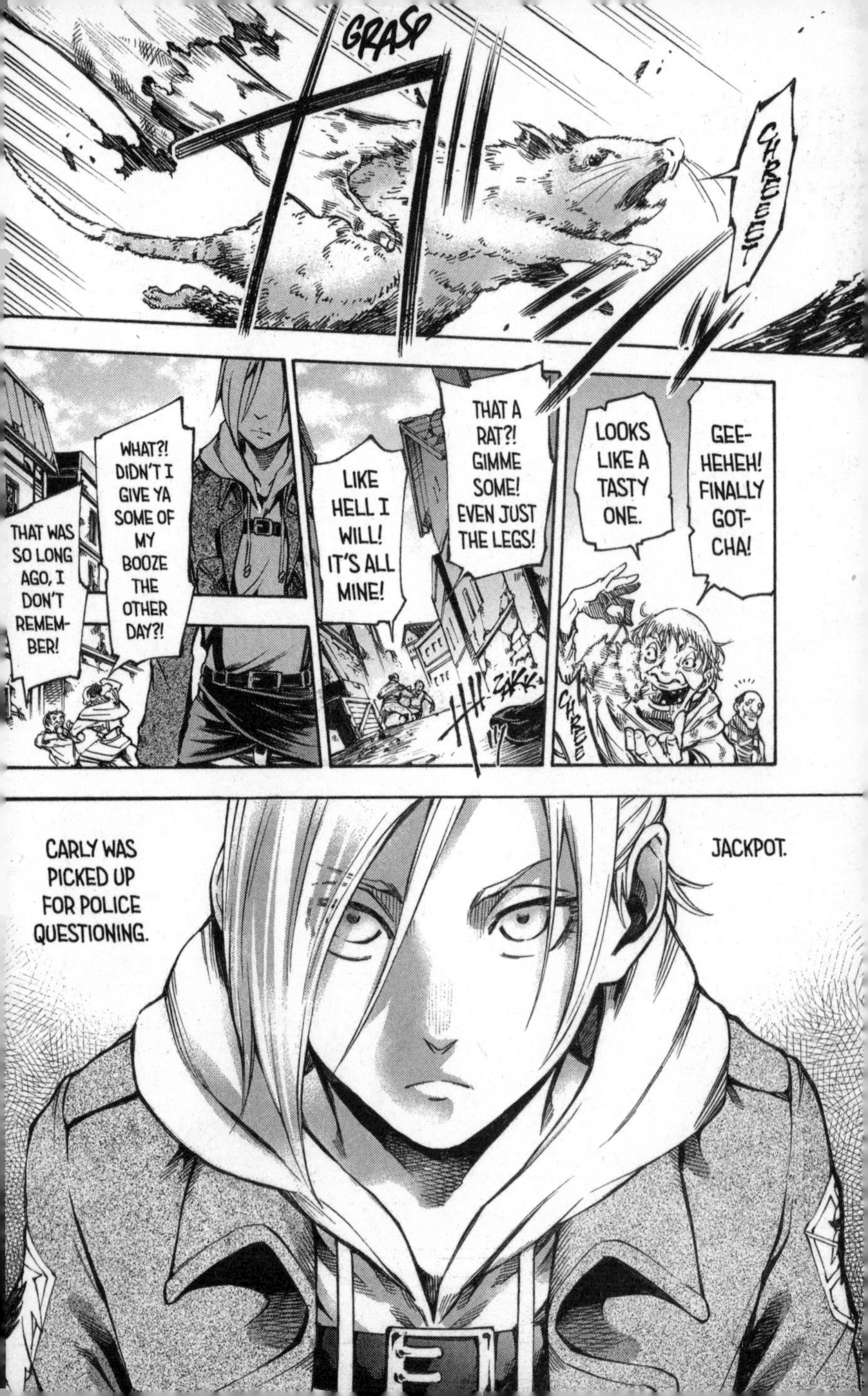
GRASP
CHREEECT
GEE-HEHEH! FINALLY GOT-CHA!
LOOKS LIKE A TASTY ONE.
CHREEE
THAT A RAT?! GIMME SOME! EVEN JUST THE LEGS!
LIKE HELL I WILL! IT'S ALL MINE!
ZAKK
WHAT?! DIDN'T I GIVE YA SOME OF MY BOOZE THE OTHER DAY?!
THAT WAS SO LONG AGO, I DON'T REMEM-BER!
JACKPOT.
CARLY WAS PICKED UP FOR POLICE QUESTIONING.

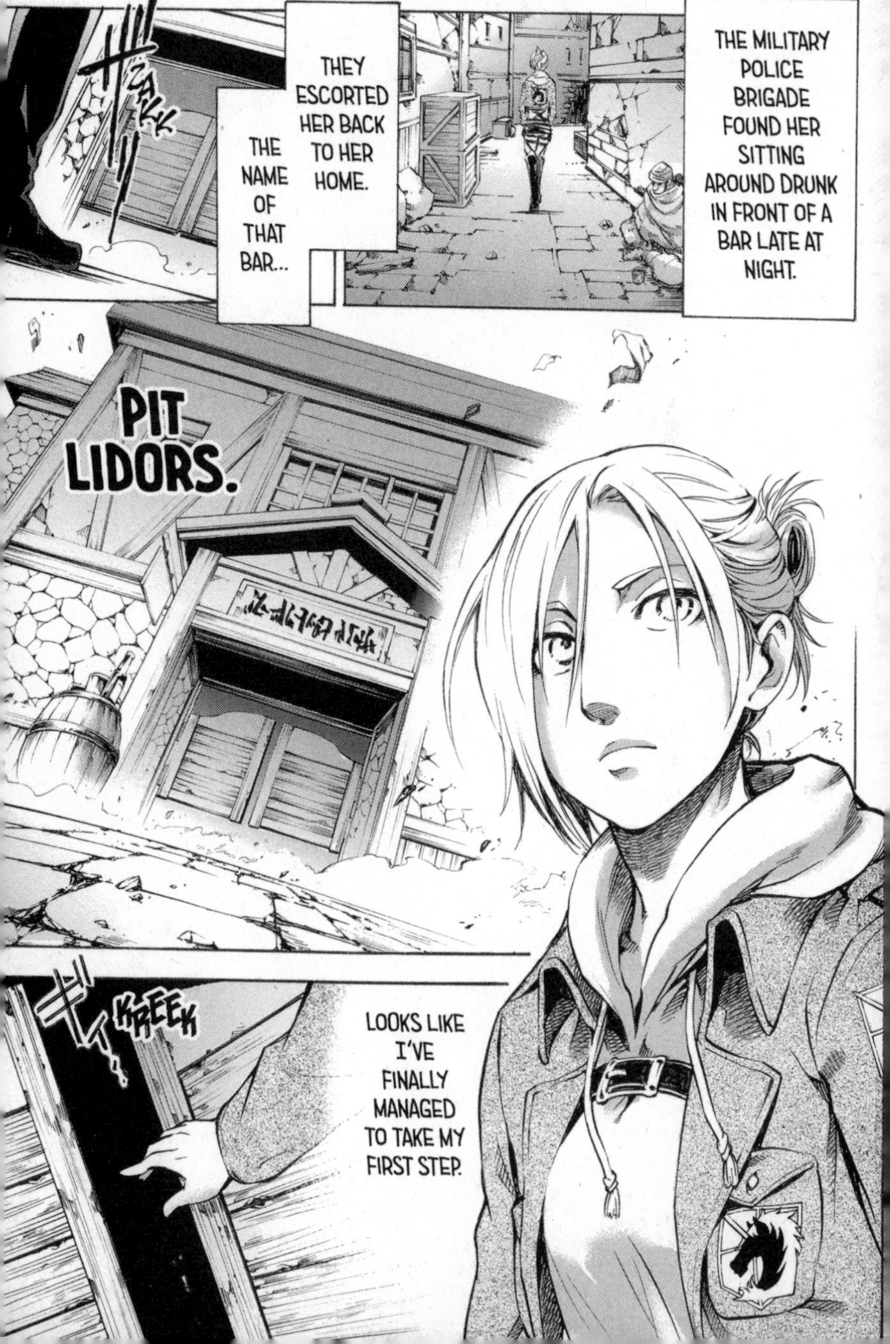
THE MILITARY POLICE BRIGADE FOUND HER SITTING AROUND DRUNK IN FRONT OF A BAR LATE AT NIGHT.
THEY ESCORTED HER BACK TO HER HOME.
THE NAME OF THAT BAR...
ZAK
PIT LIDORS.
LOOKS LIKE I'VE FINALLY MANAGED TO TAKE MY FIRST STEP.
KREEK

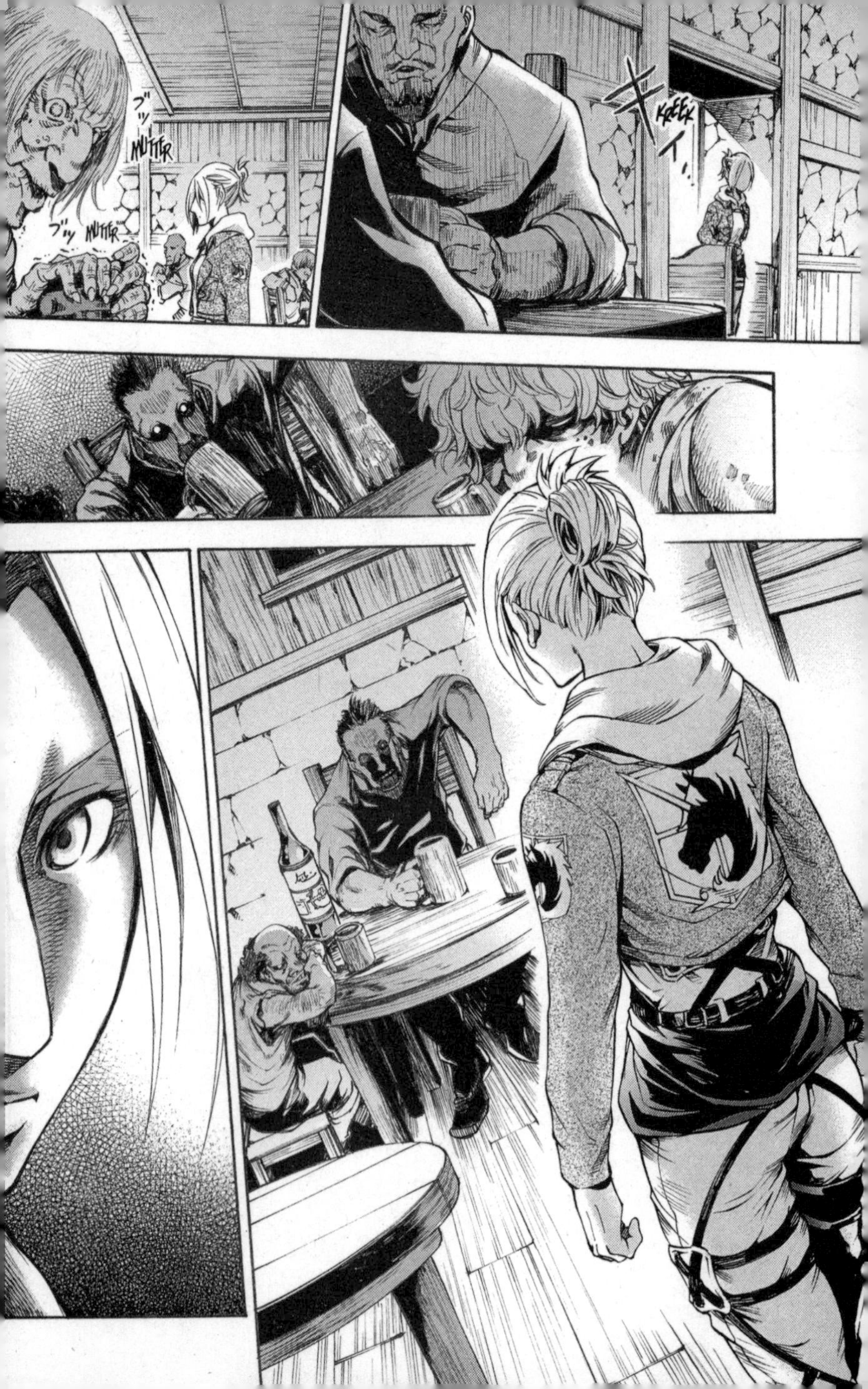
KREEK
ブツ MUTTER
ブツ MUTTER

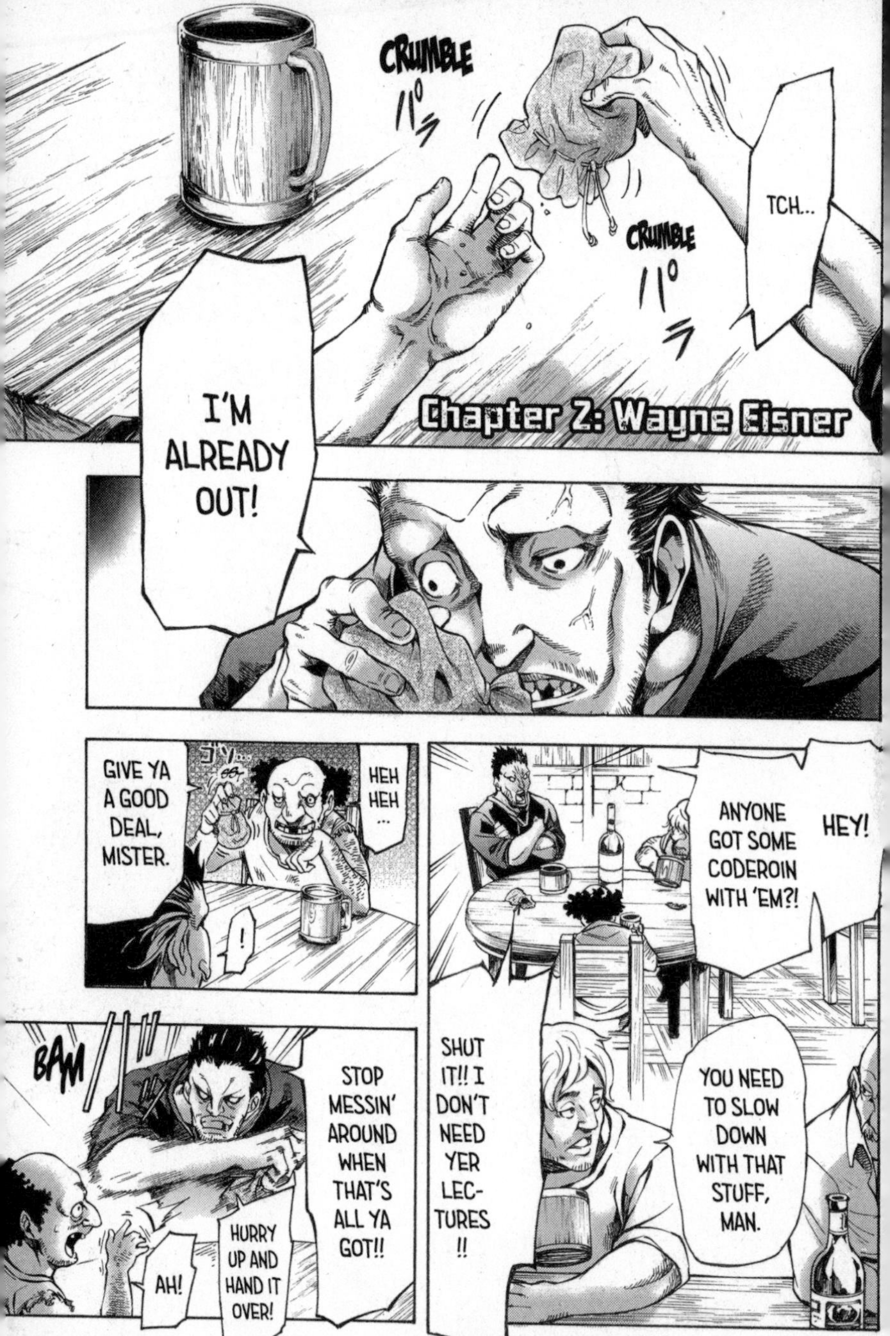
TCH...
CRUMBLE
CRUMBLE
Chapter 2: Wayne Eisner
I'M ALREADY OUT!
HEY!
ANYONE GOT SOME CODEROIN WITH 'EM?!
HEH HEH ...
GIVE YA A GOOD DEAL, MISTER.
!
YOU NEED TO SLOW DOWN WITH THAT STUFF, MAN.
SHUT IT!! I DON'T NEED YER LEC-TURES!!
STOP MESSIN' AROUND WHEN THAT'S ALL YA GOT!!
BAM
HURRY UP AND HAND IT OVER!
AH!

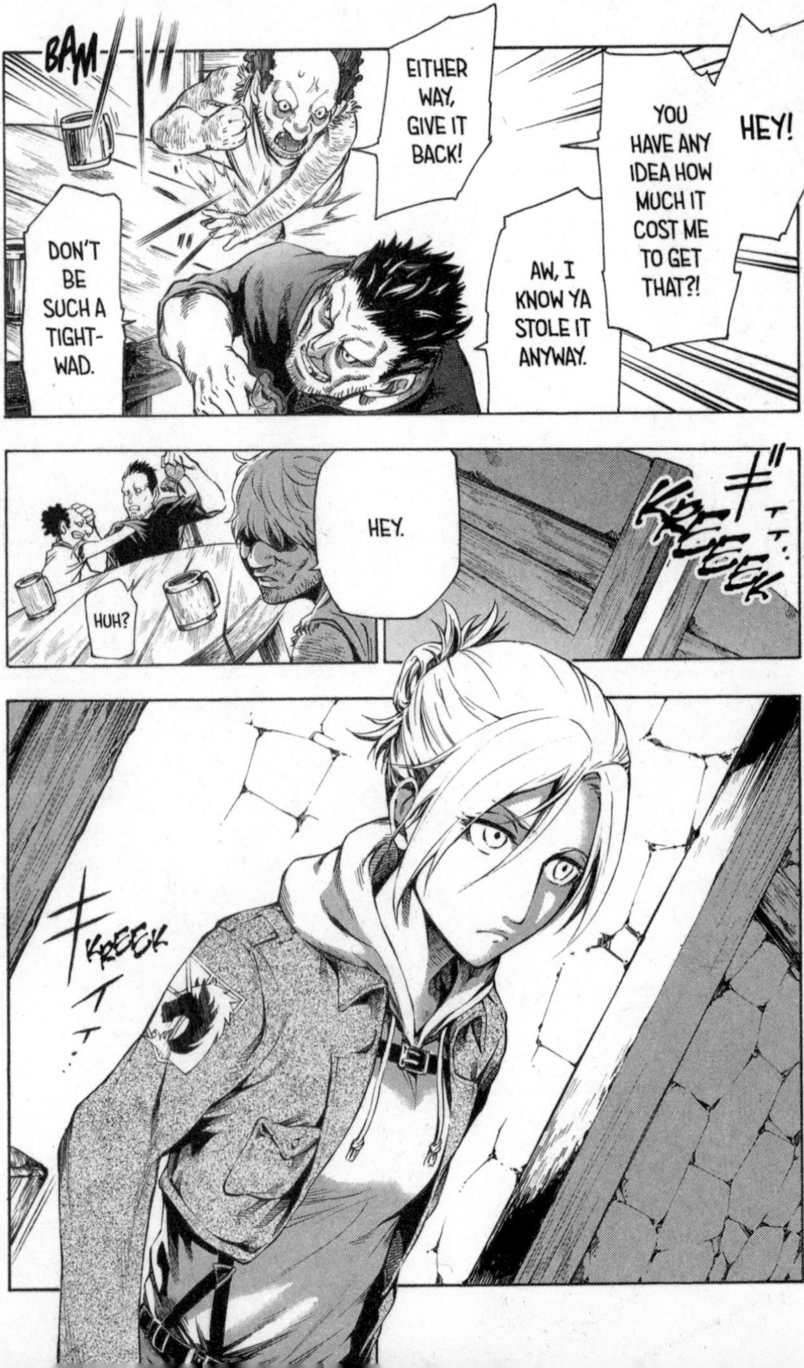
HEY!
YOU HAVE ANY IDEA HOW MUCH IT COST ME TO GET THAT?!
EITHER WAY, GIVE IT BACK!
BAM
AW, I KNOW YA STOLE IT ANYWAY.
DON'T BE SUCH A TIGHT-WAD.
KREEEEK
HEY.
HUH?
KREEK

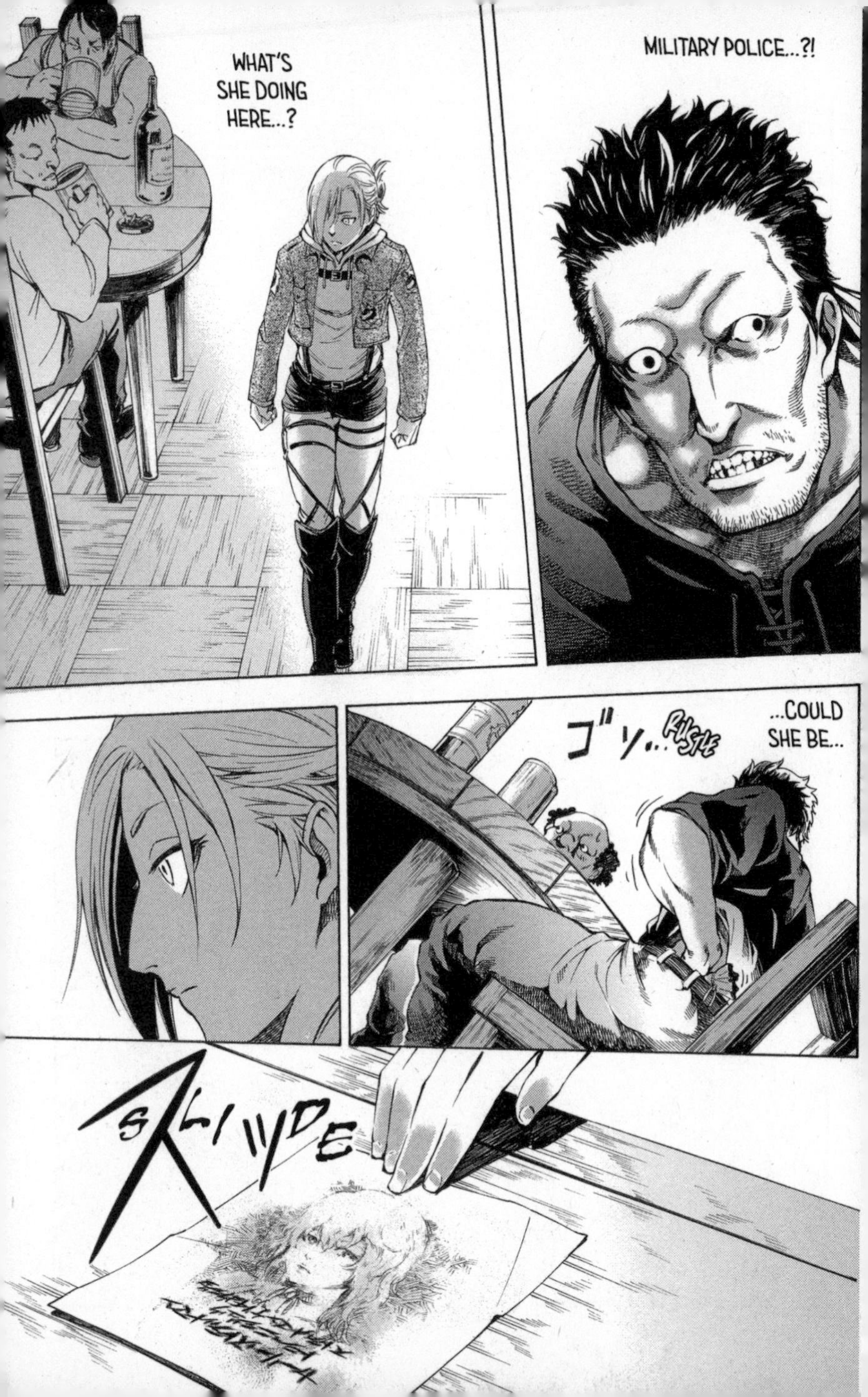
MILITARY POLICE...?!
WHAT'S SHE DOING HERE...?
...COULD SHE BE...
ゴソ...
RUSTLE
SLIIIDE

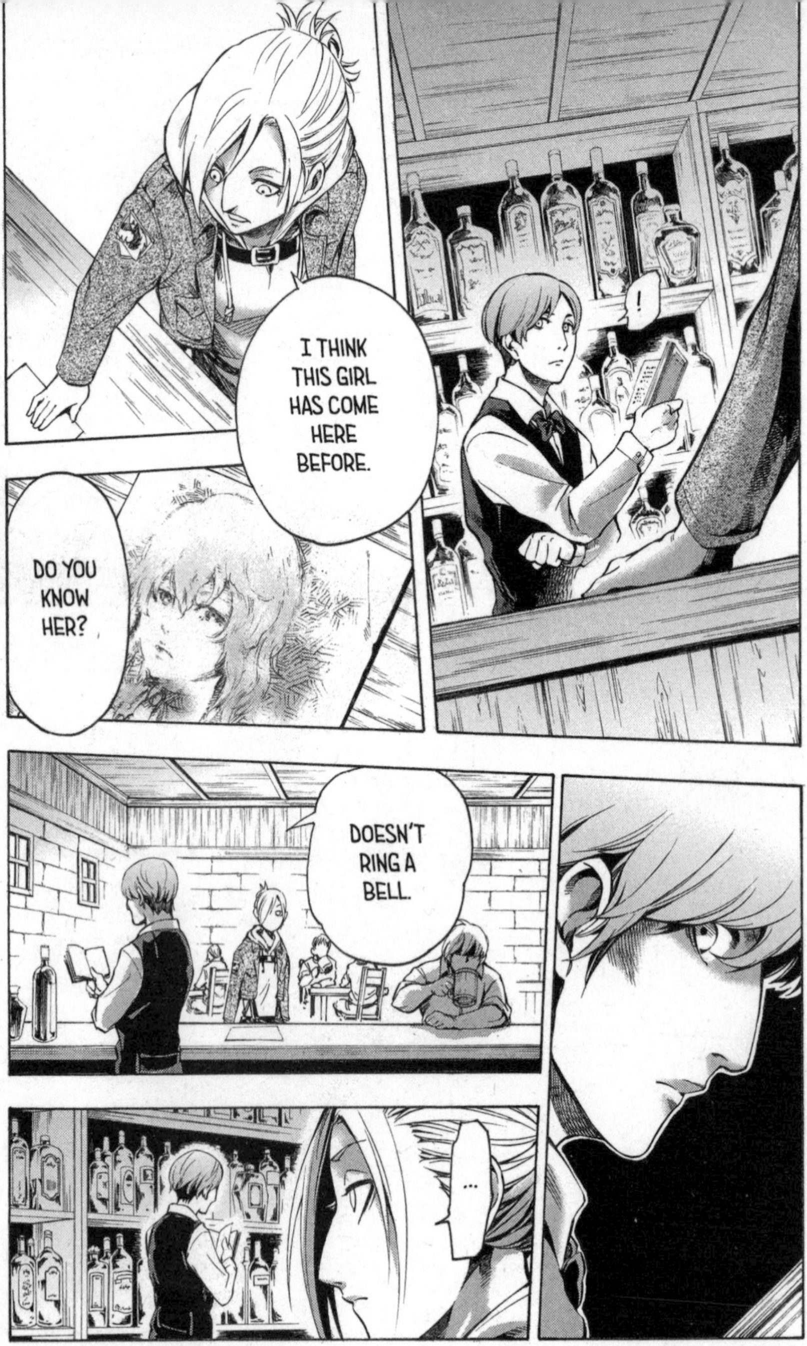
!
I THINK THIS GIRL HAS COME HERE BEFORE.
DO YOU KNOW HER?
DOESN'T RING A BELL.
...

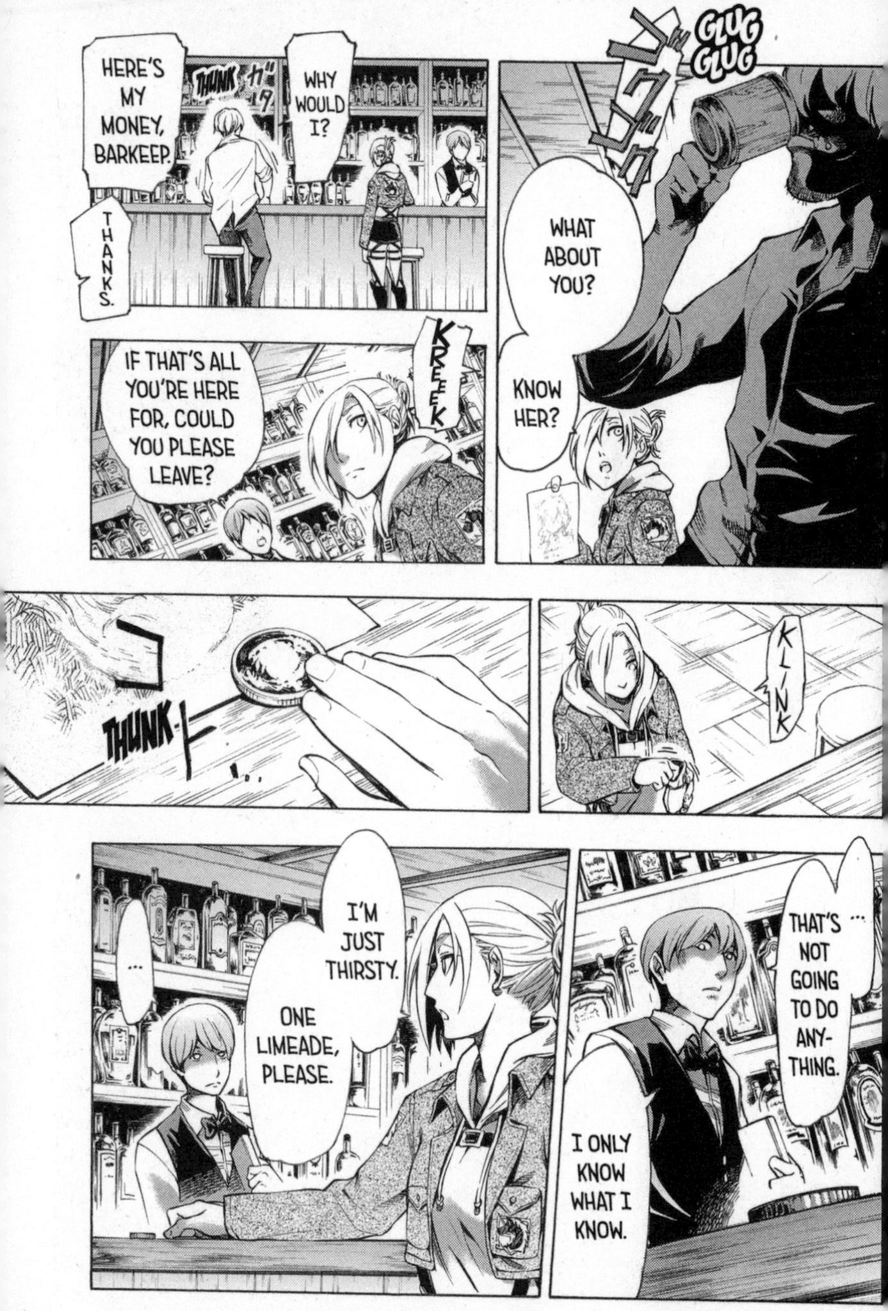
GLUG GLUG
WHAT ABOUT YOU?
KNOW HER?
WHY WOULD I?
THUNK ガタ
HERE'S MY MONEY, BARKEEP.
THANKS.
KREEEK
IF THAT'S ALL YOU'RE HERE FOR, COULD YOU PLEASE LEAVE?
KLINK
THUNK
... THAT'S NOT GOING TO DO ANYTHING.
I ONLY KNOW WHAT I KNOW.
I'M JUST THIRSTY.
ONE LIMEADE, PLEASE.
...

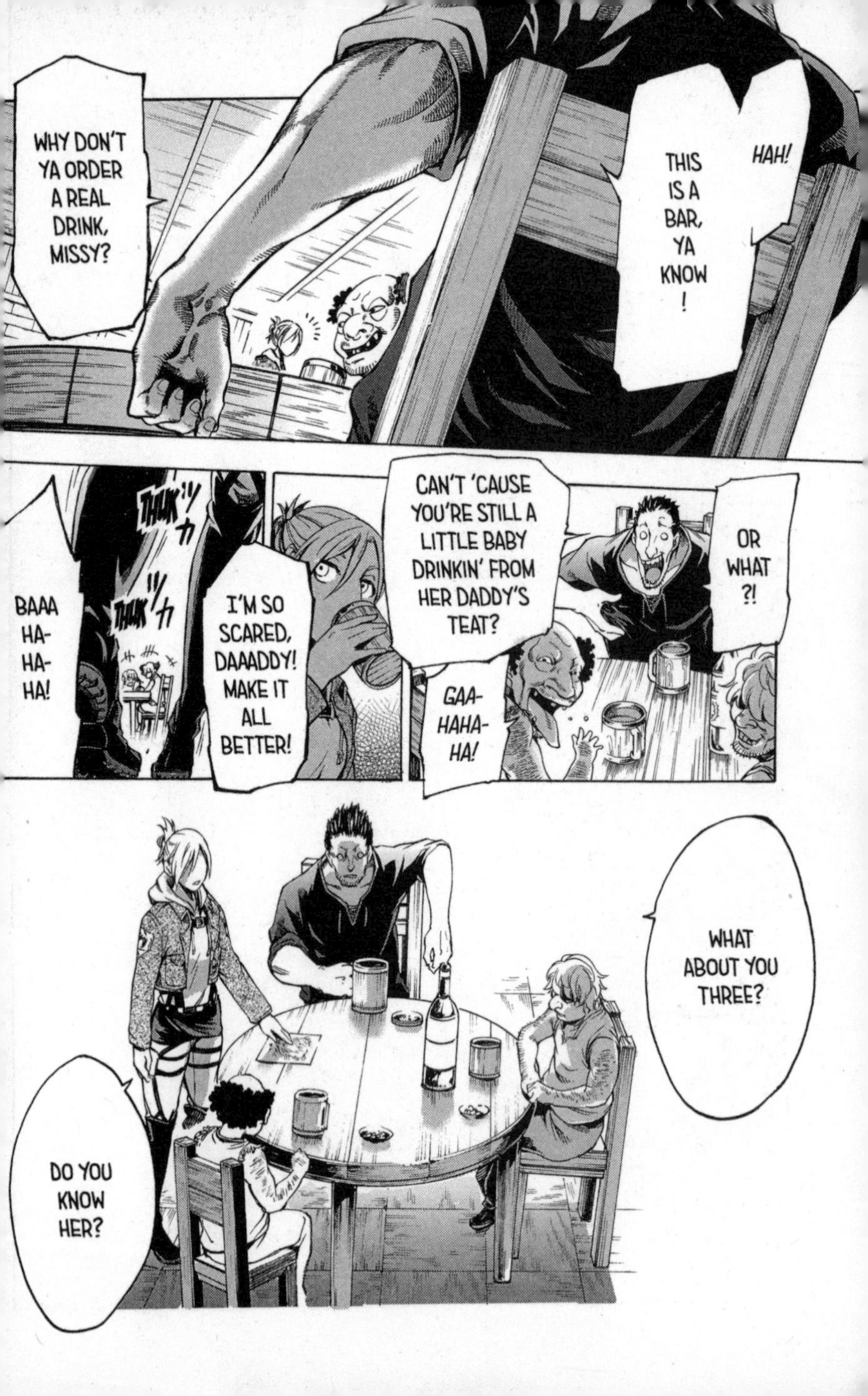
HAH!
THIS IS A BAR, YA KNOW!
WHY DON'T YA ORDER A REAL DRINK, MISSY?
CAN'T 'CAUSE YOU'RE STILL A LITTLE BABY DRINKIN' FROM HER DADDY'S TEAT?
OR WHAT?!
GAA-HAHA-HA!
I'M SO SCARED, DAAADDY! MAKE IT ALL BETTER!
THUK
THUK
BAAA HA-HA-HA!
WHAT ABOUT YOU THREE?
DO YOU KNOW HER?

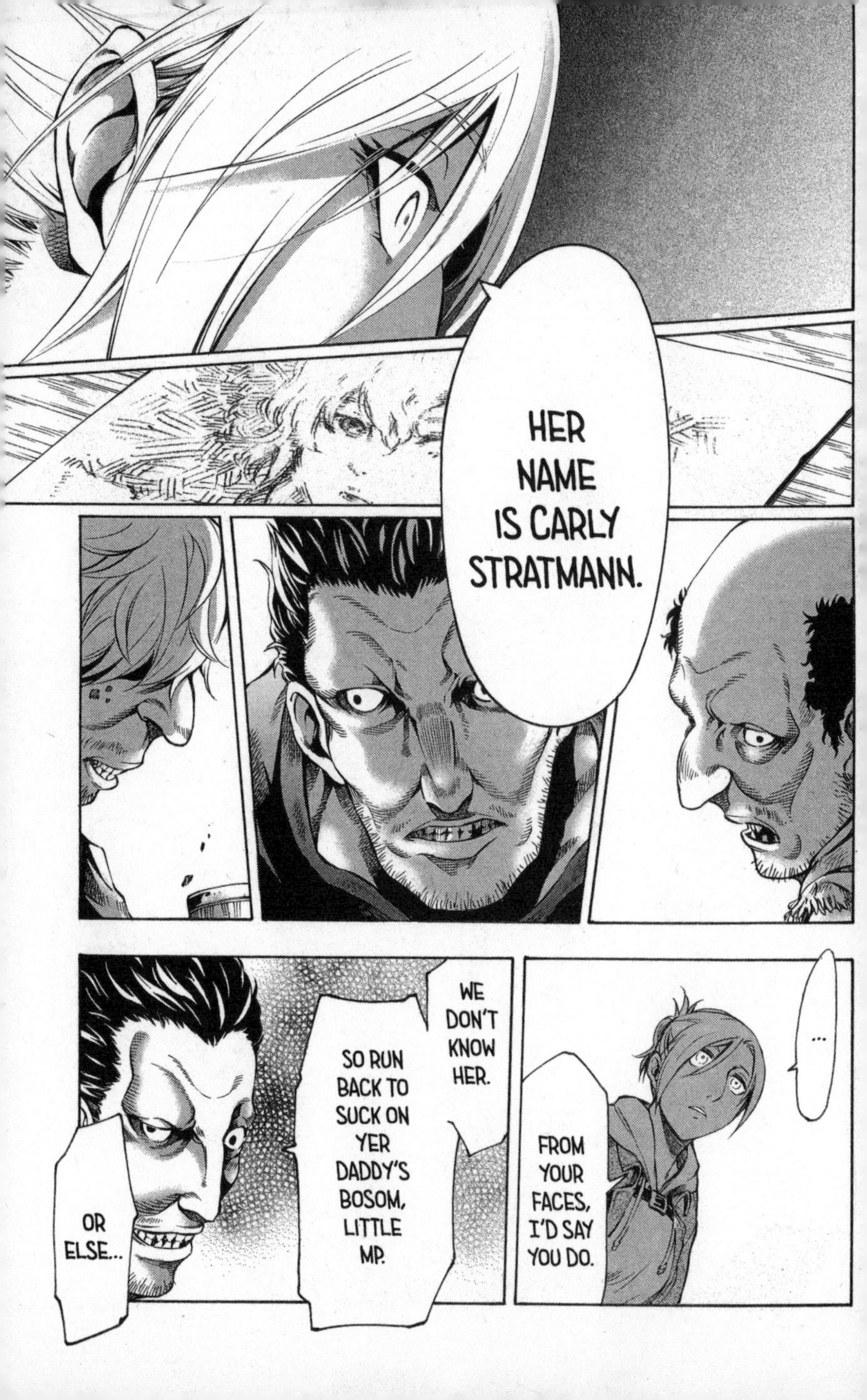
HER NAME IS CARLY STRATMANN.
...
FROM YOUR FACES, I'D SAY YOU DO.
WE DON'T KNOW HER.
SO RUN BACK TO SUCK ON YER DADDY'S BOSOM, LITTLE MP.
OR ELSE...

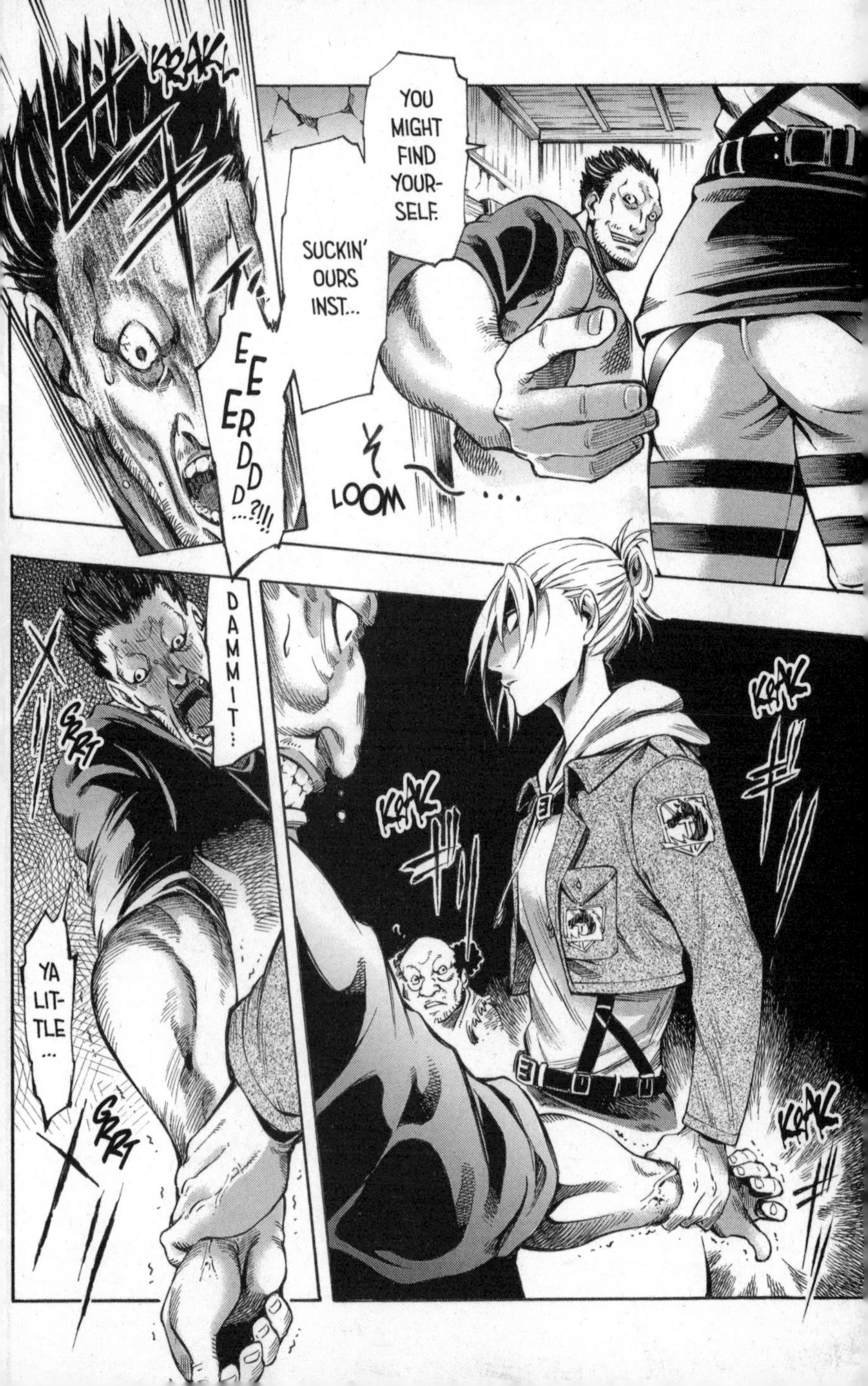
YOU MIGHT FIND YOURSELF.
SUCKIN' OURS INST...
LOOM...
KRAK
EEERDDDD...?!!!
KRAK
KRAK
KRAK
DAMMIT...
GRRT
YA LITTLE...
GRRT

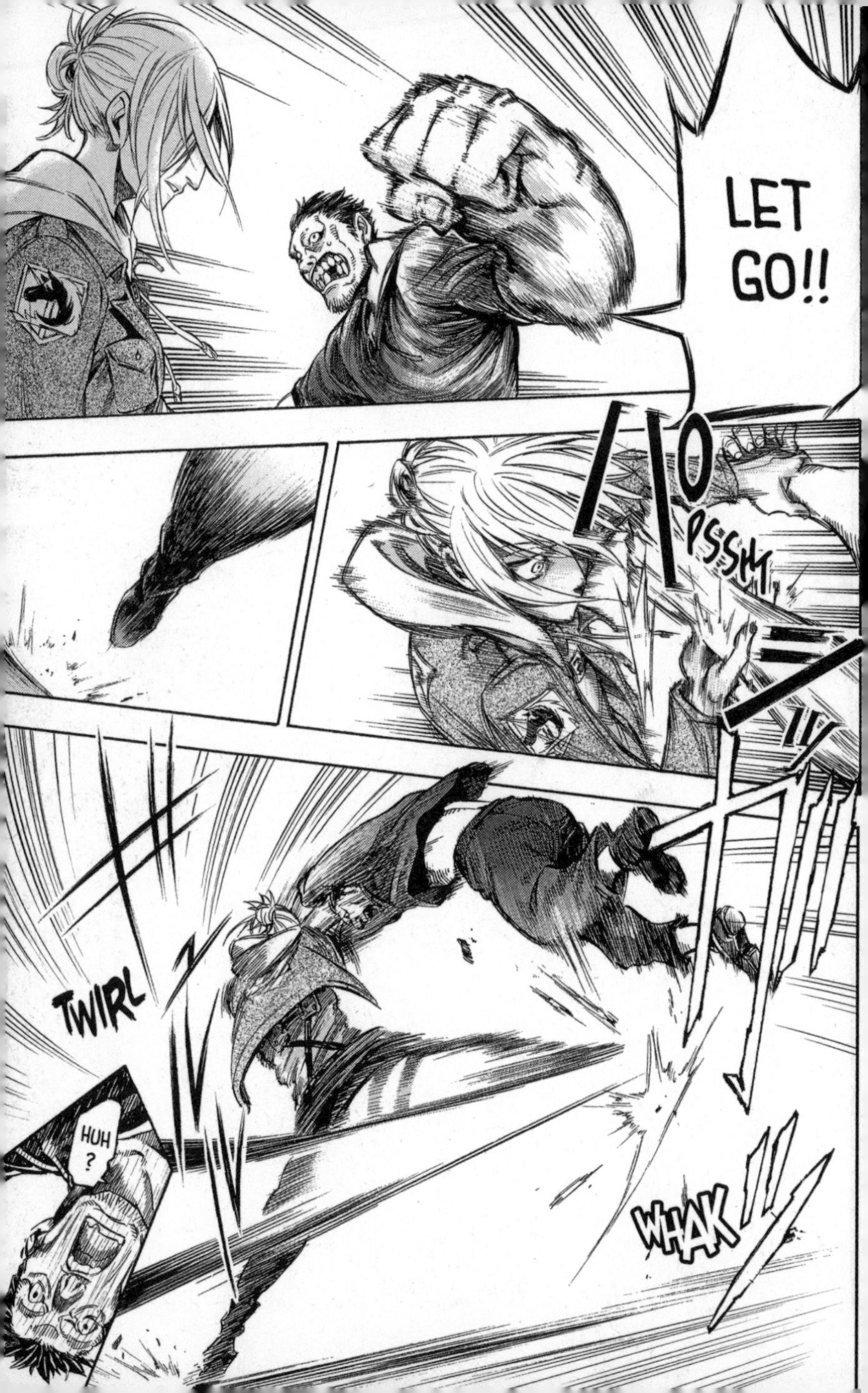
LET GO!!
PSSH
TWIRL
WHAK
HUH?

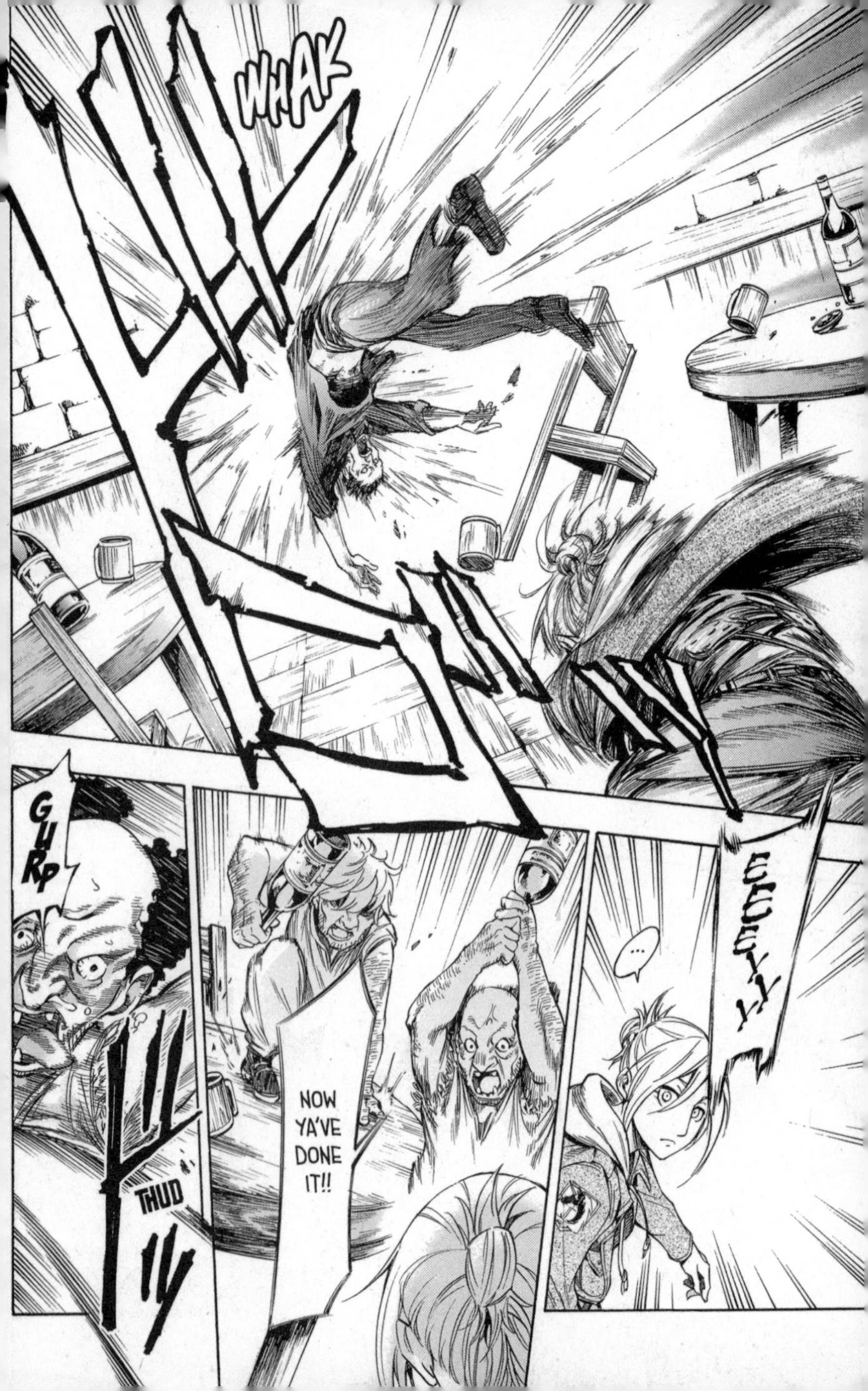
WHAK
...
NOW YA'VE DONE IT!!
GURP
THUD

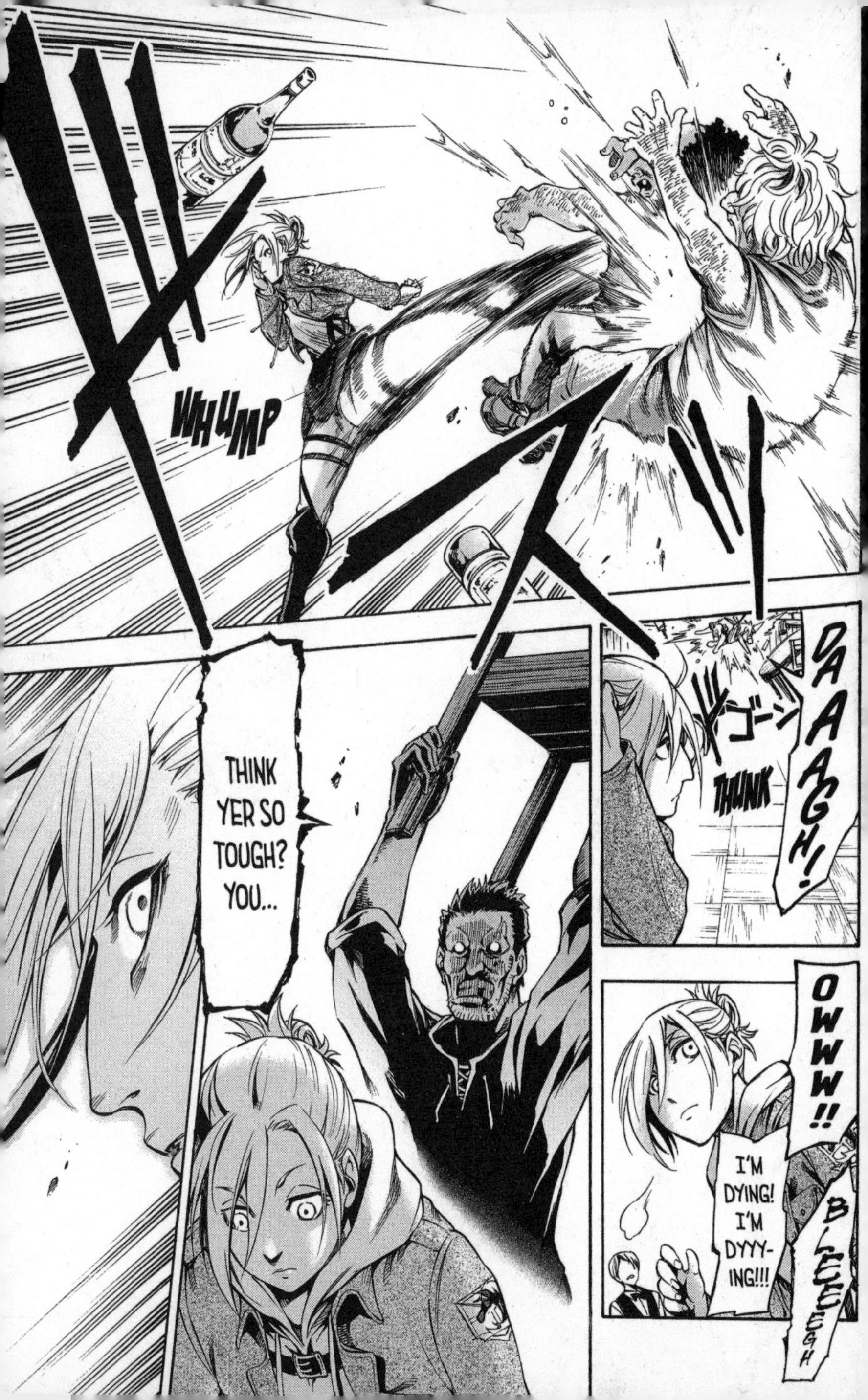
WHUMP
DAAAAGH!
ゴーン
THUNK
OWWW!!
I'M DYING! I'M DYYY-ING!!!
BLEEEEGH
THINK YER SO TOUGH? YOU...

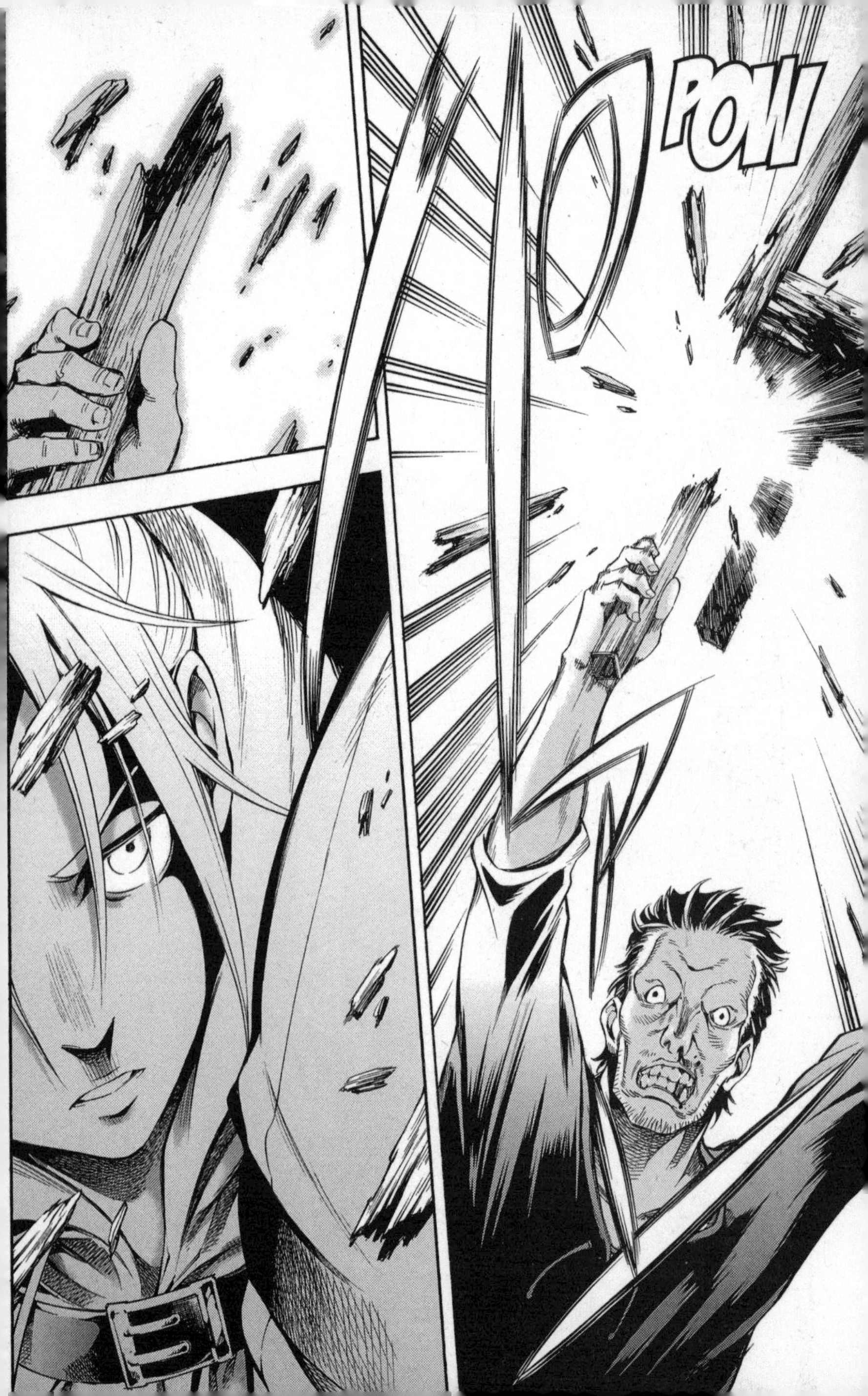
POW

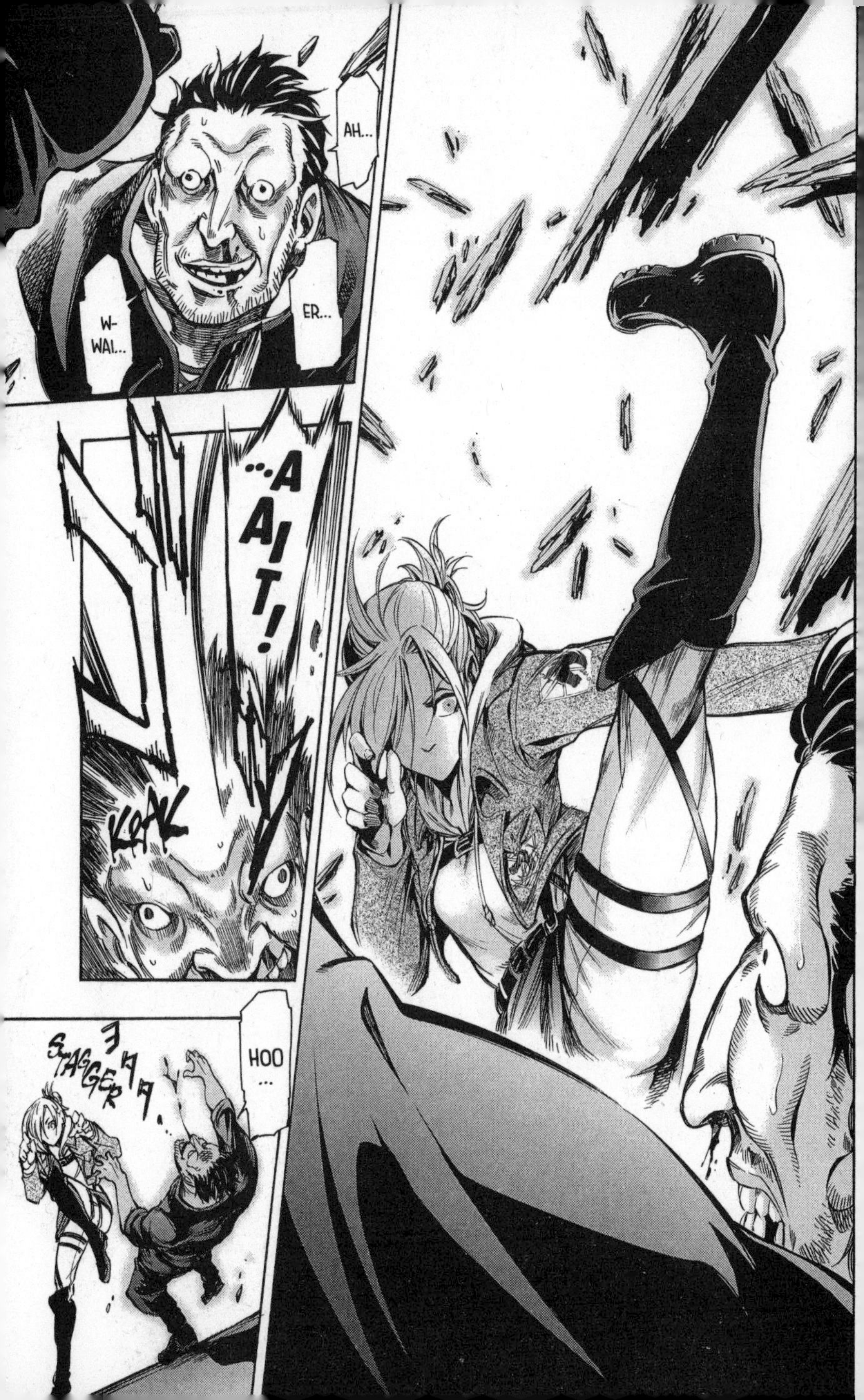

AH...
ER...
W-WAI...
...AAIT!!
KRAK
HOO...
STAGGER

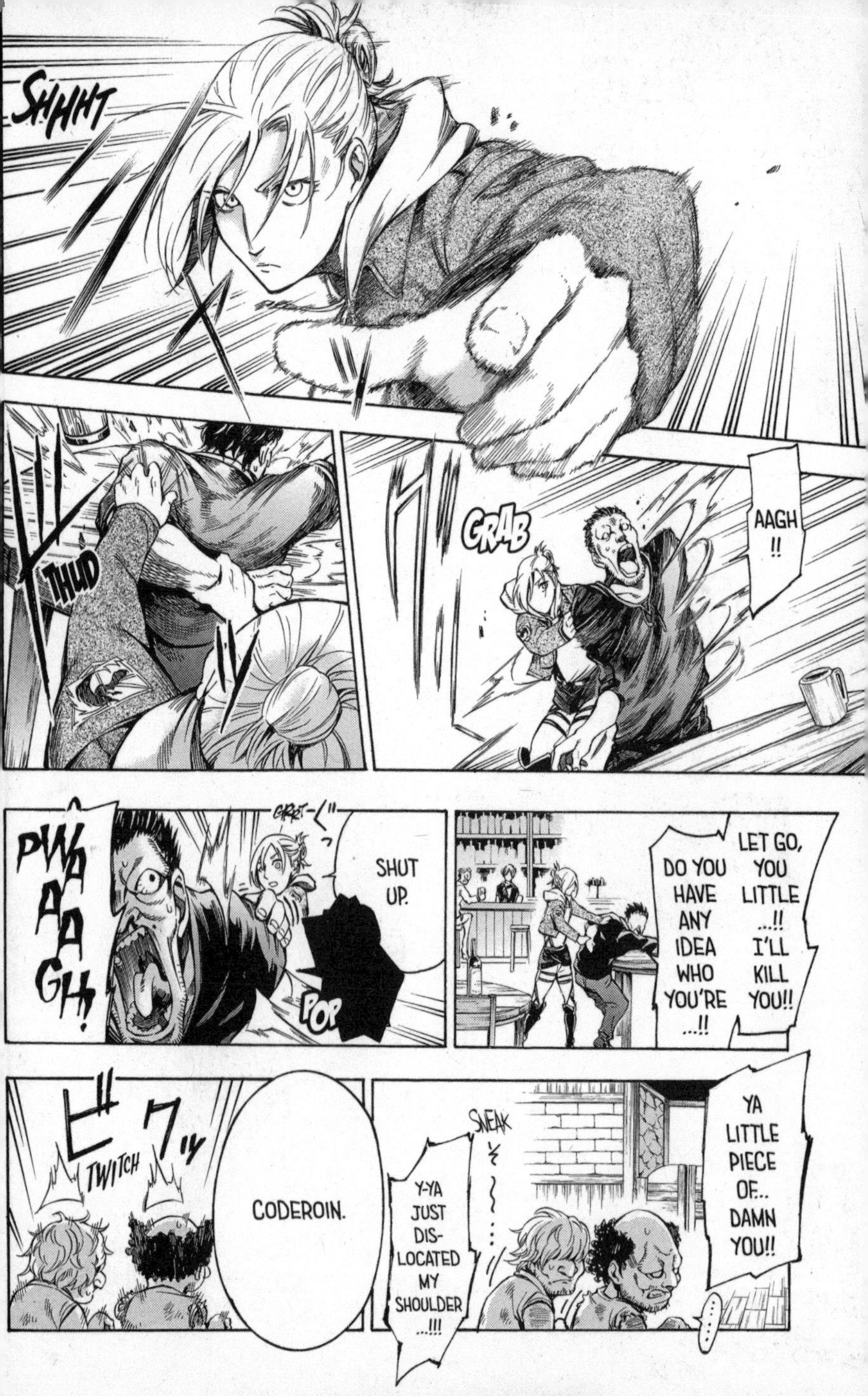
SHHHT
AAGH!!
GRAB
THUD
LET GO, YOU LITTLE ...!! I'LL KILL YOU!!
DO YOU HAVE ANY IDEA WHO YOU'RE ...!!
SHUT UP.
POP
PWAAAGH!!
YA LITTLE PIECE OF.. DAMN YOU!!
......
SNEAK
Y-YA JUST DIS-LOCATED MY SHOULDER ...!!!
CODEROIN.
ビクッ
TWITCH

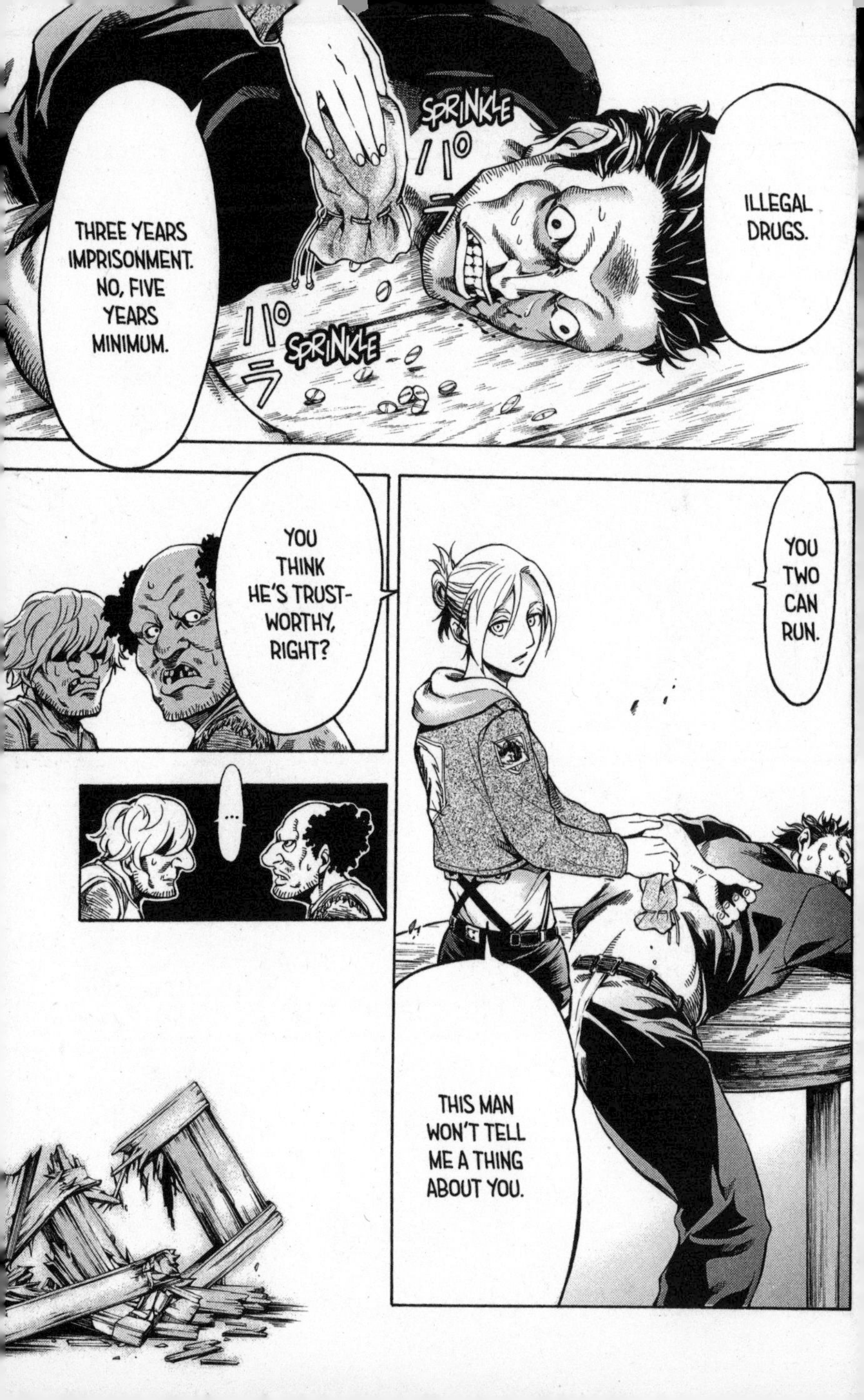
ILLEGAL DRUGS.
SPRINKLE
SPRINKLE
THREE YEARS IMPRISONMENT. NO, FIVE YEARS MINIMUM.
YOU TWO CAN RUN.
THIS MAN WON'T TELL ME A THING ABOUT YOU.
YOU THINK HE'S TRUST-WORTHY, RIGHT?
...

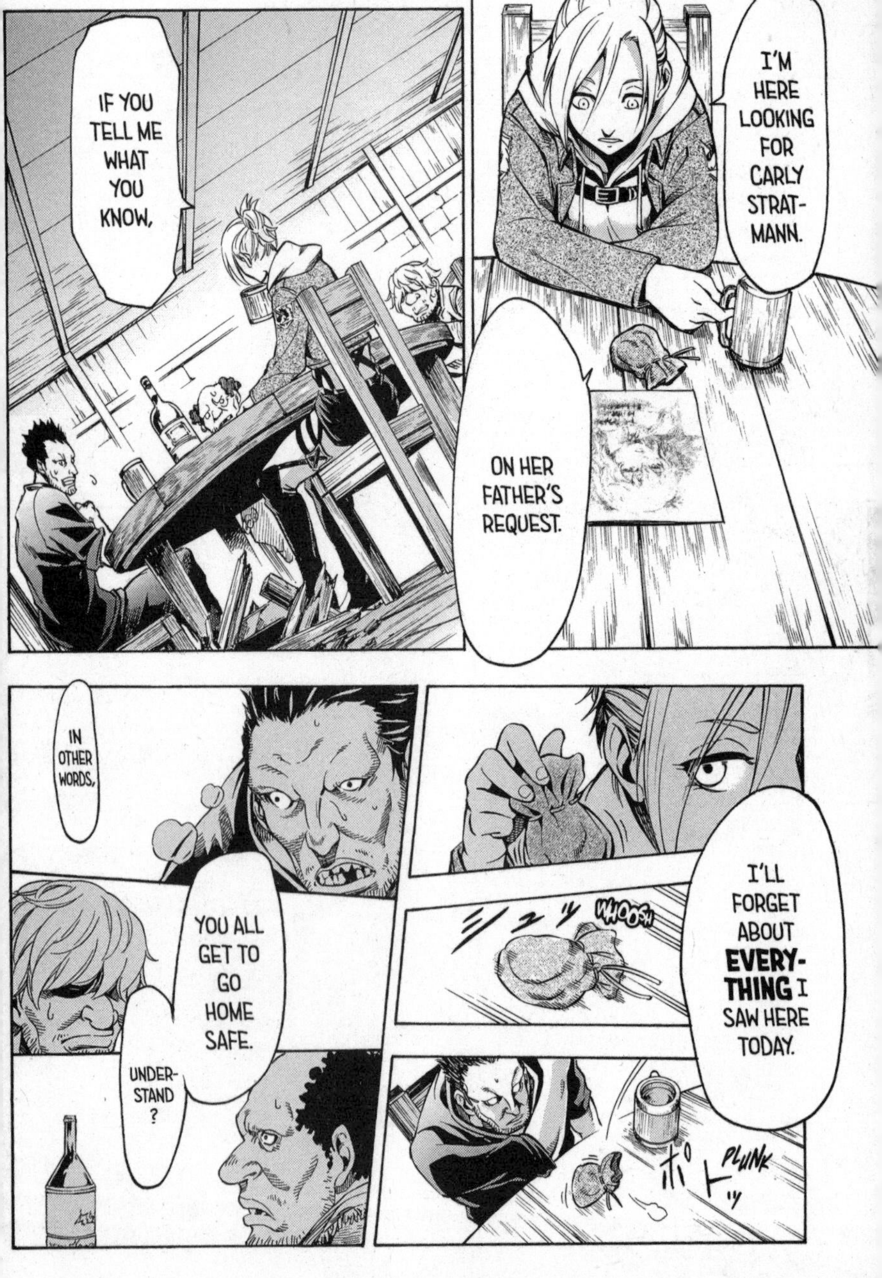
I'M HERE LOOKING FOR CARLY STRAT-MANN.
ON HER FATHER'S REQUEST.
IF YOU TELL ME WHAT YOU KNOW,
I'LL FORGET ABOUT **EVERY-THING** I SAW HERE TODAY.
WHOOSH
PLUNK
IN OTHER WORDS,
YOU ALL GET TO GO HOME SAFE.
UNDER-STAND?

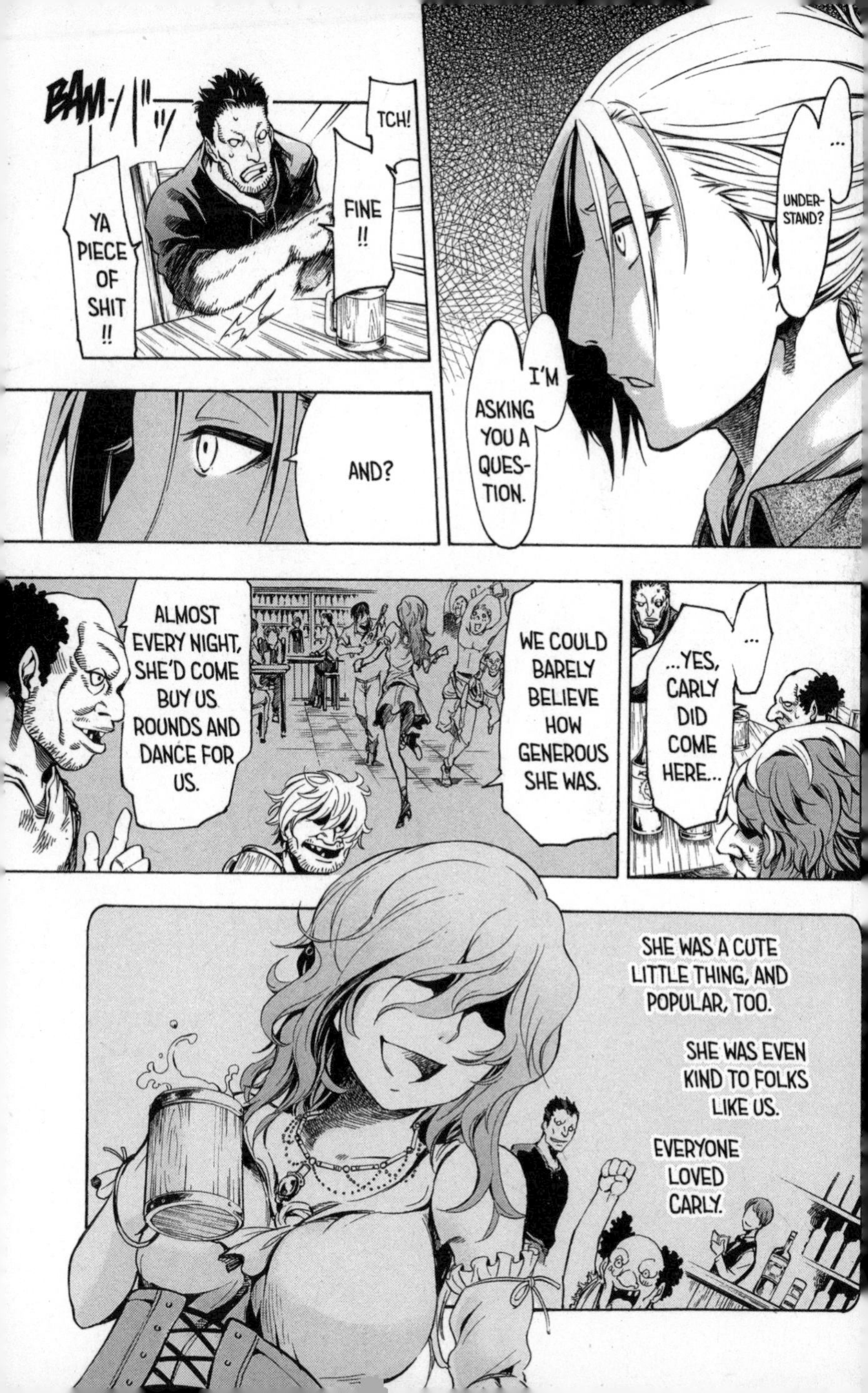
...
UNDERSTAND?
I'M ASKING YOU A QUESTION.
TCH!
FINE!!
BAM
YA PIECE OF SHIT!!
AND?
...
...YES, CARLY DID COME HERE...
WE COULD BARELY BELIEVE HOW GENEROUS SHE WAS.
ALMOST EVERY NIGHT, SHE'D COME BUY US ROUNDS AND DANCE FOR US.
SHE WAS A CUTE LITTLE THING, AND POPULAR, TOO.
SHE WAS EVEN KIND TO FOLKS LIKE US.
EVERYONE LOVED CARLY.

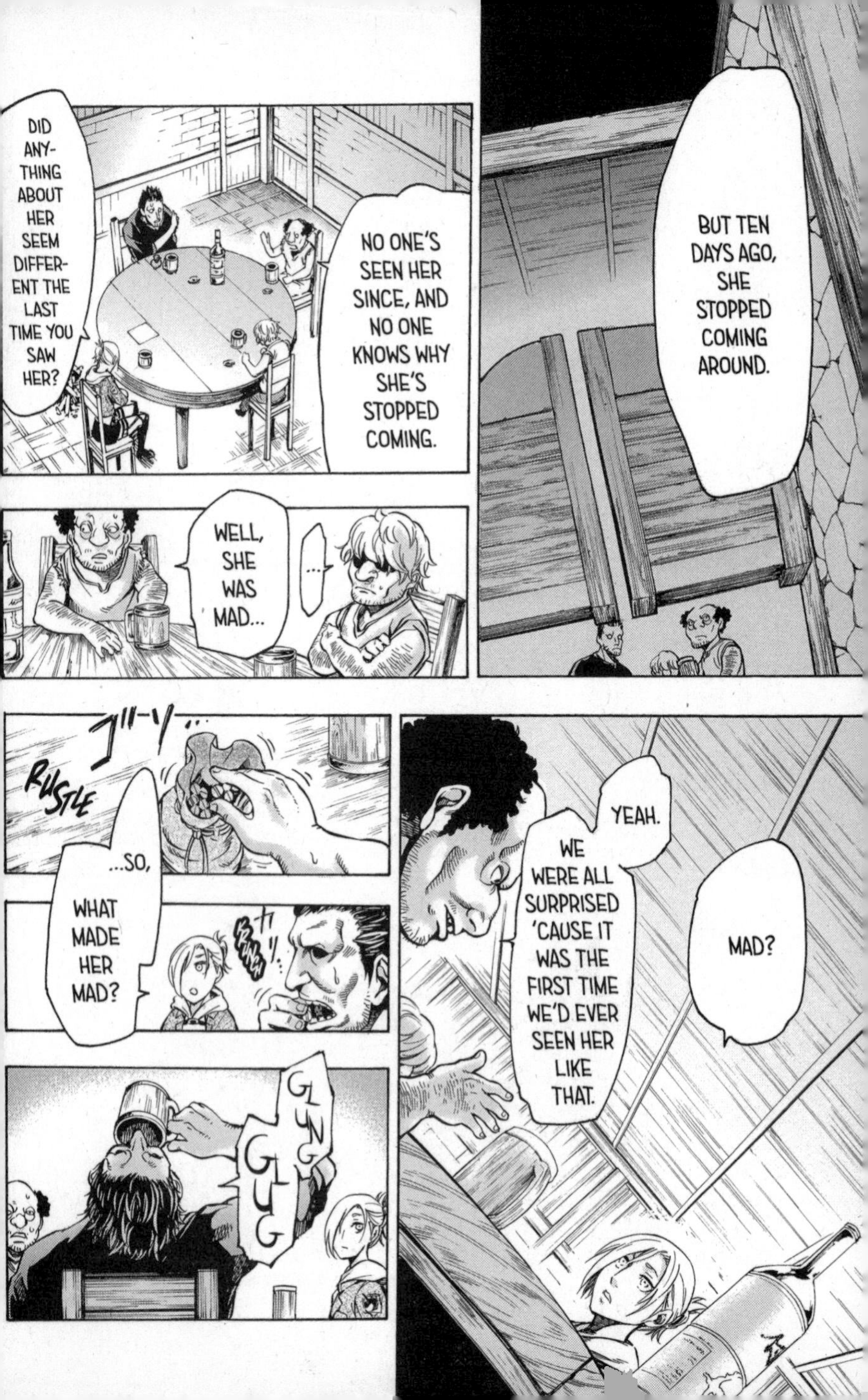
BUT TEN DAYS AGO, SHE STOPPED COMING AROUND.
NO ONE'S SEEN HER SINCE, AND NO ONE KNOWS WHY SHE'S STOPPED COMING.
DID ANYTHING ABOUT HER SEEM DIFFERENT THE LAST TIME YOU SAW HER?
...
WELL, SHE WAS MAD...
MAD?
YEAH.
WE WERE ALL SURPRISED 'CAUSE IT WAS THE FIRST TIME WE'D EVER SEEN HER LIKE THAT.
RUSTLE
...SO,
WHAT MADE HER MAD?
KRUNCH
GLUNG
GLUG

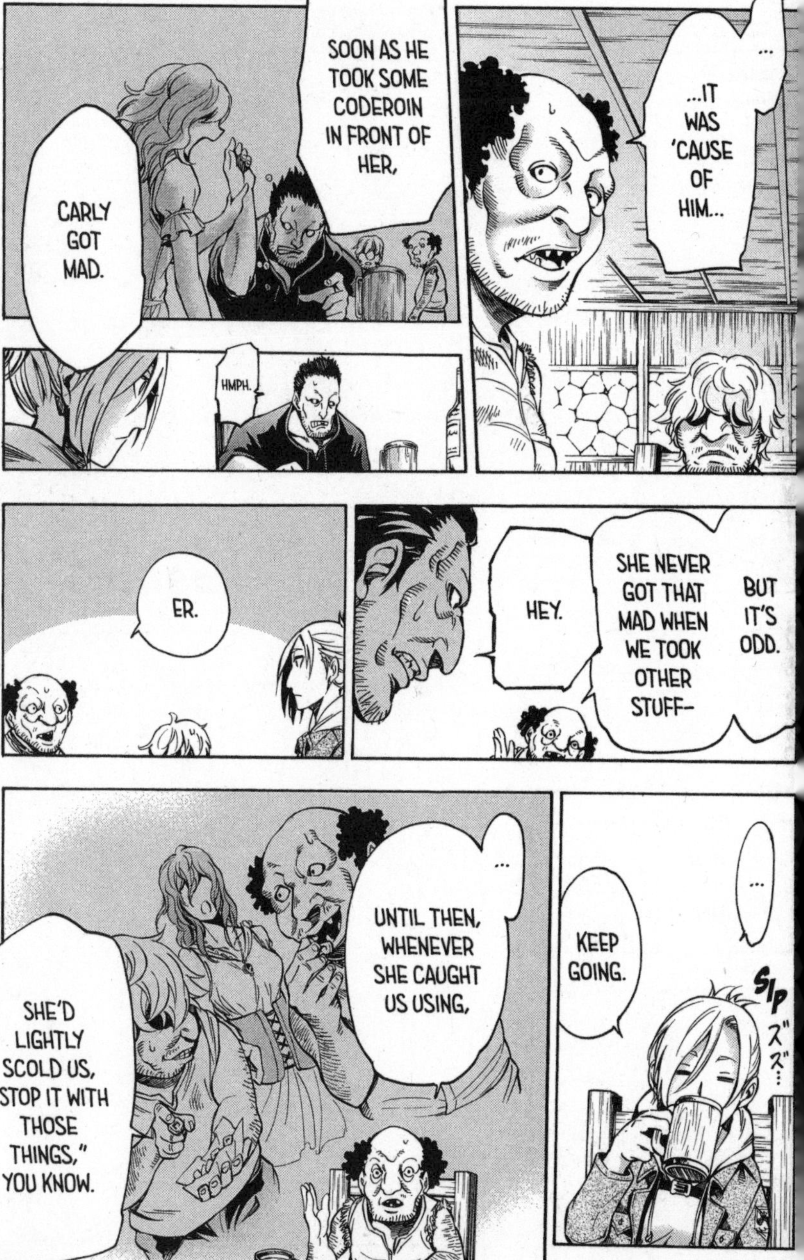
...
...IT WAS 'CAUSE OF HIM...
SOON AS HE TOOK SOME CODEROIN IN FRONT OF HER,
CARLY GOT MAD.
HMPH.
BUT IT'S ODD.
SHE NEVER GOT THAT MAD WHEN WE TOOK OTHER STUFF-
HEY.
ER.
...
KEEP GOING.
SIP
ズズ…
...
UNTIL THEN, WHENEVER SHE CAUGHT US USING,
SHE'D LIGHTLY SCOLD US, "STOP IT WITH THOSE THINGS," YOU KNOW.

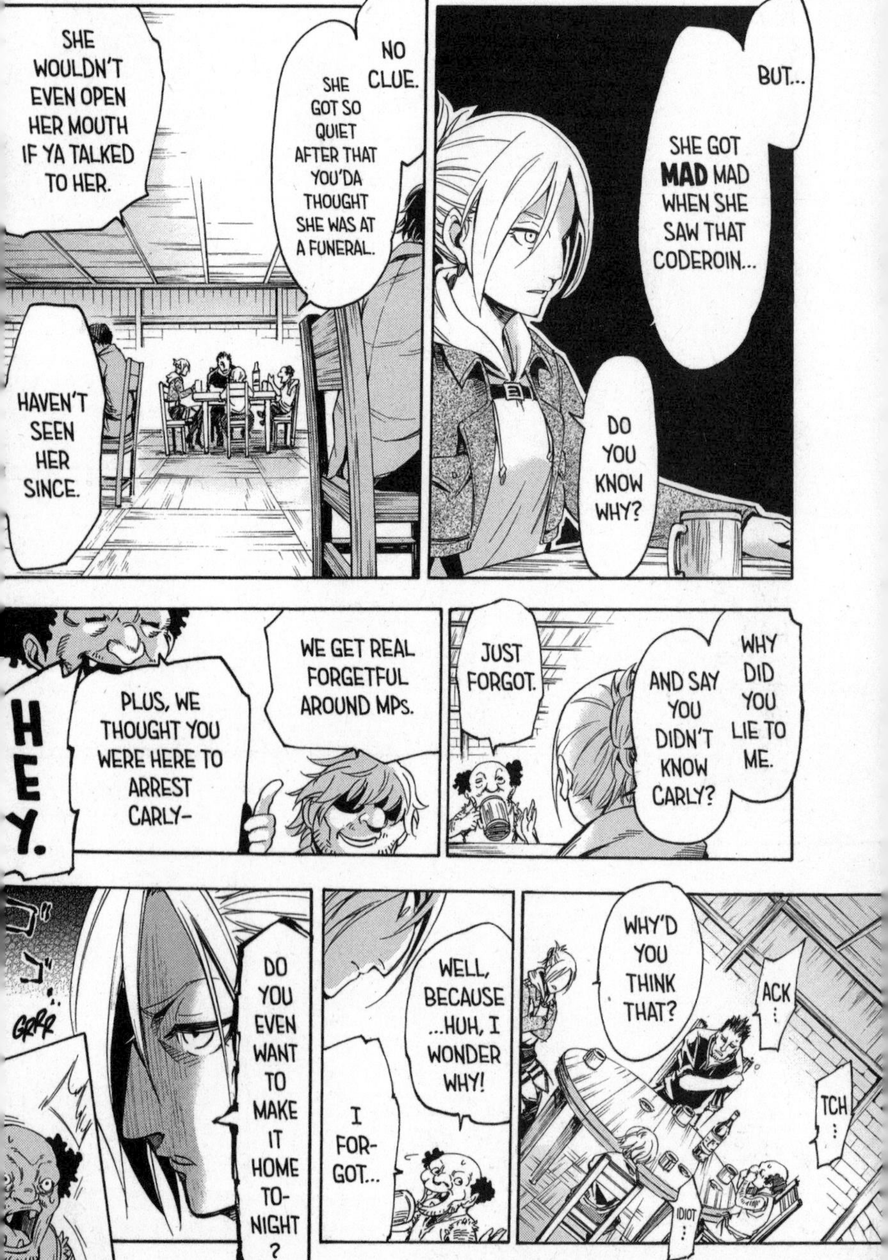
BUT...
SHE GOT **MAD** MAD WHEN SHE SAW THAT CODEROIN...
DO YOU KNOW WHY?
NO CLUE.
SHE GOT SO QUIET AFTER THAT YOU'DA THOUGHT SHE WAS AT A FUNERAL.
SHE WOULDN'T EVEN OPEN HER MOUTH IF YA TALKED TO HER.
HAVEN'T SEEN HER SINCE.
WHY DID YOU LIE TO ME.
AND SAY YOU DIDN'T KNOW CARLY?
JUST FORGOT.
WE GET REAL FORGETFUL AROUND MPs.
PLUS, WE THOUGHT YOU WERE HERE TO ARREST CARLY-
HEY.
WHY'D YOU THINK THAT?
ACK...
TCH...
IDIOT...
WELL, BECAUSE ...HUH, I WONDER WHY!
I FORGOT...
DO YOU EVEN WANT TO MAKE IT HOME TONIGHT?
GRRR

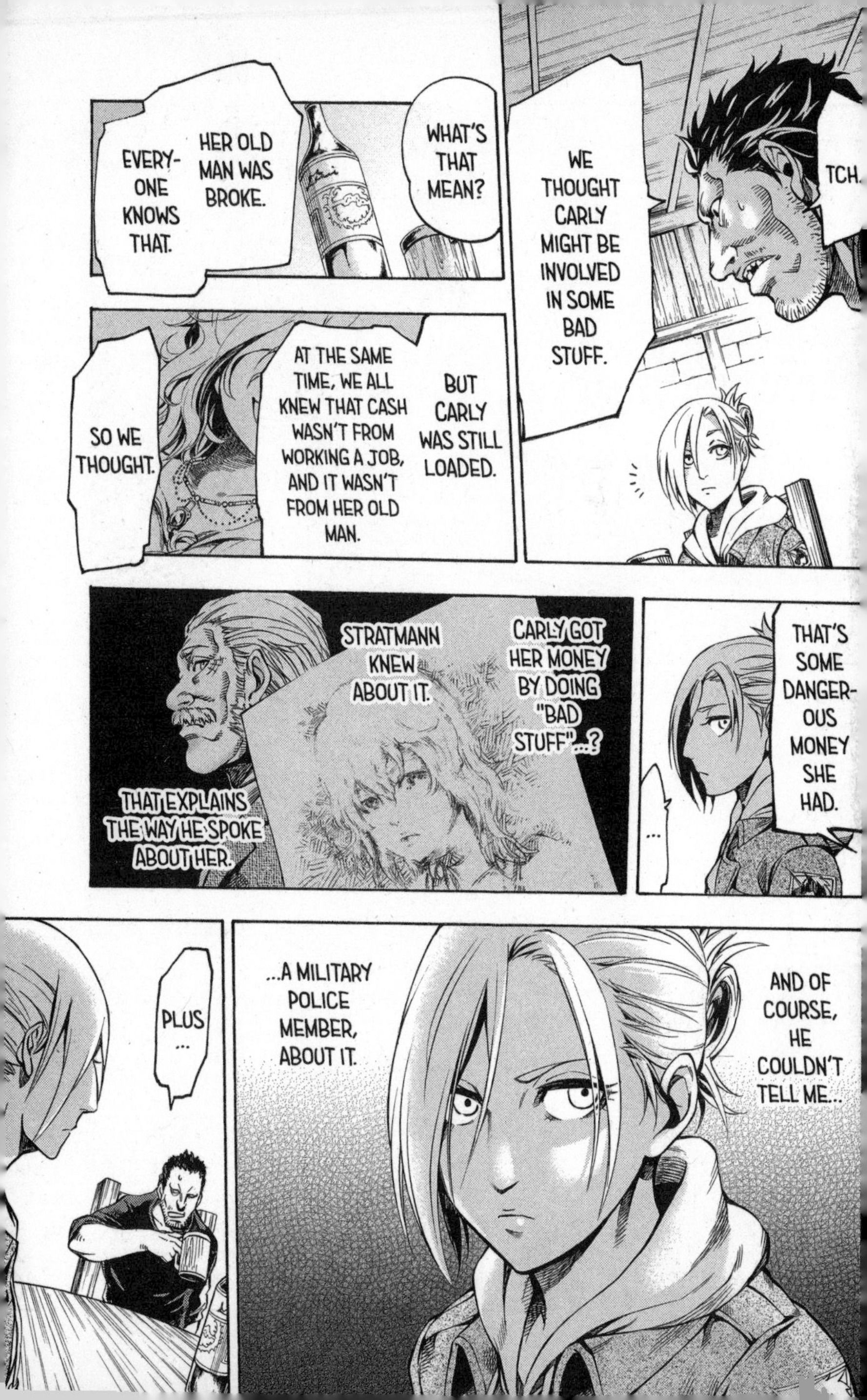
TCH.
WE THOUGHT CARLY MIGHT BE INVOLVED IN SOME BAD STUFF.
WHAT'S THAT MEAN?
HER OLD MAN WAS BROKE.
EVERY-ONE KNOWS THAT.
BUT CARLY WAS STILL LOADED.
AT THE SAME TIME, WE ALL KNEW THAT CASH WASN'T FROM WORKING A JOB, AND IT WASN'T FROM HER OLD MAN.
SO WE THOUGHT.
THAT'S SOME DANGER-OUS MONEY SHE HAD.
...
CARLY GOT HER MONEY BY DOING "BAD STUFF"...?
STRATMANN KNEW ABOUT IT.
THAT EXPLAINS THE WAY HE SPOKE ABOUT HER.
AND OF COURSE, HE COULDN'T TELL ME...
...A MILITARY POLICE MEMBER, ABOUT IT.
PLUS ...

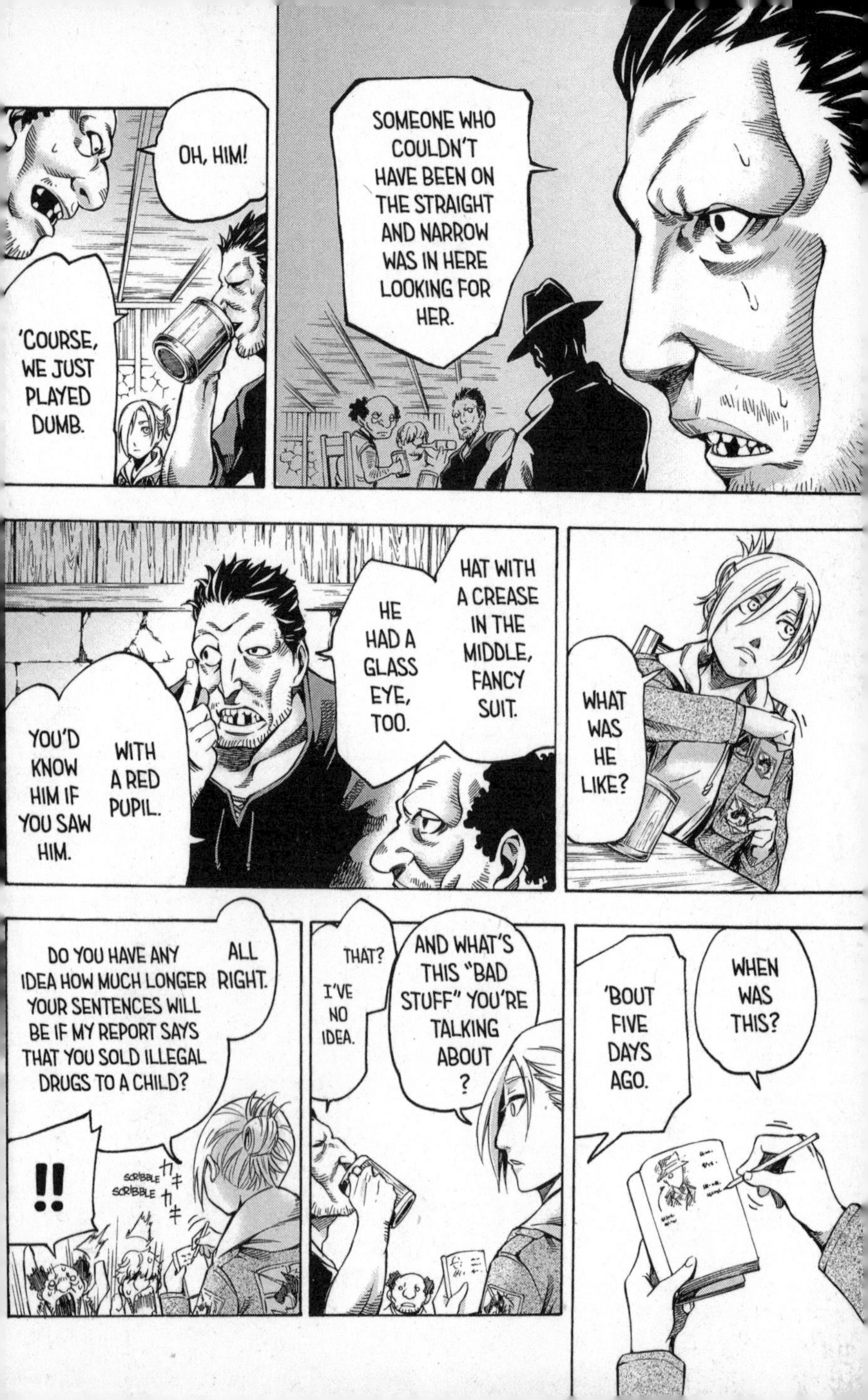
SOMEONE WHO COULDN'T HAVE BEEN ON THE STRAIGHT AND NARROW WAS IN HERE LOOKING FOR HER.
OH, HIM!
'COURSE, WE JUST PLAYED DUMB.
WHAT WAS HE LIKE?
HAT WITH A CREASE IN THE MIDDLE, FANCY SUIT.
HE HAD A GLASS EYE, TOO.
WITH A RED PUPIL.
YOU'D KNOW HIM IF YOU SAW HIM.
WHEN WAS THIS?
'BOUT FIVE DAYS AGO.
AND WHAT'S THIS "BAD STUFF" YOU'RE TALKING ABOUT?
THAT? I'VE NO IDEA.
ALL RIGHT.
DO YOU HAVE ANY IDEA HOW MUCH LONGER YOUR SENTENCES WILL BE IF MY REPORT SAYS THAT YOU SOLD ILLEGAL DRUGS TO A CHILD?
SCRIBBLE SCRIBBLE
!!

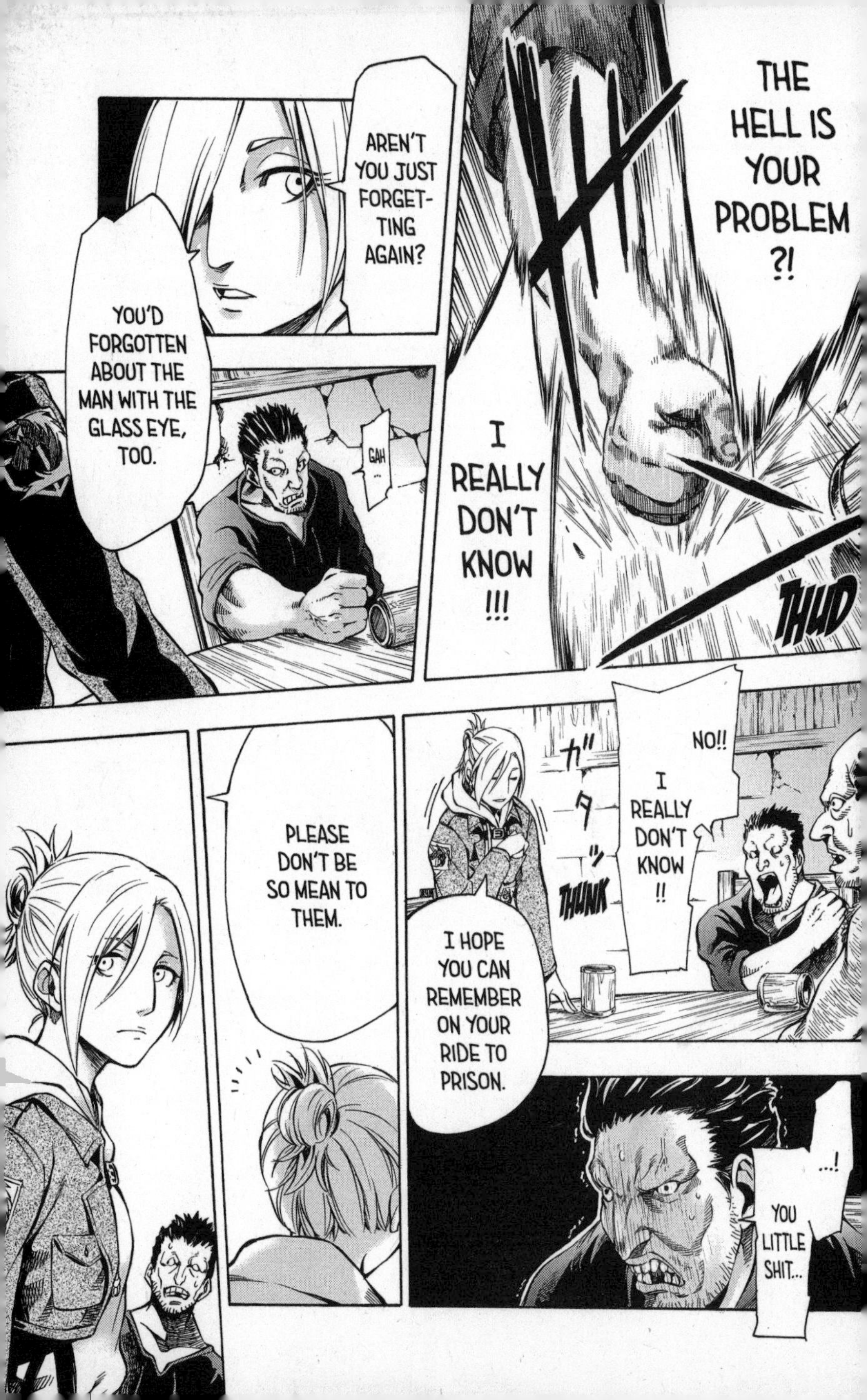

THE HELL IS YOUR PROBLEM?!
I REALLY DON'T KNOW!!!
THUD
AREN'T YOU JUST FORGETTING AGAIN?
YOU'D FORGOTTEN ABOUT THE MAN WITH THE GLASS EYE, TOO.
GAH...
NO!! I REALLY DON'T KNOW!!
ガタッ
THUNK
I HOPE YOU CAN REMEMBER ON YOUR RIDE TO PRISON.
...!
YOU LITTLE SHIT...
PLEASE DON'T BE SO MEAN TO THEM.

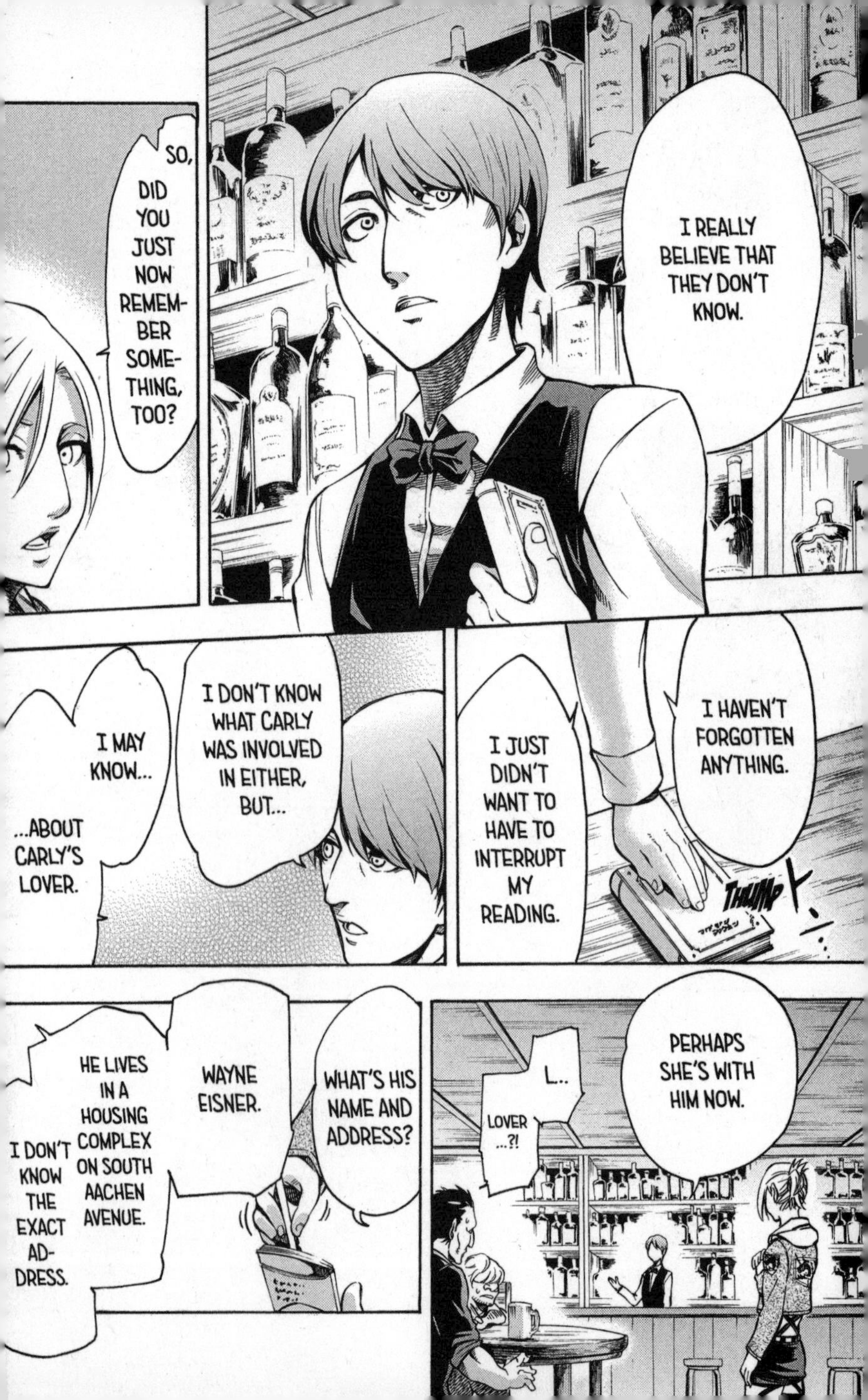
I REALLY BELIEVE THAT THEY DON'T KNOW.
SO, DID YOU JUST NOW REMEMBER SOMETHING, TOO?
I HAVEN'T FORGOTTEN ANYTHING.
I JUST DIDN'T WANT TO HAVE TO INTERRUPT MY READING.
THUMP
I DON'T KNOW WHAT CARLY WAS INVOLVED IN EITHER, BUT...
I MAY KNOW...
...ABOUT CARLY'S LOVER.
PERHAPS SHE'S WITH HIM NOW.
L..
LOVER ...?!
WHAT'S HIS NAME AND ADDRESS?
WAYNE EISNER.
HE LIVES IN A HOUSING COMPLEX ON SOUTH AACHEN AVENUE.
I DON'T KNOW THE EXACT ADDRESS.

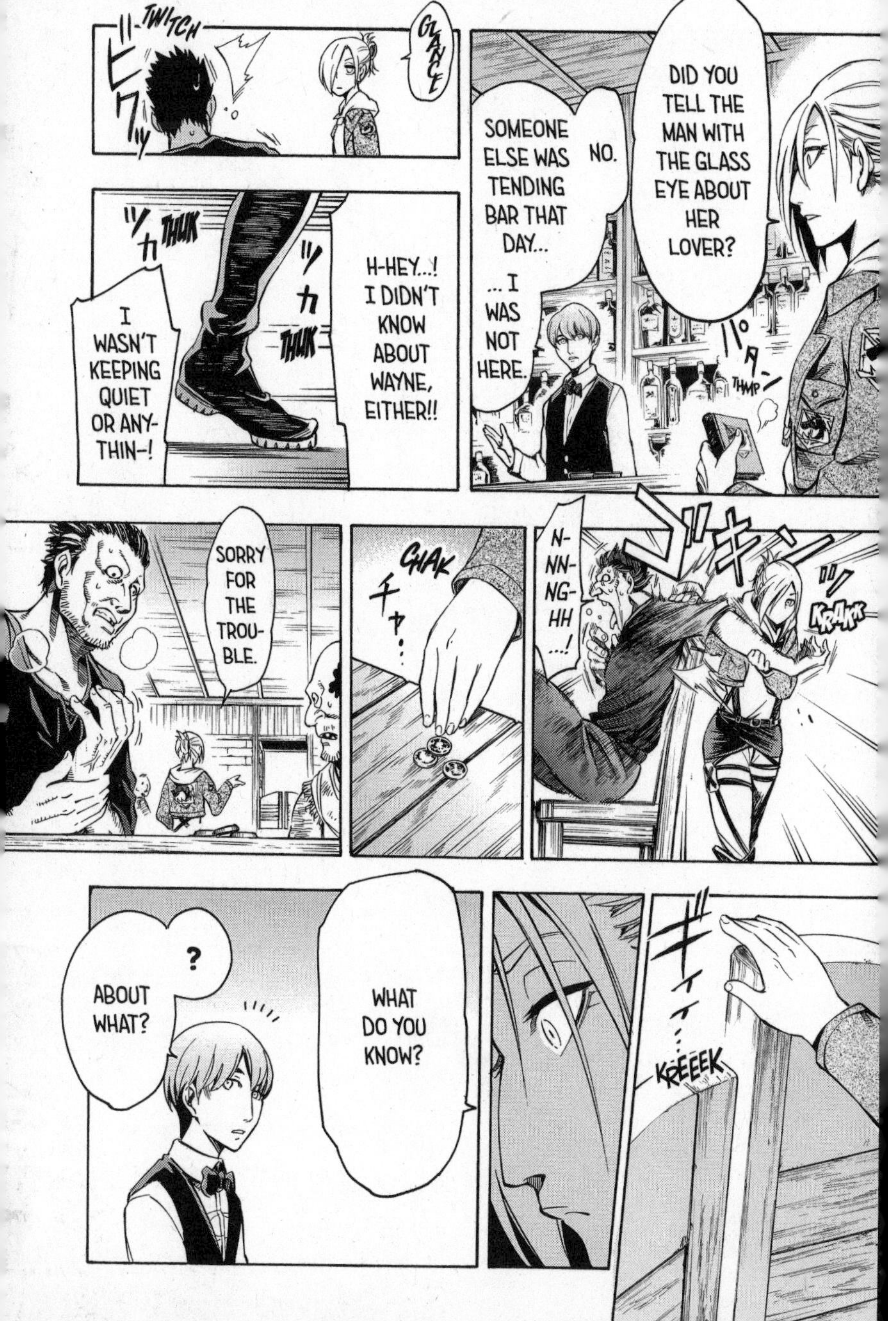
DID YOU TELL THE MAN WITH THE GLASS EYE ABOUT HER LOVER?
NO.
SOMEONE ELSE WAS TENDING BAR THAT DAY...
...I WAS NOT HERE.
THMP
GLANCE
TWITCH
H-HEY...! I DIDN'T KNOW ABOUT WAYNE, EITHER!!
THUK
THUK
I WASN'T KEEPING QUIET OR ANY-THIN-!
KRAKK
N-NN-NG-HH...!
CHAK
SORRY FOR THE TROUBLE.
KREEEK
WHAT DO YOU KNOW?
?
ABOUT WHAT?

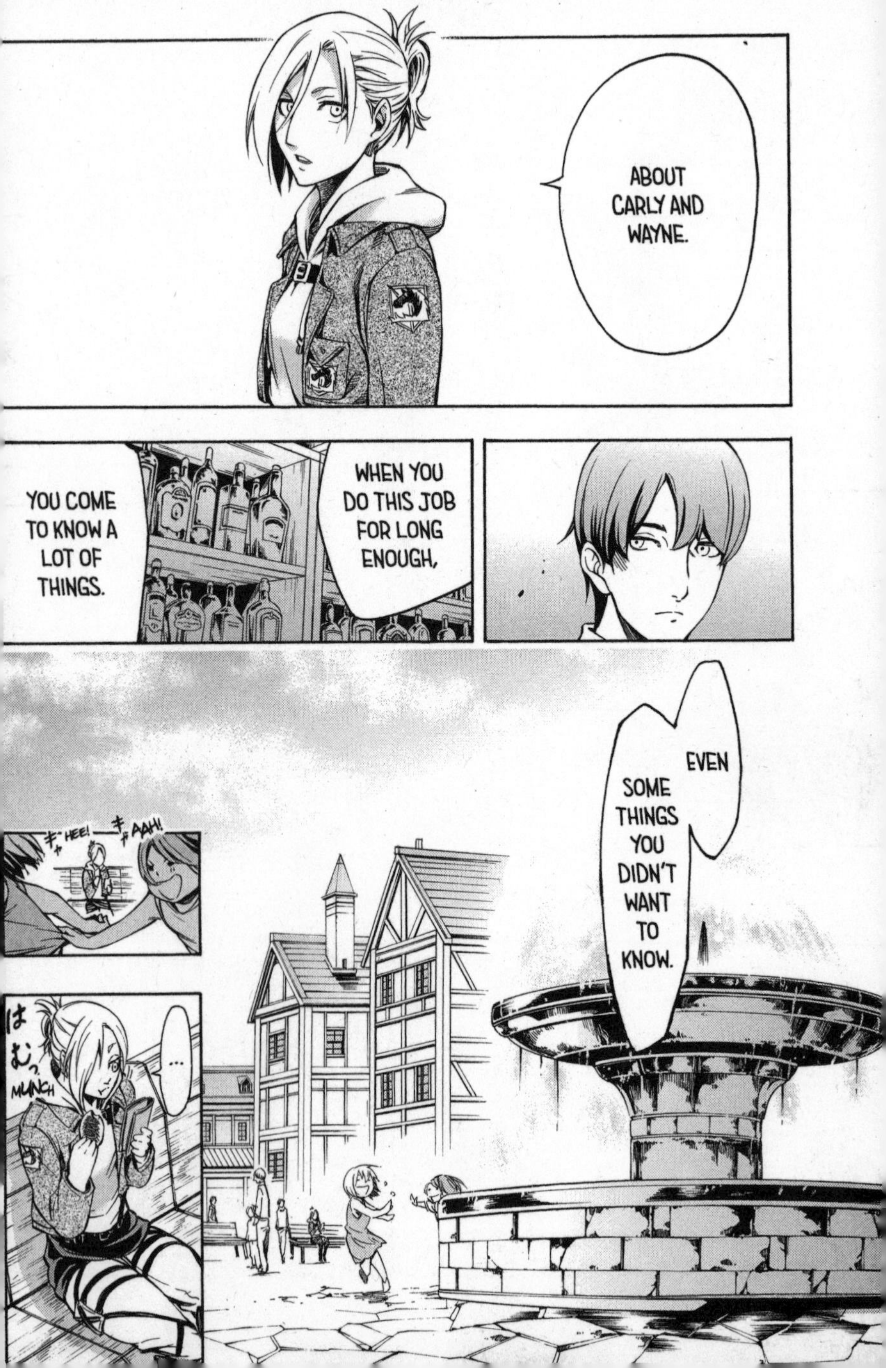
ABOUT CARLY AND WAYNE.
WHEN YOU DO THIS JOB FOR LONG ENOUGH,
YOU COME TO KNOW A LOT OF THINGS.
EVEN SOME THINGS YOU DIDN'T WANT TO KNOW.
ギャ HEE!
ギャ AAH!
...
はむっ MUNCH

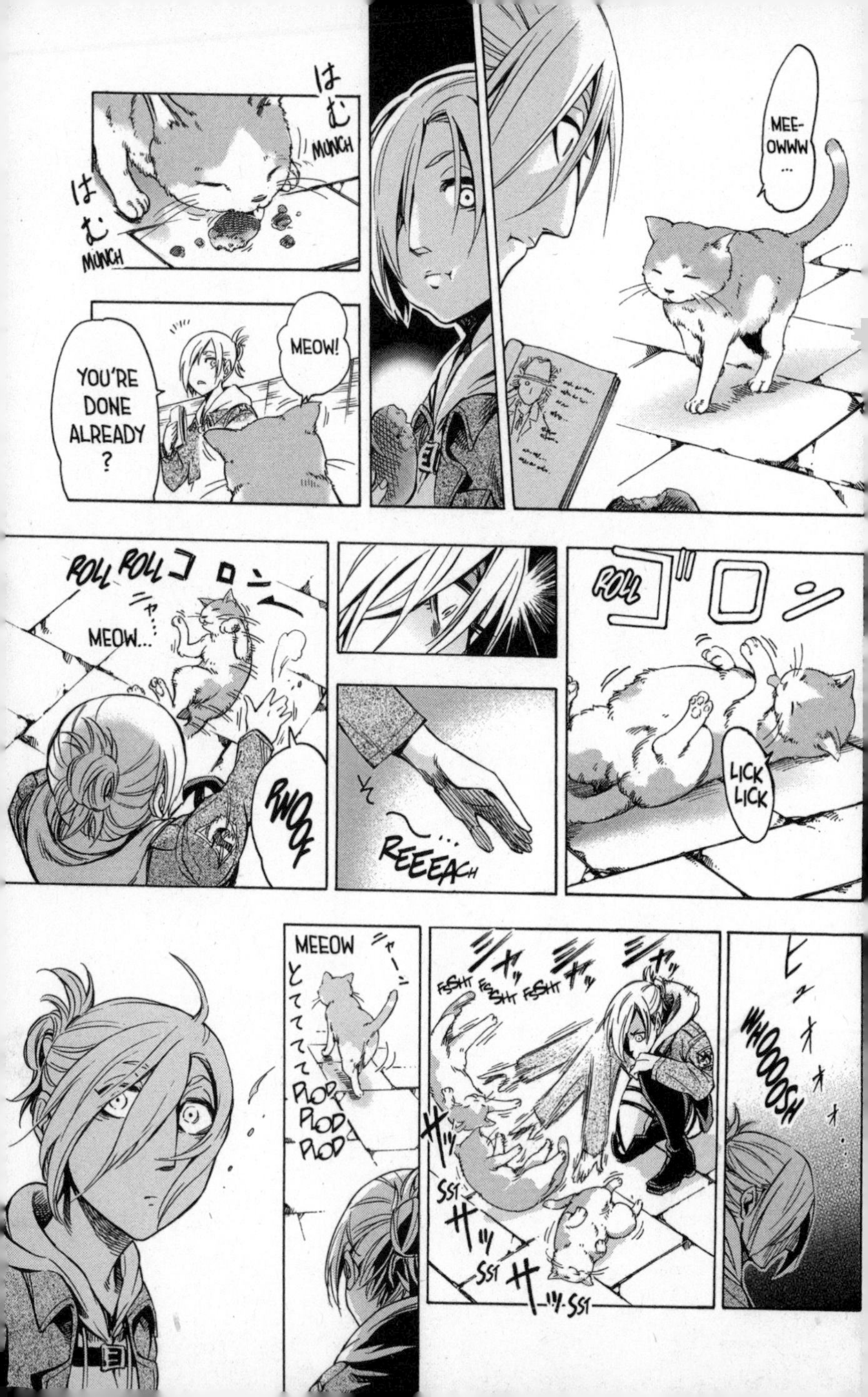
MEE-OWWW ...
はむ
MUNCH
はむ
MUNCH
MEOW!
YOU'RE DONE ALREADY ?
ROLL
ゴロン
LICK LICK
そ
REEEACH
ROLL ROLL コロン
ニャ…
MEOW...
ヒュオオオ
WHOOOOSH
シャッ
FSSHT FSSHT FSSHT
シャッ
ザッ
SSST
ザッ
SSST
ザッ
ザッ SSST
MEEOW
ニャーン
とててててて
PLOD
PLOD
PLOD

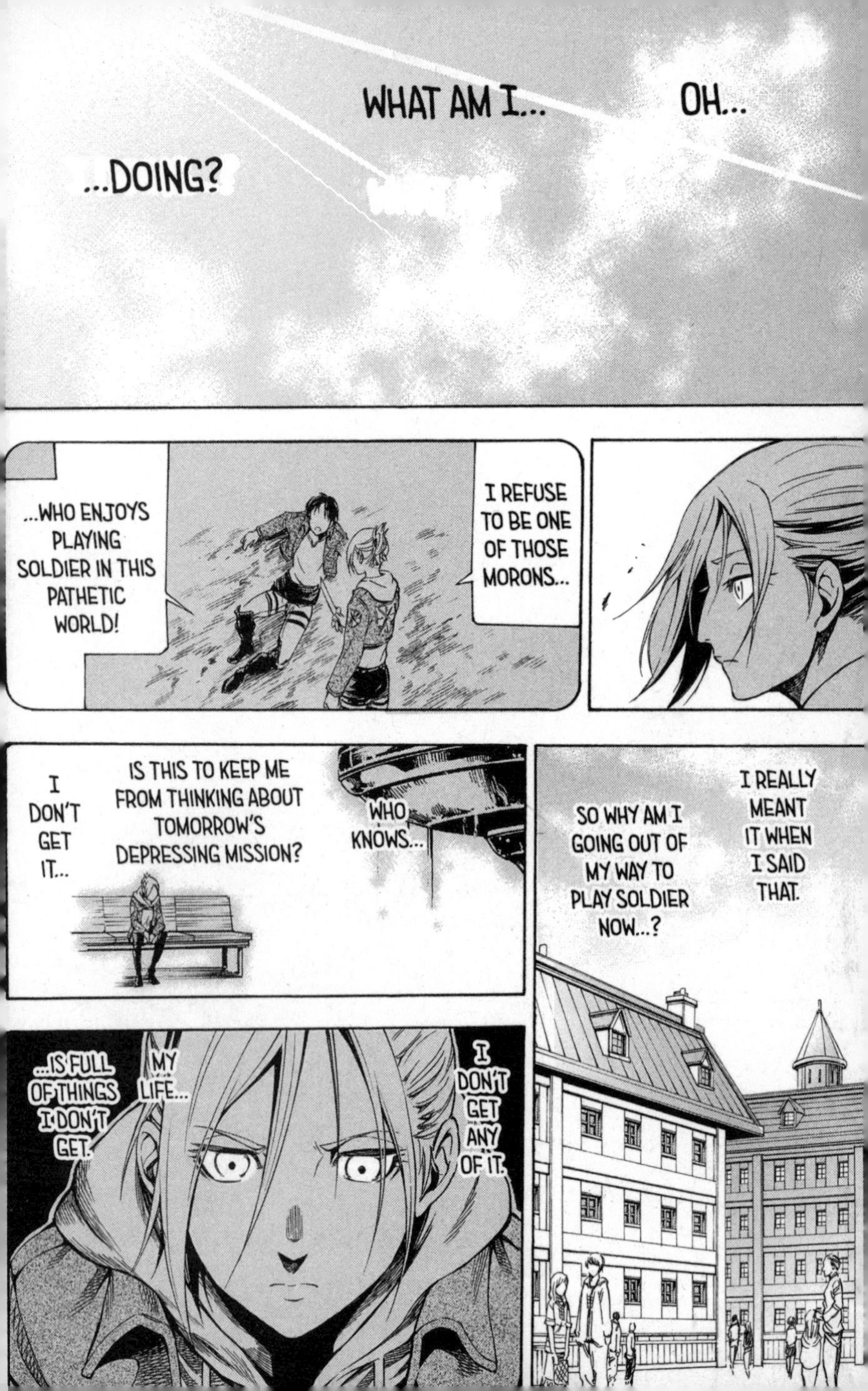
OH...
WHAT AM I...
...DOING?
I REFUSE TO BE ONE OF THOSE MORONS...
...WHO ENJOYS PLAYING SOLDIER IN THIS PATHETIC WORLD!
I REALLY MEANT IT WHEN I SAID THAT.
SO WHY AM I GOING OUT OF MY WAY TO PLAY SOLDIER NOW...?
WHO KNOWS...
IS THIS TO KEEP ME FROM THINKING ABOUT TOMORROW'S DEPRESSING MISSION?
I DON'T GET IT...
I DON'T GET ANY OF IT.
MY LIFE...
...IS FULL OF THINGS I DON'T GET.

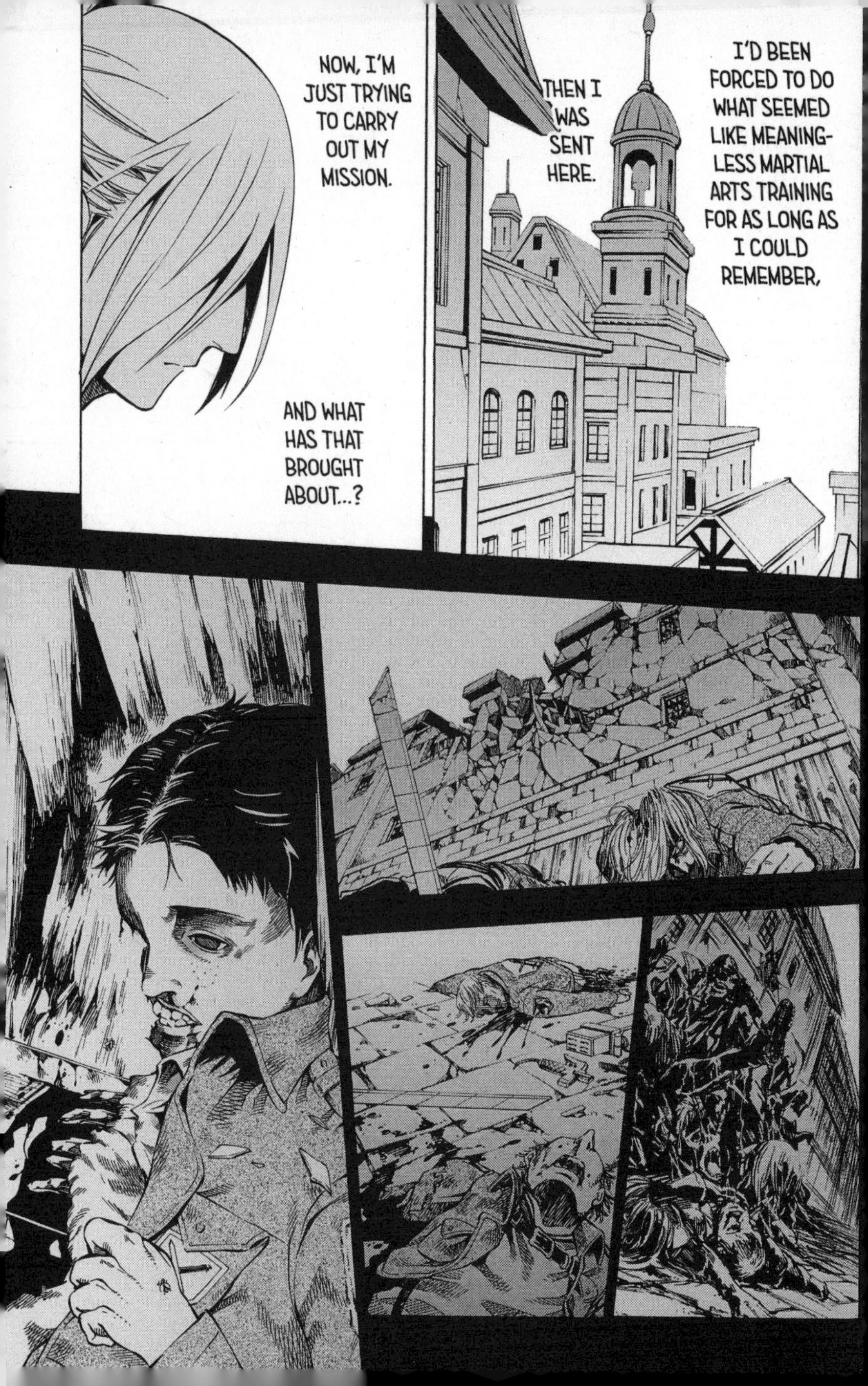
I'D BEEN FORCED TO DO WHAT SEEMED LIKE MEANING-LESS MARTIAL ARTS TRAINING FOR AS LONG AS I COULD REMEMBER,
THEN I WAS SENT HERE.
NOW, I'M JUST TRYING TO CARRY OUT MY MISSION.
AND WHAT HAS THAT BROUGHT ABOUT...?

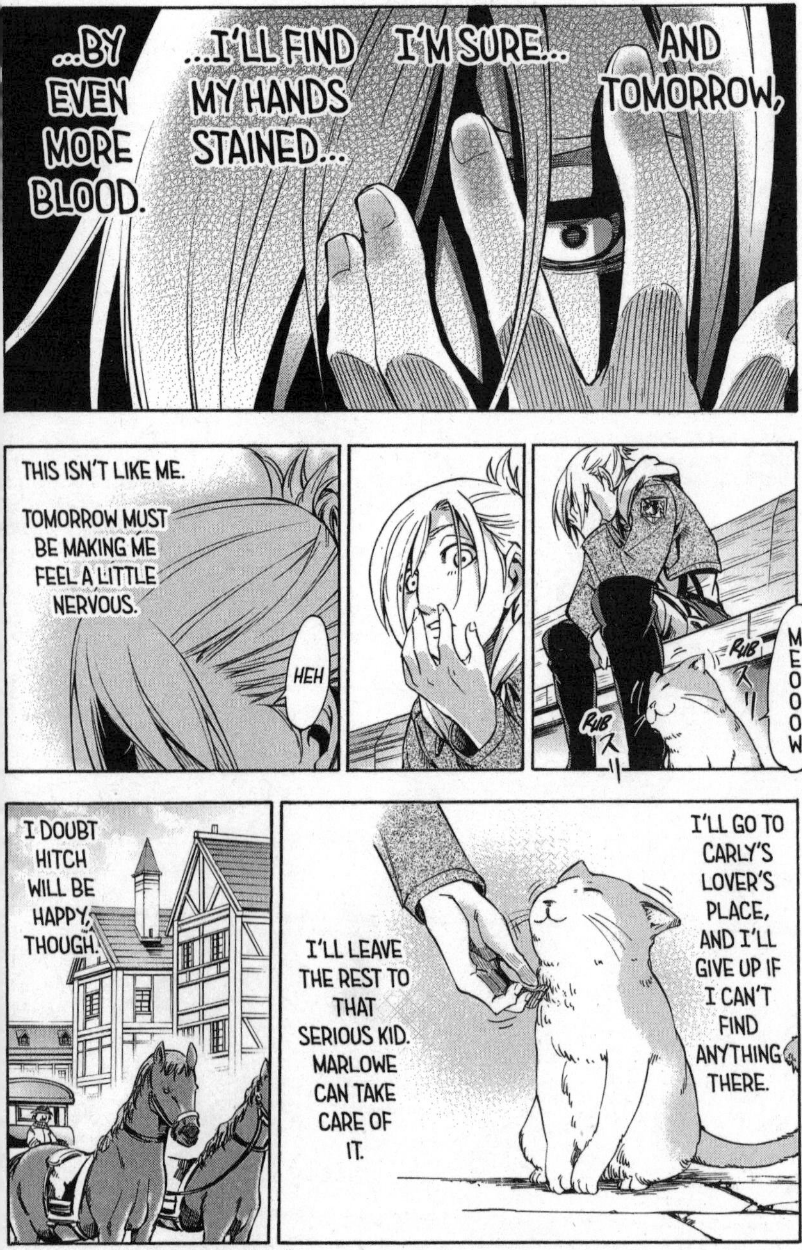
AND TOMORROW,
I'M SURE...
...I'LL FIND MY HANDS STAINED...
...BY EVEN MORE BLOOD.
MEOOOOW
RUB
RUB
THIS ISN'T LIKE ME.
TOMORROW MUST BE MAKING ME FEEL A LITTLE NERVOUS.
HEH
I'LL GO TO CARLY'S LOVER'S PLACE, AND I'LL GIVE UP IF I CAN'T FIND ANYTHING THERE.
I'LL LEAVE THE REST TO THAT SERIOUS KID. MARLOWE CAN TAKE CARE OF IT.
I DOUBT HITCH WILL BE HAPPY, THOUGH.

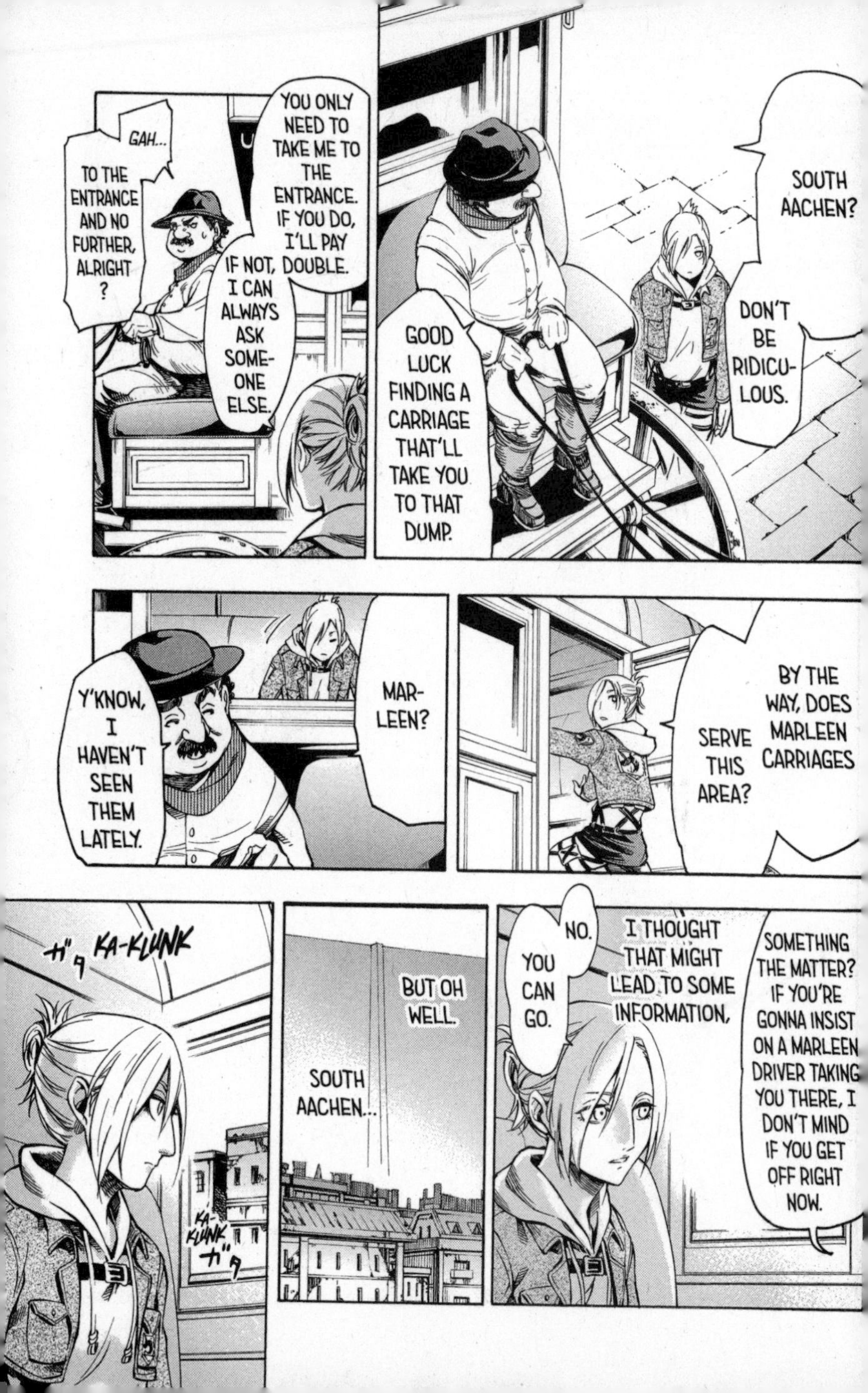
SOUTH AACHEN?
DON'T BE RIDICULOUS.
GOOD LUCK FINDING A CARRIAGE THAT'LL TAKE YOU TO THAT DUMP.
YOU ONLY NEED TO TAKE ME TO THE ENTRANCE. IF YOU DO, I'LL PAY DOUBLE.
IF NOT, I CAN ALWAYS ASK SOMEONE ELSE.
GAH...
TO THE ENTRANCE AND NO FURTHER, ALRIGHT?
BY THE WAY, DOES MARLEEN CARRIAGES SERVE THIS AREA?
MARLEEN?
Y'KNOW, I HAVEN'T SEEN THEM LATELY.
SOMETHING THE MATTER? IF YOU'RE GONNA INSIST ON A MARLEEN DRIVER TAKING YOU THERE, I DON'T MIND IF YOU GET OFF RIGHT NOW.
NO.
YOU CAN GO.
I THOUGHT THAT MIGHT LEAD TO SOME INFORMATION,
BUT OH WELL.
SOUTH AACHEN...
ガタ KA-KLUNK
KA-KLUNK ガタ

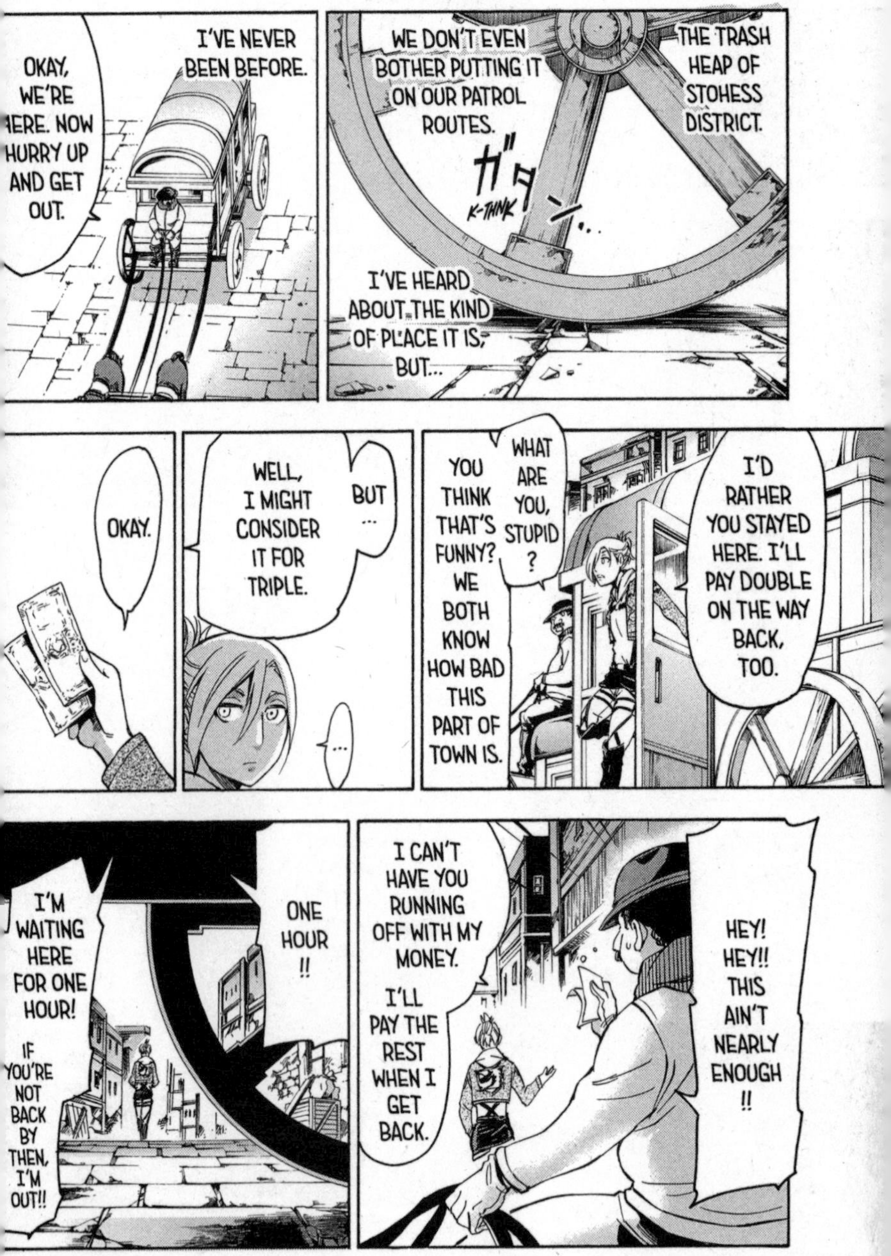
THE TRASH HEAP OF STOHESS DISTRICT.
WE DON'T EVEN BOTHER PUTTING IT ON OUR PATROL ROUTES.
ガタン
K-THINK
I'VE HEARD ABOUT THE KIND OF PLACE IT IS, BUT...
I'VE NEVER BEEN BEFORE.
OKAY, WE'RE HERE. NOW HURRY UP AND GET OUT.
I'D RATHER YOU STAYED HERE. I'LL PAY DOUBLE ON THE WAY BACK, TOO.
WHAT ARE YOU, STUPID?
YOU THINK THAT'S FUNNY? WE BOTH KNOW HOW BAD THIS PART OF TOWN IS.
BUT...
WELL, I MIGHT CONSIDER IT FOR TRIPLE.
...
OKAY.
HEY! HEY!! THIS AIN'T NEARLY ENOUGH!!
I CAN'T HAVE YOU RUNNING OFF WITH MY MONEY.
I'LL PAY THE REST WHEN I GET BACK.
ONE HOUR!!
I'M WAITING HERE FOR ONE HOUR!
IF YOU'RE NOT BACK BY THEN, I'M OUT!!

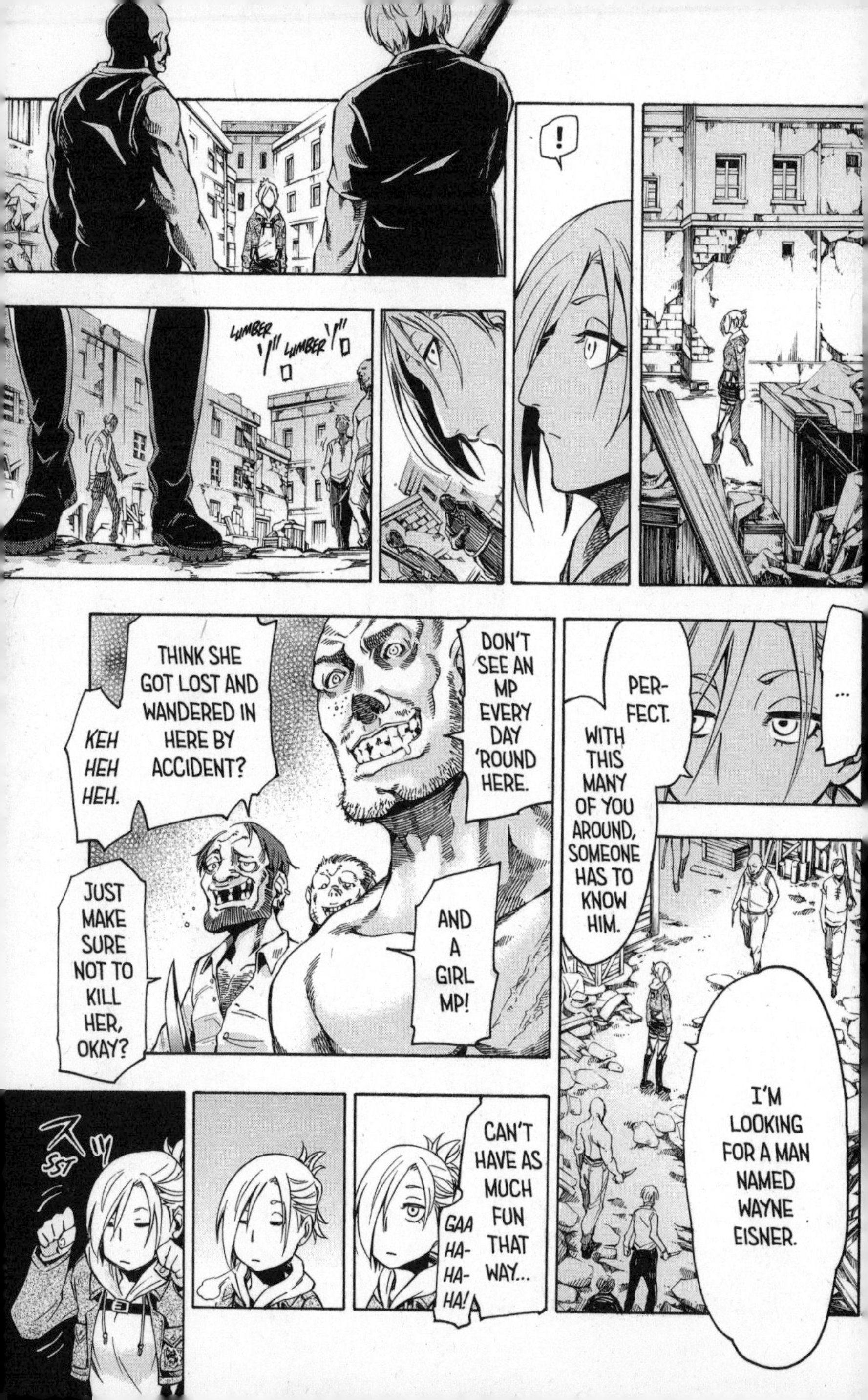
!
LUMBER
LUMBER
...
PER-FECT. WITH THIS MANY OF YOU AROUND, SOMEONE HAS TO KNOW HIM.
I'M LOOKING FOR A MAN NAMED WAYNE EISNER.
DON'T SEE AN MP EVERY DAY 'ROUND HERE.
THINK SHE GOT LOST AND WANDERED IN HERE BY ACCIDENT?
KEH HEH HEH.
AND A GIRL MP!
JUST MAKE SURE NOT TO KILL HER, OKAY?
CAN'T HAVE AS MUCH FUN THAT WAY...
GAA HA-HA-HA!
スッ
SST

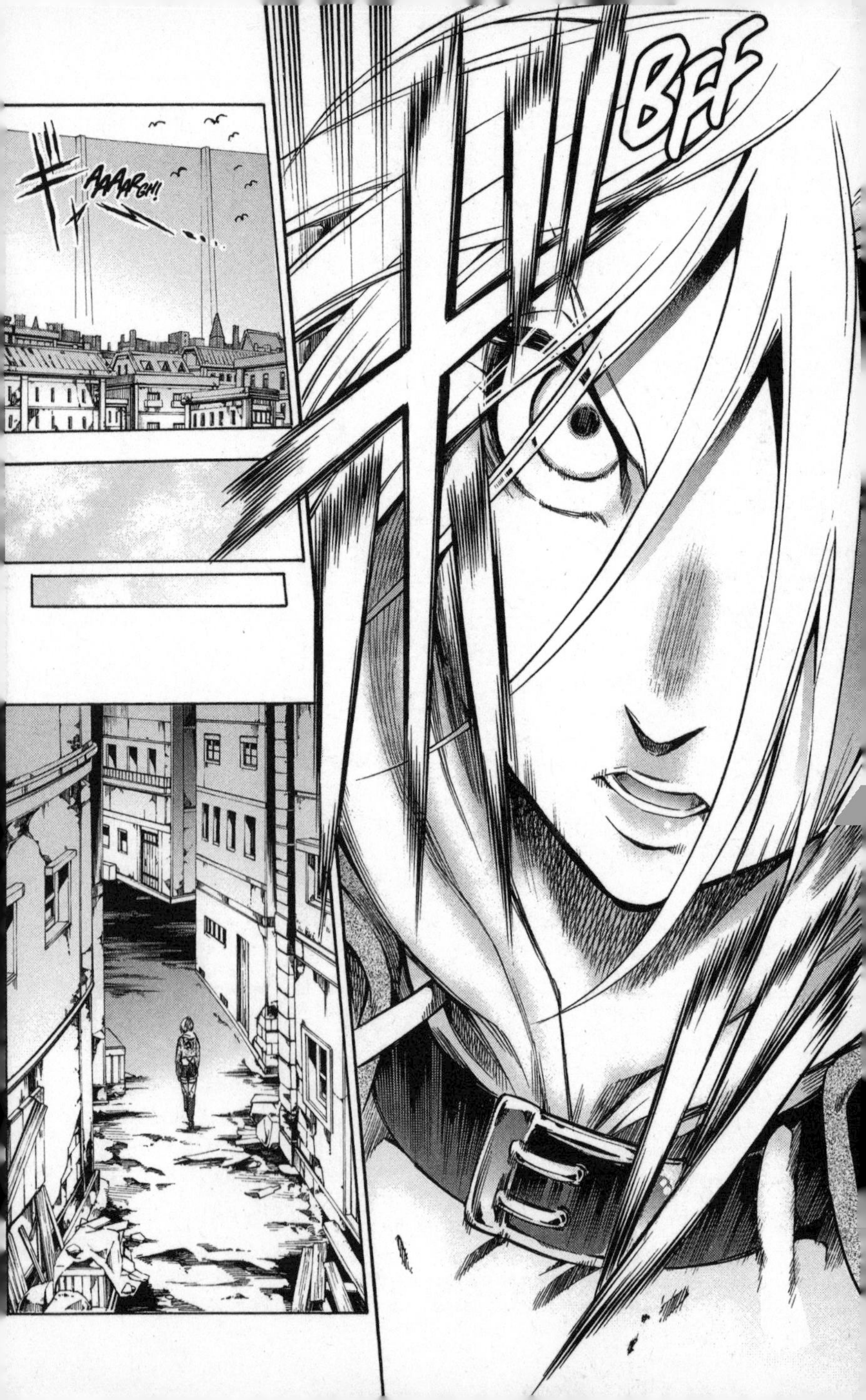
BFF
AAAARGH!

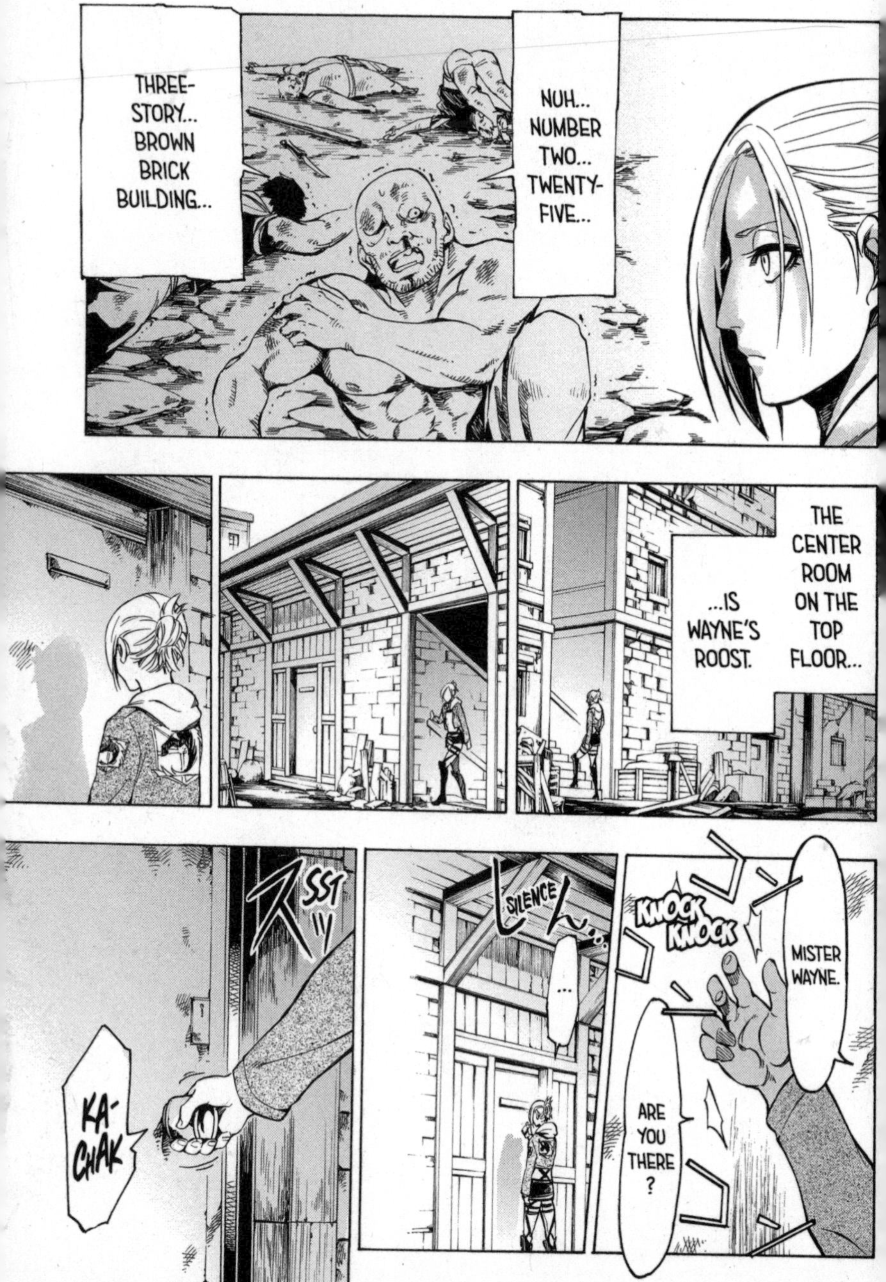
NUH... NUMBER TWO... TWENTY-FIVE...
THREE-STORY... BROWN BRICK BUILDING...
THE CENTER ROOM ON THE TOP FLOOR...
...IS WAYNE'S ROOST.
KNOCK KNOCK
MISTER WAYNE.
ARE YOU THERE?
SILENCE
...
SSST
KA-CHAK

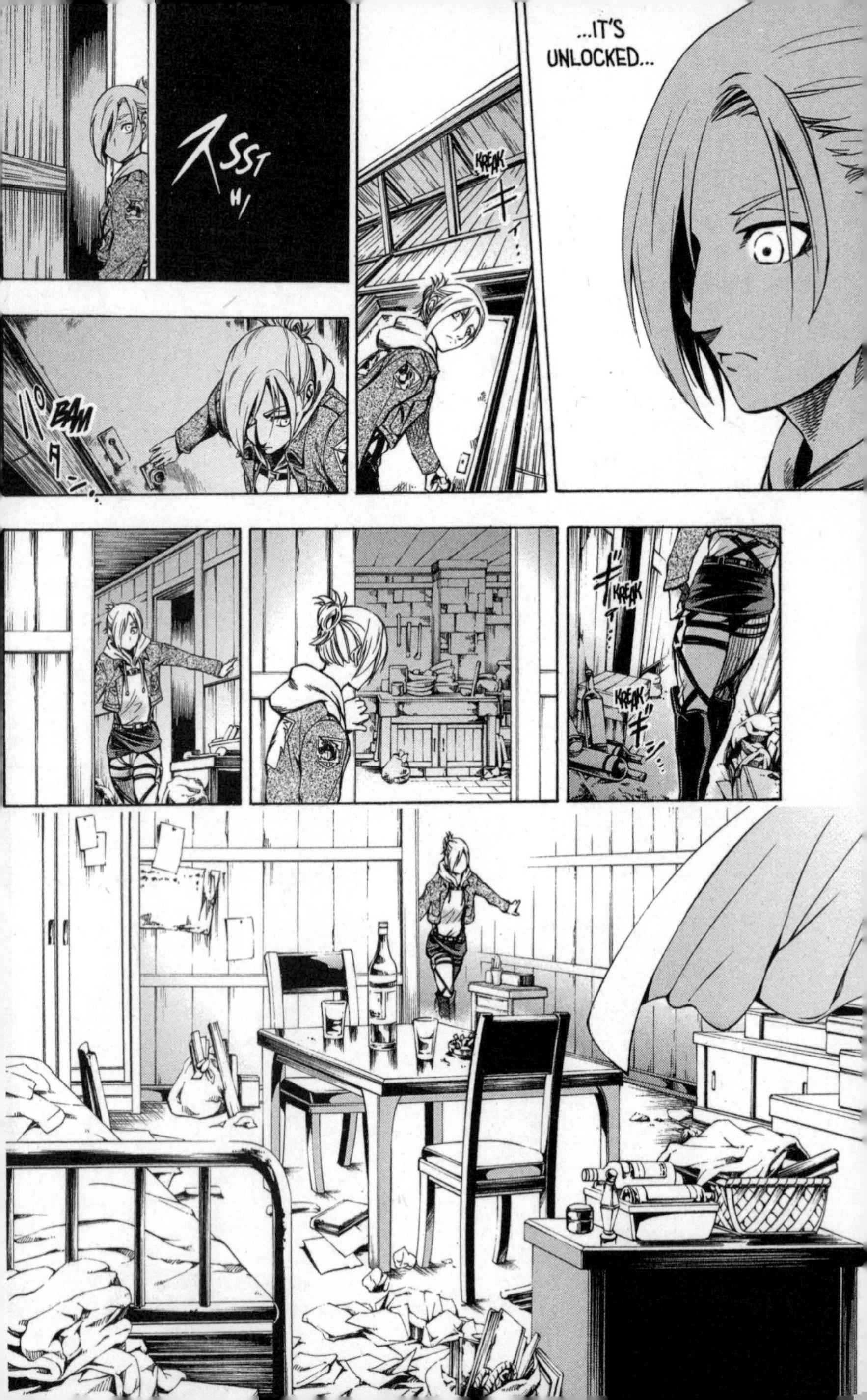
...IT'S UNLOCKED...
KREAK
SST
BAM
KREAK
KREAK

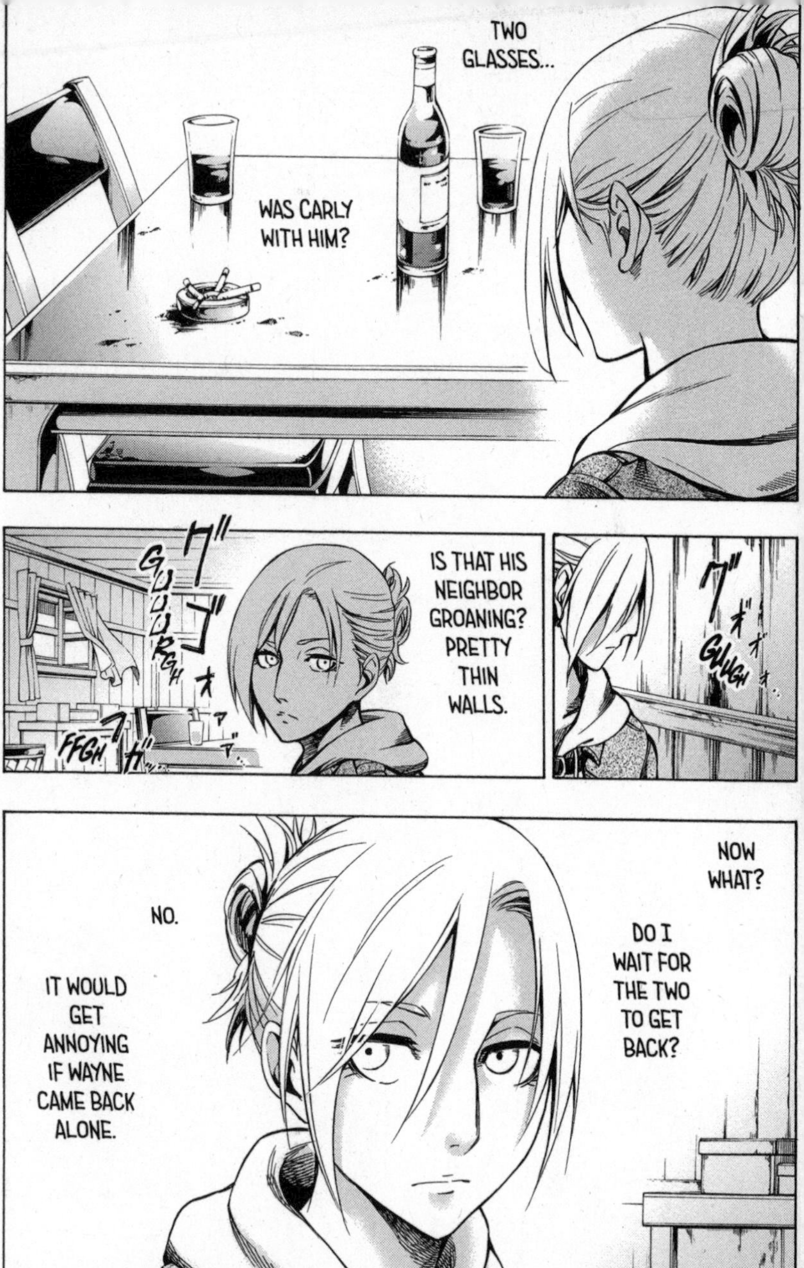
TWO GLASSES...
WAS CARLY WITH HIM?
GUUGH
IS THAT HIS NEIGHBOR GROANING? PRETTY THIN WALLS.
GUUURGH
FFGH
NOW WHAT?
DO I WAIT FOR THE TWO TO GET BACK?
NO.
IT WOULD GET ANNOYING IF WAYNE CAME BACK ALONE.

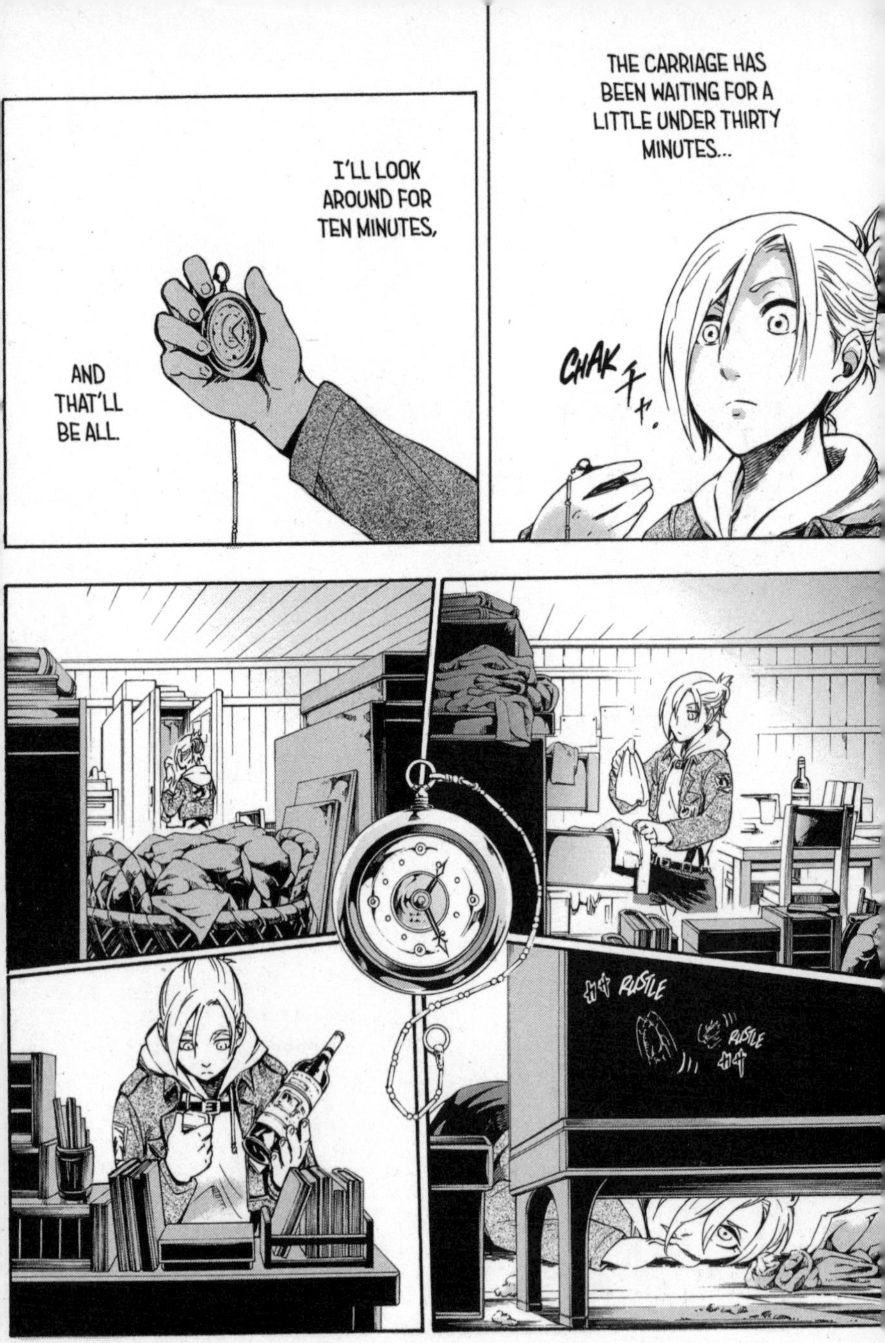
THE CARRIAGE HAS BEEN WAITING FOR A LITTLE UNDER THIRTY MINUTES...
CHAK
チャ
I'LL LOOK AROUND FOR TEN MINUTES,
AND THAT'LL BE ALL.
RUSTLE
RUSTLE

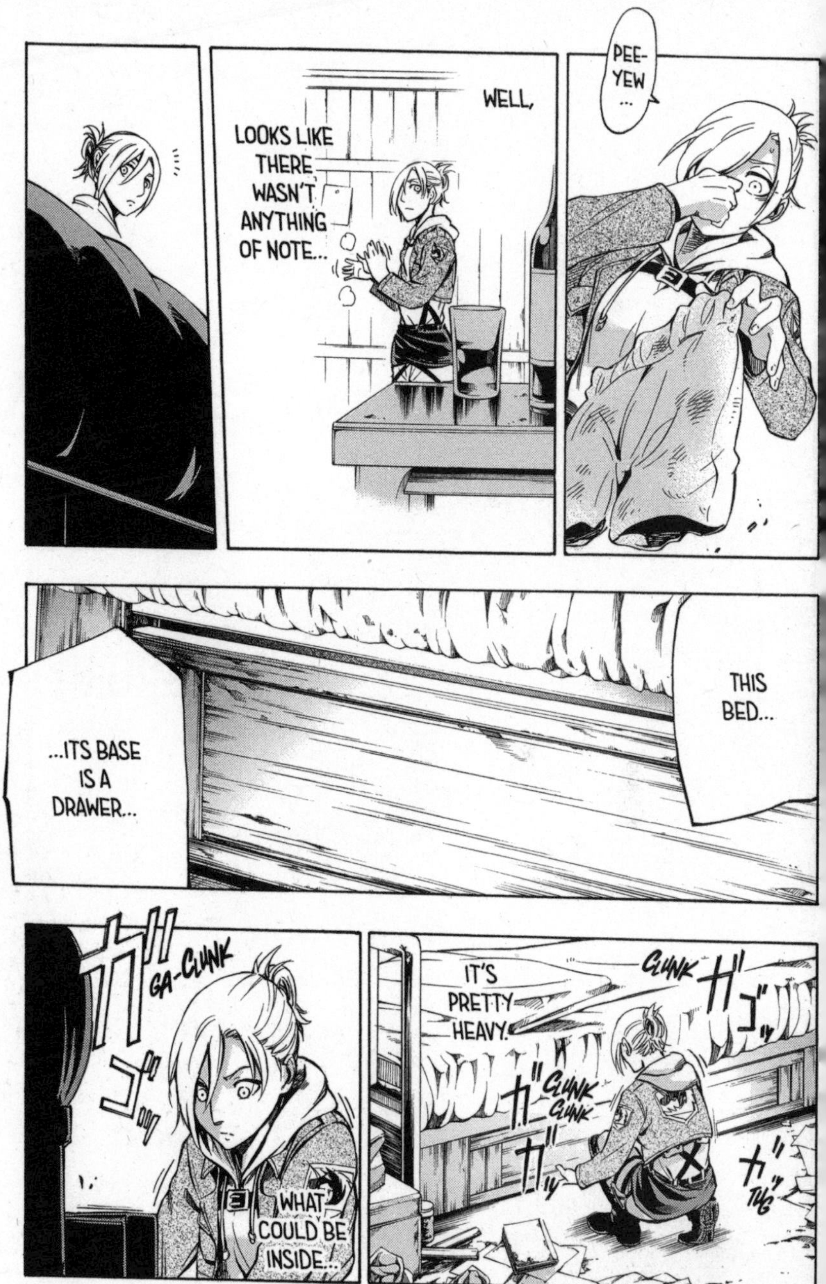
PEE-YEW...
WELL,
LOOKS LIKE THERE WASN'T ANYTHING OF NOTE...
THIS BED...
...ITS BASE IS A DRAWER...
CLUNK
IT'S PRETTY HEAVY.
CLUNK CLUNK
TUG
GA-CLUNK
WHAT COULD BE INSIDE...

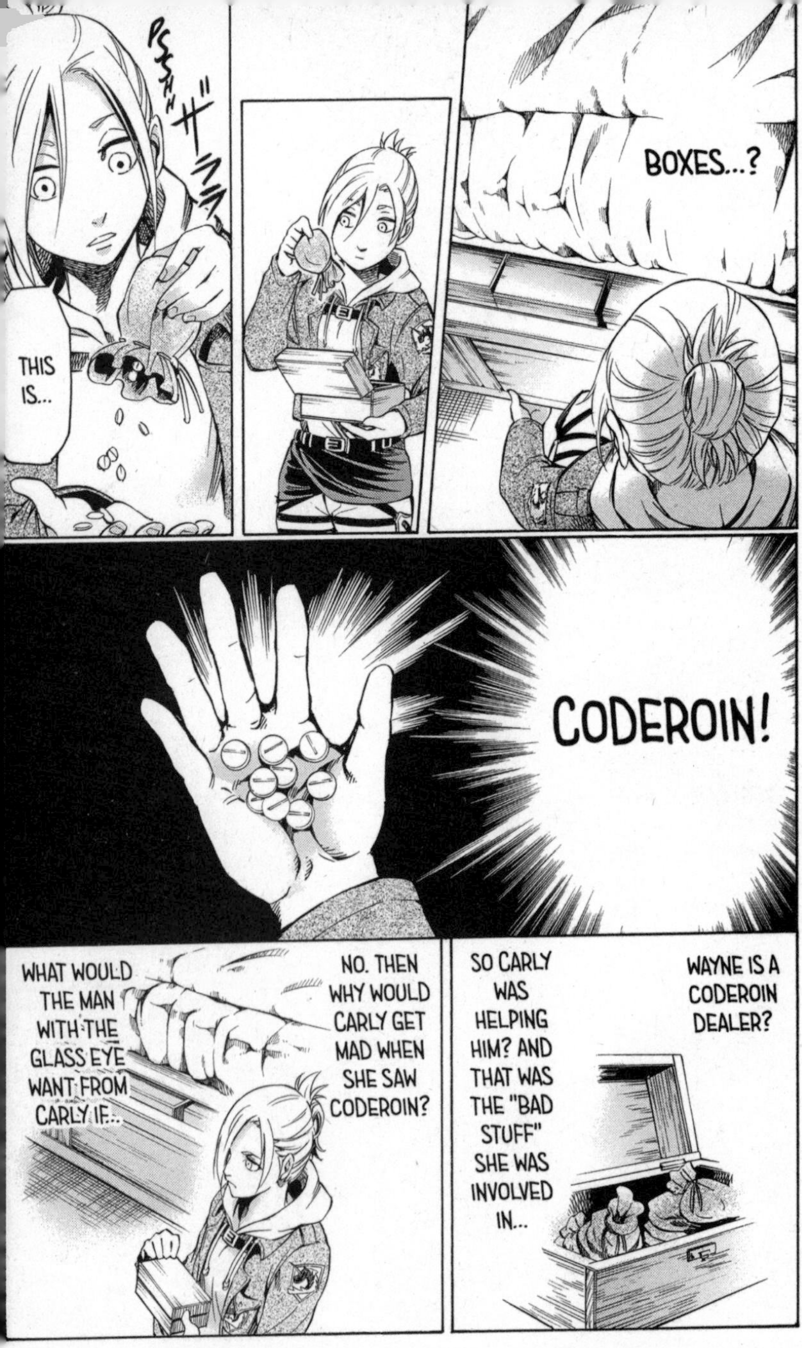
BOXES...?
PSSHHH
ザラ
THIS IS...
CODEROIN!
WAYNE IS A CODEROIN DEALER?
SO CARLY WAS HELPING HIM? AND THAT WAS THE "BAD STUFF" SHE WAS INVOLVED IN...
NO. THEN WHY WOULD CARLY GET MAD WHEN SHE SAW CODEROIN?
WHAT WOULD THE MAN WITH THE GLASS EYE WANT FROM CARLY IF...

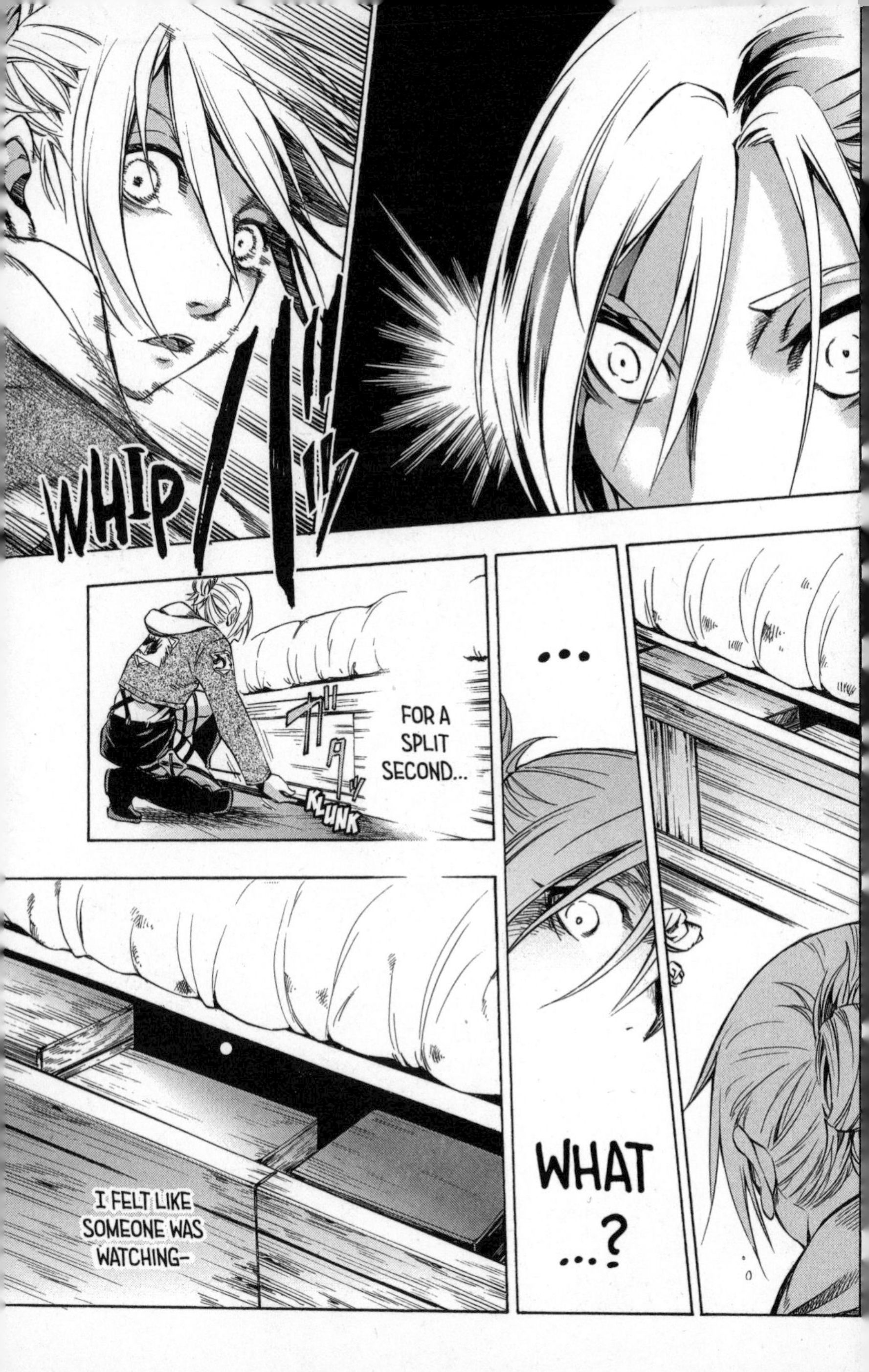
WHIP
...
WHAT
...?
FOR A SPLIT SECOND...
KLUNK
I FELT LIKE SOMEONE WAS WATCHING–

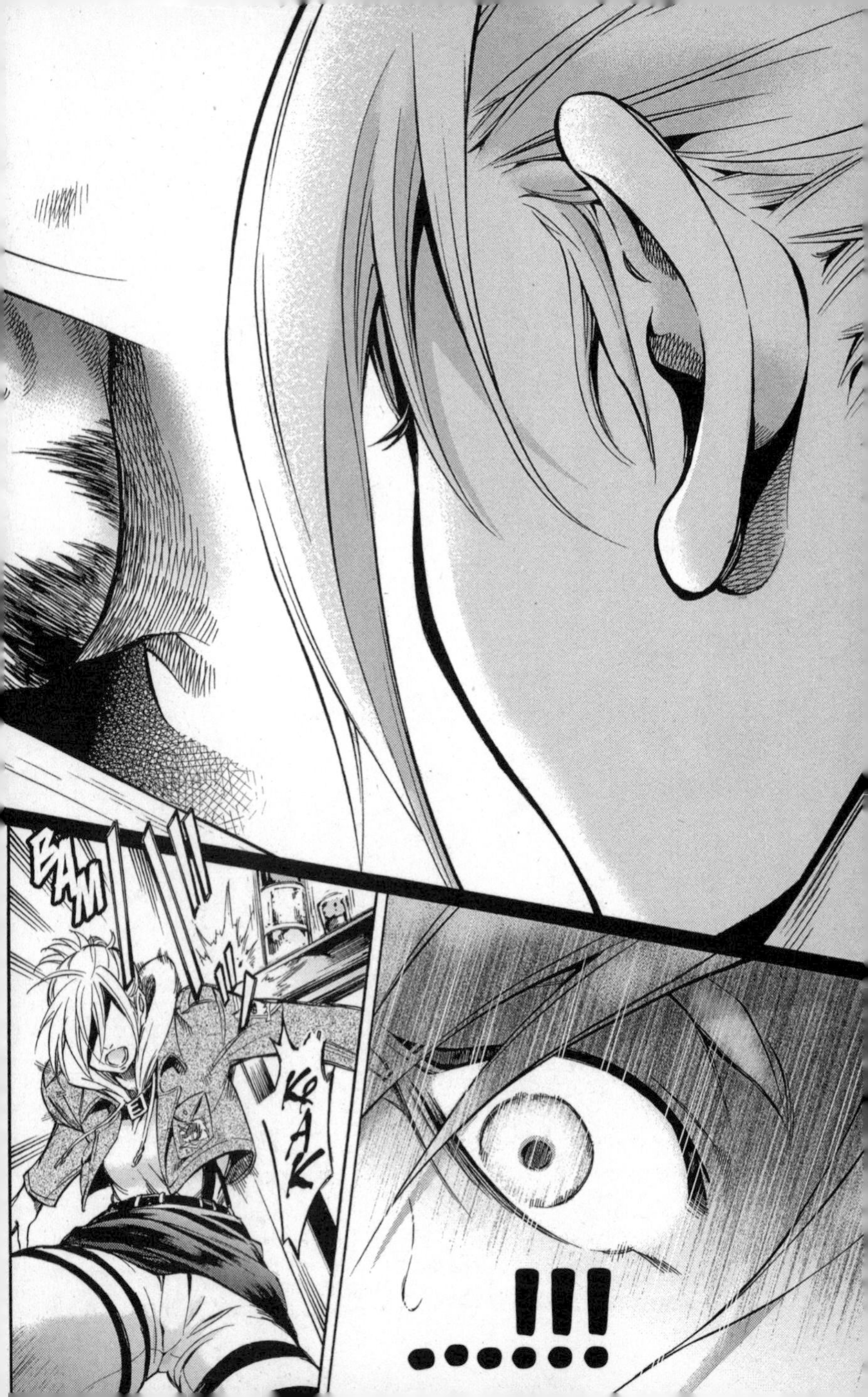
BAM
KRAK
.....!!!

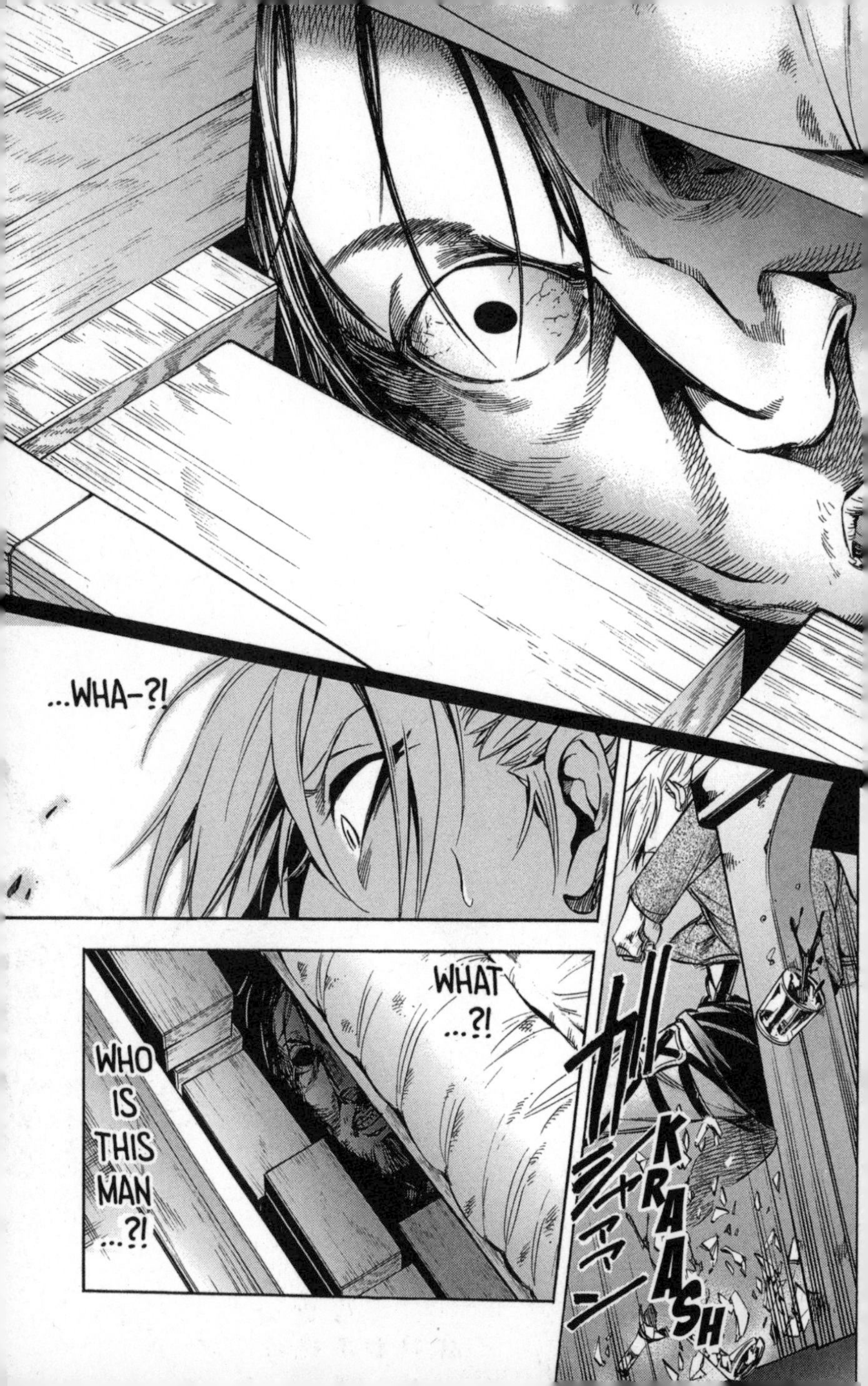
...WHA-?!
ガシャァーン
KRAASH
WHAT ...?!
WHO IS THIS MAN ...?!

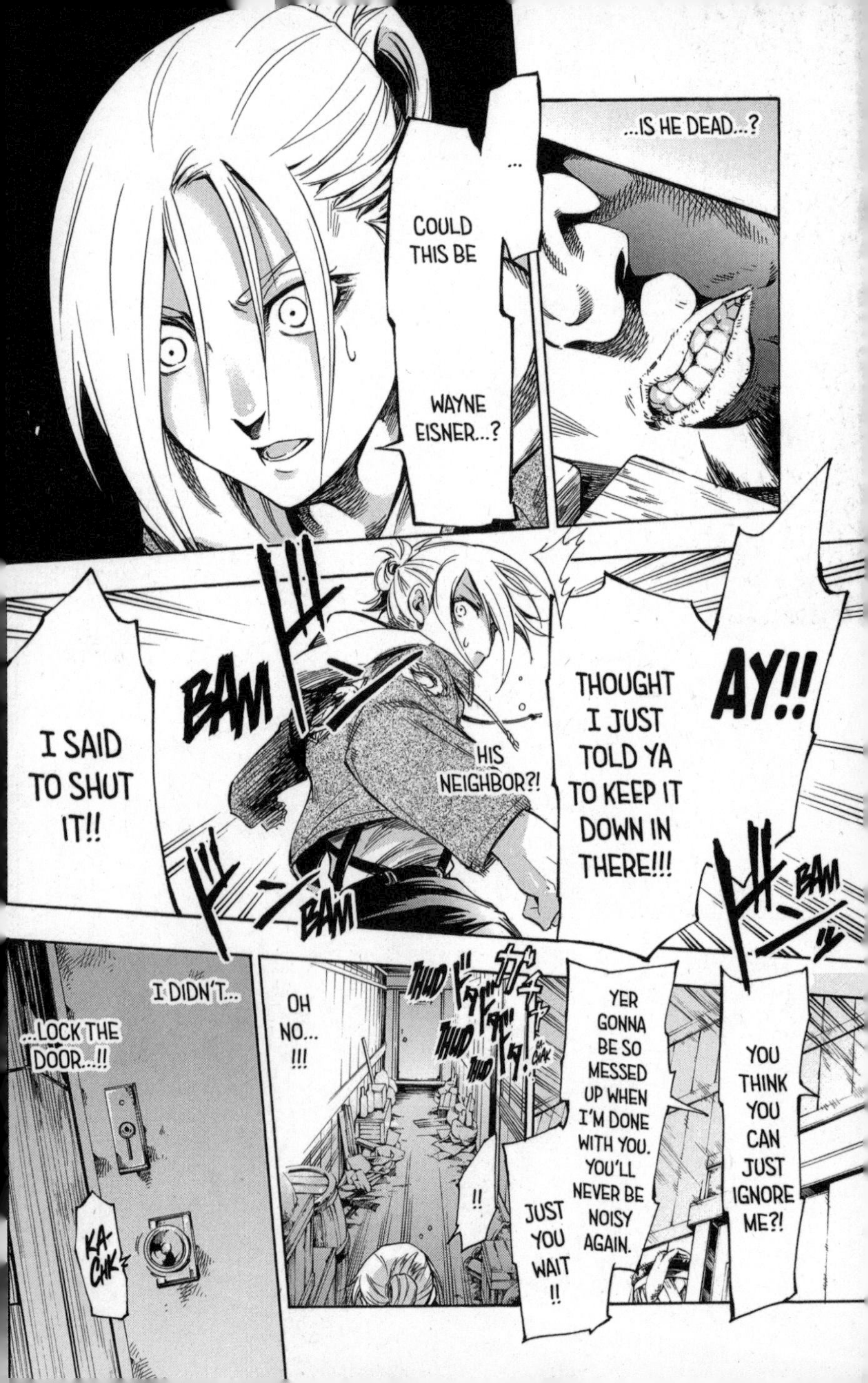
...IS HE DEAD...?
...
COULD THIS BE
WAYNE EISNER...?
AY!!
THOUGHT I JUST TOLD YA TO KEEP IT DOWN IN THERE!!!
BAM
HIS NEIGHBOR?!
BAM
I SAID TO SHUT IT!!
BAM
YOU THINK YOU CAN JUST IGNORE ME?!
YER GONNA BE SO MESSED UP WHEN I'M DONE WITH YOU. YOU'LL NEVER BE NOISY AGAIN.
JUST YOU WAIT !!
THUD
THUD
THUD
KA-CHAK
OH NO... !!!
!!
I DIDN'T...
...LOCK THE DOOR...!!
KA-CHK

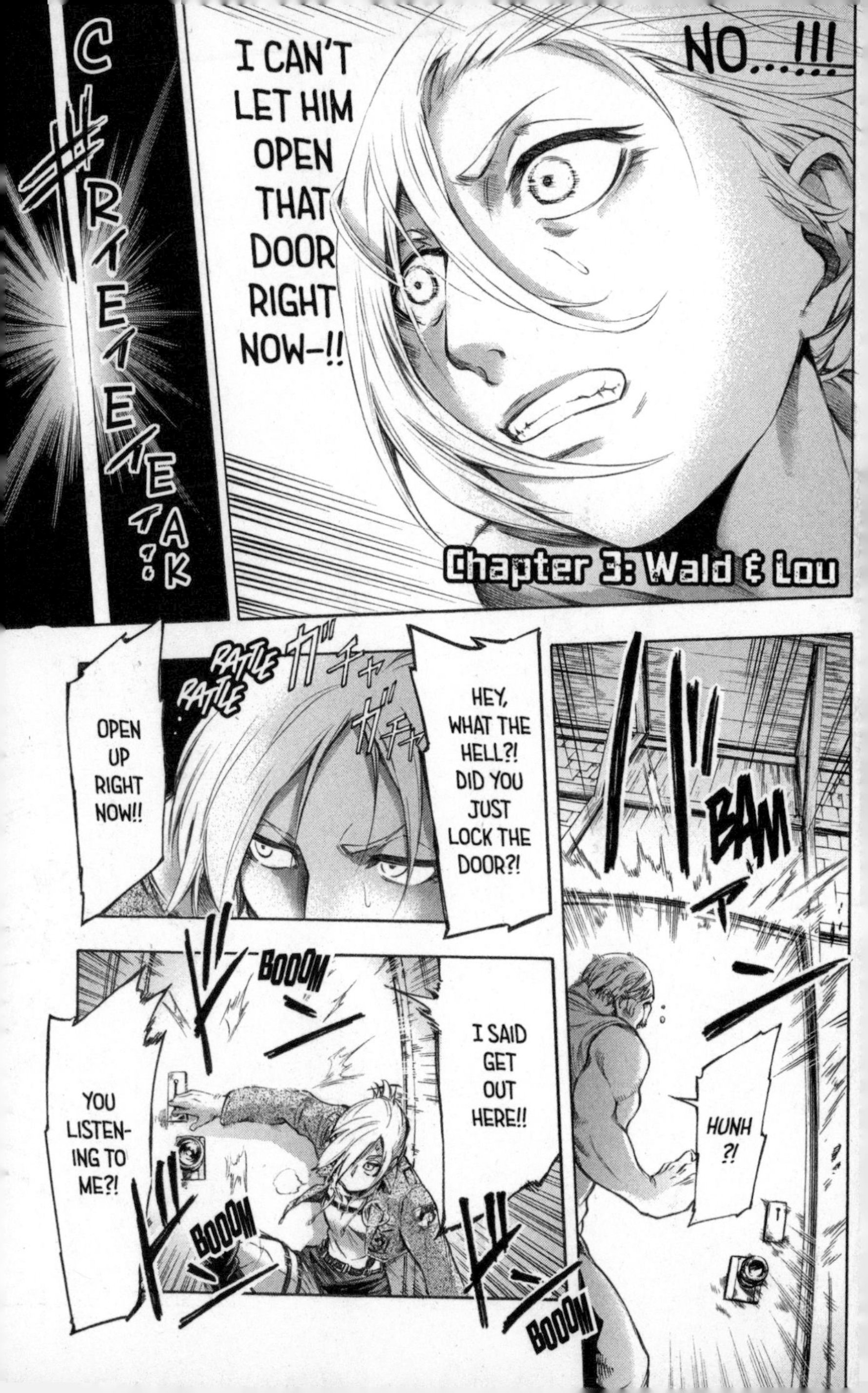
NO......!!!
I CAN'T LET HIM OPEN THAT DOOR RIGHT NOW-!!
CREEEAK
Chapter 3: Wald & Lou
BAM
HUNH?!
RATTLE RATTLE
HEY, WHAT THE HELL?! DID YOU JUST LOCK THE DOOR?!
OPEN UP RIGHT NOW!!
BOOOM
I SAID GET OUT HERE!!
YOU LISTEN-ING TO ME?!
BOOOM
BOOOM

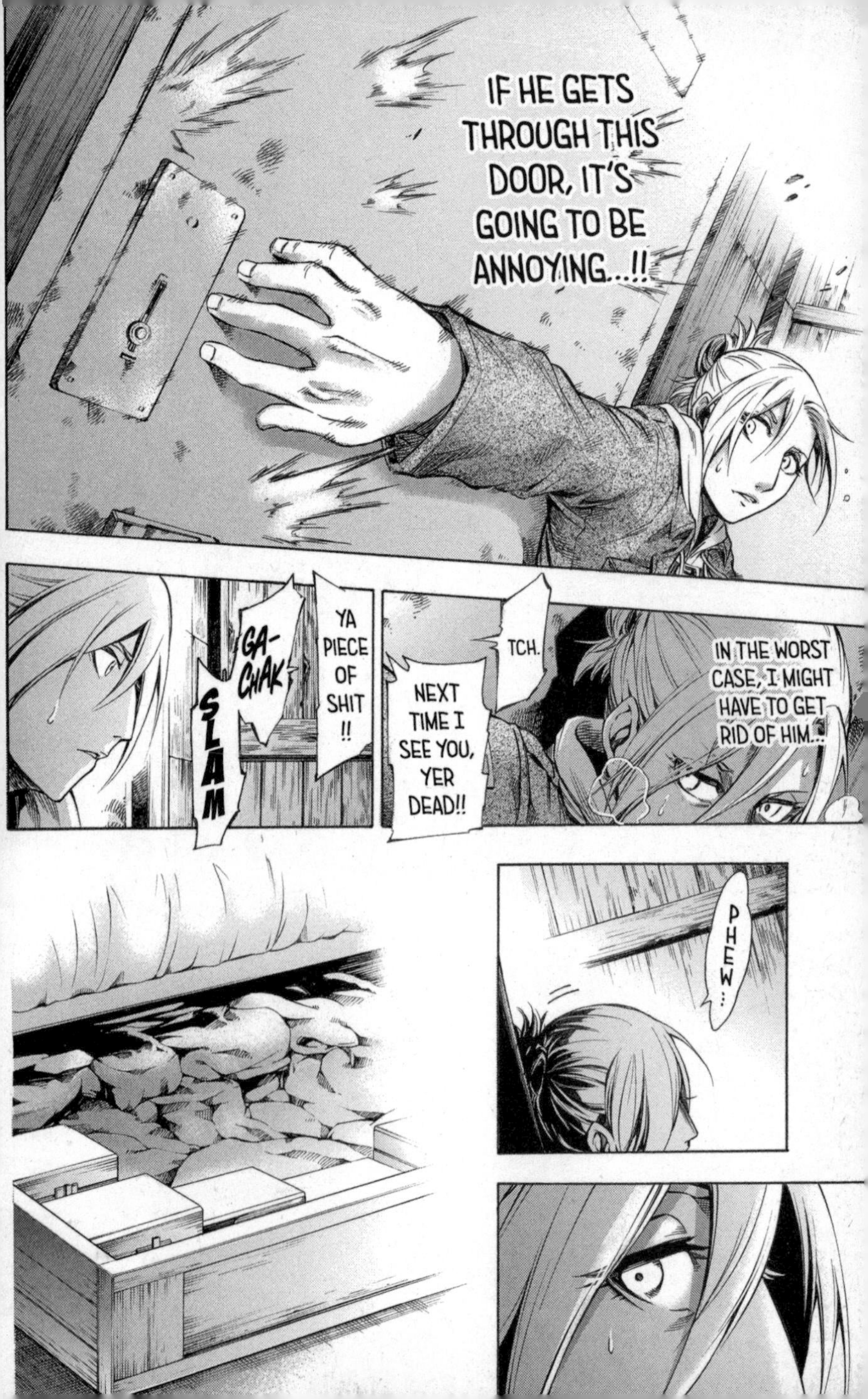
IF HE GETS THROUGH THIS DOOR, IT'S GOING TO BE ANNOYING...!!
IN THE WORST CASE, I MIGHT HAVE TO GET RID OF HIM...
TCH.
NEXT TIME I SEE YOU, YER DEAD!!
YA PIECE OF SHIT!!
GA-CHAK
SLAM
PHEW...

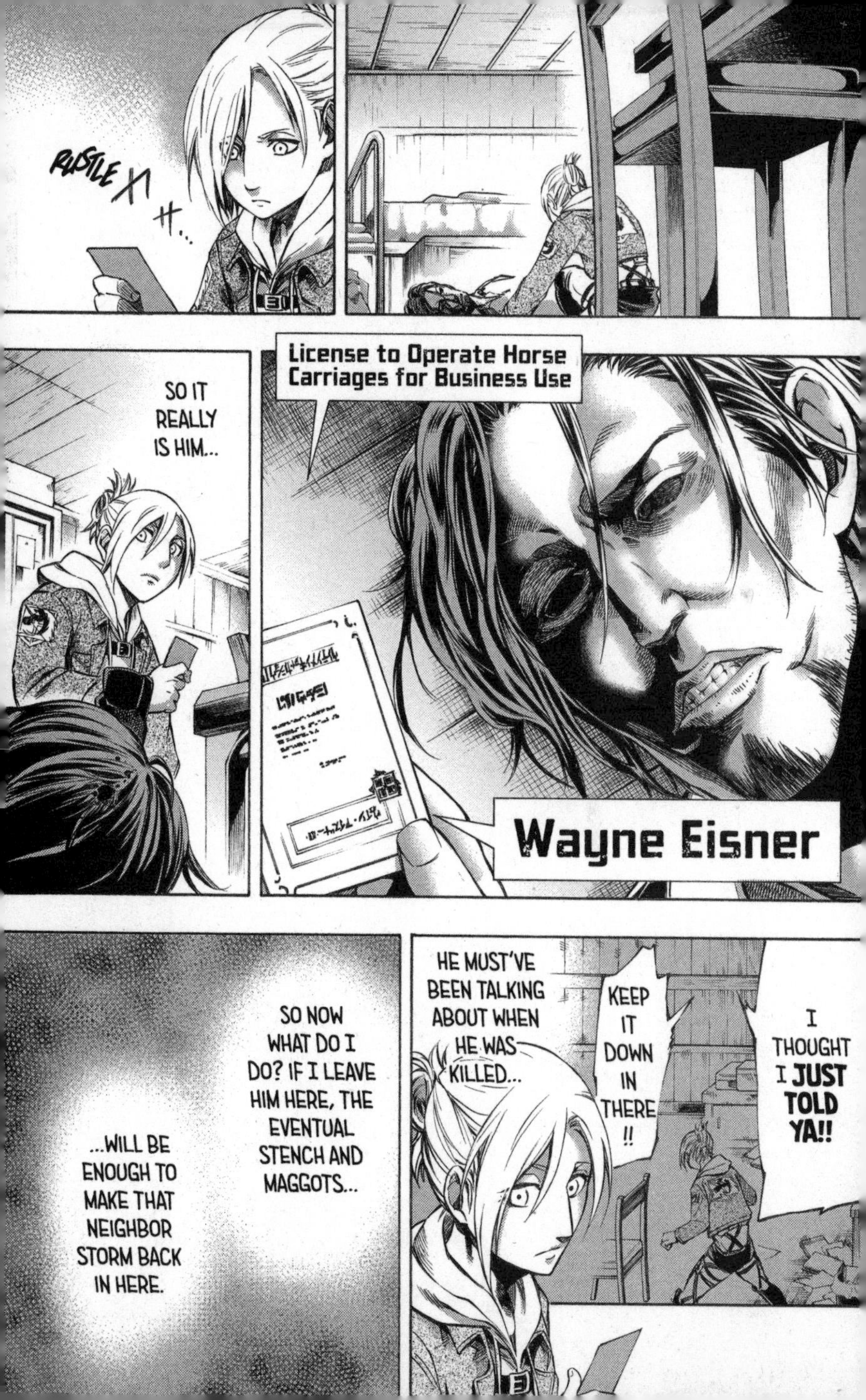
RUSTLE
License to Operate Horse Carriages for Business Use
Wayne Eisner
SO IT REALLY IS HIM...
I THOUGHT I **JUST TOLD YA!!**
KEEP IT DOWN IN THERE!!
HE MUST'VE BEEN TALKING ABOUT WHEN HE WAS KILLED...
SO NOW WHAT DO I DO? IF I LEAVE HIM HERE, THE EVENTUAL STENCH AND MAGGOTS...
...WILL BE ENOUGH TO MAKE THAT NEIGHBOR STORM BACK IN HERE.

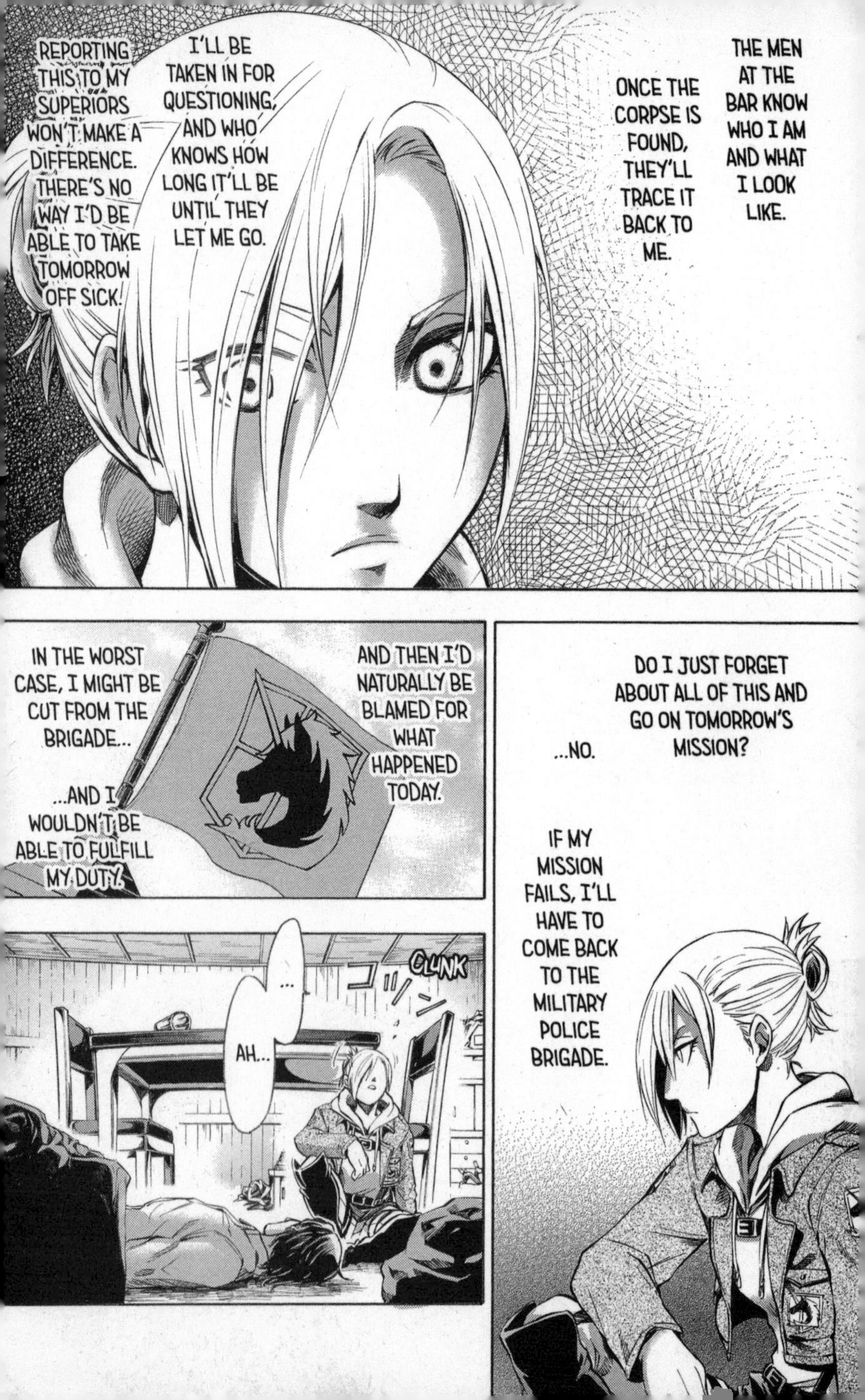
THE MEN AT THE BAR KNOW WHO I AM AND WHAT I LOOK LIKE.
ONCE THE CORPSE IS FOUND, THEY'LL TRACE IT BACK TO ME.
I'LL BE TAKEN IN FOR QUESTIONING, AND WHO KNOWS HOW LONG IT'LL BE UNTIL THEY LET ME GO.
REPORTING THIS TO MY SUPERIORS WON'T MAKE A DIFFERENCE. THERE'S NO WAY I'D BE ABLE TO TAKE TOMORROW OFF SICK.
DO I JUST FORGET ABOUT ALL OF THIS AND GO ON TOMORROW'S MISSION?
...NO.
IF MY MISSION FAILS, I'LL HAVE TO COME BACK TO THE MILITARY POLICE BRIGADE.
AND THEN I'D NATURALLY BE BLAMED FOR WHAT HAPPENED TODAY.
IN THE WORST CASE, I MIGHT BE CUT FROM THE BRIGADE...
...AND I WOULDN'T BE ABLE TO FULFILL MY DUTY.
CLUNK
...
AH...

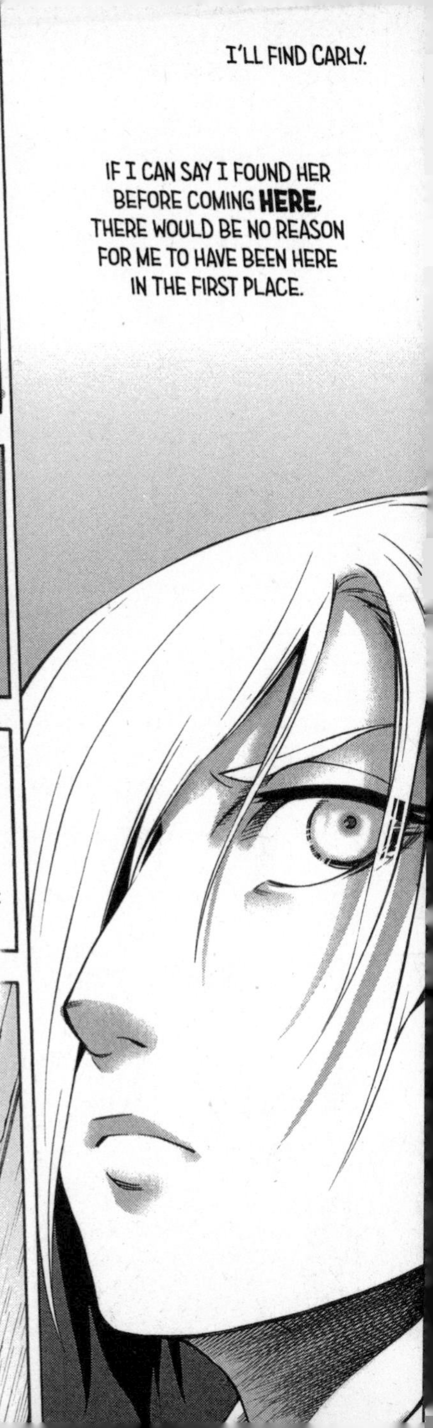
I'LL FIND CARLY.
IF I CAN SAY I FOUND HER BEFORE COMING **HERE**, THERE WOULD BE NO REASON FOR ME TO HAVE BEEN HERE IN THE FIRST PLACE.

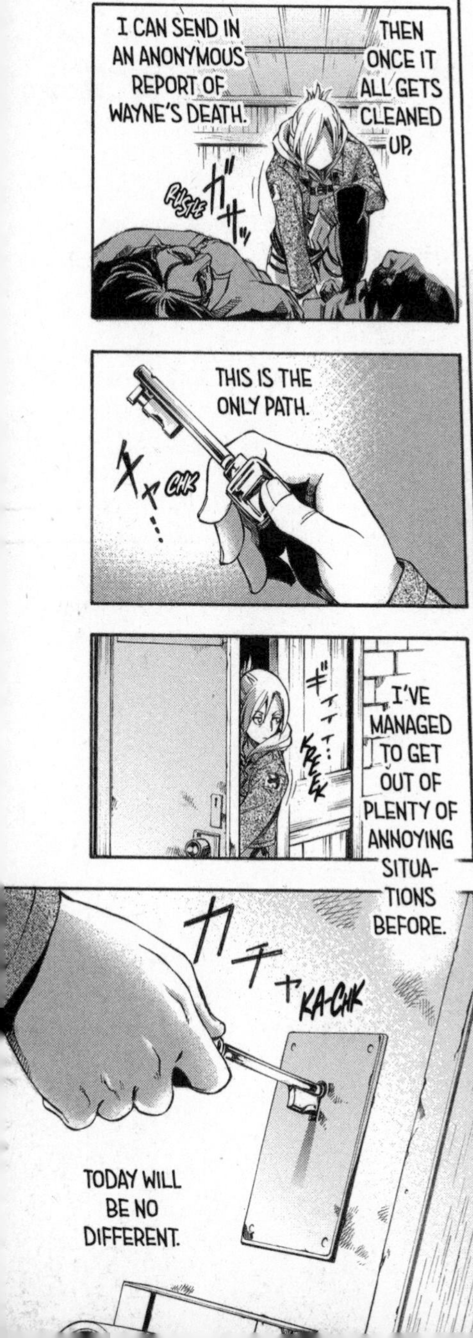
THEN ONCE IT ALL GETS CLEANED UP,
I CAN SEND IN AN ANONYMOUS REPORT OF WAYNE'S DEATH.
RUSTLE
THIS IS THE ONLY PATH.
CHK
I'VE MANAGED TO GET OUT OF PLENTY OF ANNOYING SITUATIONS BEFORE.
KREEK
KA-CHK
TODAY WILL BE NO DIFFERENT.

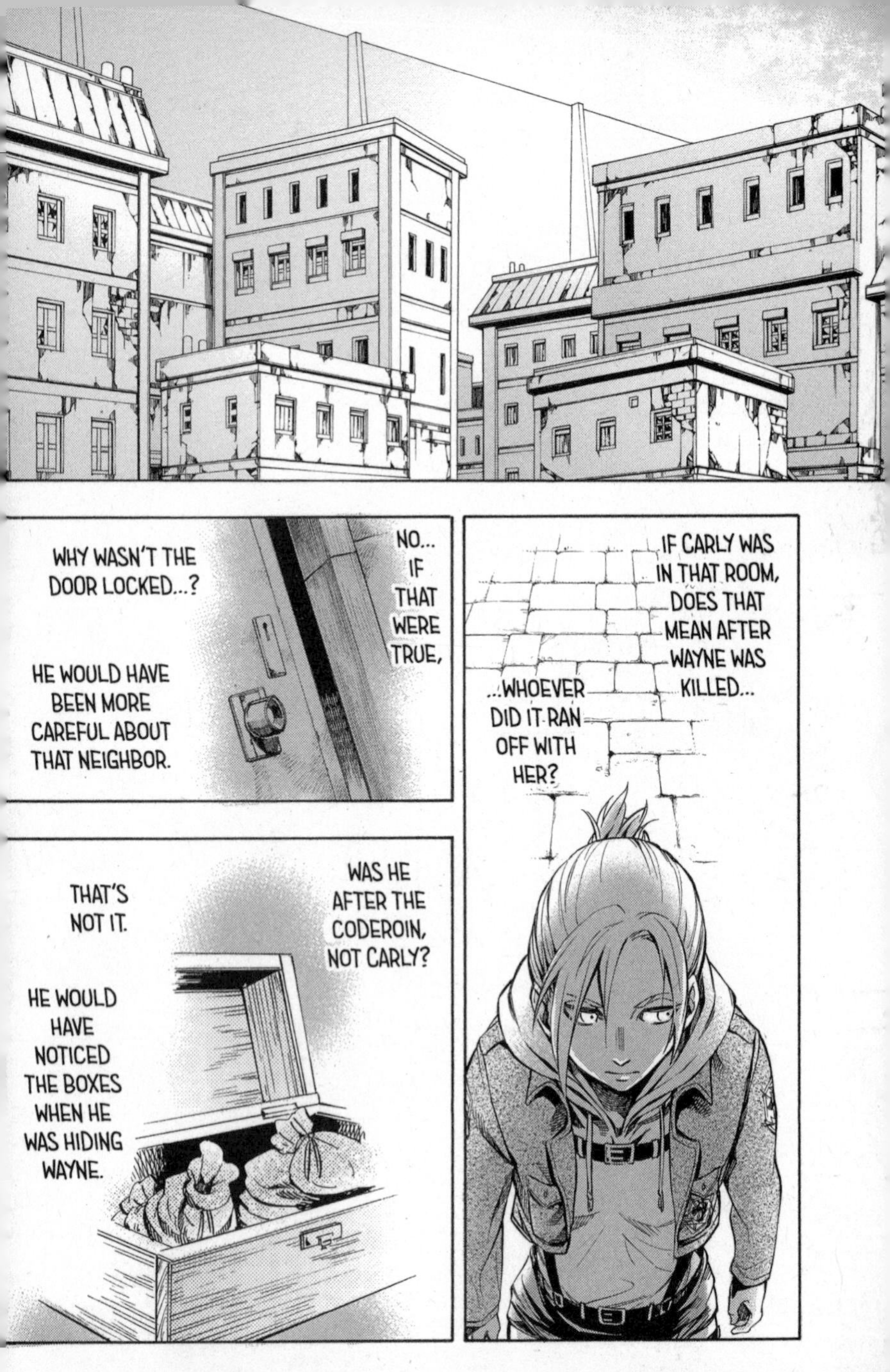
IF CARLY WAS IN THAT ROOM, DOES THAT MEAN AFTER WAYNE WAS KILLED...
...WHOEVER DID IT RAN OFF WITH HER?
NO... IF THAT WERE TRUE,
WHY WASN'T THE DOOR LOCKED...?
HE WOULD HAVE BEEN MORE CAREFUL ABOUT THAT NEIGHBOR.
WAS HE AFTER THE CODEROIN, NOT CARLY?
THAT'S NOT IT.
HE WOULD HAVE NOTICED THE BOXES WHEN HE WAS HIDING WAYNE.

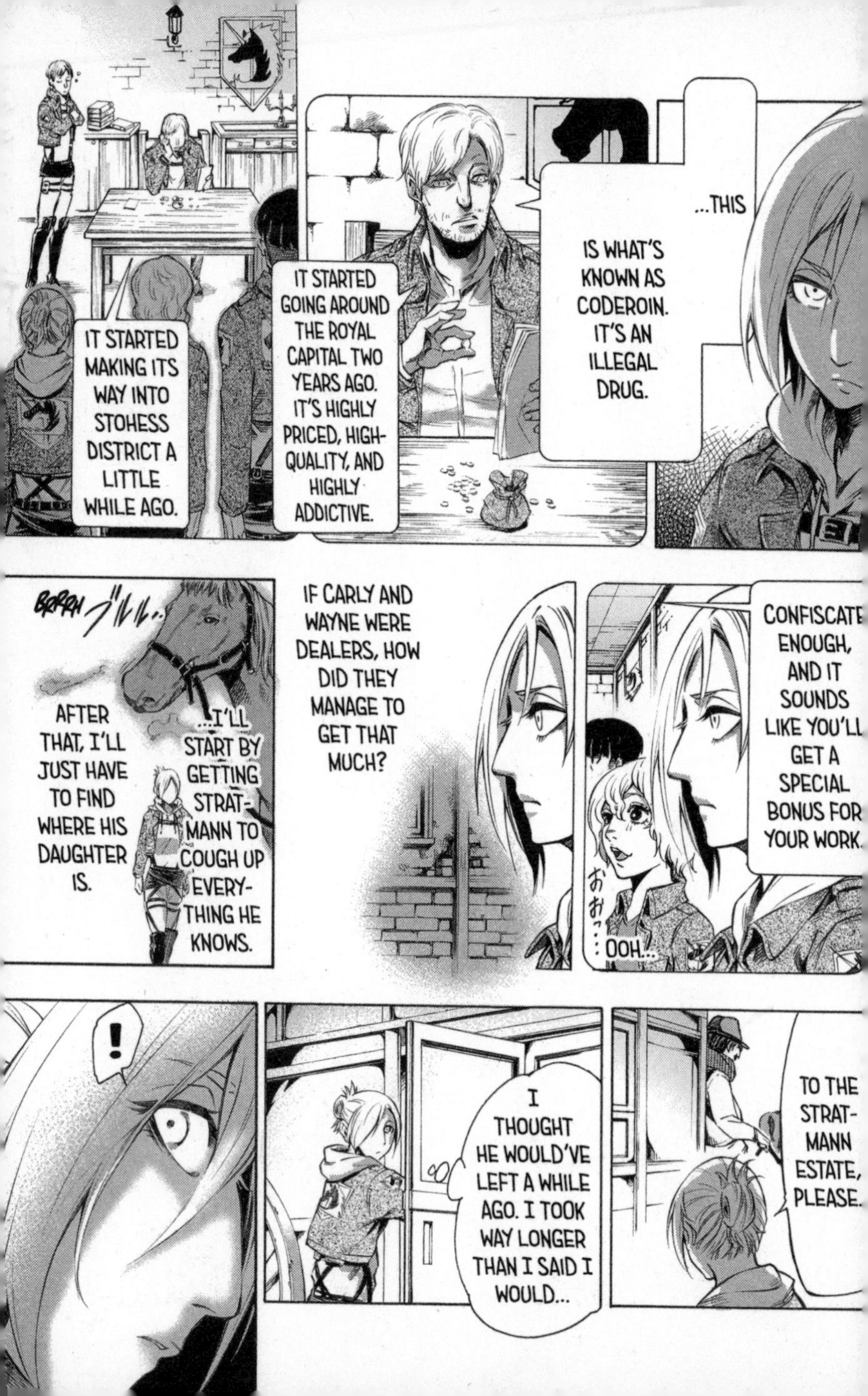
...THIS
IS WHAT'S KNOWN AS CODEROIN. IT'S AN ILLEGAL DRUG.
IT STARTED GOING AROUND THE ROYAL CAPITAL TWO YEARS AGO. IT'S HIGHLY PRICED, HIGH-QUALITY, AND HIGHLY ADDICTIVE.
IT STARTED MAKING ITS WAY INTO STOHESS DISTRICT A LITTLE WHILE AGO.
CONFISCATE ENOUGH, AND IT SOUNDS LIKE YOU'LL GET A SPECIAL BONUS FOR YOUR WORK.
おおっ…
OOH...
IF CARLY AND WAYNE WERE DEALERS, HOW DID THEY MANAGE TO GET THAT MUCH?
BRRRH
ブルル…
...I'LL START BY GETTING STRAT-MANN TO COUGH UP EVERY-THING HE KNOWS.
AFTER THAT, I'LL JUST HAVE TO FIND WHERE HIS DAUGHTER IS.
TO THE STRAT-MANN ESTATE, PLEASE.
I THOUGHT HE WOULD'VE LEFT A WHILE AGO. I TOOK WAY LONGER THAN I SAID I WOULD...
!

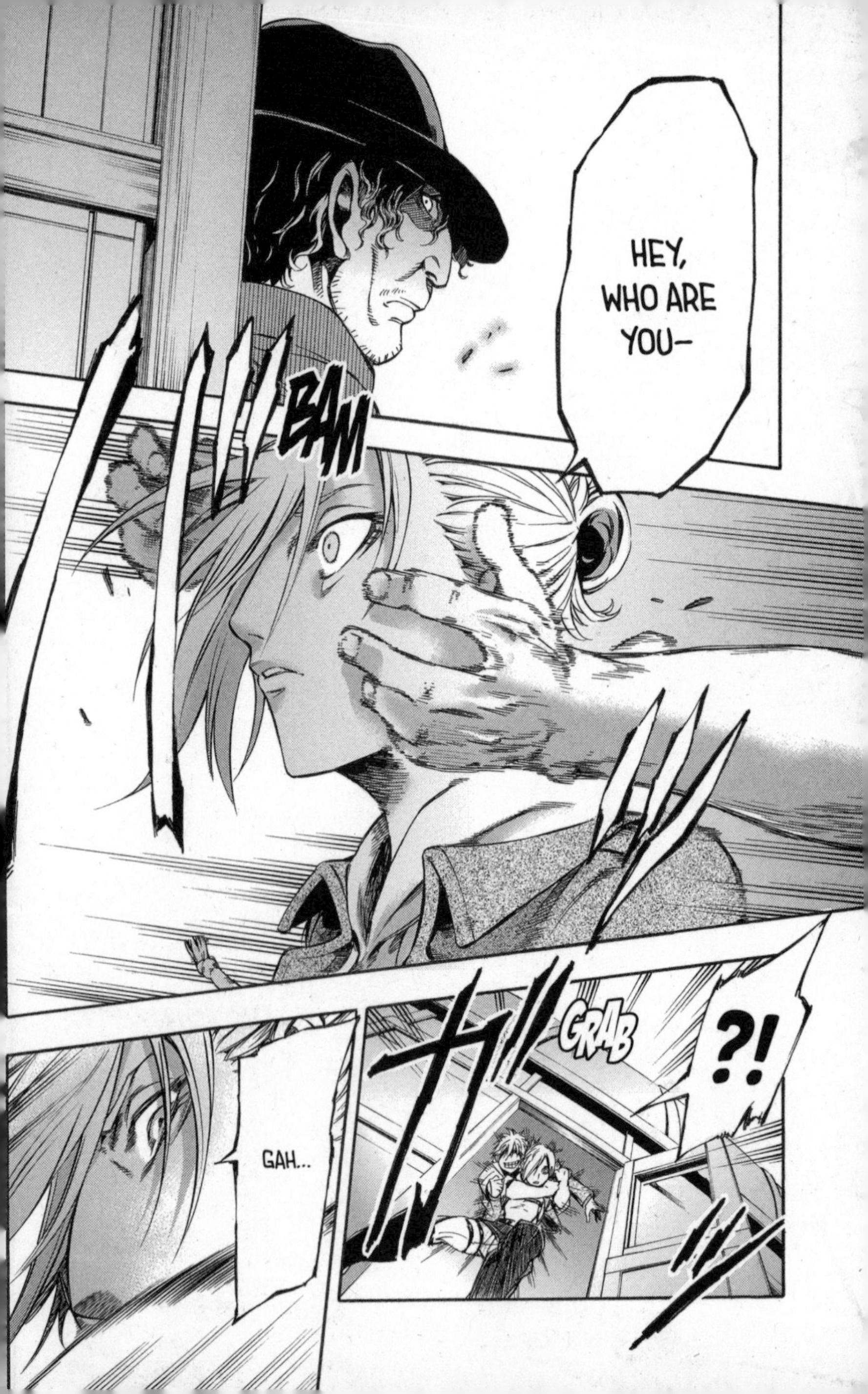
HEY, WHO ARE YOU–
BAM
?!
GRAB
GAH...

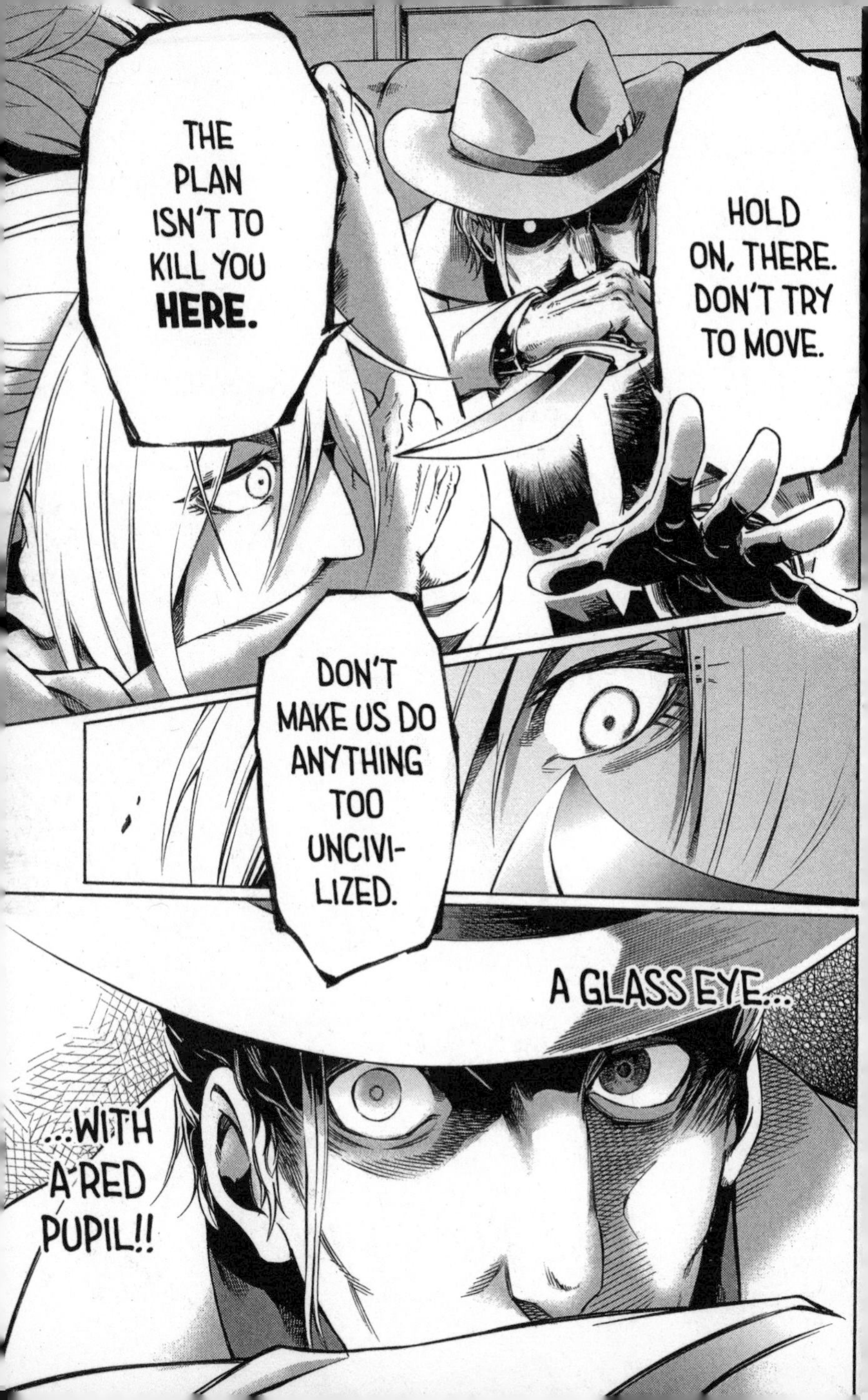
HOLD ON, THERE. DON'T TRY TO MOVE.
THE PLAN ISN'T TO KILL YOU **HERE.**
DON'T MAKE US DO ANYTHING TOO UNCIVILIZED.
A GLASS EYE...
...WITH A RED PUPIL!!

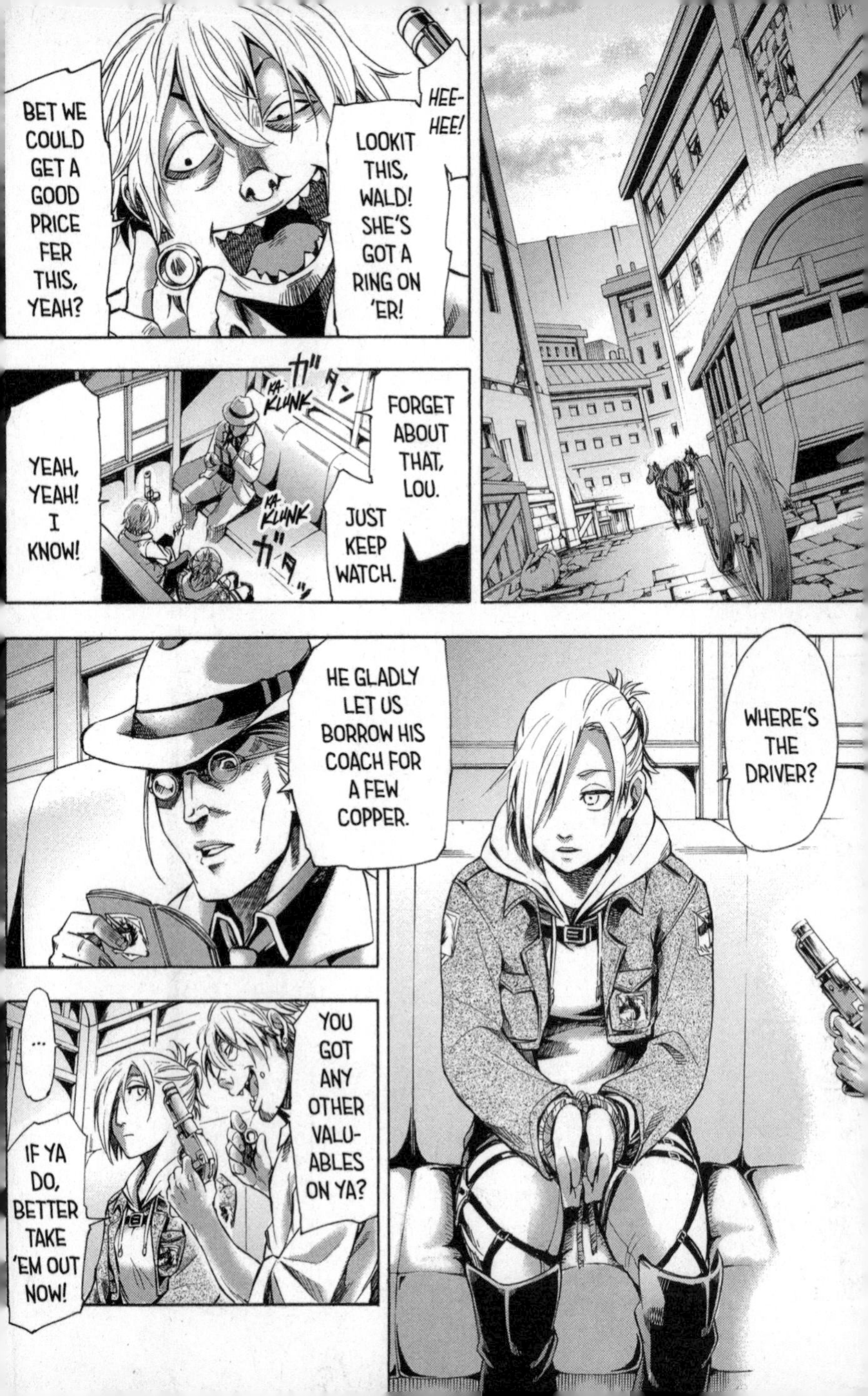
HEE-HEE!
LOOKIT THIS, WALD! SHE'S GOT A RING ON 'ER!
BET WE COULD GET A GOOD PRICE FER THIS, YEAH?
KA-KLUNK
FORGET ABOUT THAT, LOU.
JUST KEEP WATCH.
KA-KLUNK
YEAH, YEAH! I KNOW!
WHERE'S THE DRIVER?
HE GLADLY LET US BORROW HIS COACH FOR A FEW COPPER.
YOU GOT ANY OTHER VALU-ABLES ON YA?
...
IF YA DO, BETTER TAKE 'EM OUT NOW!

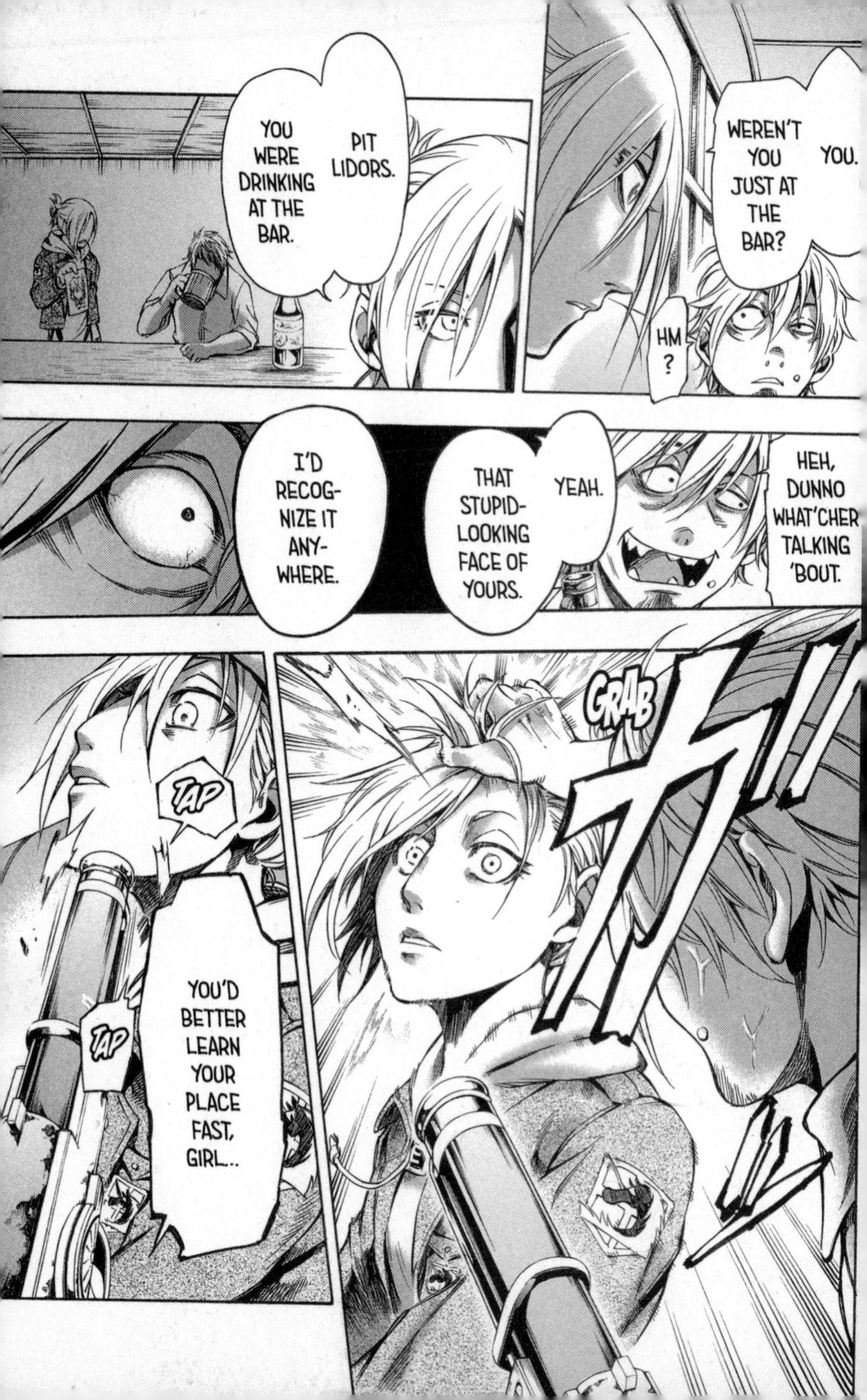
YOU.
WEREN'T YOU JUST AT THE BAR?
HM?
PIT LIDORS.
YOU WERE DRINKING AT THE BAR.
HEH, DUNNO WHAT'CHER TALKING 'BOUT.
YEAH.
THAT STUPID-LOOKING FACE OF YOURS.
I'D RECOG-NIZE IT ANY-WHERE.
GRAB
TAP
TAP
YOU'D BETTER LEARN YOUR PLACE FAST, GIRL...

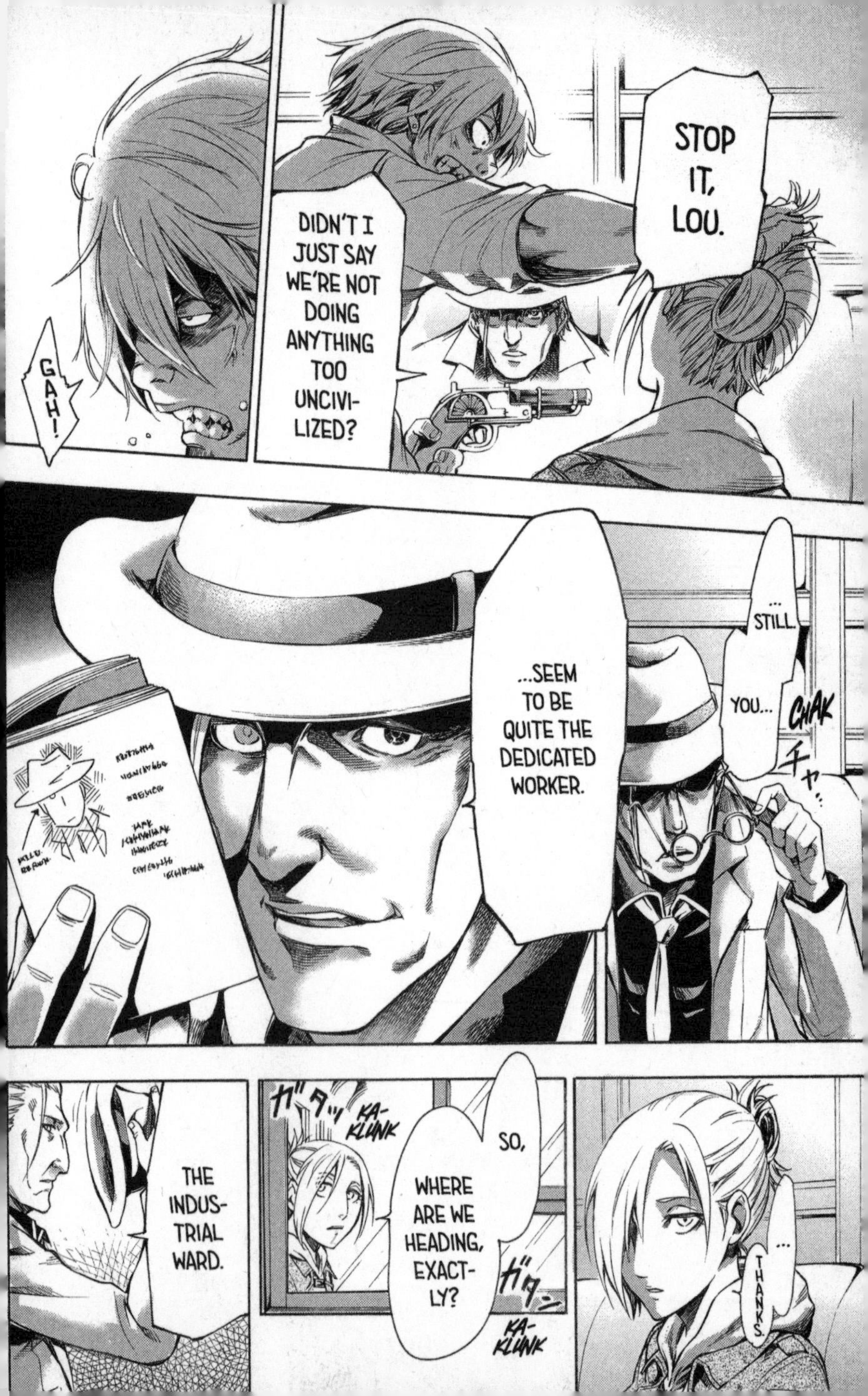
STOP IT, LOU.
DIDN'T I JUST SAY WE'RE NOT DOING ANYTHING TOO UNCIVI-LIZED?
GAH!
...STILL.
YOU...
CHAK
チャ...
...SEEM TO BE QUITE THE DEDICATED WORKER.
...
THANKS.
ガタッ
KA-KLUNK
SO,
WHERE ARE WE HEADING, EXACT-LY?
ガタン
KA-KLUNK
THE INDUS-TRIAL WARD.

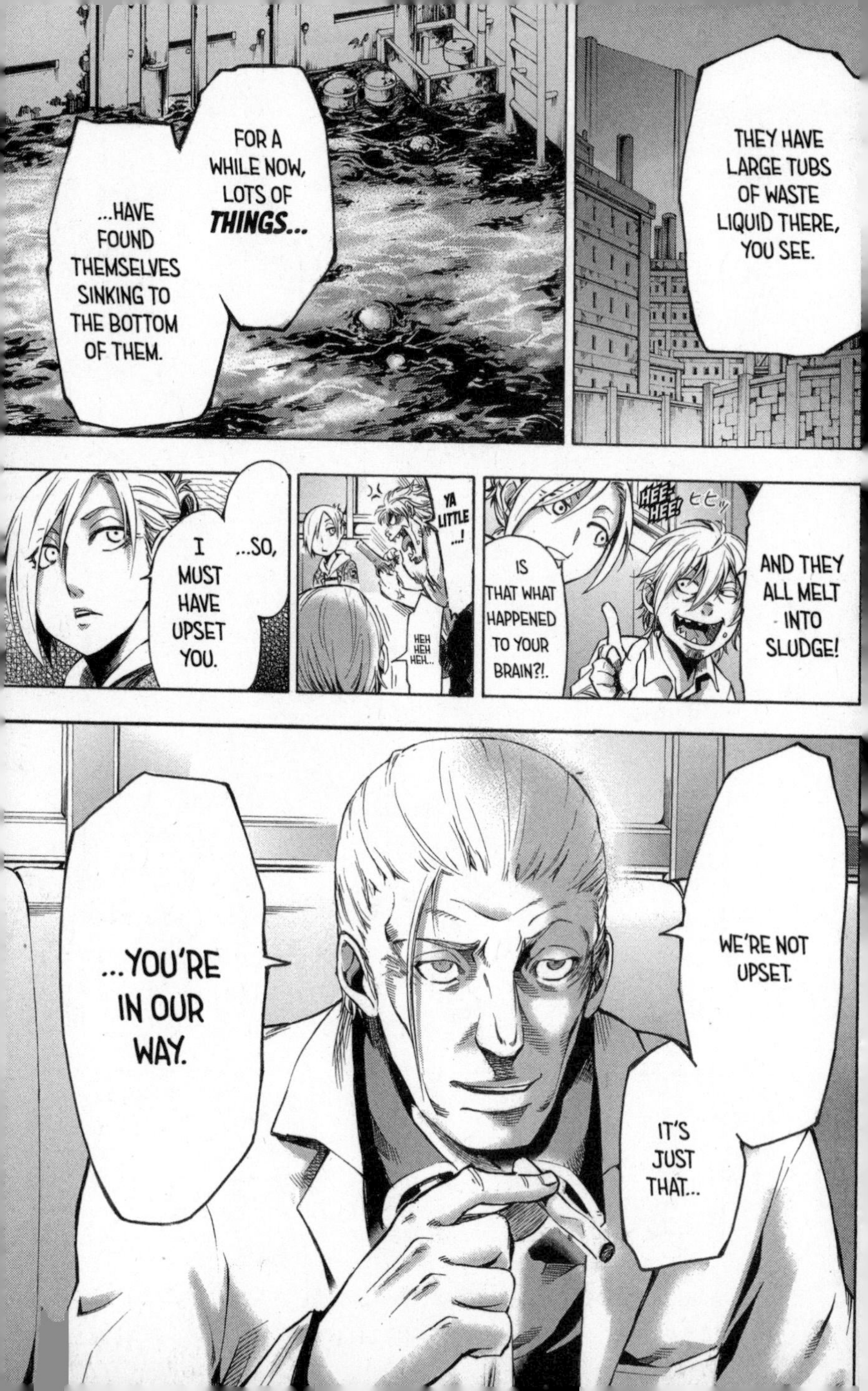
THEY HAVE LARGE TUBS OF WASTE LIQUID THERE, YOU SEE.
FOR A WHILE NOW, LOTS OF THINGS...
...HAVE FOUND THEMSELVES SINKING TO THE BOTTOM OF THEM.
AND THEY ALL MELT INTO SLUDGE!
HEE-HEE!
ヒヒッ
IS THAT WHAT HAPPENED TO YOUR BRAIN?!.
YA LITTLE ...!
HEH HEH HEH...
...SO,
I MUST HAVE UPSET YOU.
WE'RE NOT UPSET.
IT'S JUST THAT...
...YOU'RE IN OUR WAY.

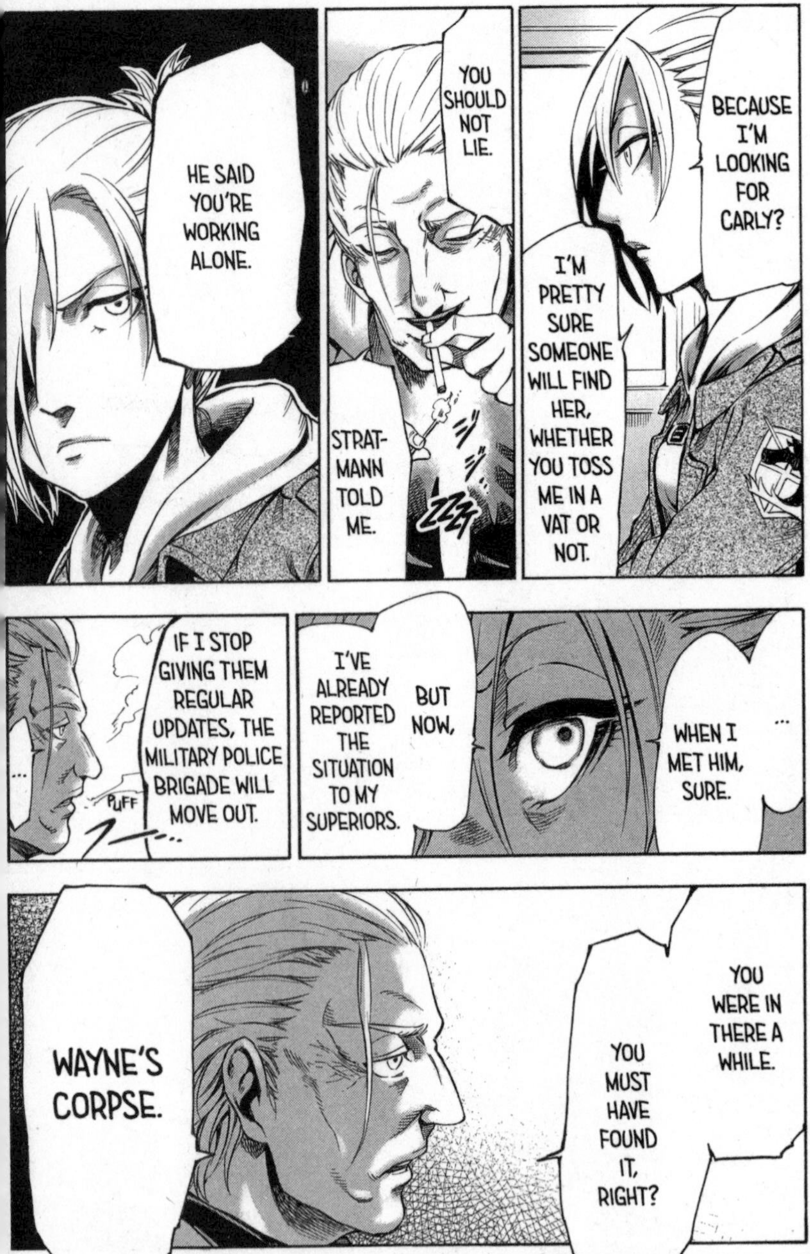
BECAUSE I'M LOOKING FOR CARLY?
I'M PRETTY SURE SOMEONE WILL FIND HER, WHETHER YOU TOSS ME IN A VAT OR NOT.
YOU SHOULD NOT LIE.
STRAT-MANN TOLD ME.
HE SAID YOU'RE WORKING ALONE.
...
WHEN I MET HIM, SURE.
BUT NOW,
I'VE ALREADY REPORTED THE SITUATION TO MY SUPERIORS.
IF I STOP GIVING THEM REGULAR UPDATES, THE MILITARY POLICE BRIGADE WILL MOVE OUT.
...
PUFF
YOU WERE IN THERE A WHILE.
YOU MUST HAVE FOUND IT, RIGHT?
WAYNE'S CORPSE.

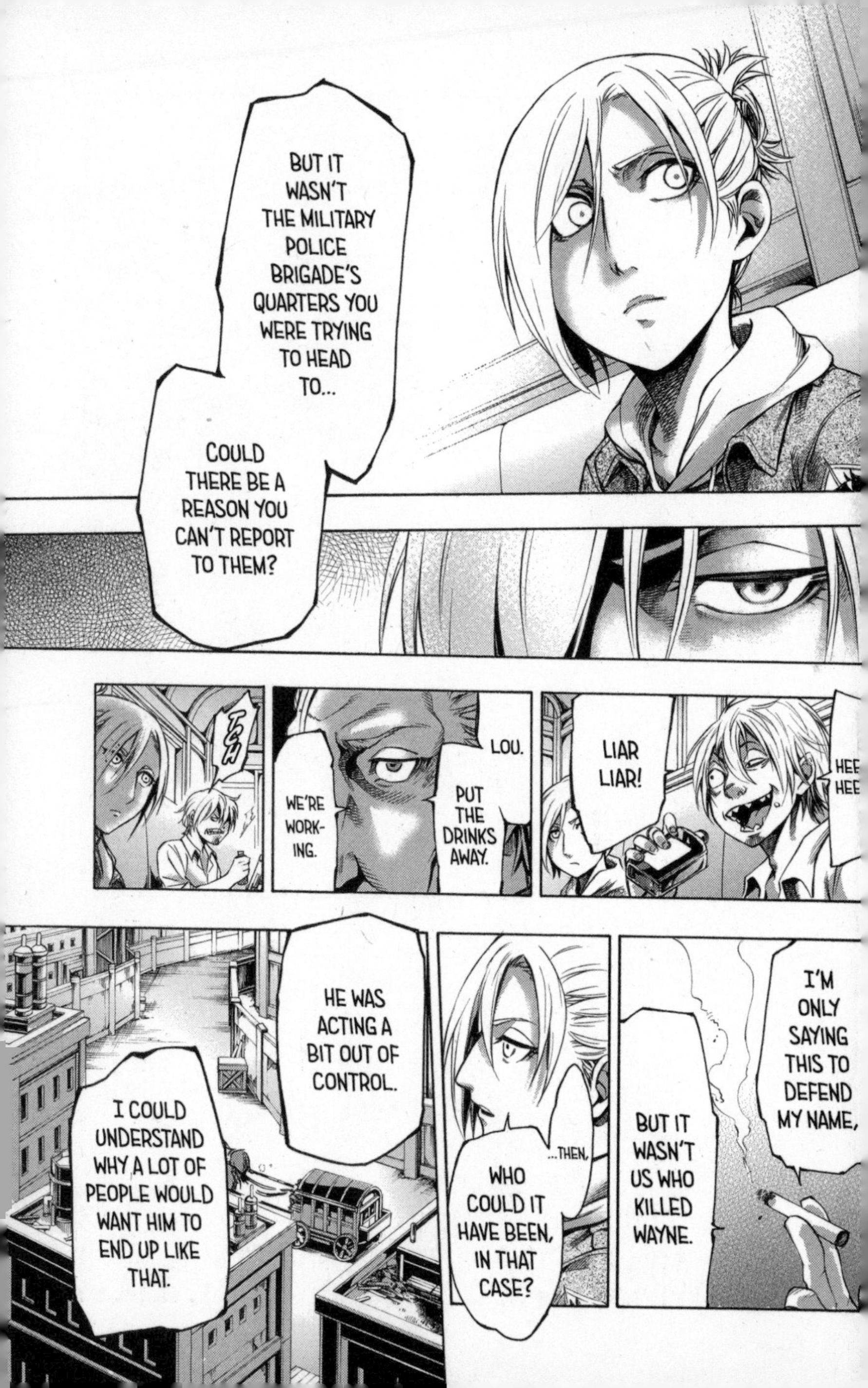
BUT IT WASN'T THE MILITARY POLICE BRIGADE'S QUARTERS YOU WERE TRYING TO HEAD TO...
COULD THERE BE A REASON YOU CAN'T REPORT TO THEM?
HEE HEE
LIAR LIAR!
LOU.
PUT THE DRINKS AWAY.
WE'RE WORK-ING.
TCH
I'M ONLY SAYING THIS TO DEFEND MY NAME,
BUT IT WASN'T US WHO KILLED WAYNE.
...THEN,
WHO COULD IT HAVE BEEN, IN THAT CASE?
HE WAS ACTING A BIT OUT OF CONTROL.
I COULD UNDERSTAND WHY A LOT OF PEOPLE WOULD WANT HIM TO END UP LIKE THAT.

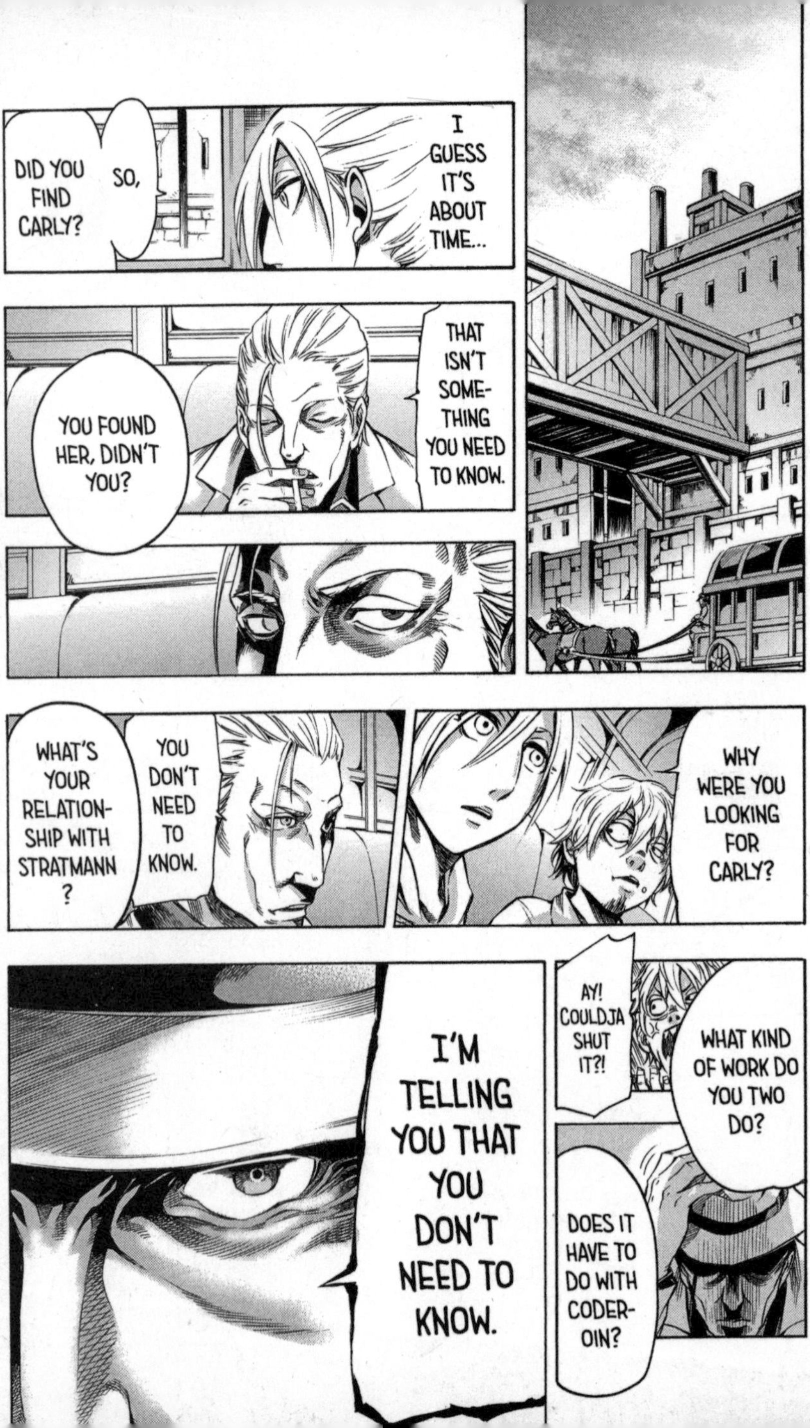
I GUESS IT'S ABOUT TIME...
SO,
DID YOU FIND CARLY?
THAT ISN'T SOME-THING YOU NEED TO KNOW.
YOU FOUND HER, DIDN'T YOU?
WHY WERE YOU LOOKING FOR CARLY?
YOU DON'T NEED TO KNOW.
WHAT'S YOUR RELATION-SHIP WITH STRATMANN?
WHAT KIND OF WORK DO YOU TWO DO?
AY! COULDJA SHUT IT?!
DOES IT HAVE TO DO WITH CODER-OIN?
I'M TELLING YOU THAT YOU DON'T NEED TO KNOW.

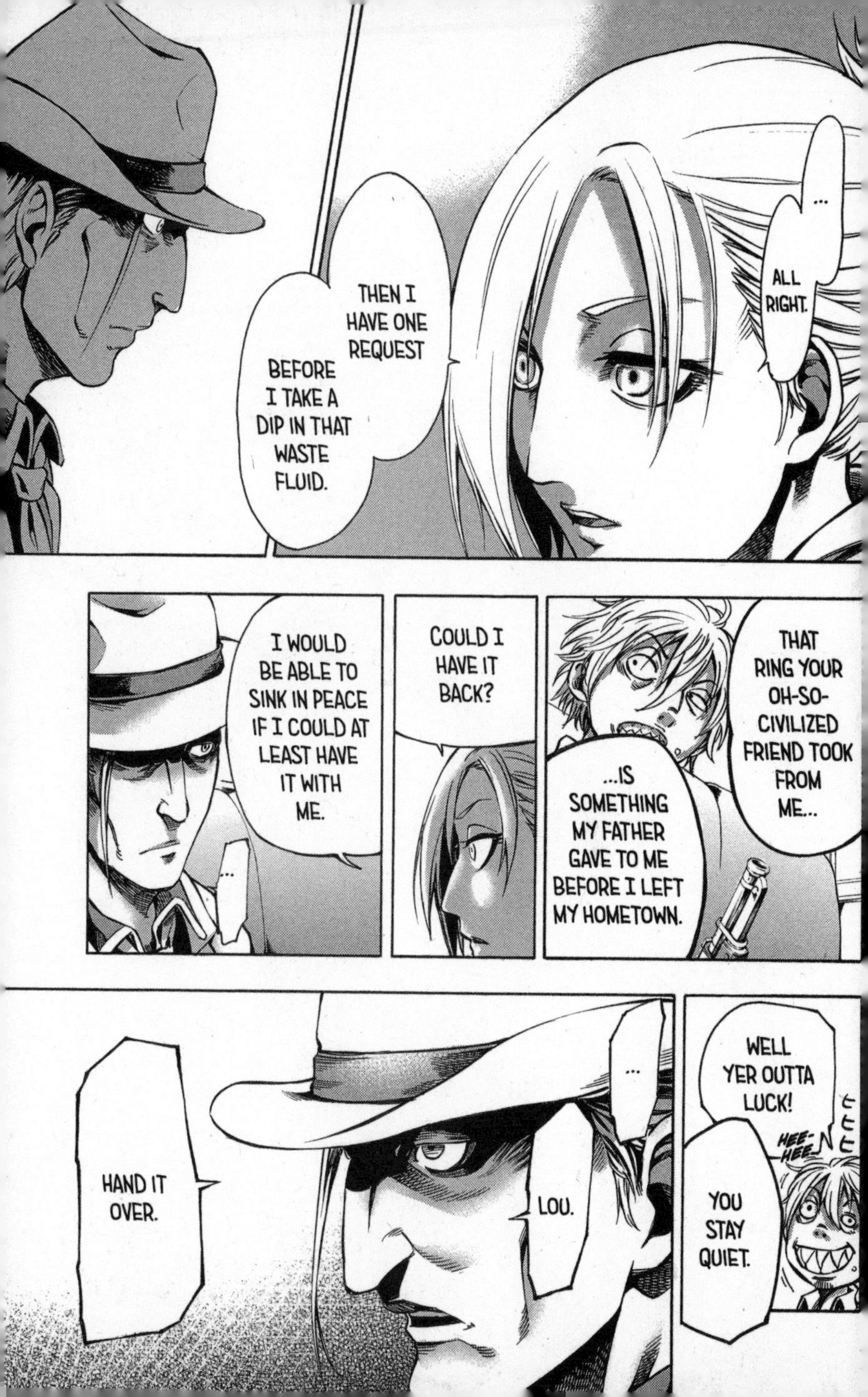
...
ALL RIGHT.
THEN I HAVE ONE REQUEST
BEFORE I TAKE A DIP IN THAT WASTE FLUID.
THAT RING YOUR OH-SO-CIVILIZED FRIEND TOOK FROM ME...
...IS SOMETHING MY FATHER GAVE TO ME BEFORE I LEFT MY HOMETOWN.
COULD I HAVE IT BACK?
I WOULD BE ABLE TO SINK IN PEACE IF I COULD AT LEAST HAVE IT WITH ME.
...
WELL YER OUTTA LUCK!
ヒヒヒ
HEE-HEE
YOU STAY QUIET.
...
LOU.
HAND IT OVER.

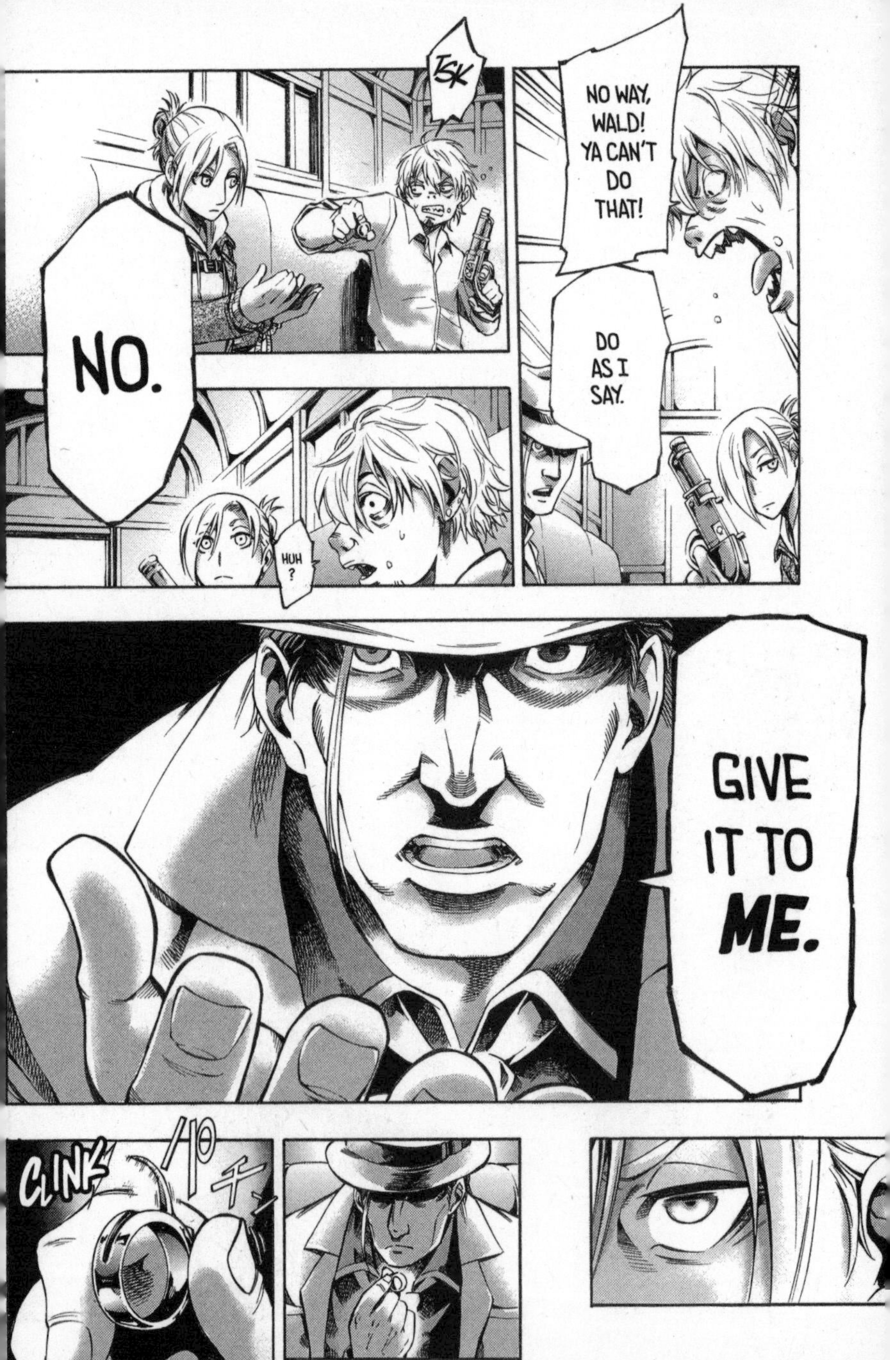

NO WAY, WALD! YA CAN'T DO THAT!
DO AS I SAY.
TSK
NO.
HUH ?
GIVE IT TO **ME.**
CLINK

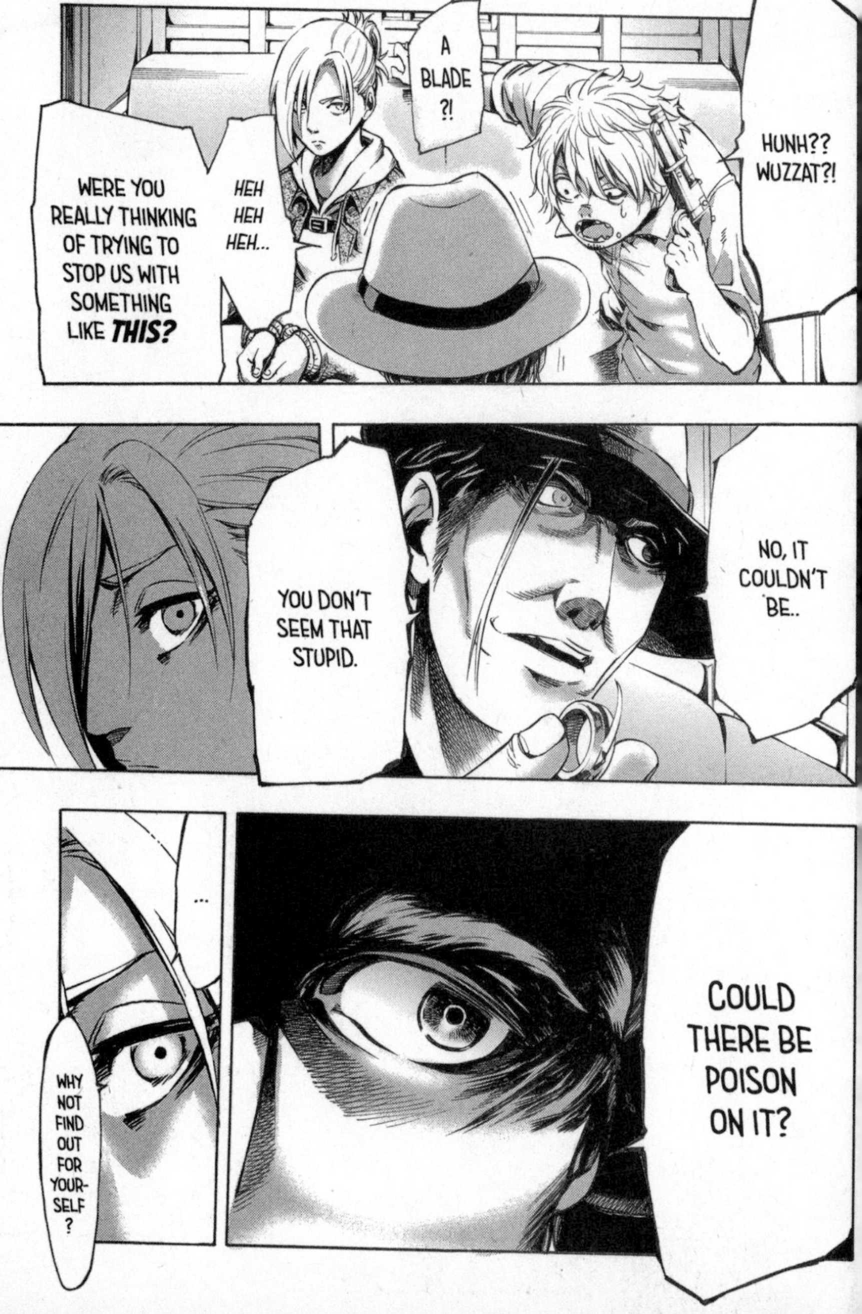
HUNH?? WUZZAT?!
A BLADE ?!
HEH HEH HEH...
WERE YOU REALLY THINKING OF TRYING TO STOP US WITH SOMETHING LIKE **THIS?**
NO, IT COULDN'T BE..
YOU DON'T SEEM THAT STUPID.
COULD THERE BE POISON ON IT?
...
WHY NOT FIND OUT FOR YOUR-SELF ?

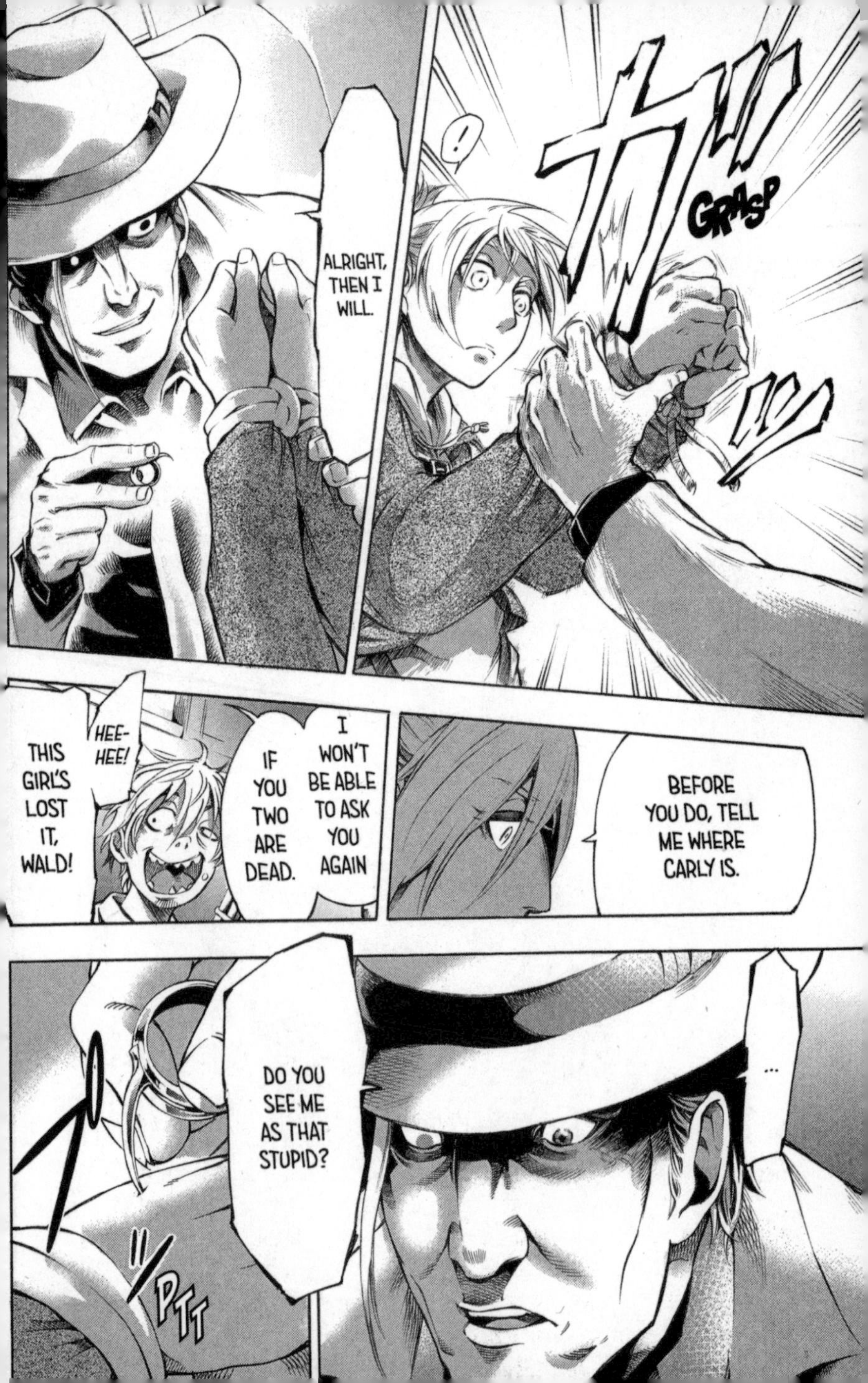
!
GRASP
ALRIGHT, THEN I WILL.
BEFORE YOU DO, TELL ME WHERE CARLY IS.
I WON'T BE ABLE TO ASK YOU AGAIN
IF YOU TWO ARE DEAD.
HEE-HEE!
THIS GIRL'S LOST IT, WALD!
...
DO YOU SEE ME AS THAT STUPID?
PTT

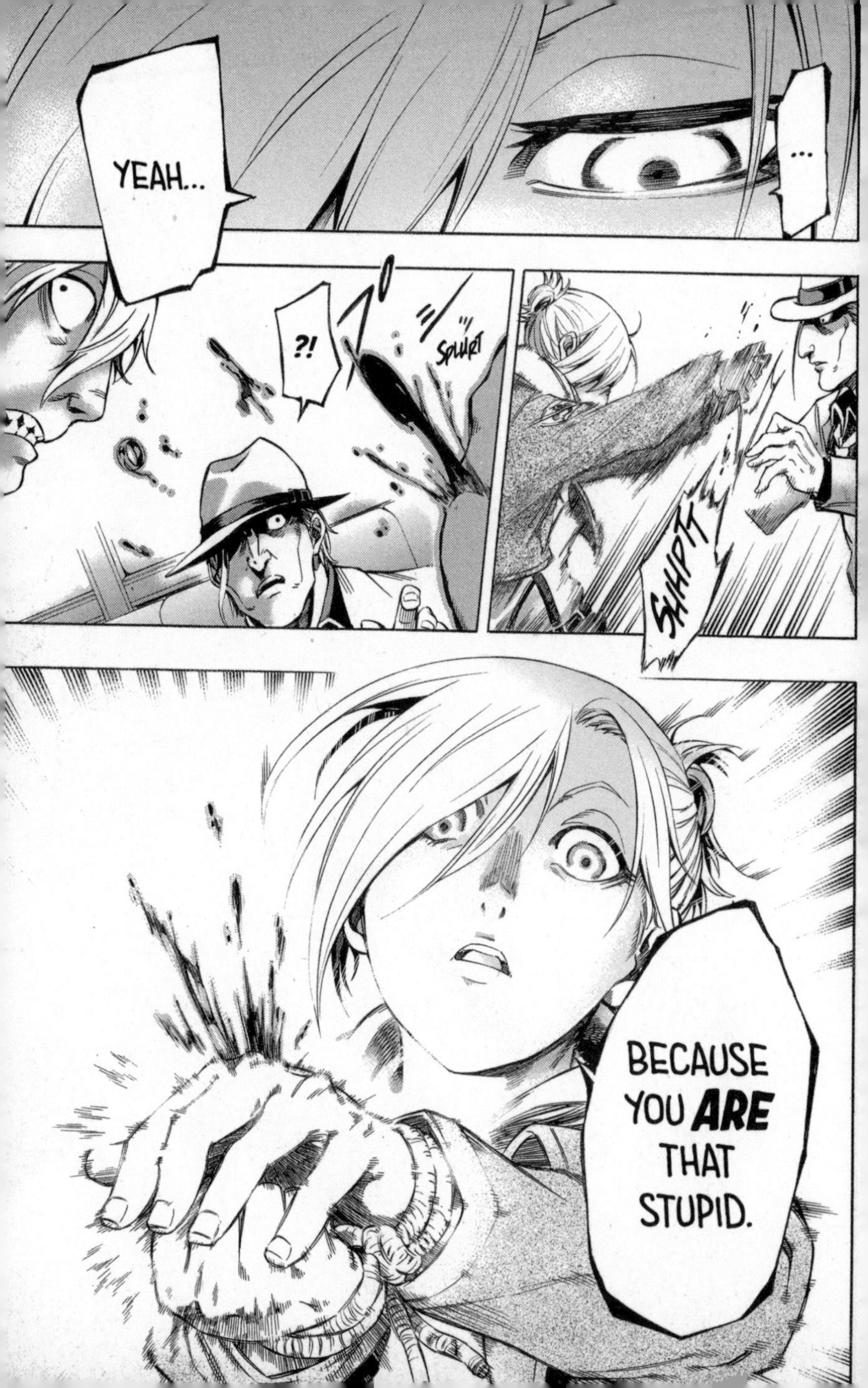
...
YEAH...
SHHPTT
SPLURT
?!
BECAUSE YOU **ARE** THAT STUPID.

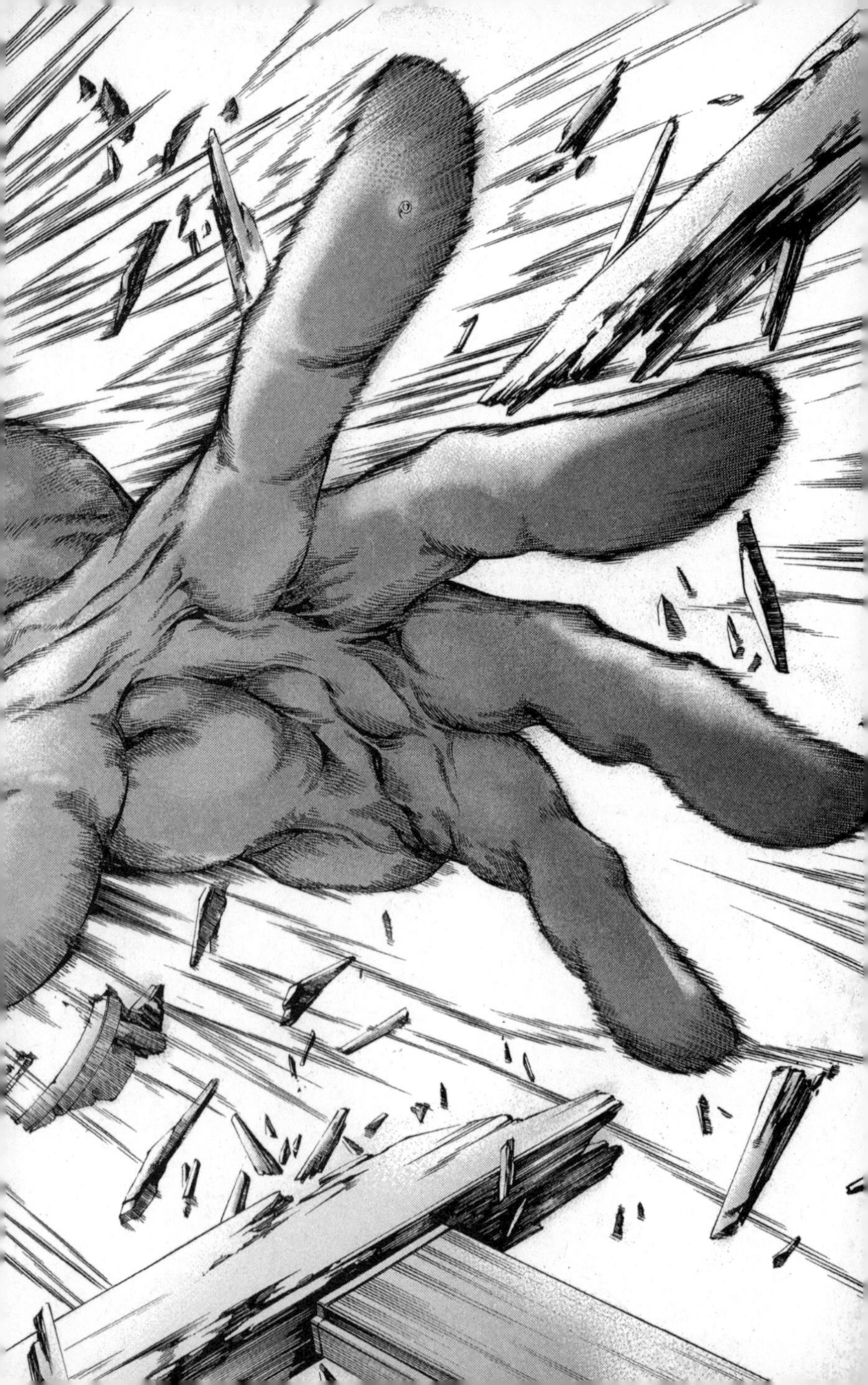

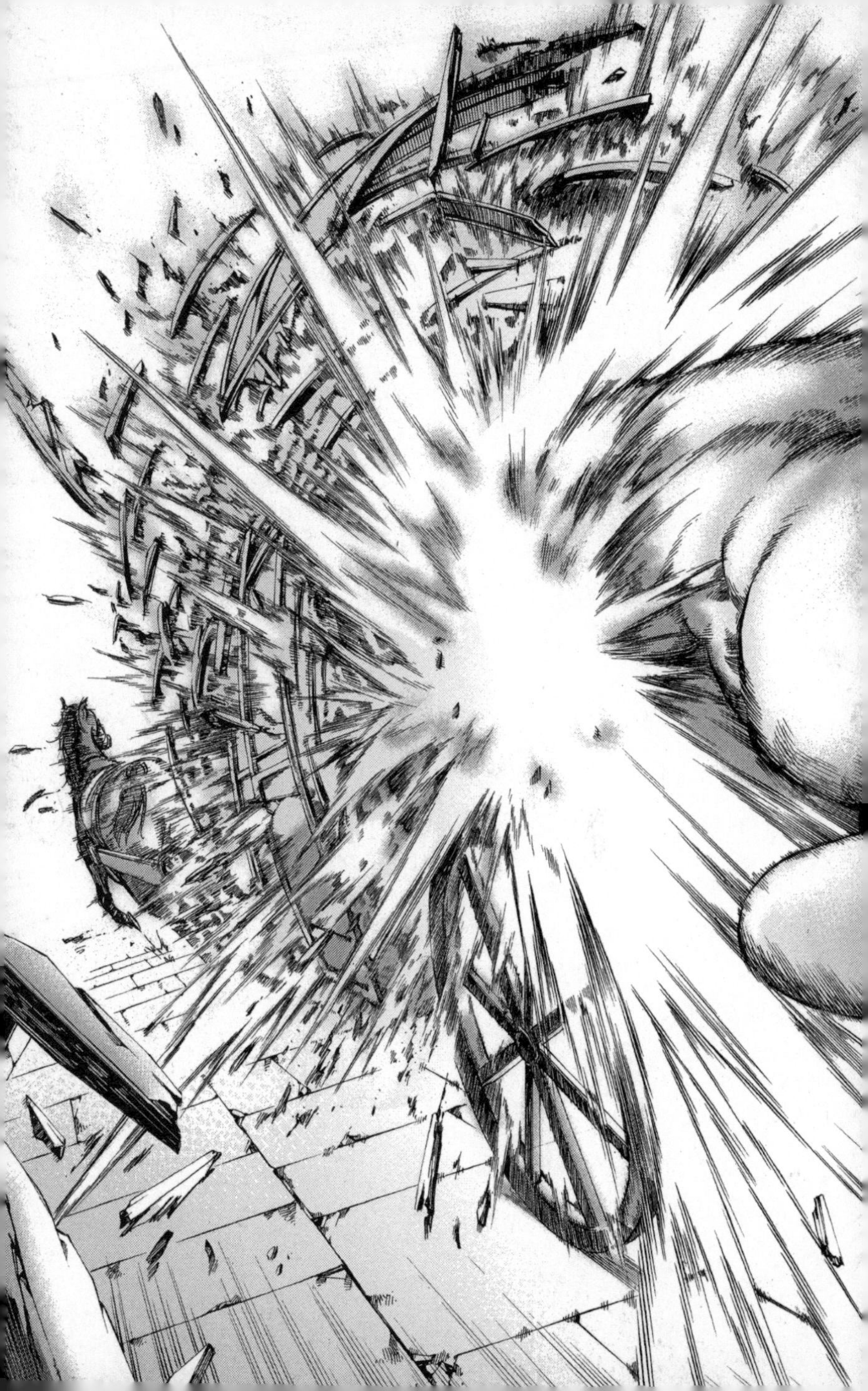

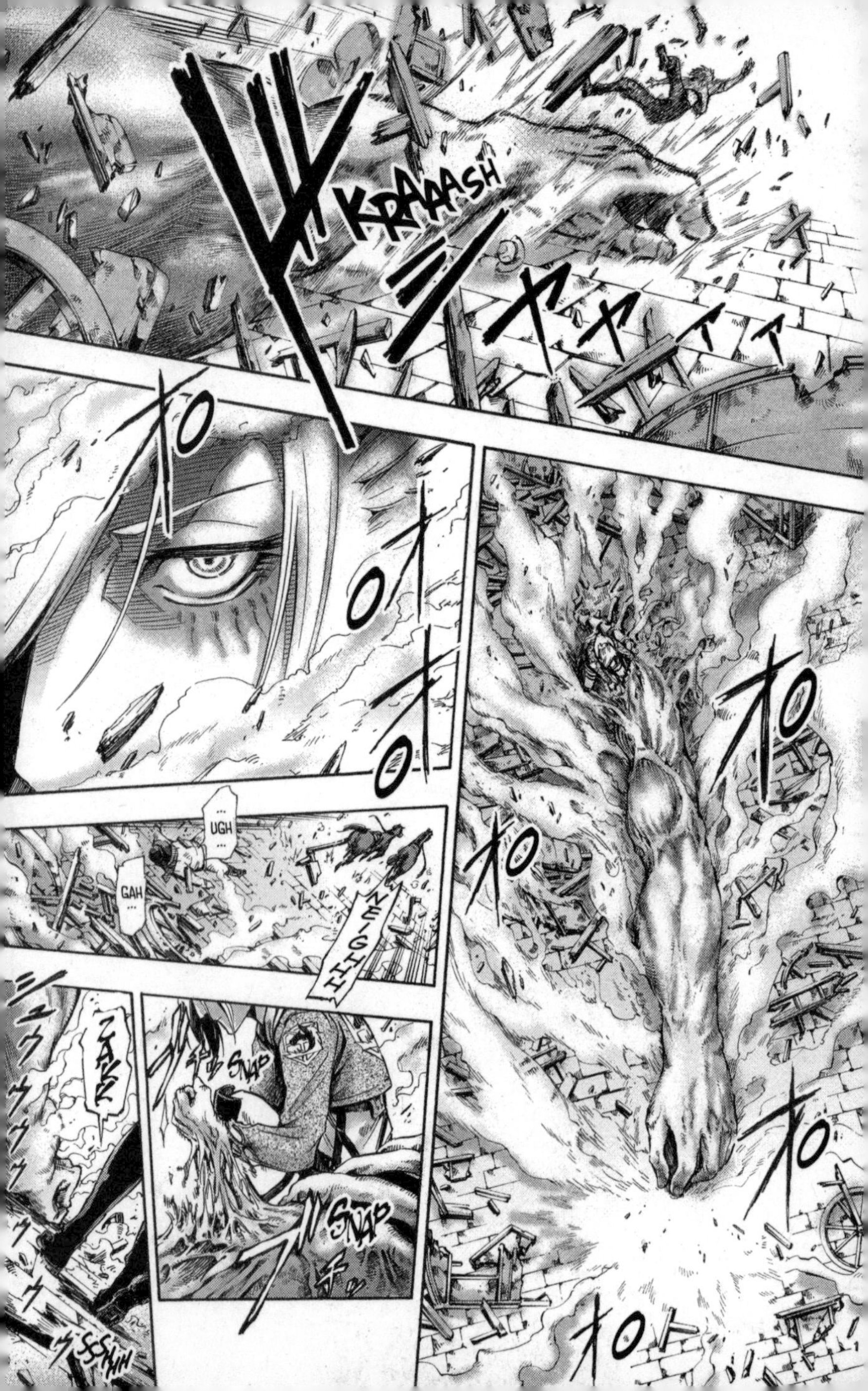
KRAAASH
NEIGHHH
...UGH...
GAH...
SNAP
SNAP
ZAKK
SSSHHH

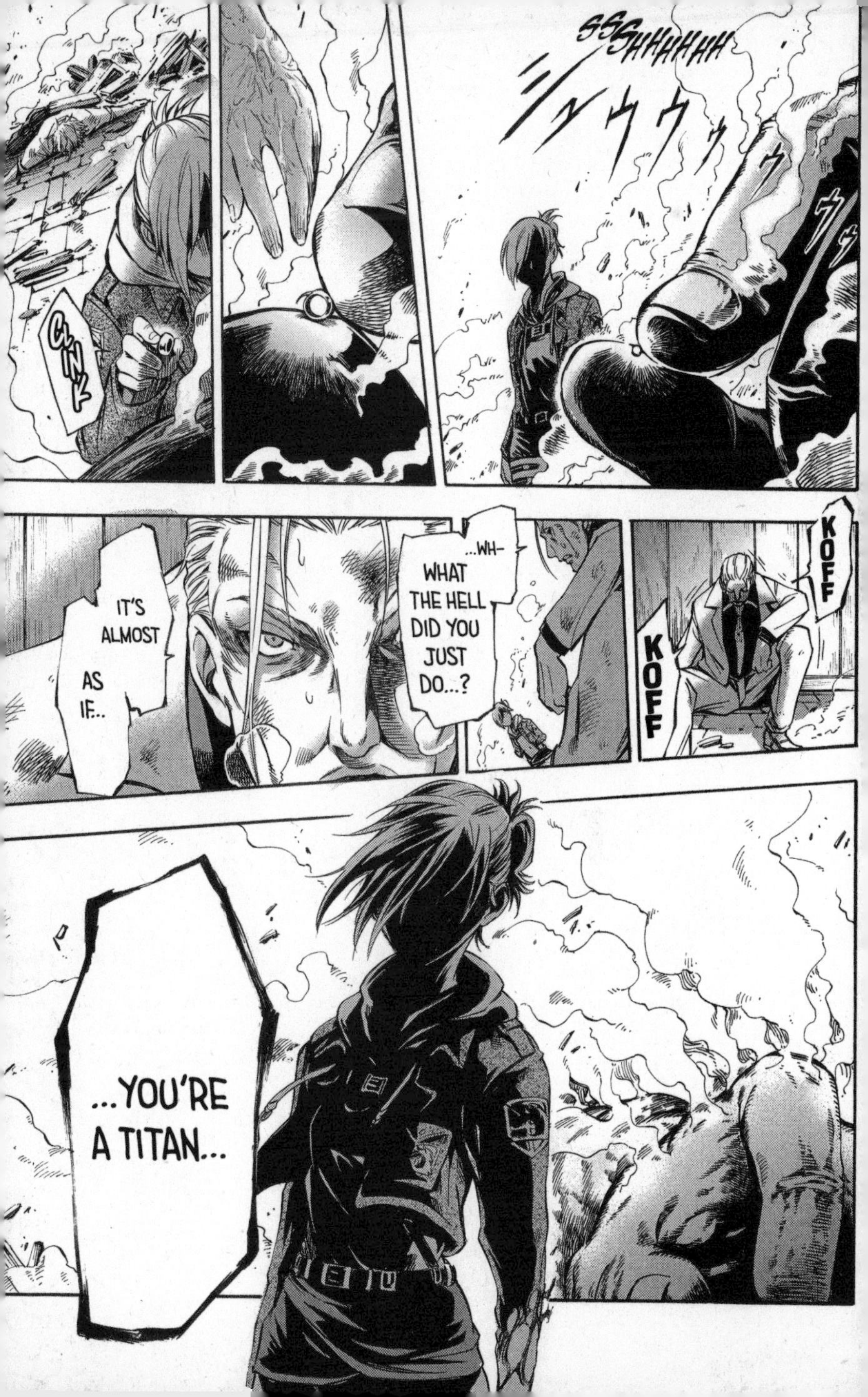
SSSHHHHAH
CLINK
KOFF
KOFF
...WH- WHAT THE HELL DID YOU JUST DO...?
IT'S ALMOST AS IF...
...YOU'RE A TITAN...

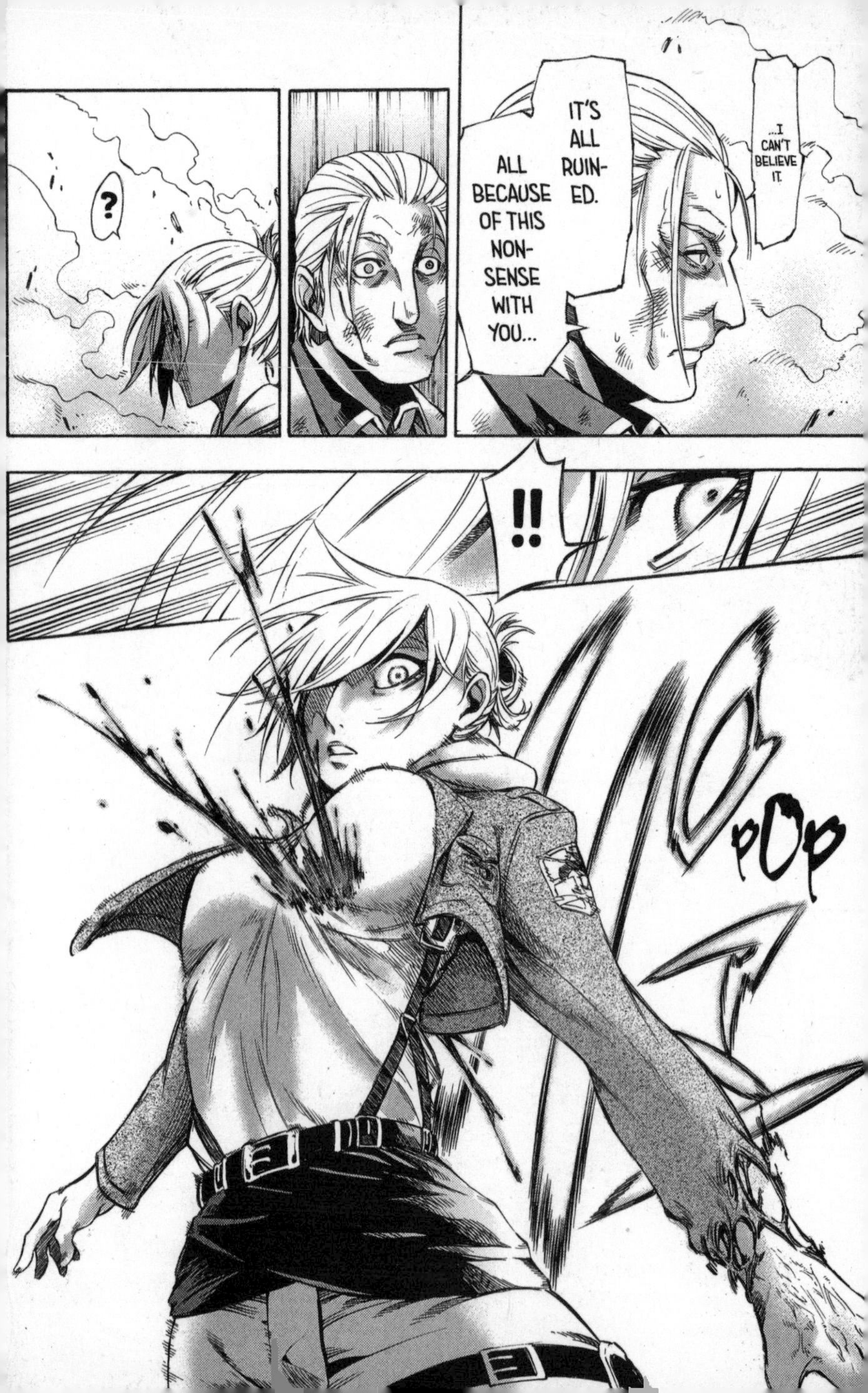
...I CAN'T BELIEVE IT.
IT'S ALL RUINED. ALL BECAUSE OF THIS NONSENSE WITH YOU...
?
!!
POP

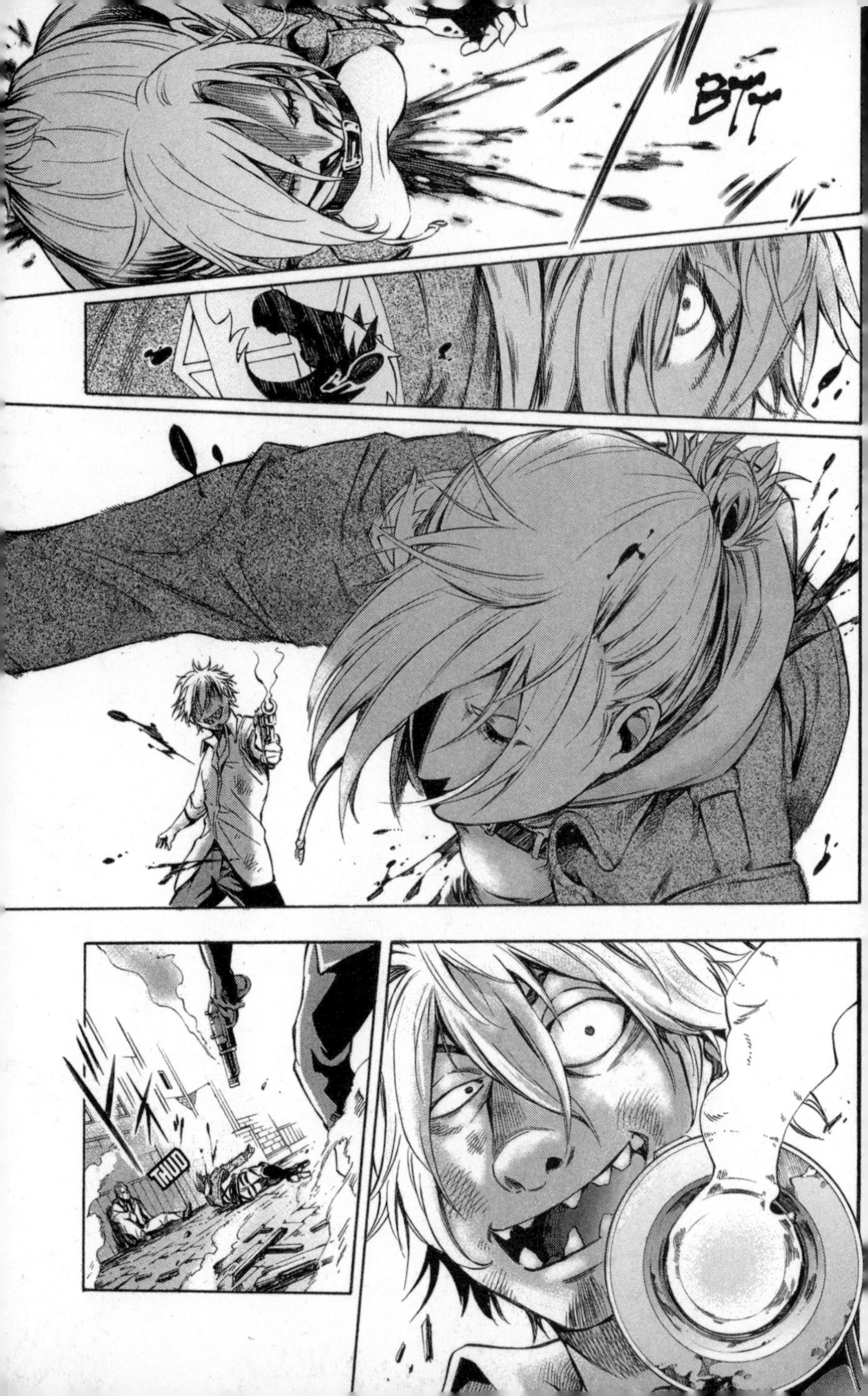
BTT
THUD

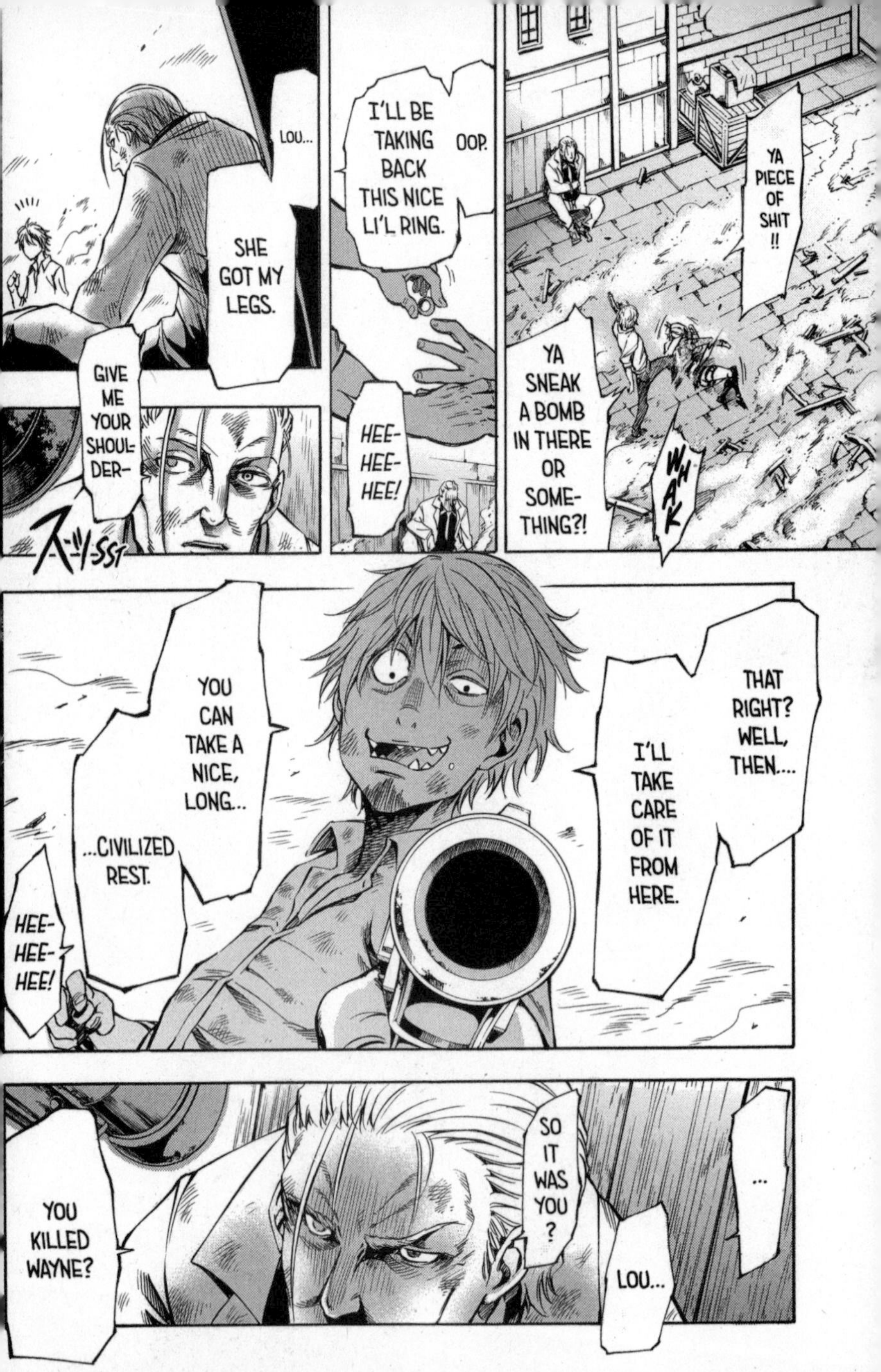

YA PIECE OF SHIT!!
YA SNEAK A BOMB IN THERE OR SOMETHING?!
WHAK
I'LL BE TAKING BACK THIS NICE LI'L RING.
OOP.
HEE-HEE-HEE!
LOU...
SHE GOT MY LEGS.
GIVE ME YOUR SHOUL-DER-
SSST
THAT RIGHT? WELL, THEN....
I'LL TAKE CARE OF IT FROM HERE.
YOU CAN TAKE A NICE, LONG...
...CIVILIZED REST.
HEE-HEE-HEE!
...
LOU...
SO IT WAS YOU?
YOU KILLED WAYNE?

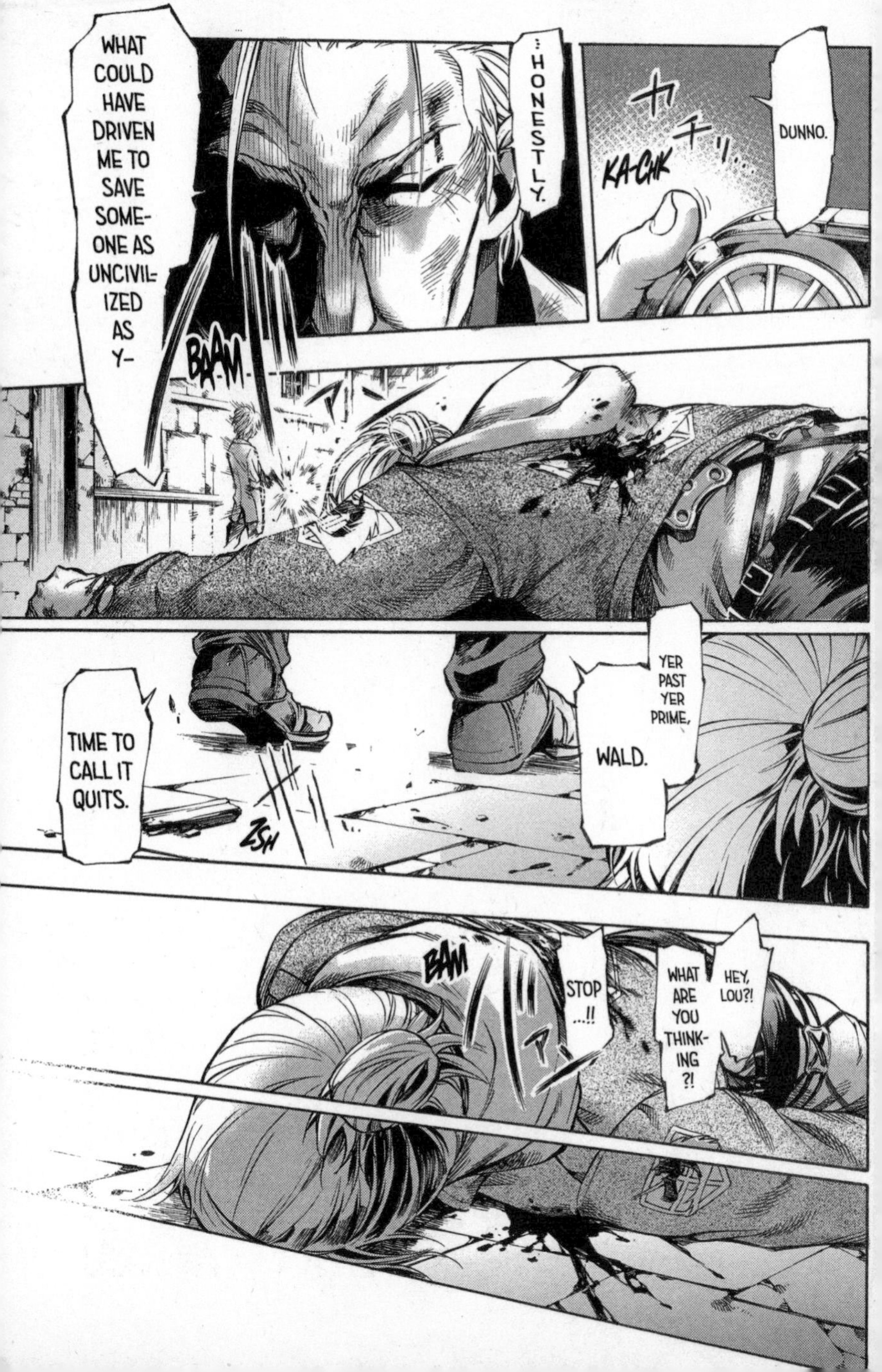
DUNNO.
カチリ…
KA-CHK
...HONESTLY.
WHAT COULD HAVE DRIVEN ME TO SAVE SOME-ONE AS UNCIVIL-IZED AS Y–
BAAM
YER PAST YER PRIME,
WALD.
TIME TO CALL IT QUITS.
ZSH
HEY, LOU?!
WHAT ARE YOU THINK-ING?!
STOP ...!!
BAM

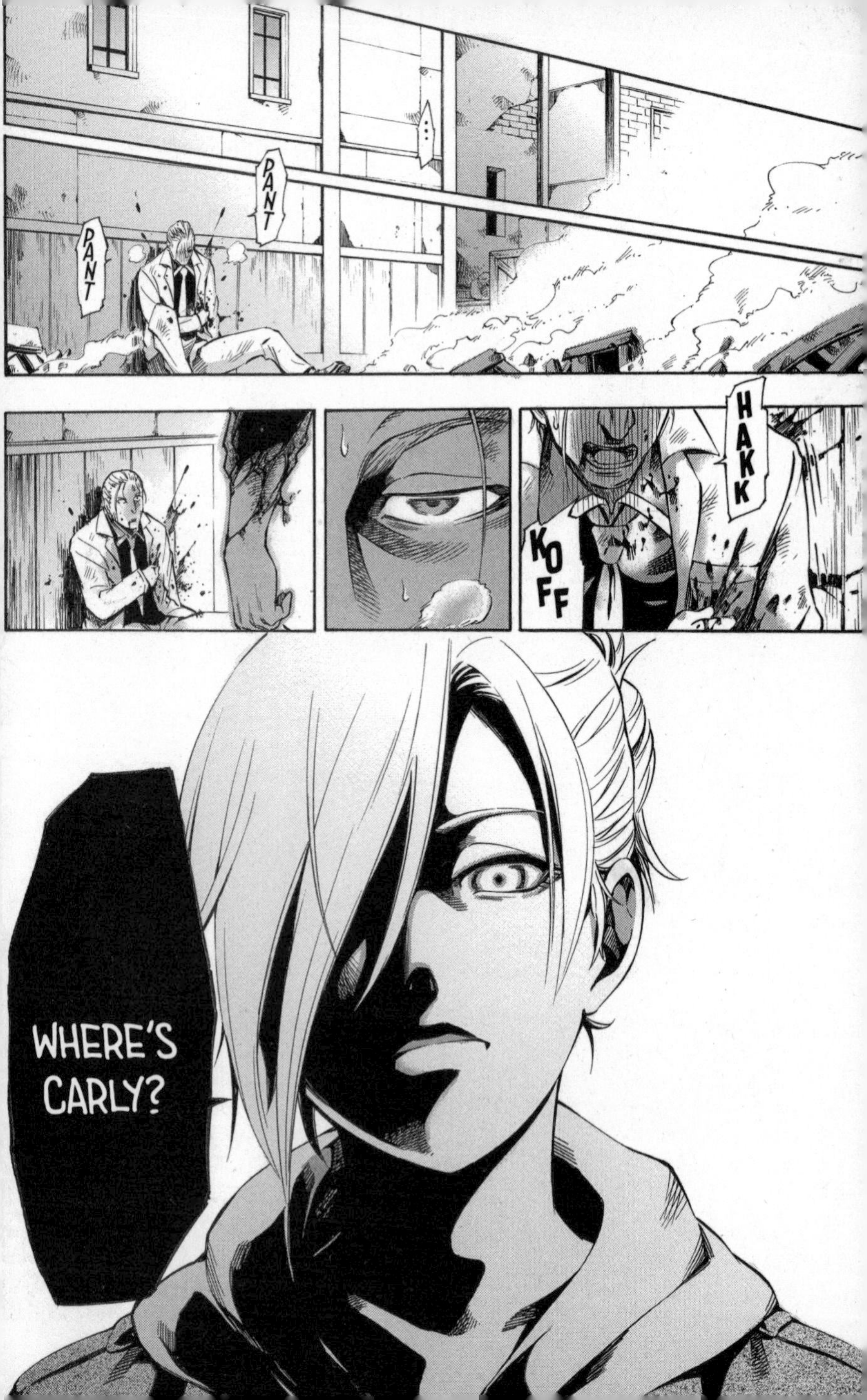
...
PANT
PANT
HAKK
KOFF
WHERE'S CARLY?

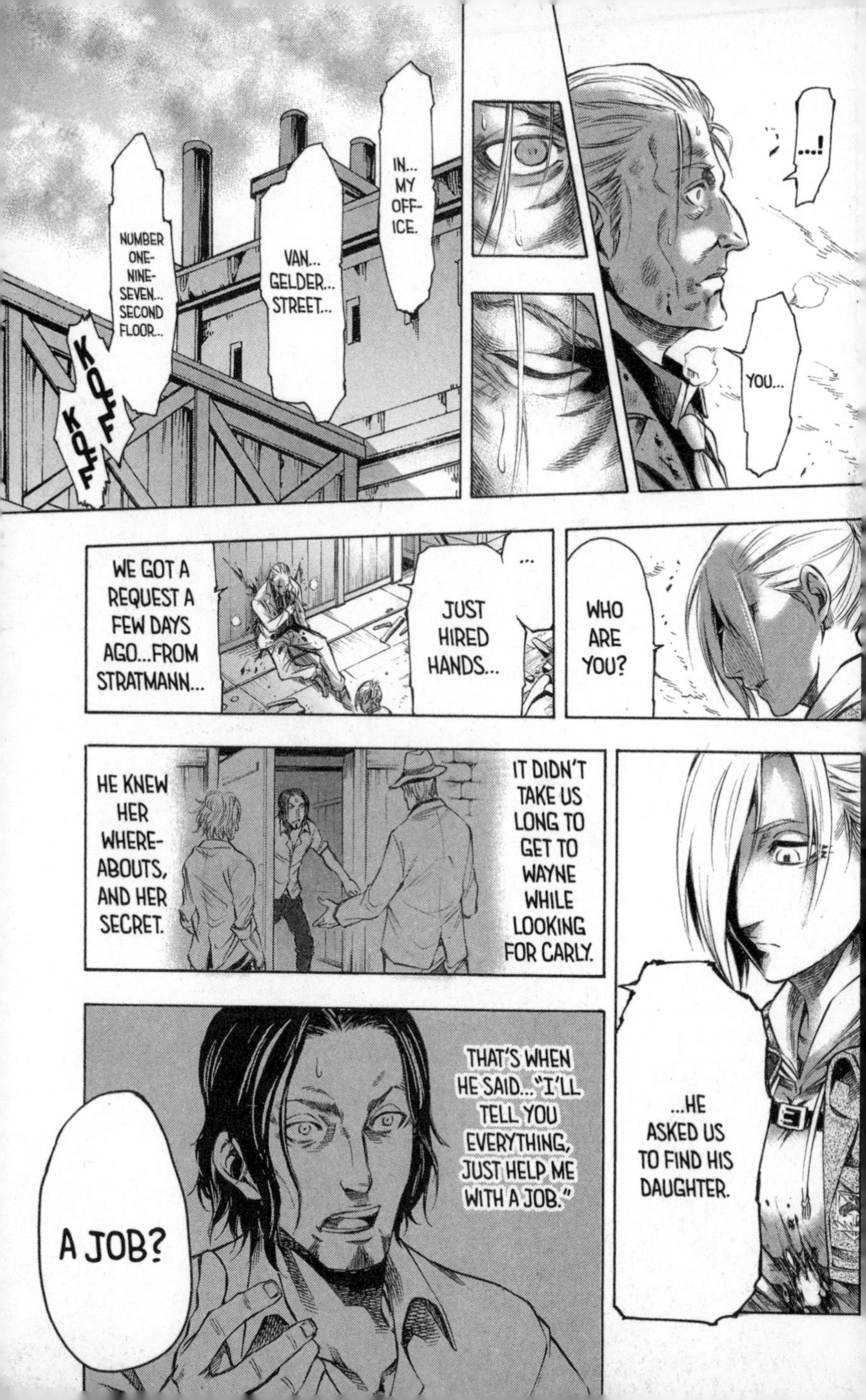
...!
YOU...
IN... MY OFF-ICE.
VAN... GELDER... STREET...
NUMBER ONE-NINE-SEVEN... SECOND FLOOR...
KOFF KOFF
WHO ARE YOU?
...
JUST HIRED HANDS...
WE GOT A REQUEST A FEW DAYS AGO...FROM STRATMANN...
...HE ASKED US TO FIND HIS DAUGHTER.
IT DIDN'T TAKE US LONG TO GET TO WAYNE WHILE LOOKING FOR CARLY.
HE KNEW HER WHERE-ABOUTS, AND HER SECRET.
THAT'S WHEN HE SAID... "I'LL TELL YOU EVERYTHING, JUST HELP ME WITH A JOB."
A JOB?

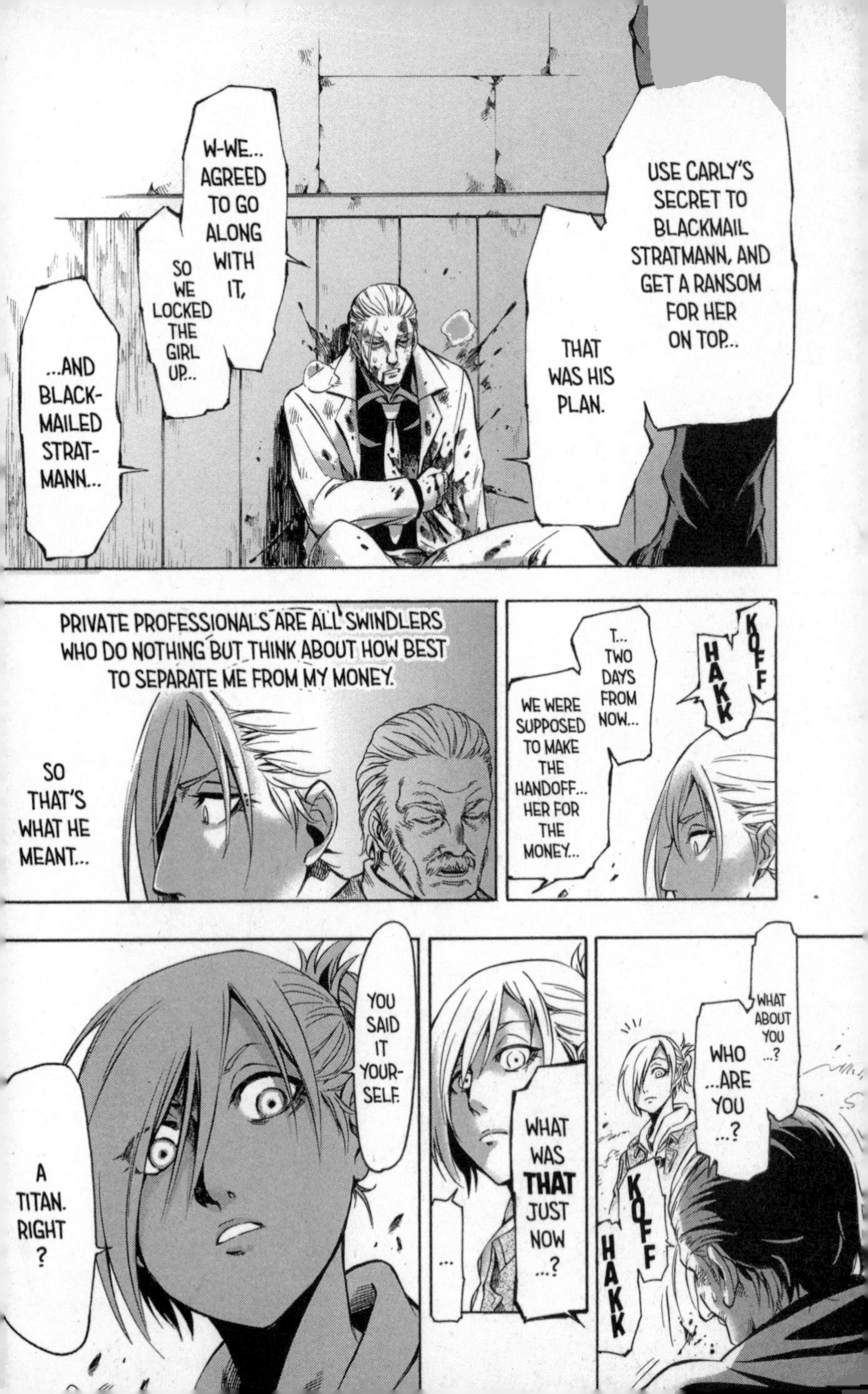
USE CARLY'S SECRET TO BLACKMAIL STRATMANN, AND GET A RANSOM FOR HER ON TOP...
THAT WAS HIS PLAN.
W-WE... AGREED TO GO ALONG WITH IT,
SO WE LOCKED THE GIRL UP...
...AND BLACK-MAILED STRAT-MANN...
HAKK KOFF
T... TWO DAYS FROM NOW...
WE WERE SUPPOSED TO MAKE THE HANDOFF... HER FOR THE MONEY...
PRIVATE PROFESSIONALS ARE ALL SWINDLERS WHO DO NOTHING BUT THINK ABOUT HOW BEST TO SEPARATE ME FROM MY MONEY.
SO THAT'S WHAT HE MEANT...
WHAT ABOUT YOU ...?
WHO ...ARE YOU ...?
HAKK KOFF
WHAT WAS **THAT** JUST NOW ...?
...
YOU SAID IT YOUR-SELF.
A TITAN. RIGHT ?

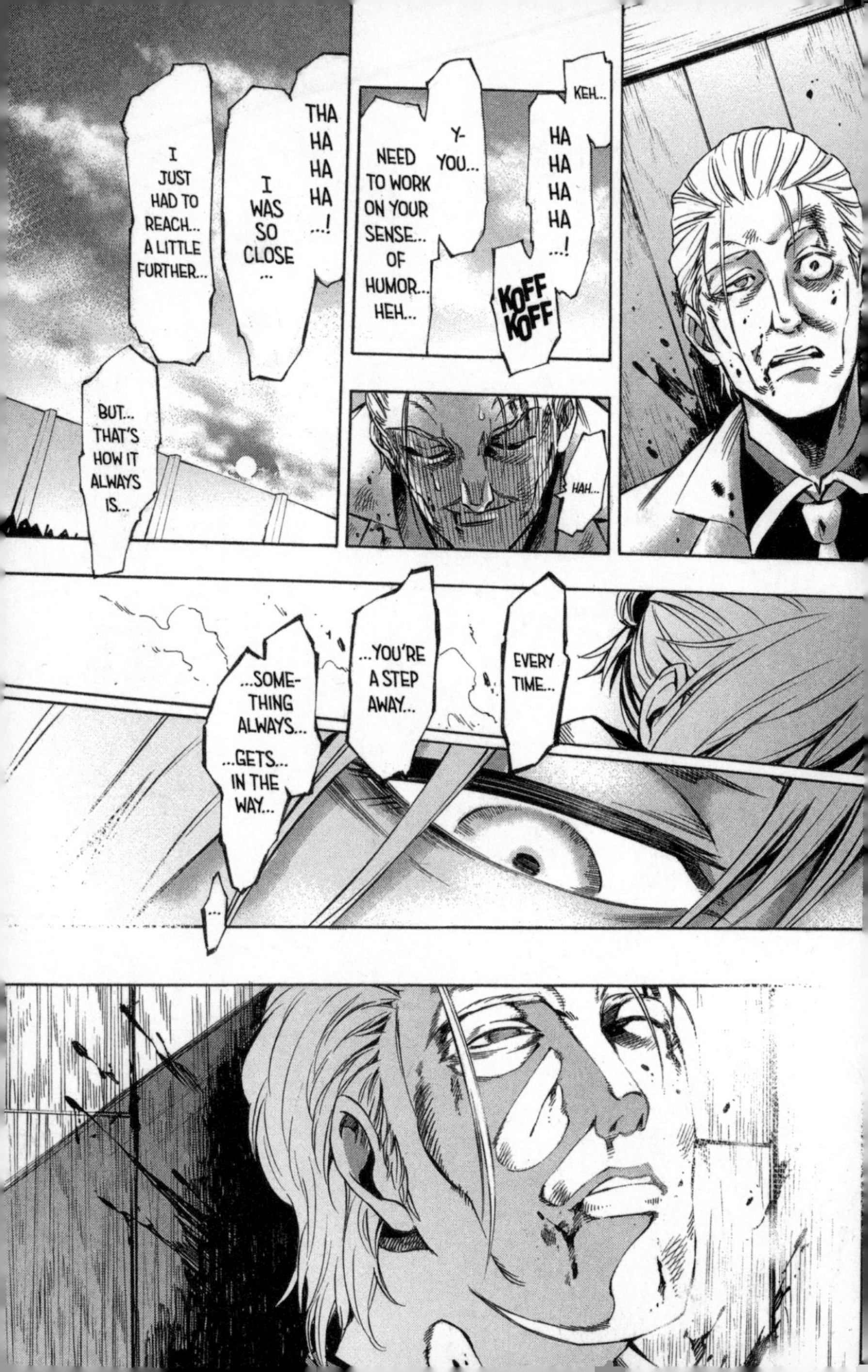
KEH...
HA HA HA HA...!
KOFF KOFF
Y- YOU...
NEED TO WORK ON YOUR SENSE... OF HUMOR... HEH...
HAH...
THA HA HA HA...!
I WAS SO CLOSE...
I JUST HAD TO REACH... A LITTLE FURTHER...
BUT... THAT'S HOW IT ALWAYS IS...
EVERY TIME...
...YOU'RE A STEP AWAY...
...SOME-THING ALWAYS...
...GETS... IN THE WAY...
...

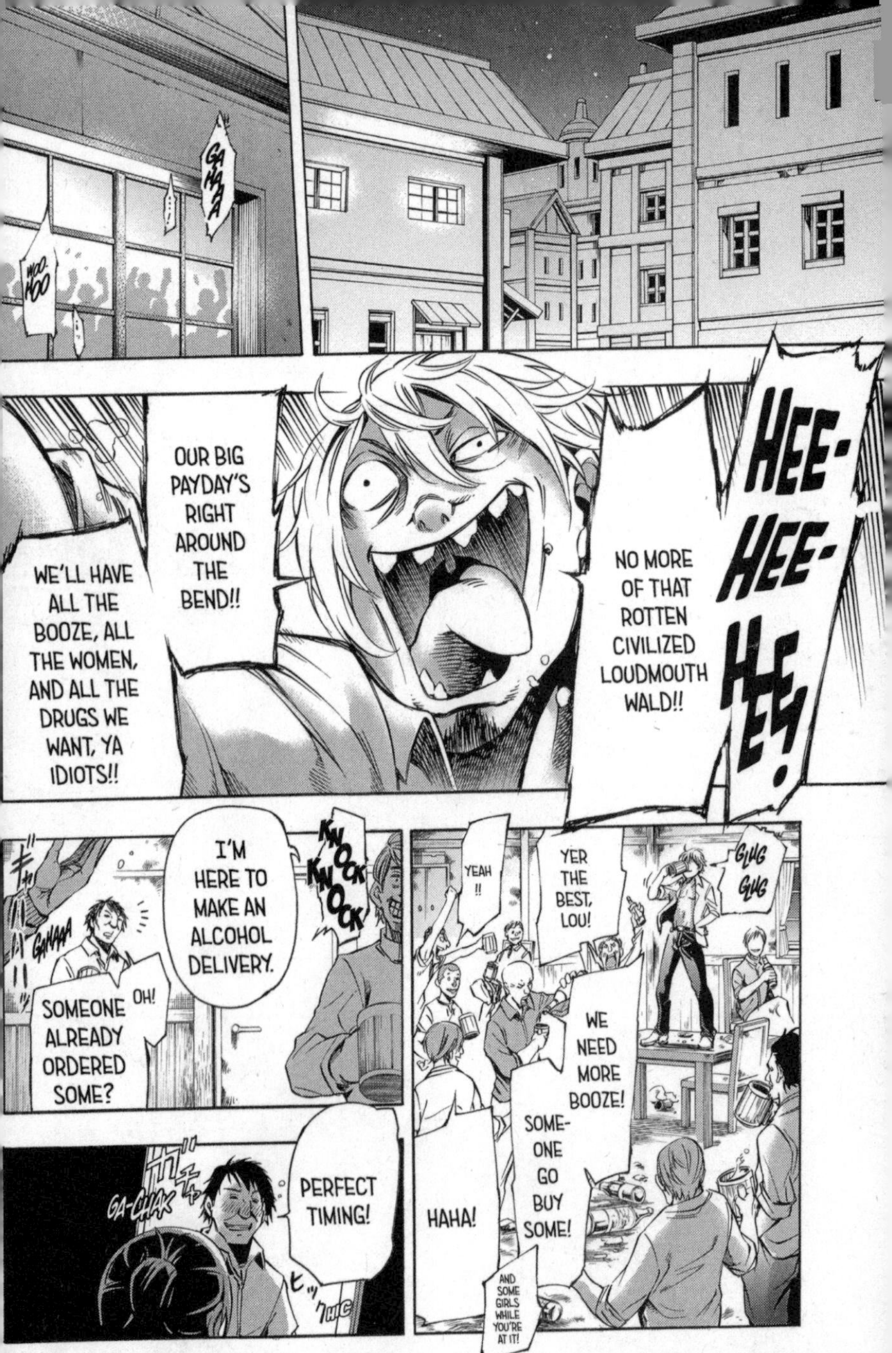
GAHAHA
WOO HOO
HEE-HEE-HEE-HEE!
NO MORE OF THAT ROTTEN CIVILIZED LOUDMOUTH WALD!!
OUR BIG PAYDAY'S RIGHT AROUND THE BEND!!
WE'LL HAVE ALL THE BOOZE, ALL THE WOMEN, AND ALL THE DRUGS WE WANT, YA IDIOTS!!
GLUG GLUG
YER THE BEST, LOU!
YEAH !!
WE NEED MORE BOOZE!
SOME-ONE GO BUY SOME!
HAHA!
AND SOME GIRLS WHILE YOU'RE AT IT!
KNOCK KNOCK
I'M HERE TO MAKE AN ALCOHOL DELIVERY.
OH!
SOMEONE ALREADY ORDERED SOME?
GAHAAA
PERFECT TIMING!
GA-CHAK
HIC

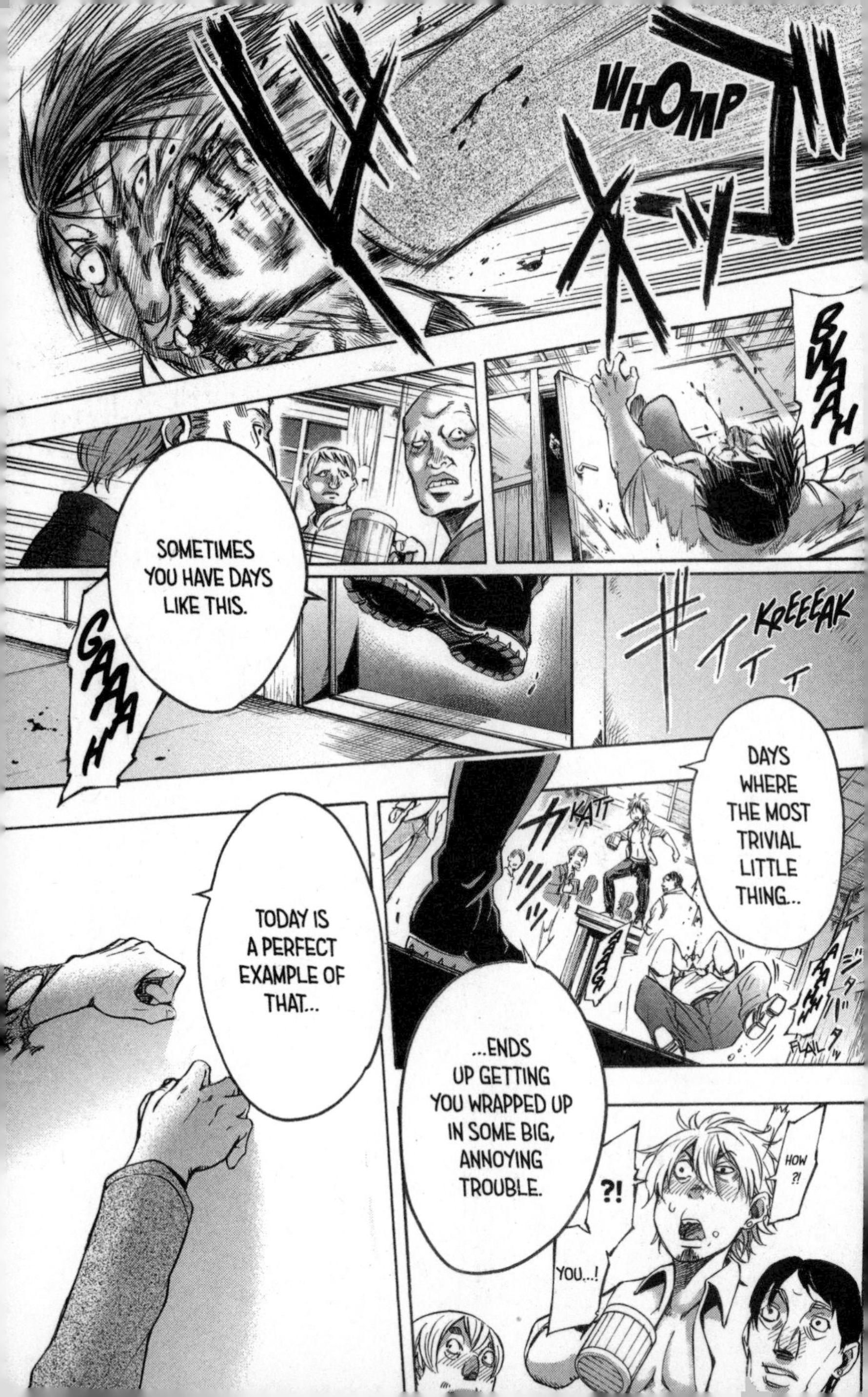
WHOMP
BWAAAH
SOMETIMES YOU HAVE DAYS LIKE THIS.
KREEEAK
GAAAAH
DAYS WHERE THE MOST TRIVIAL LITTLE THING...
KATT
FLAIL
TODAY IS A PERFECT EXAMPLE OF THAT...
...ENDS UP GETTING YOU WRAPPED UP IN SOME BIG, ANNOYING TROUBLE.
HOW ?!
?!
YOU...!

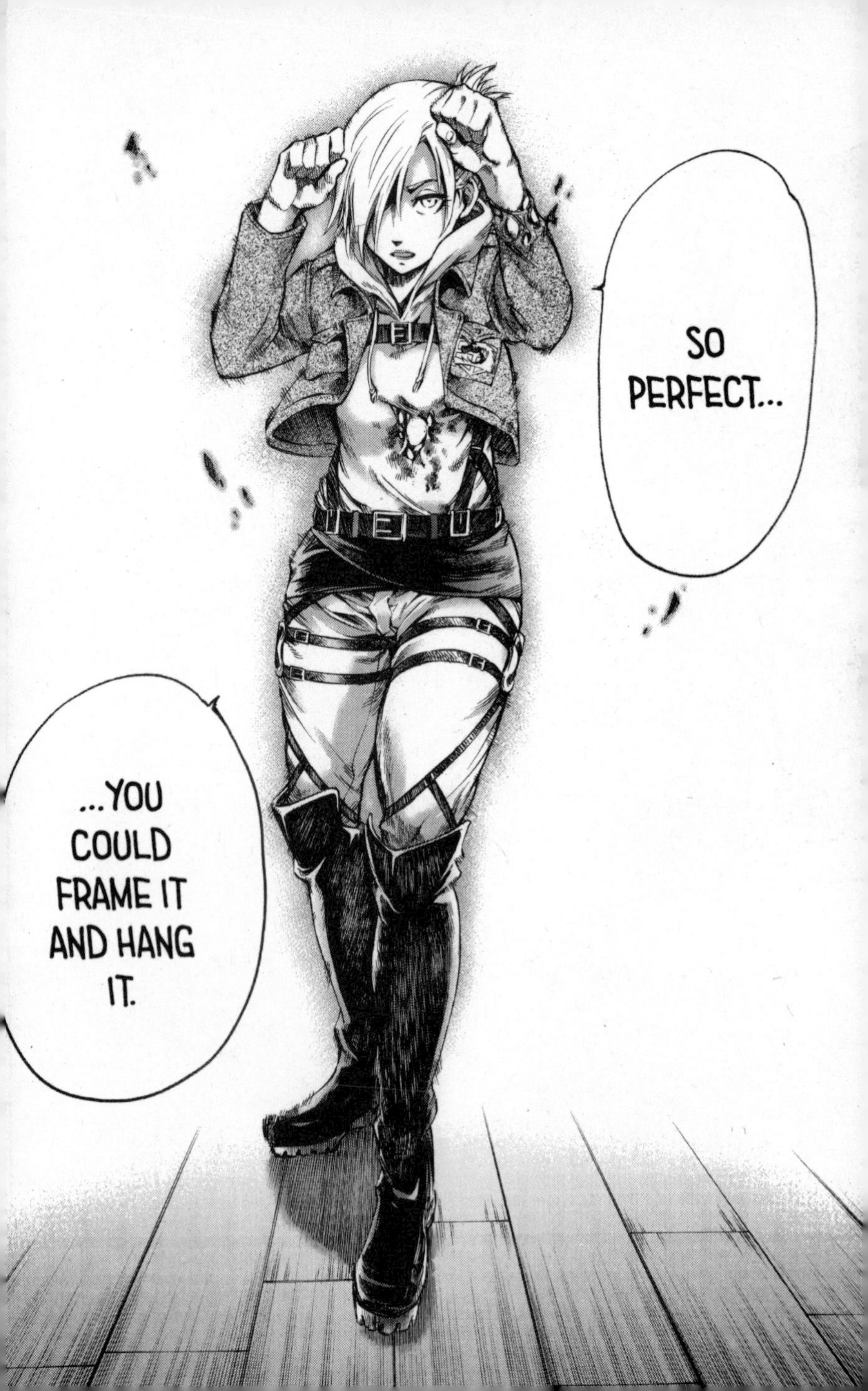
SO PERFECT...
...YOU COULD FRAME IT AND HANG IT.

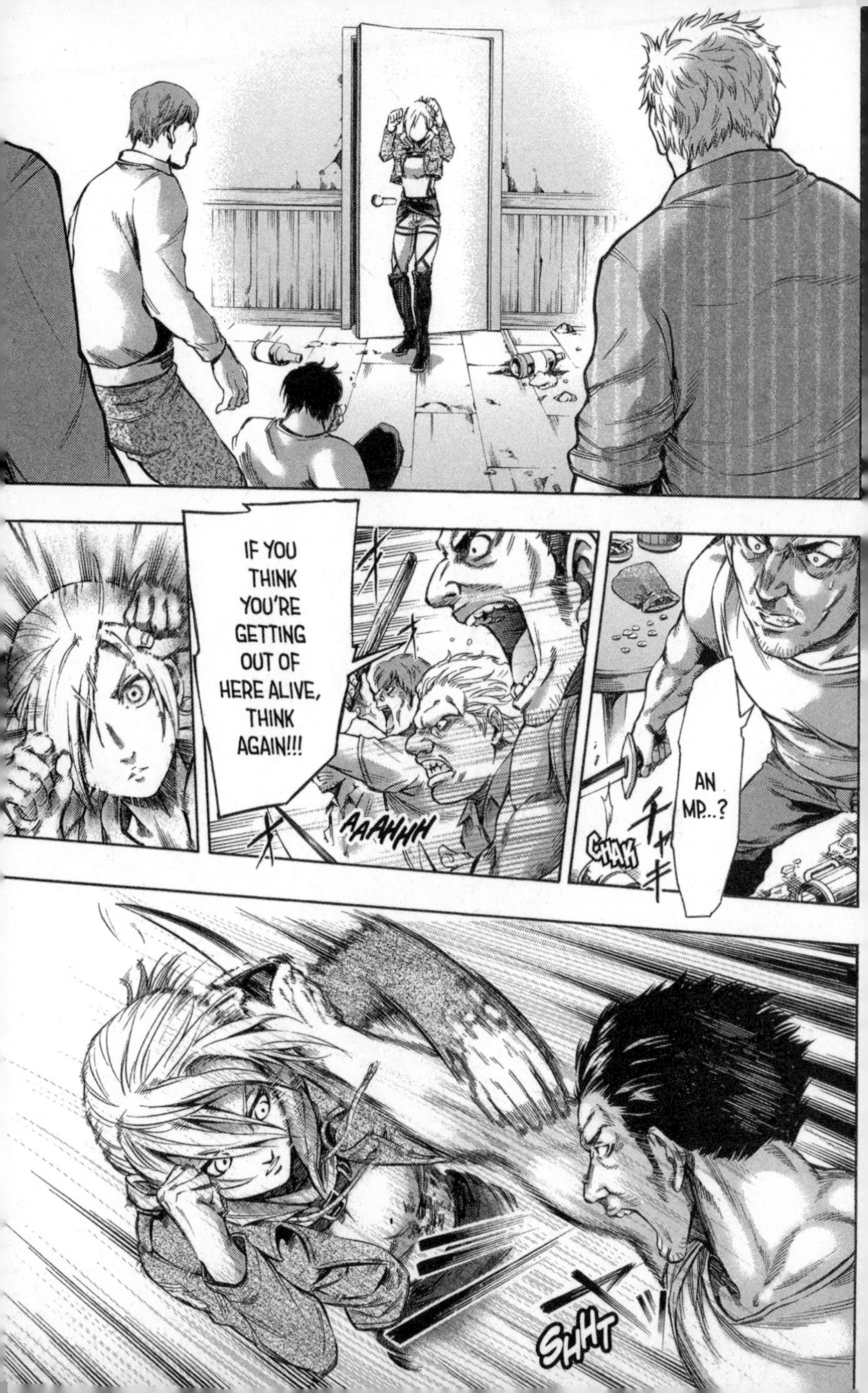
AN MP...?
CHAK
IF YOU THINK YOU'RE GETTING OUT OF HERE ALIVE, THINK AGAIN!!!
AAAHHH
SHHT

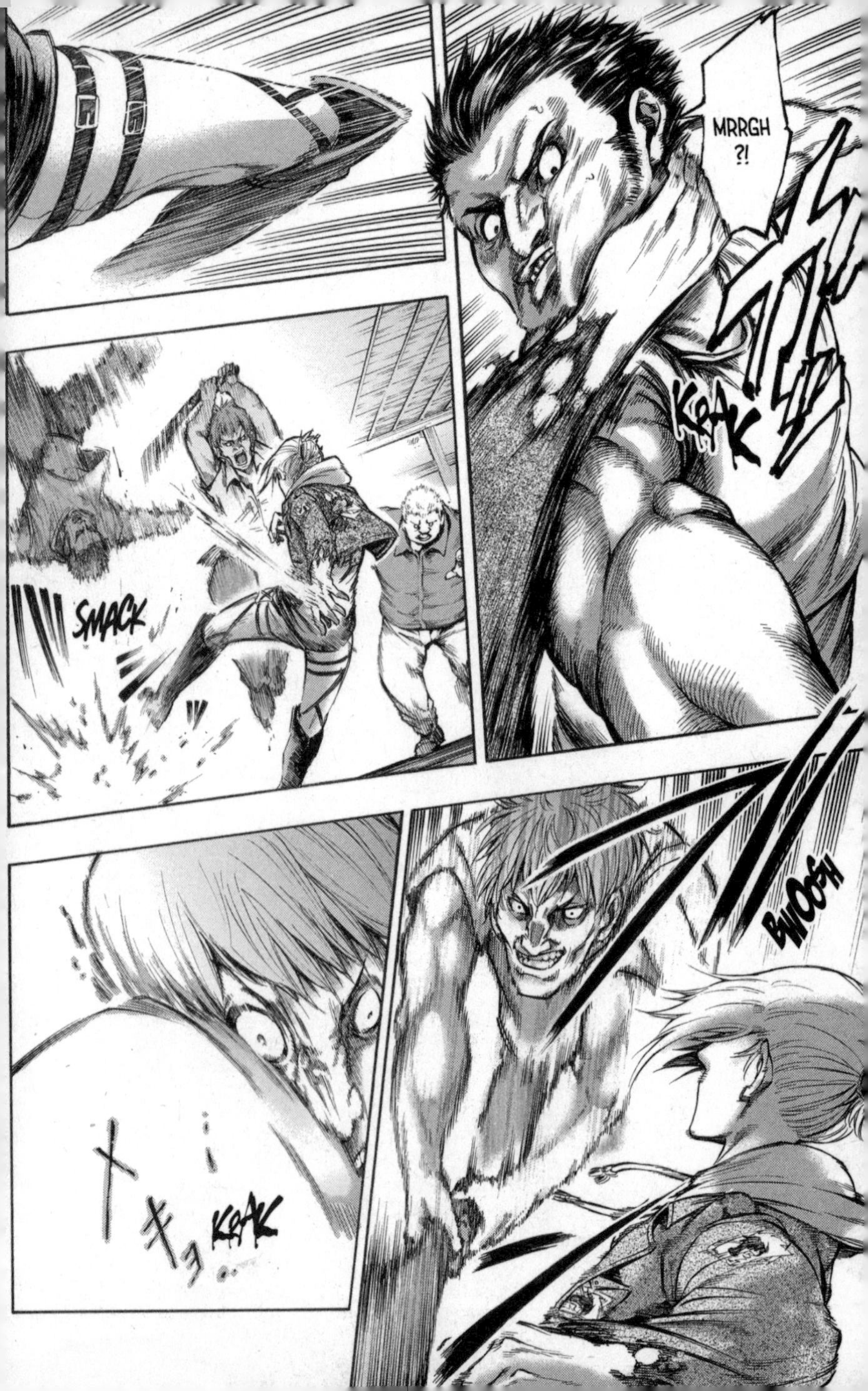
MRRGH ?!
KRAK
SMACK
BWOOSH
KRAK

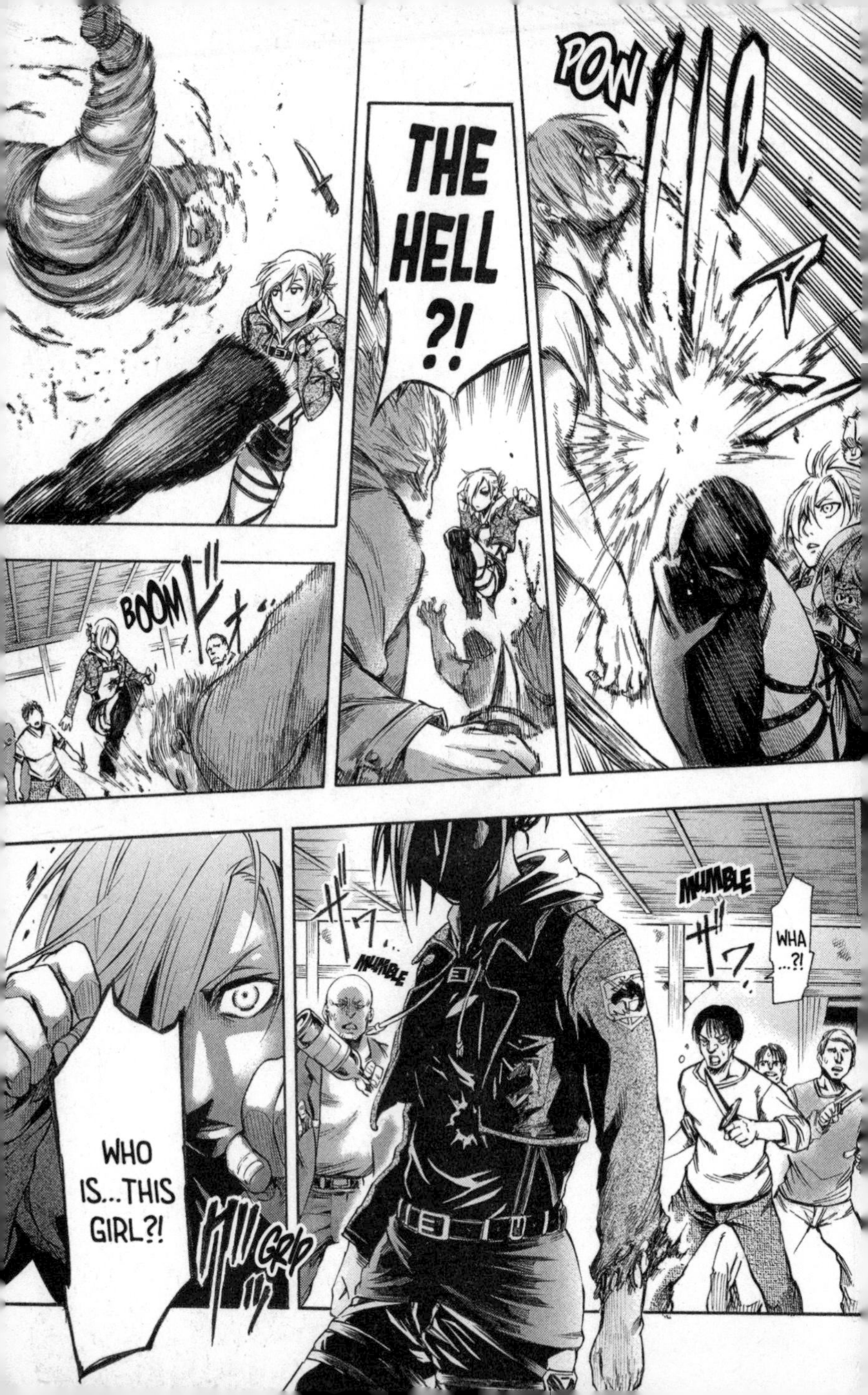
POW
THE HELL ?!
BOOM
WHA ...?!
MUMBLE
MUMBLE
WHO IS...THIS GIRL?!
GRIP

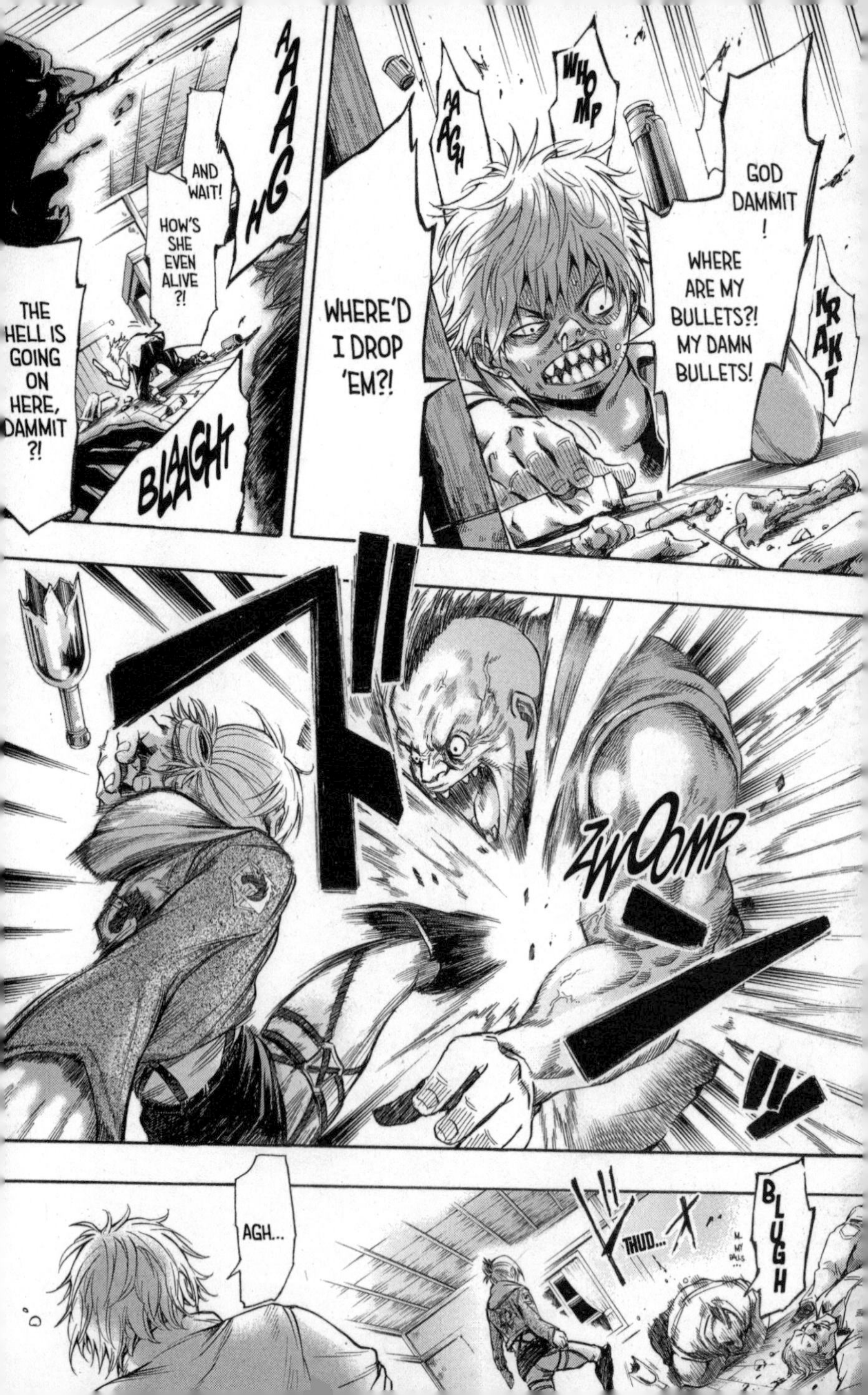
WHOMP
AAAGH
GOD DAMMIT!
WHERE ARE MY BULLETS?! MY DAMN BULLETS!
KRAKT
WHERE'D I DROP 'EM?!
AAAAGGH
AND WAIT!
HOW'S SHE EVEN ALIVE?!
THE HELL IS GOING ON HERE, DAMMIT?!
BLAAGHT
ZWOOMP
BLUGH
M... MY BALLS...
THUD...
AGH...

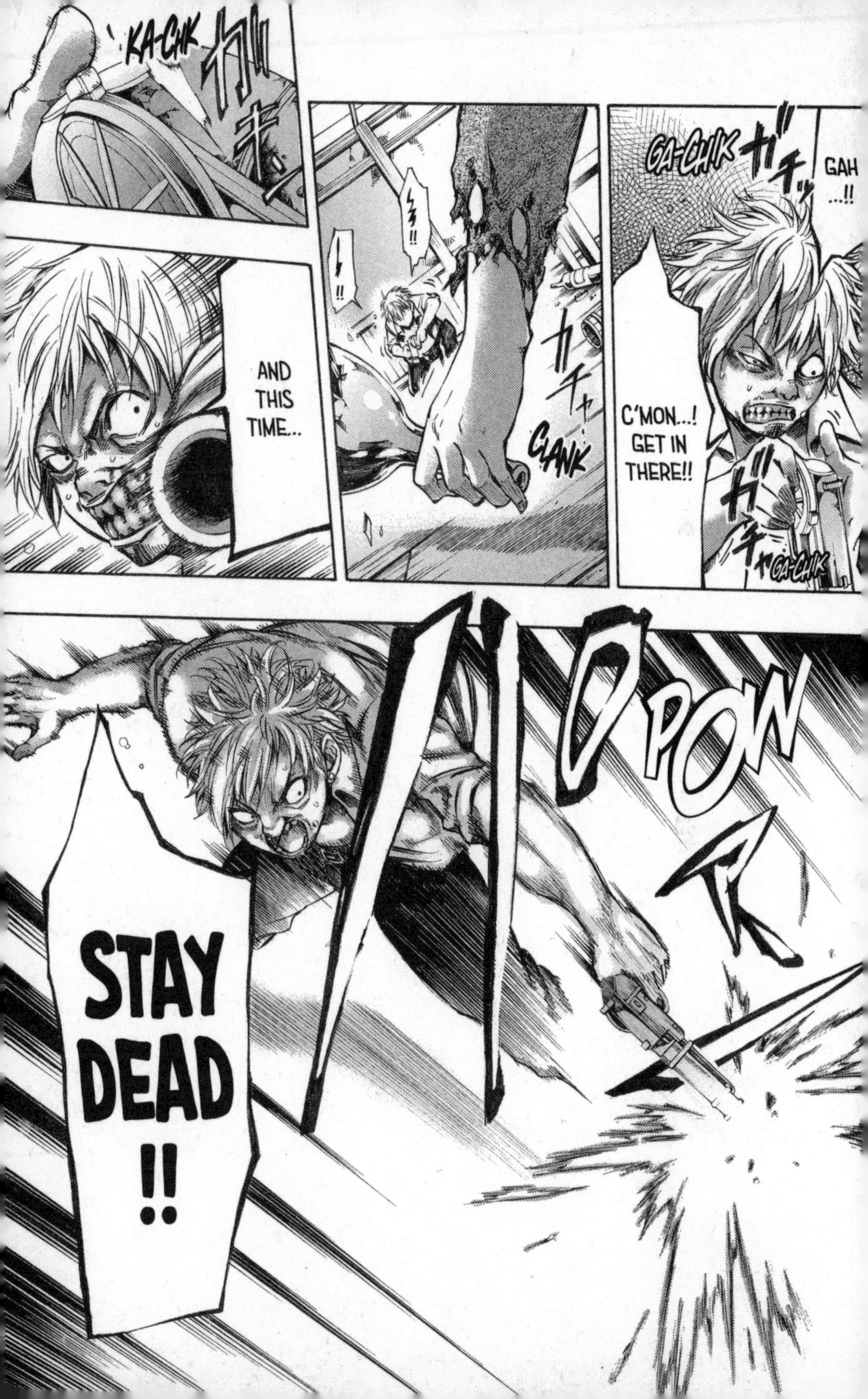
GA-CHIK
GAH ...!!
C'MON...! GET IN THERE!!
GA-CHIK
!!
!!
CLANK
KA-CHK
AND THIS TIME...
POW
STAY DEAD !!

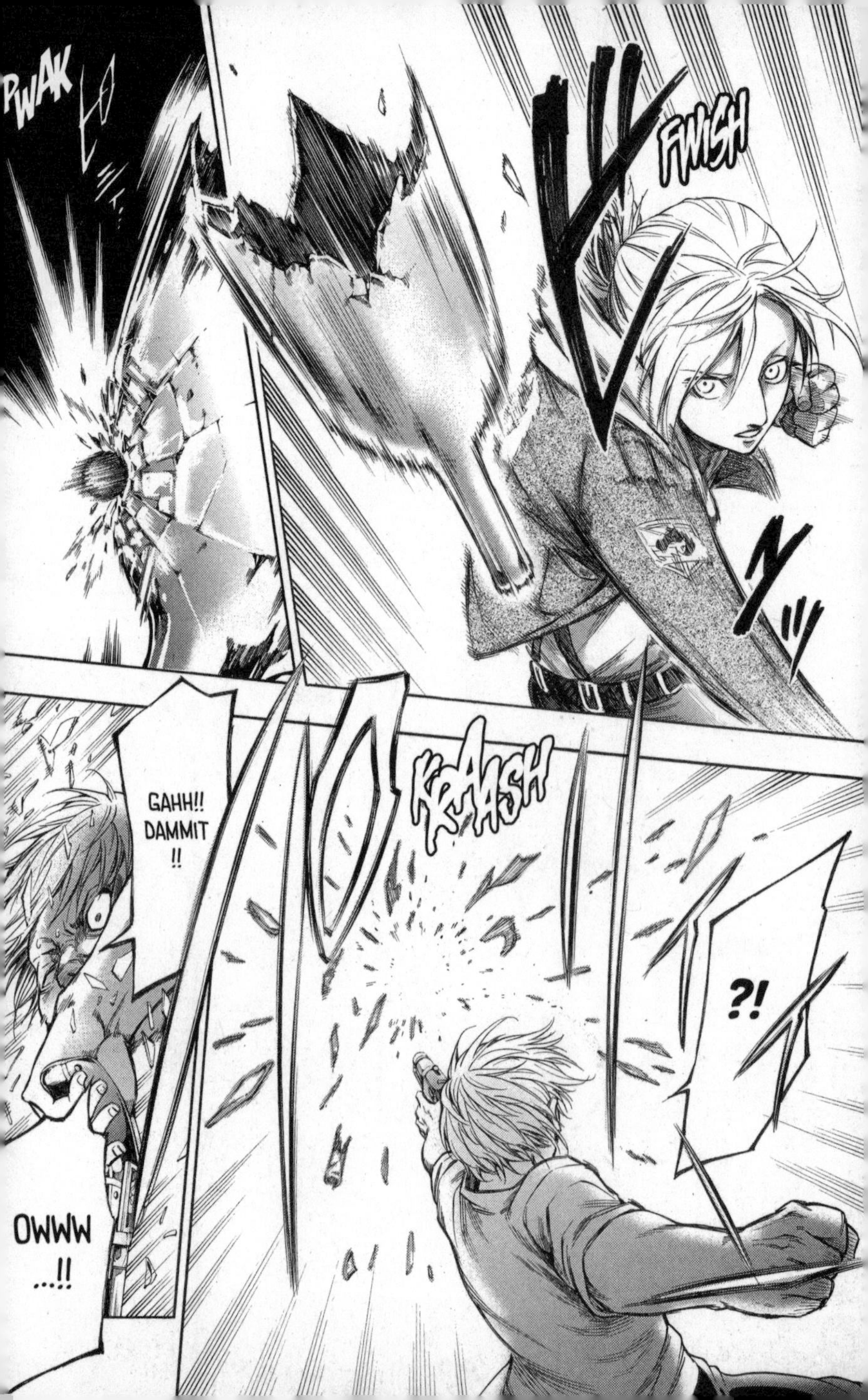
FWISH
PWAK
KRASH
?!
GAHH!! DAMMIT !!
OWWW ...!!

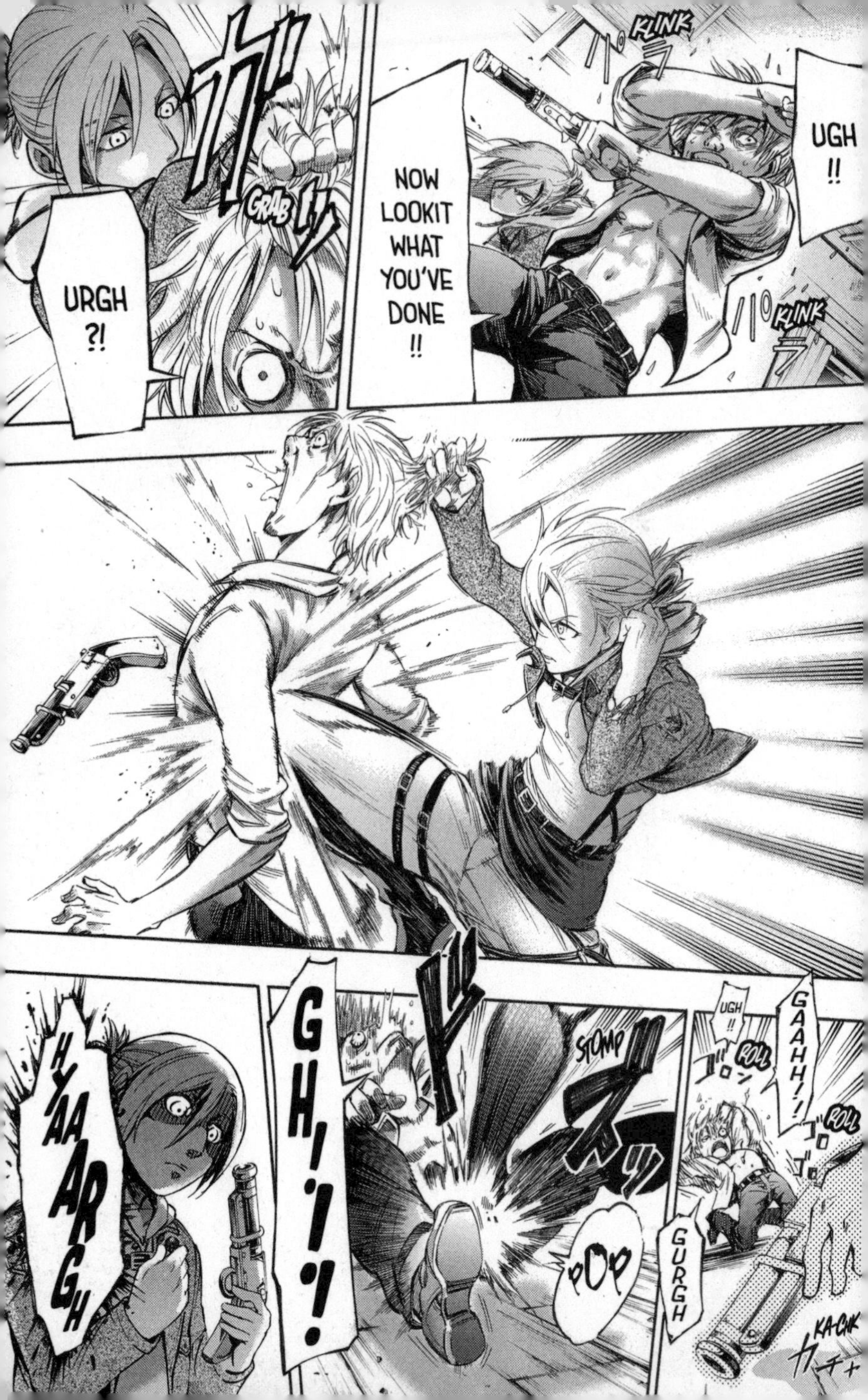

KLINK
UGH !!
NOW LOOKIT WHAT YOU'VE DONE !!
KLINK
GRAB
URGH ?!
UGH !!
GAAHH!!
ROLL
ROLL
GURGH
KA-CHK
STOMP
GHI!!!
POP
HYAAARGH

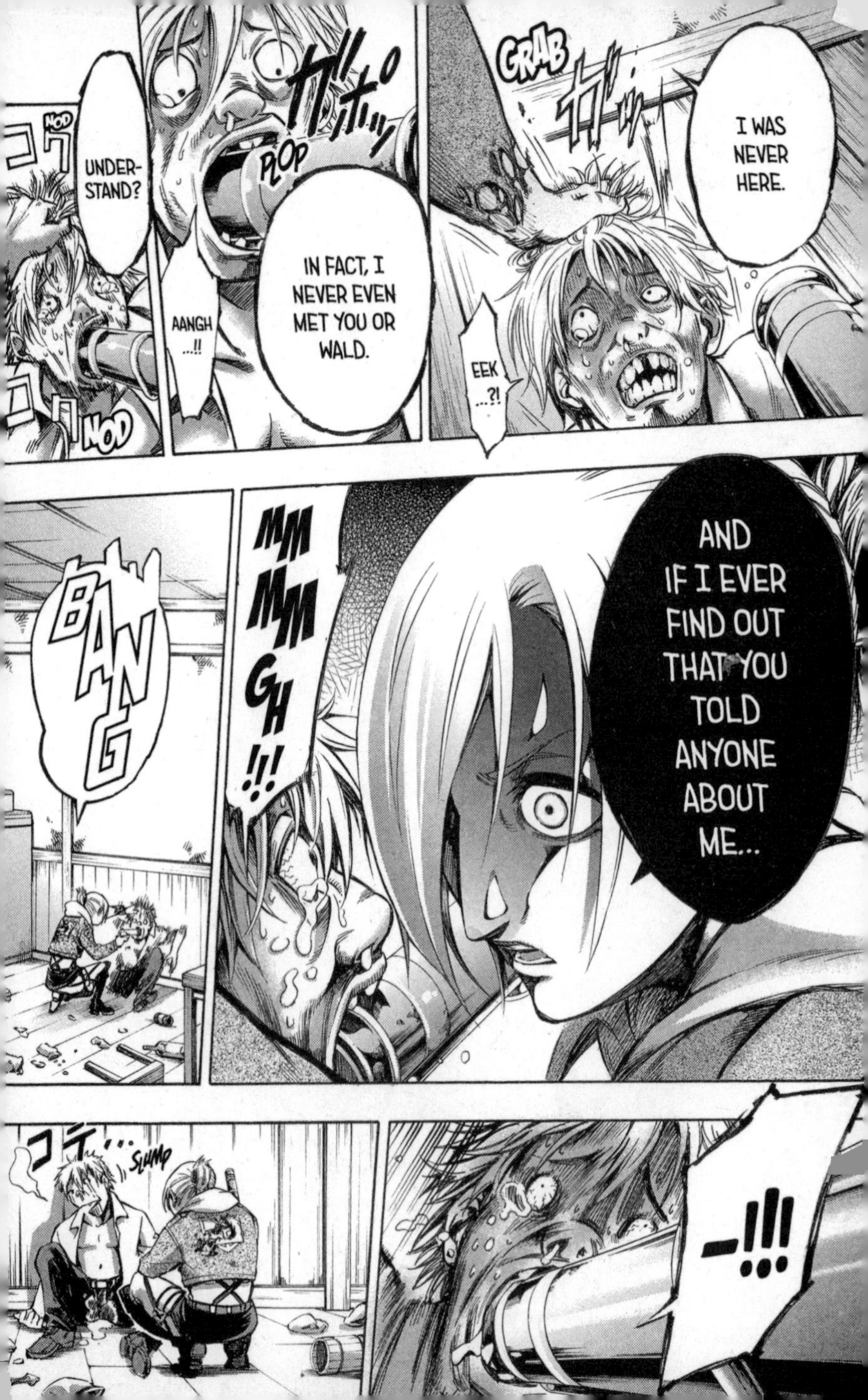
GRAB
I WAS NEVER HERE.
EEK ...?!
PLOP
IN FACT, I NEVER EVEN MET YOU OR WALD.
AANGH ...!!
NOD
UNDER-STAND?
NOD
AND IF I EVER FIND OUT THAT YOU TOLD ANYONE ABOUT ME...
MMMMMMGH!!!
BANG
—!!!
SLUMP

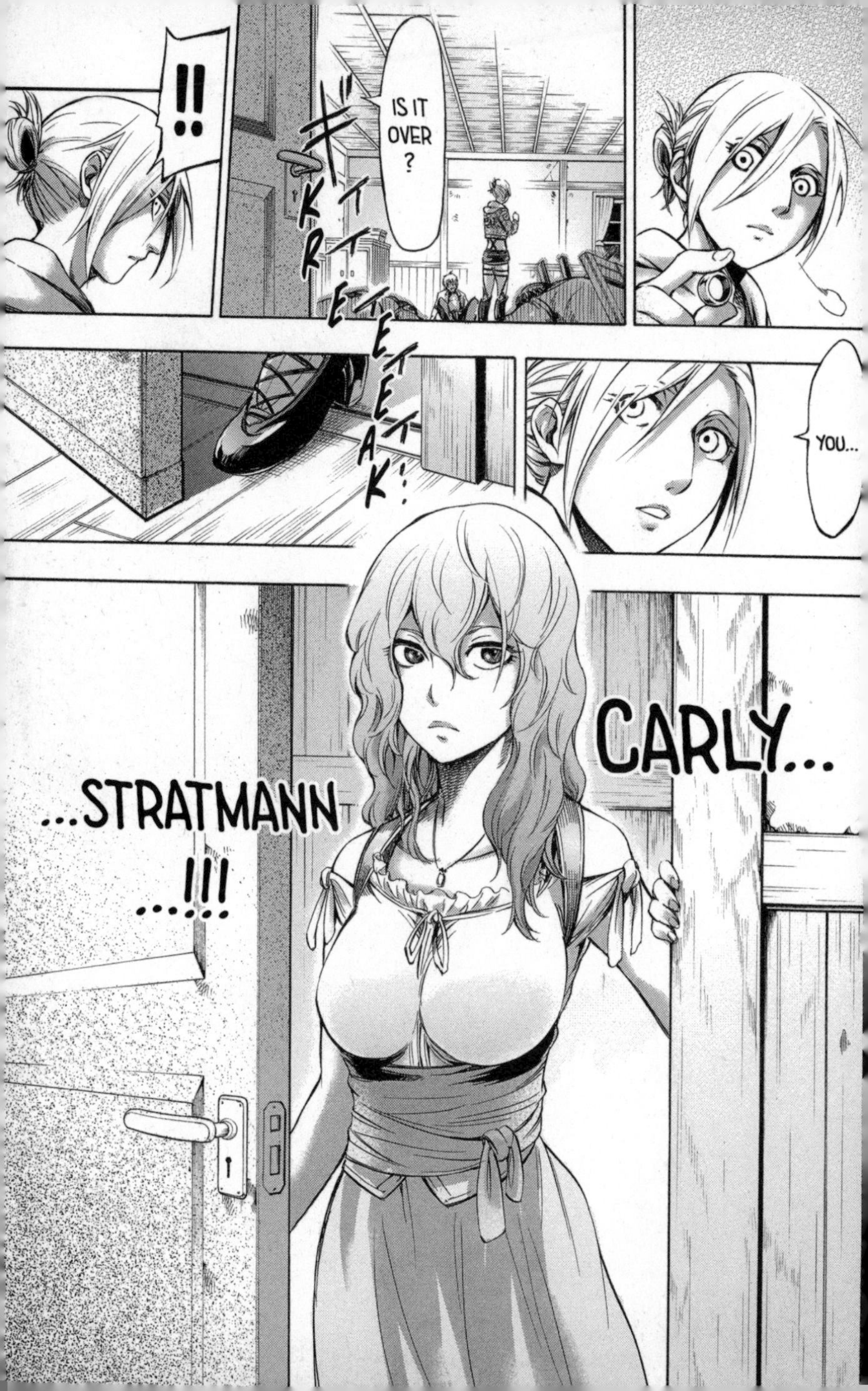
IS IT OVER?
KREEEAK!
!!
YOU...
CARLY...
...STRATMANN
...!!!

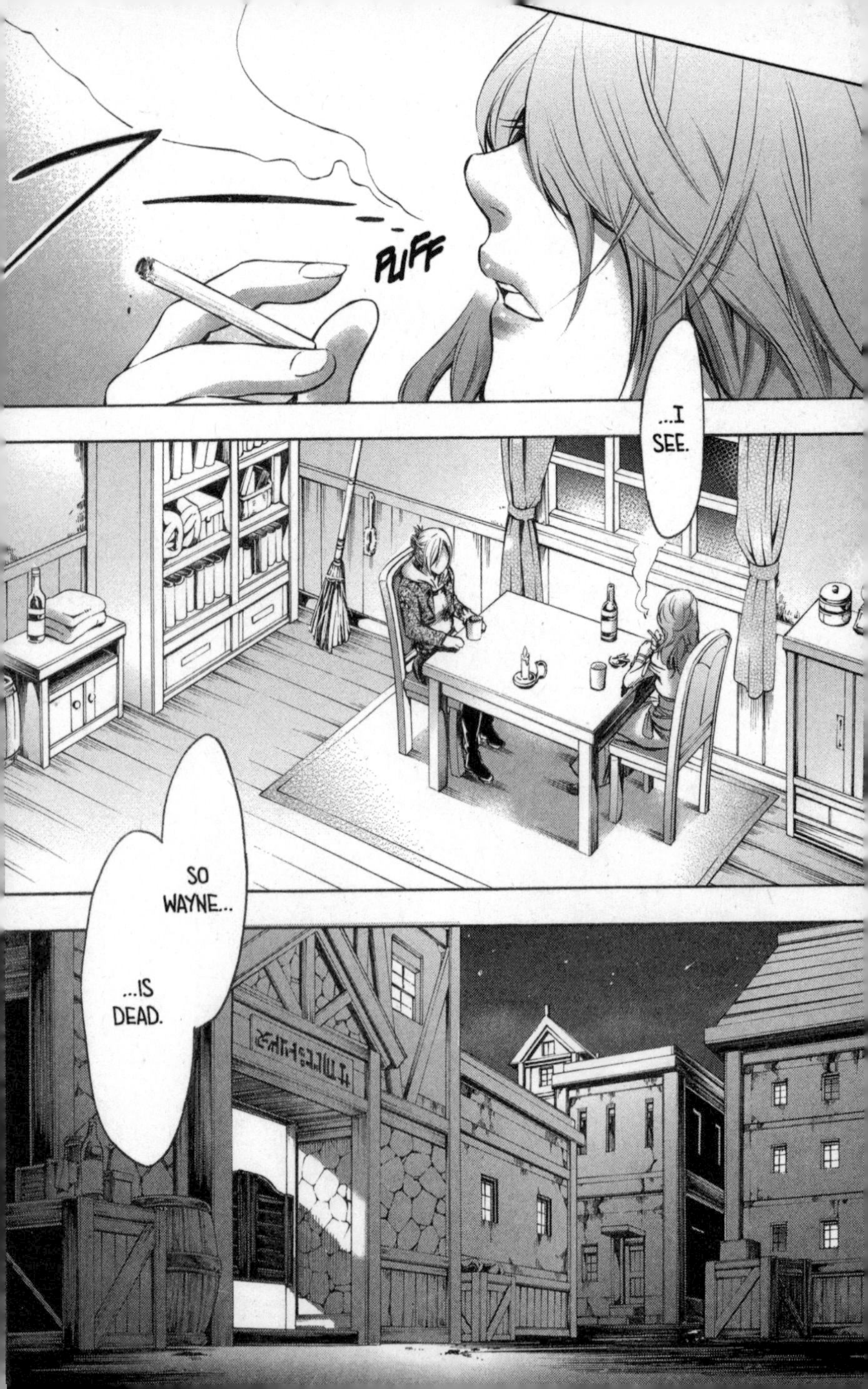
PUFF
...I SEE.
SO WAYNE...
...IS DEAD.

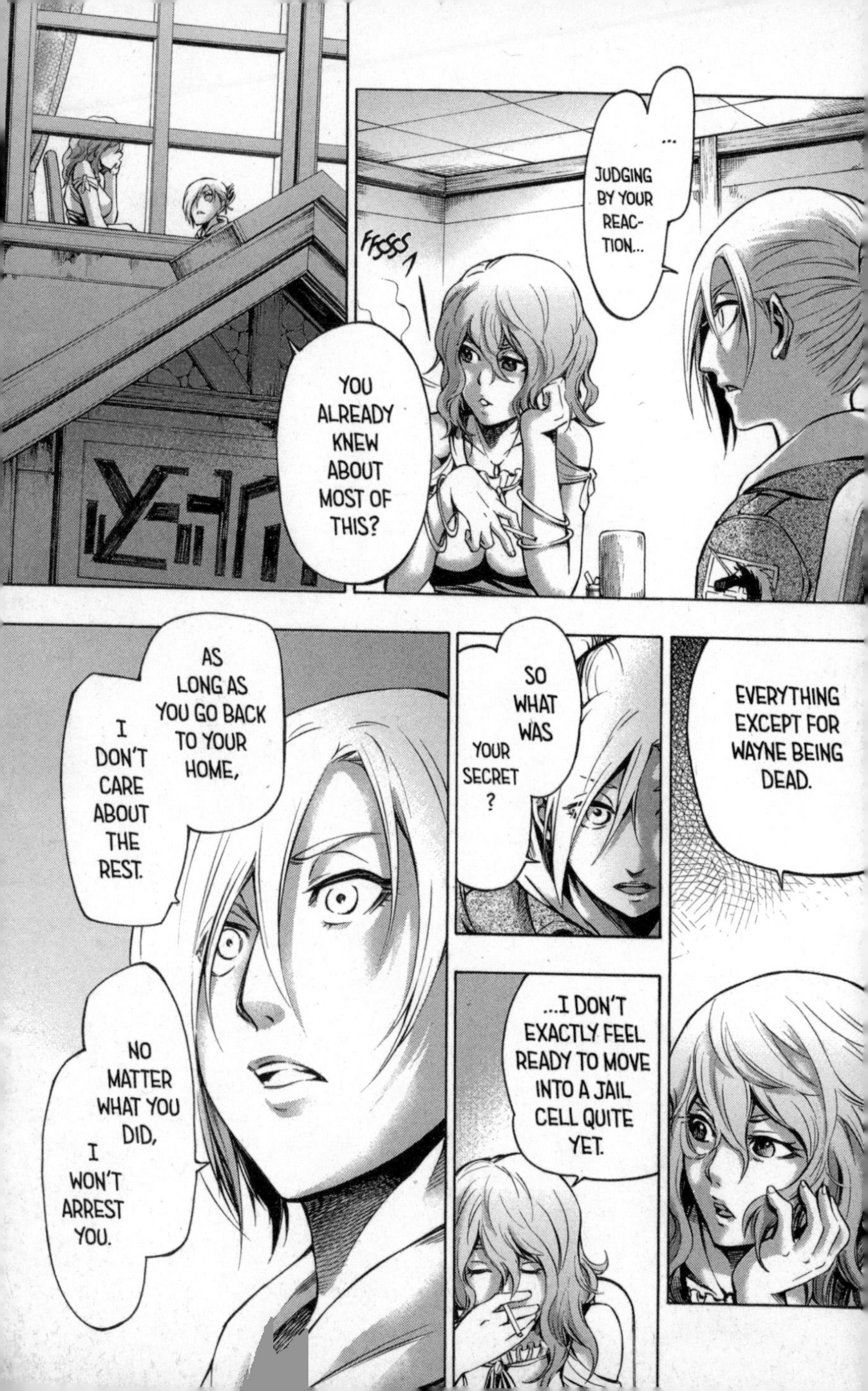
...
JUDGING BY YOUR REACTION...
FSSSS
YOU ALREADY KNEW ABOUT MOST OF THIS?
EVERYTHING EXCEPT FOR WAYNE BEING DEAD.
SO WHAT WAS YOUR SECRET?
...I DON'T EXACTLY FEEL READY TO MOVE INTO A JAIL CELL QUITE YET.
AS LONG AS YOU GO BACK TO YOUR HOME,
I DON'T CARE ABOUT THE REST.
NO MATTER WHAT YOU DID,
I WON'T ARREST YOU.

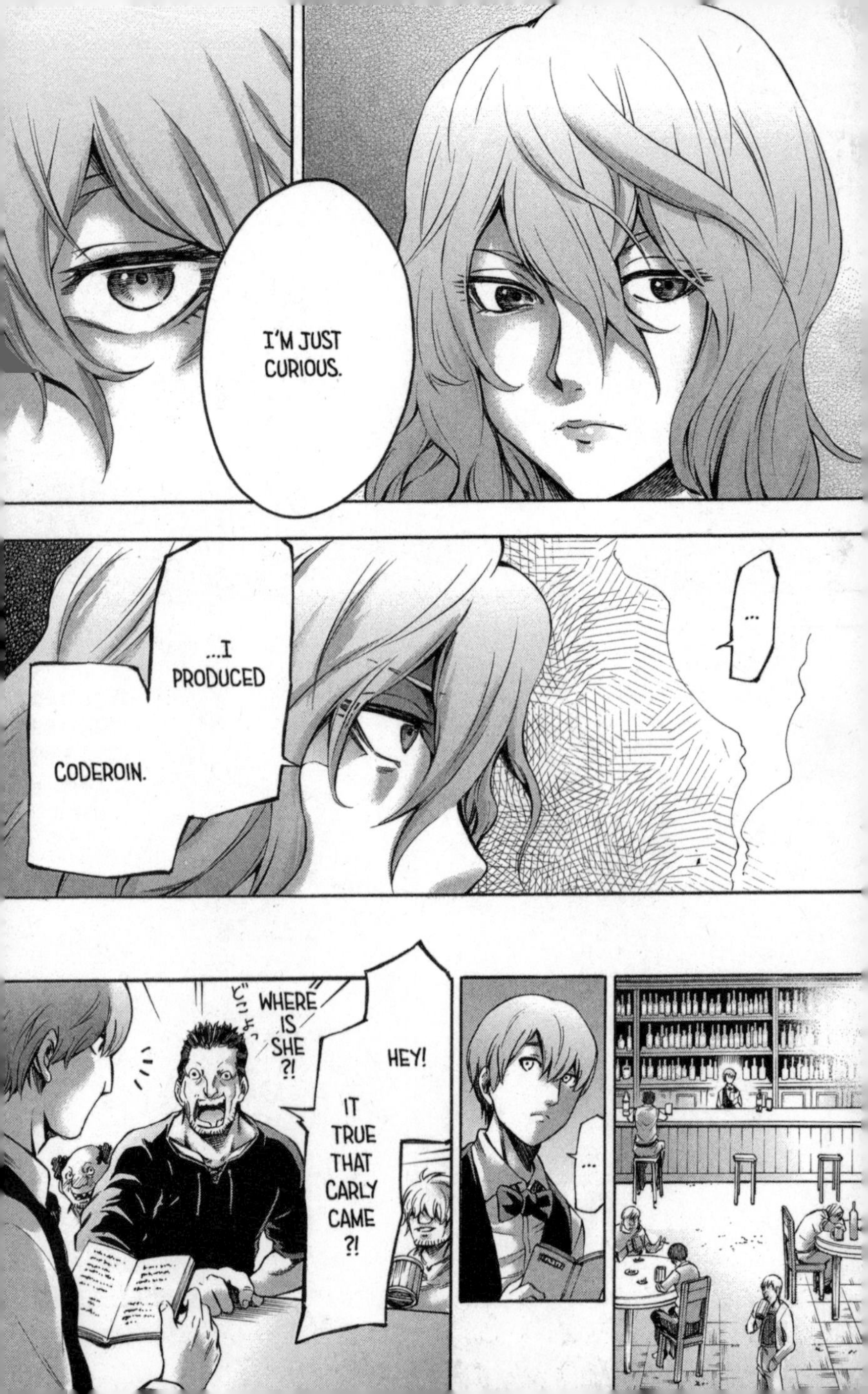

I'M JUST CURIOUS.
...
...I PRODUCED CODEROIN.
...
HEY! IT TRUE THAT CARLY CAME?!
WHERE IS SHE?!
どこよっ

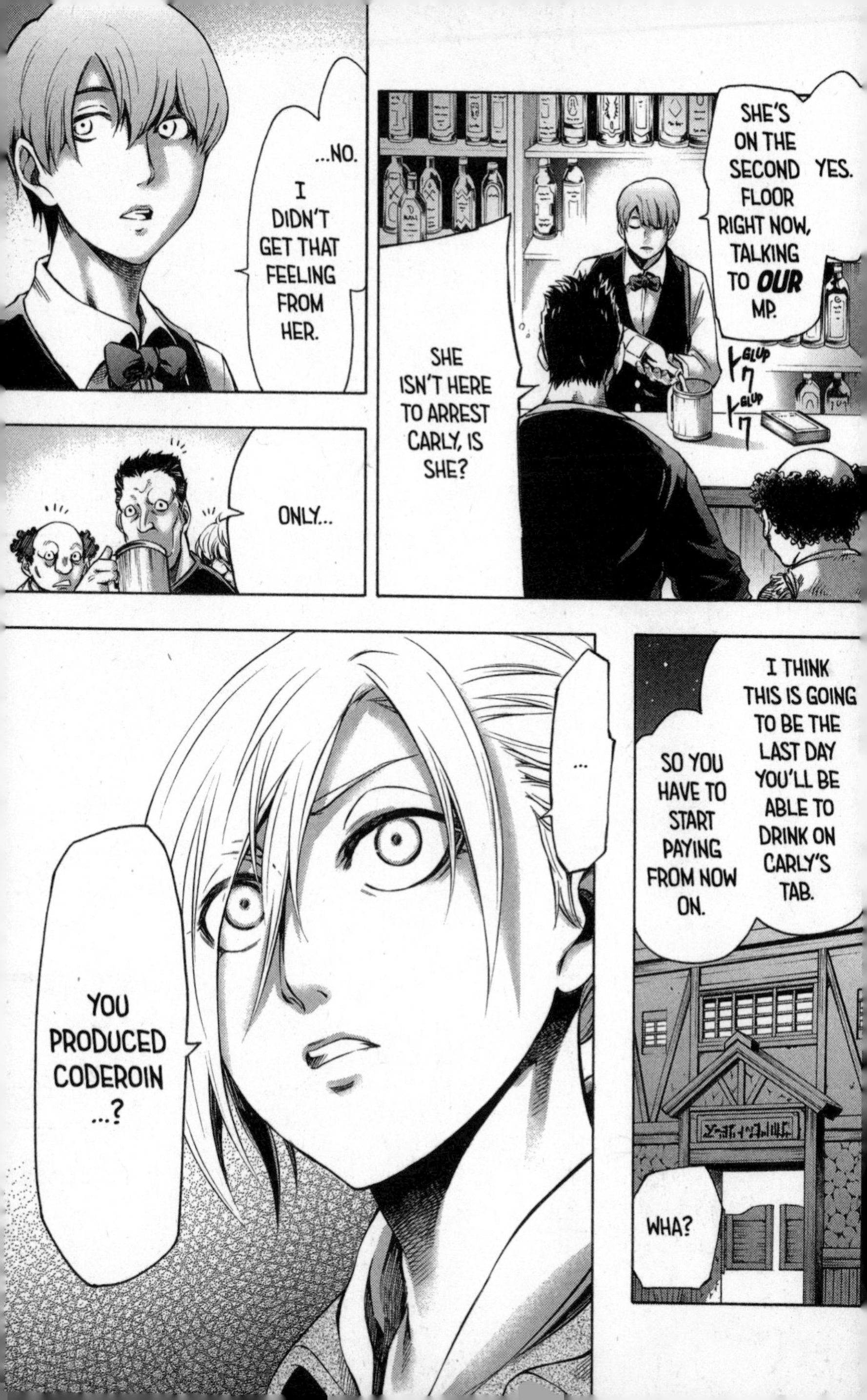
YES.
SHE'S ON THE SECOND FLOOR RIGHT NOW, TALKING TO *OUR* MP.
GLUP
GLUP
SHE ISN'T HERE TO ARREST CARLY, IS SHE?
...NO.
I DIDN'T GET THAT FEELING FROM HER.
ONLY...
I THINK THIS IS GOING TO BE THE LAST DAY YOU'LL BE ABLE TO DRINK ON CARLY'S TAB.
SO YOU HAVE TO START PAYING FROM NOW ON.
WHA?
...
YOU PRODUCED CODEROIN ...?

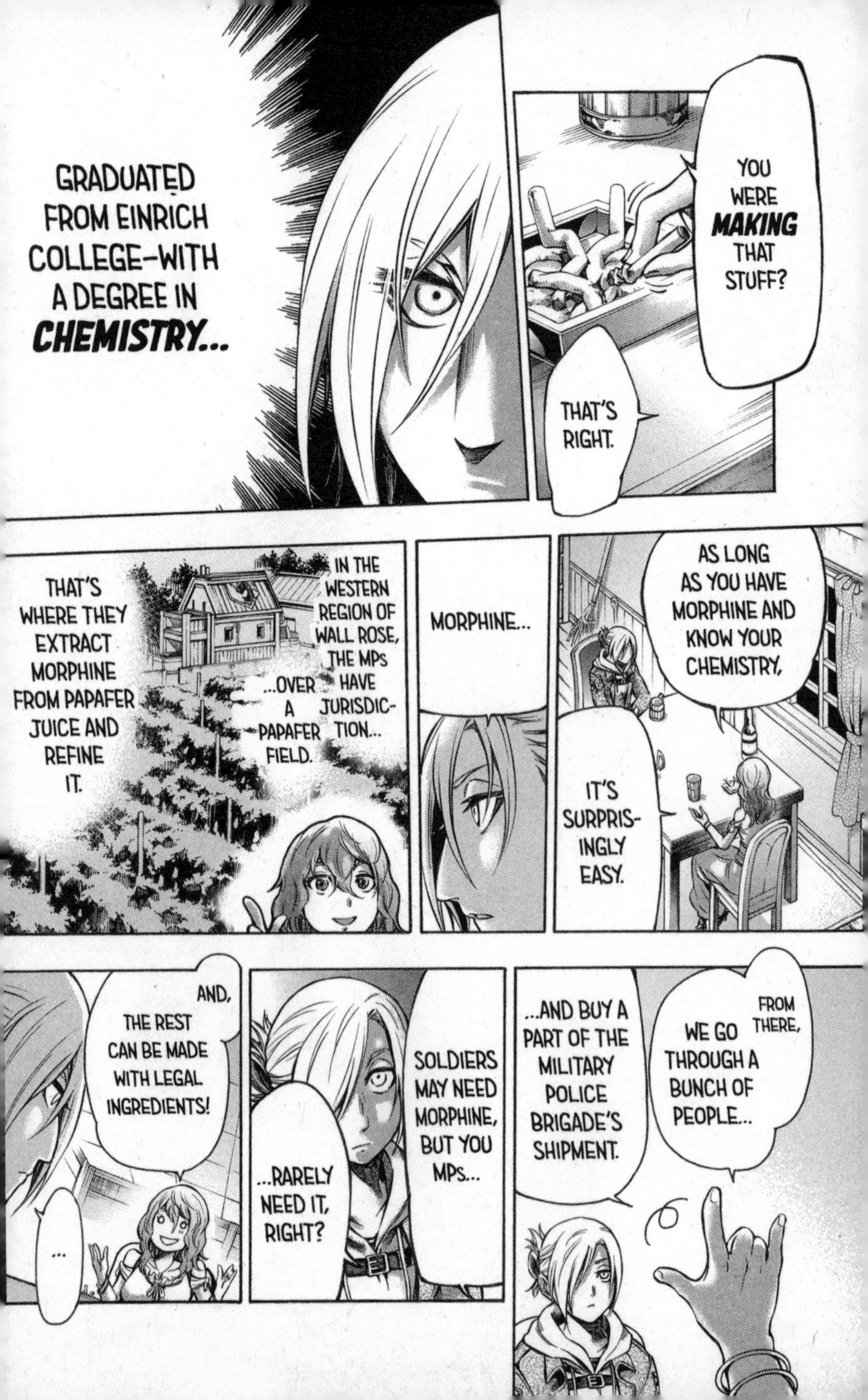
YOU WERE MAKING THAT STUFF?
THAT'S RIGHT.
GRADUATED FROM EINRICH COLLEGE—WITH A DEGREE IN CHEMISTRY...
AS LONG AS YOU HAVE MORPHINE AND KNOW YOUR CHEMISTRY,
IT'S SURPRISINGLY EASY.
MORPHINE...
IN THE WESTERN REGION OF WALL ROSE, THE MPs HAVE JURISDICTION...
...OVER A PAPAFER FIELD.
THAT'S WHERE THEY EXTRACT MORPHINE FROM PAPAFER JUICE AND REFINE IT.
FROM THERE,
WE GO THROUGH A BUNCH OF PEOPLE...
...AND BUY A PART OF THE MILITARY POLICE BRIGADE'S SHIPMENT.
SOLDIERS MAY NEED MORPHINE, BUT YOU MPs...
...RARELY NEED IT, RIGHT?
AND, THE REST CAN BE MADE WITH LEGAL INGREDIENTS!
...

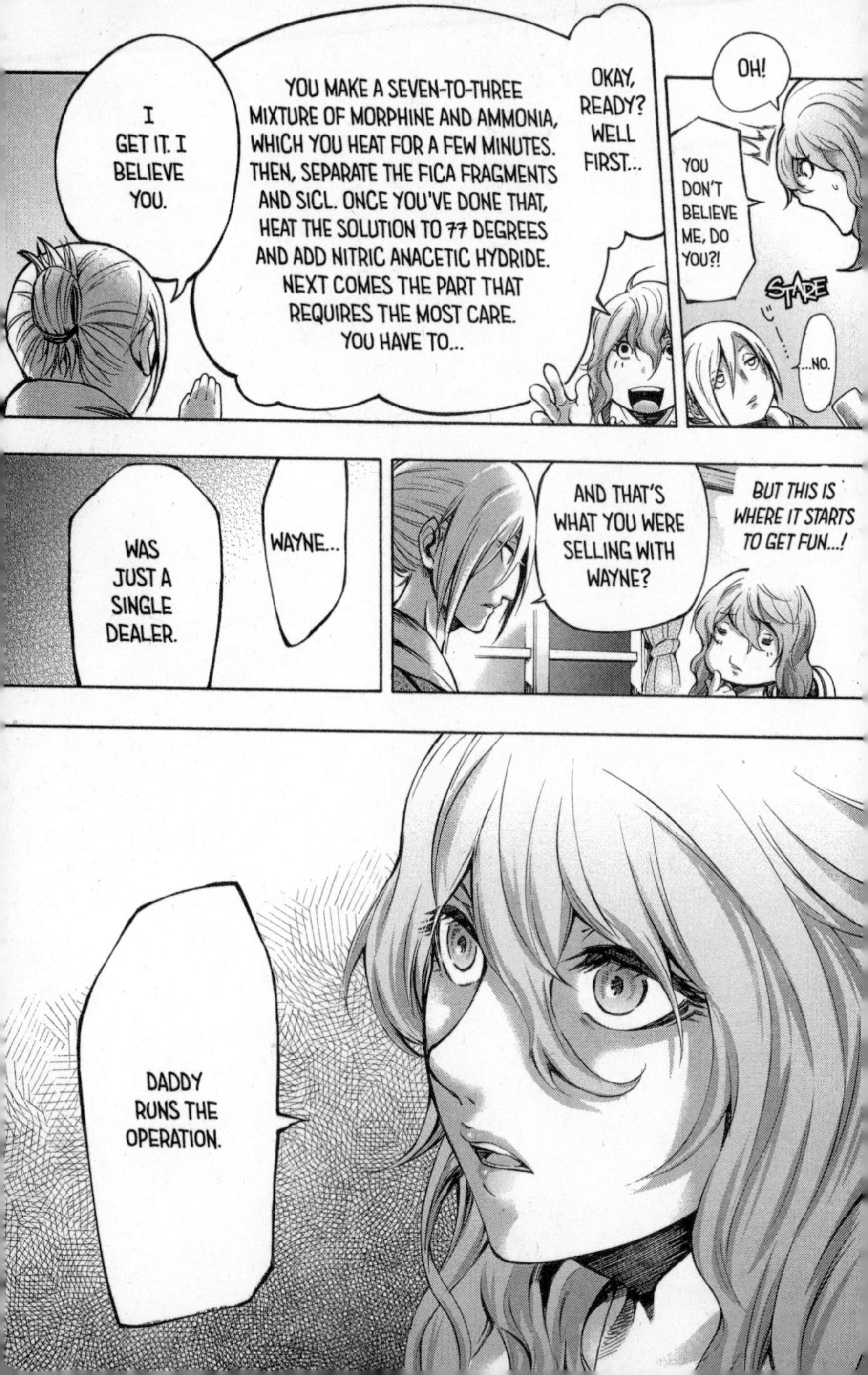
OH!
YOU DON'T BELIEVE ME, DO YOU?!
STARE
...NO.
OKAY, READY? WELL FIRST...
YOU MAKE A SEVEN-TO-THREE MIXTURE OF MORPHINE AND AMMONIA, WHICH YOU HEAT FOR A FEW MINUTES. THEN, SEPARATE THE FICA FRAGMENTS AND SICL. ONCE YOU'VE DONE THAT, HEAT THE SOLUTION TO 77 DEGREES AND ADD NITRIC ANACETIC HYDRIDE. NEXT COMES THE PART THAT REQUIRES THE MOST CARE. YOU HAVE TO...
I GET IT. I BELIEVE YOU.
BUT THIS IS WHERE IT STARTS TO GET FUN...!
AND THAT'S WHAT YOU WERE SELLING WITH WAYNE?
WAYNE...
WAS JUST A SINGLE DEALER.
DADDY RUNS THE OPERATION.

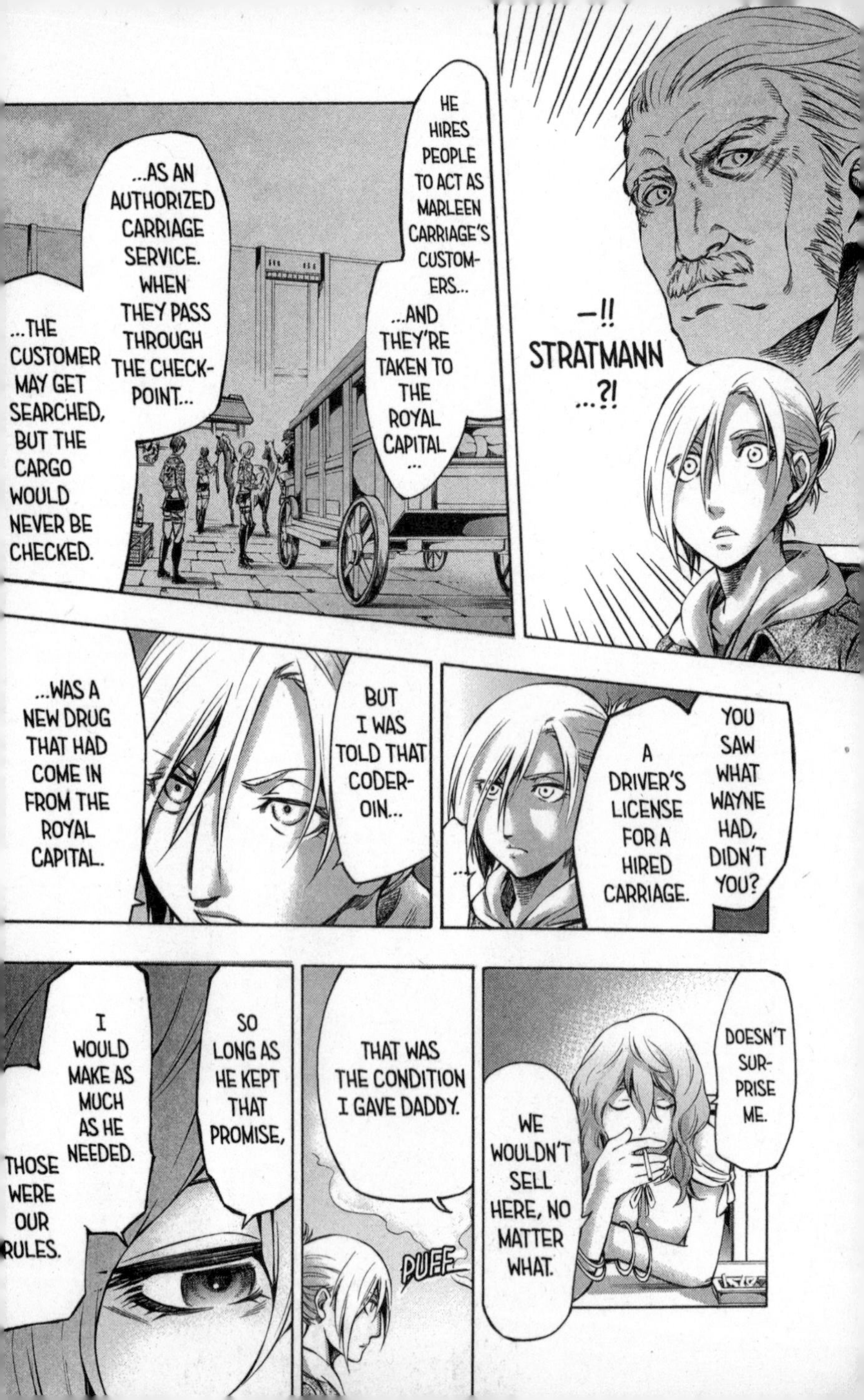
—!! STRATMANN ...?!
HE HIRES PEOPLE TO ACT AS MARLEEN CARRIAGE'S CUSTOMERS...
...AND THEY'RE TAKEN TO THE ROYAL CAPITAL...
...AS AN AUTHORIZED CARRIAGE SERVICE. WHEN THEY PASS THROUGH THE CHECKPOINT...
...THE CUSTOMER MAY GET SEARCHED, BUT THE CARGO WOULD NEVER BE CHECKED.
YOU SAW WHAT WAYNE HAD, DIDN'T YOU?
A DRIVER'S LICENSE FOR A HIRED CARRIAGE.
...
BUT I WAS TOLD THAT CODEROIN...
...WAS A NEW DRUG THAT HAD COME IN FROM THE ROYAL CAPITAL.
DOESN'T SURPRISE ME.
WE WOULDN'T SELL HERE, NO MATTER WHAT.
THAT WAS THE CONDITION I GAVE DADDY.
PUFF
SO LONG AS HE KEPT THAT PROMISE,
I WOULD MAKE AS MUCH AS HE NEEDED.
THOSE WERE OUR RULES.

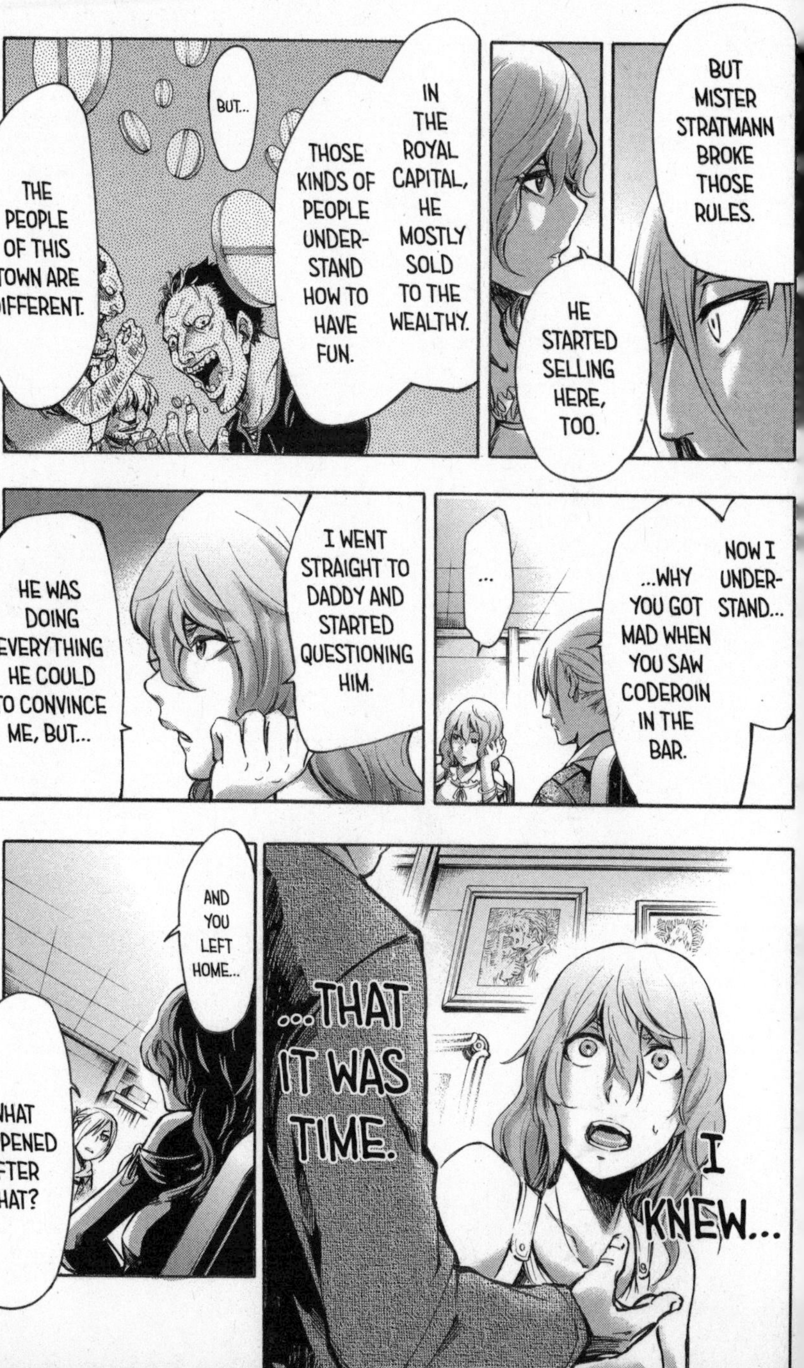
BUT MISTER STRATMANN BROKE THOSE RULES.
HE STARTED SELLING HERE, TOO.
IN THE ROYAL CAPITAL, HE MOSTLY SOLD TO THE WEALTHY.
THOSE KINDS OF PEOPLE UNDER-STAND HOW TO HAVE FUN.
BUT...
THE PEOPLE OF THIS TOWN ARE DIFFERENT.
NOW I UNDER-STAND...
...WHY YOU GOT MAD WHEN YOU SAW CODEROIN IN THE BAR.
...
I WENT STRAIGHT TO DADDY AND STARTED QUESTIONING HIM.
HE WAS DOING EVERYTHING HE COULD TO CONVINCE ME, BUT...
I KNEW...
...THAT IT WAS TIME.
AND YOU LEFT HOME...
WHAT HAPPENED AFTER THAT?

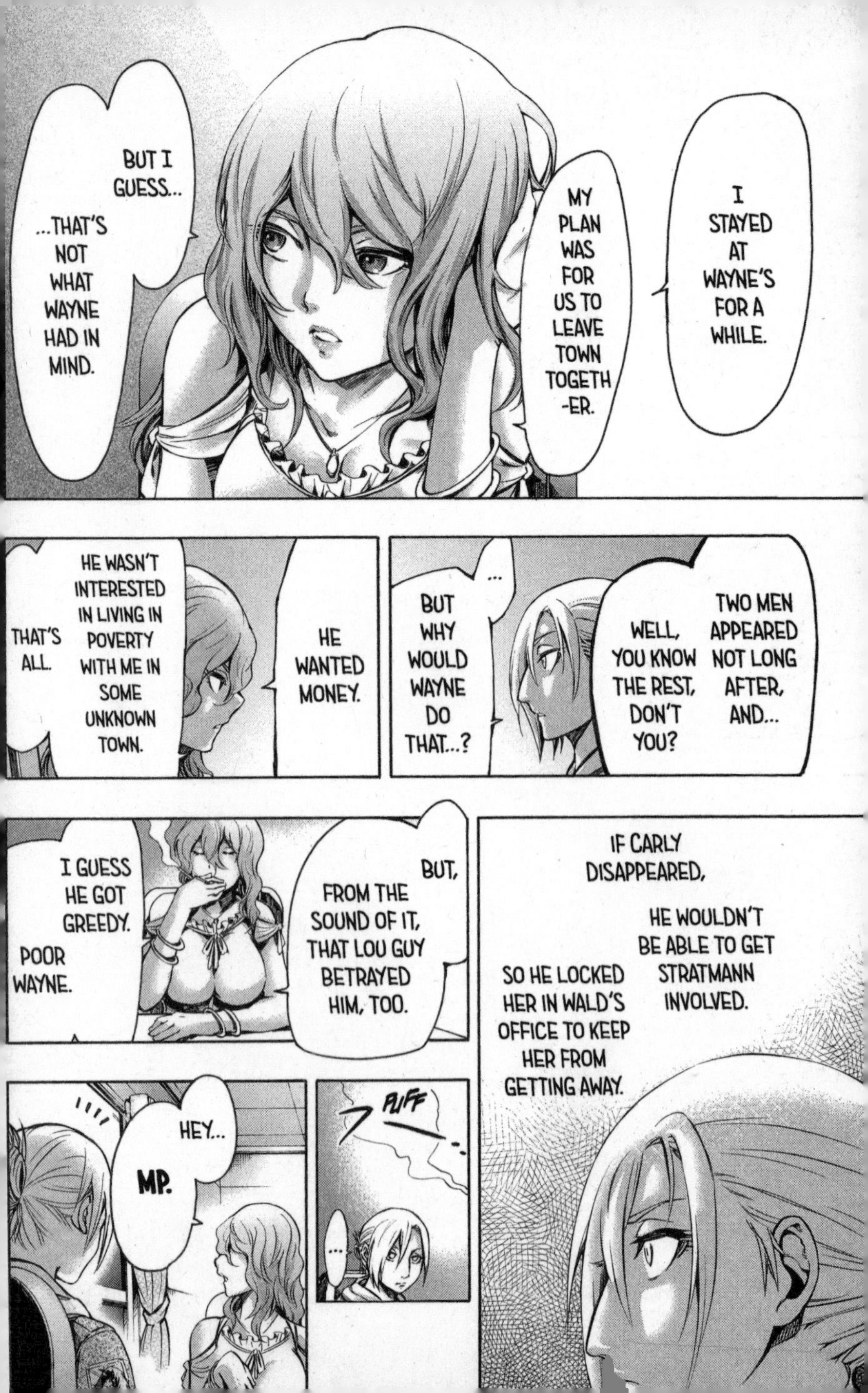
I STAYED AT WAYNE'S FOR A WHILE.
MY PLAN WAS FOR US TO LEAVE TOWN TOGETH-ER.
BUT I GUESS...
...THAT'S NOT WHAT WAYNE HAD IN MIND.
TWO MEN APPEARED NOT LONG AFTER, AND...
WELL, YOU KNOW THE REST, DON'T YOU?
...
BUT WHY WOULD WAYNE DO THAT...?
HE WANTED MONEY.
HE WASN'T INTERESTED IN LIVING IN POVERTY WITH ME IN SOME UNKNOWN TOWN.
THAT'S ALL.
IF CARLY DISAPPEARED,
HE WOULDN'T BE ABLE TO GET STRATMANN INVOLVED.
SO HE LOCKED HER IN WALD'S OFFICE TO KEEP HER FROM GETTING AWAY.
BUT, FROM THE SOUND OF IT, THAT LOU GUY BETRAYED HIM, TOO.
I GUESS HE GOT GREEDY.
POOR WAYNE.
PUFF
...
HEY...
MP.

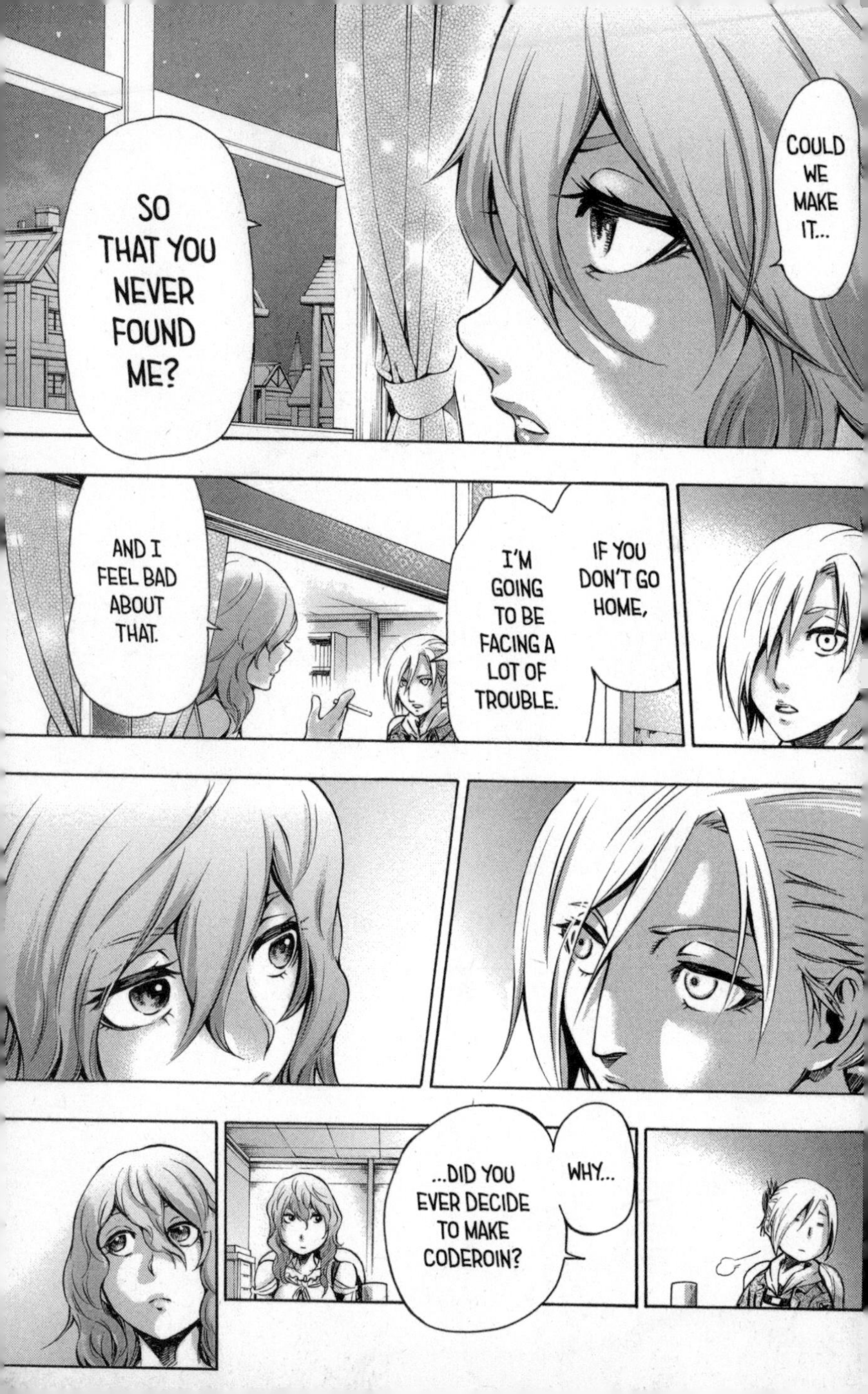
COULD WE MAKE IT...
SO THAT YOU NEVER FOUND ME?
IF YOU DON'T GO HOME,
I'M GOING TO BE FACING A LOT OF TROUBLE.
AND I FEEL BAD ABOUT THAT.
WHY...
...DID YOU EVER DECIDE TO MAKE CODEROIN?

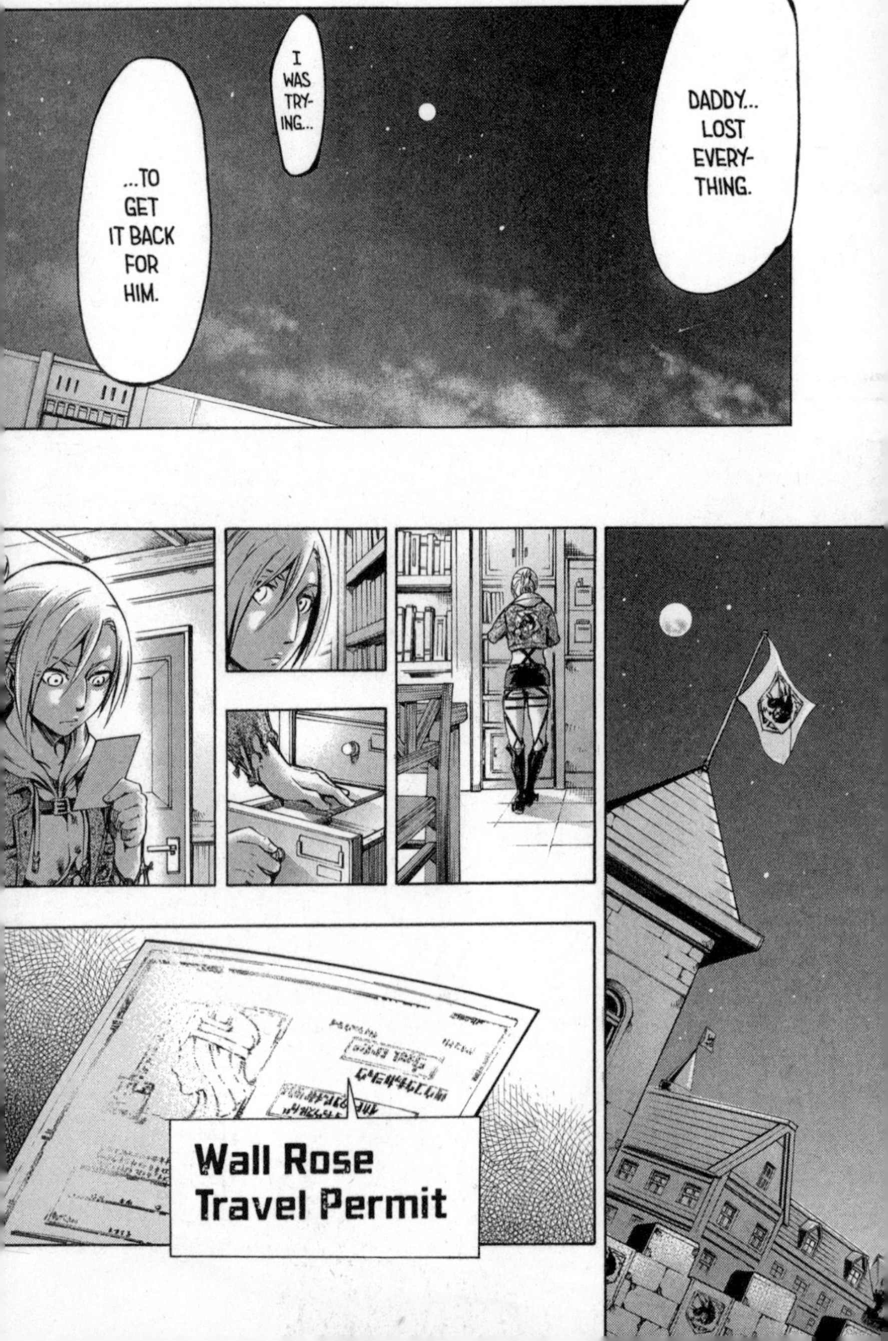
DADDY... LOST EVERY-THING.
I WAS TRY-ING...
...TO GET IT BACK FOR HIM.
Wall Rose Travel Permit

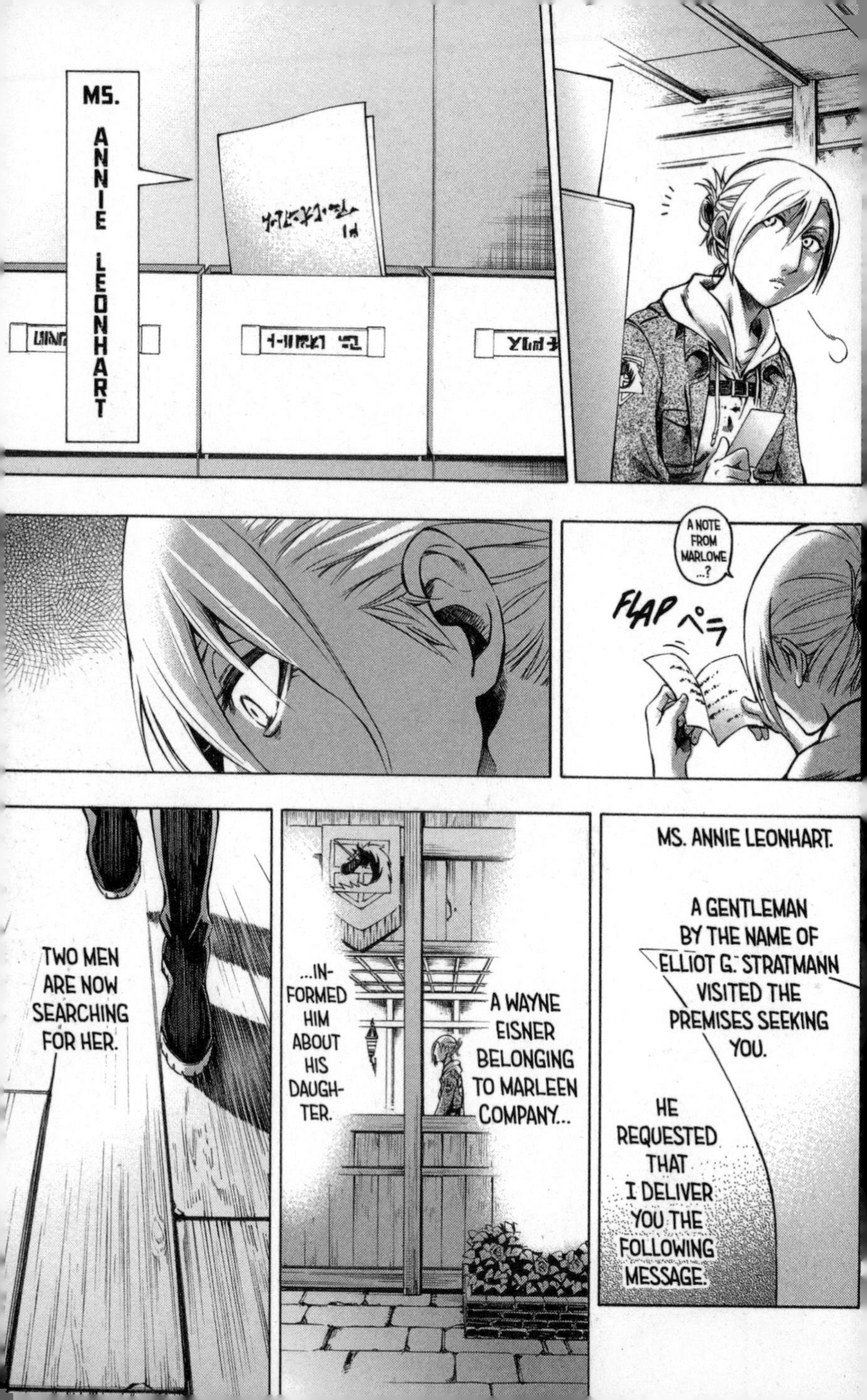
MS. ANNIE LEONHART
A NOTE FROM MARLOWE ...?
FLAP ペラ
MS. ANNIE LEONHART.
A GENTLEMAN BY THE NAME OF ELLIOT G. STRATMANN VISITED THE PREMISES SEEKING YOU.
HE REQUESTED THAT I DELIVER YOU THE FOLLOWING MESSAGE.
A WAYNE EISNER BELONGING TO MARLEEN COMPANY...
...INFORMED HIM ABOUT HIS DAUGHTER.
TWO MEN ARE NOW SEARCHING FOR HER.

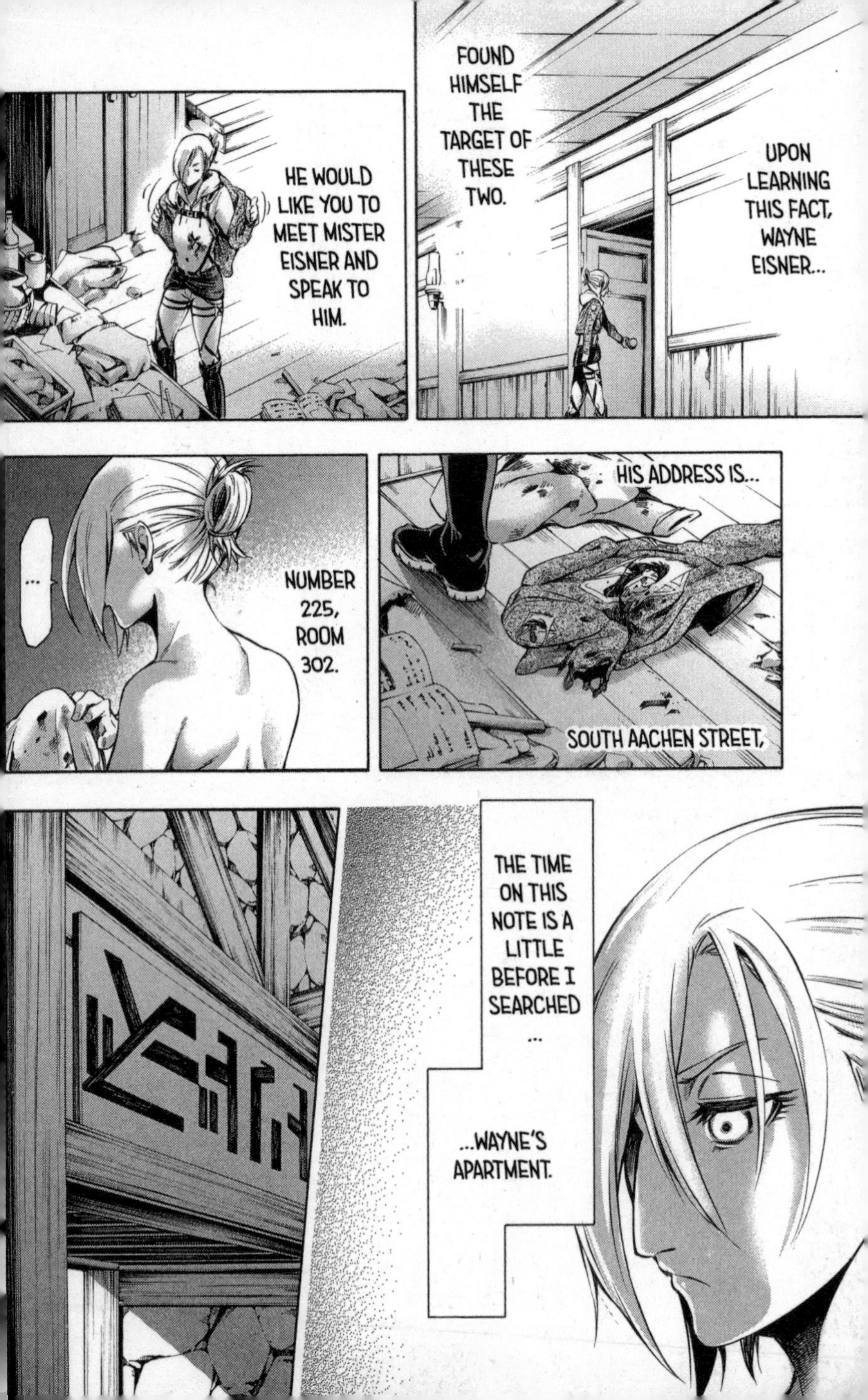
UPON LEARNING THIS FACT, WAYNE EISNER...
FOUND HIMSELF THE TARGET OF THESE TWO.
HE WOULD LIKE YOU TO MEET MISTER EISNER AND SPEAK TO HIM.
HIS ADDRESS IS...
SOUTH AACHEN STREET,
NUMBER 225, ROOM 302.
...
THE TIME ON THIS NOTE IS A LITTLE BEFORE I SEARCHED ...
...WAYNE'S APARTMENT.

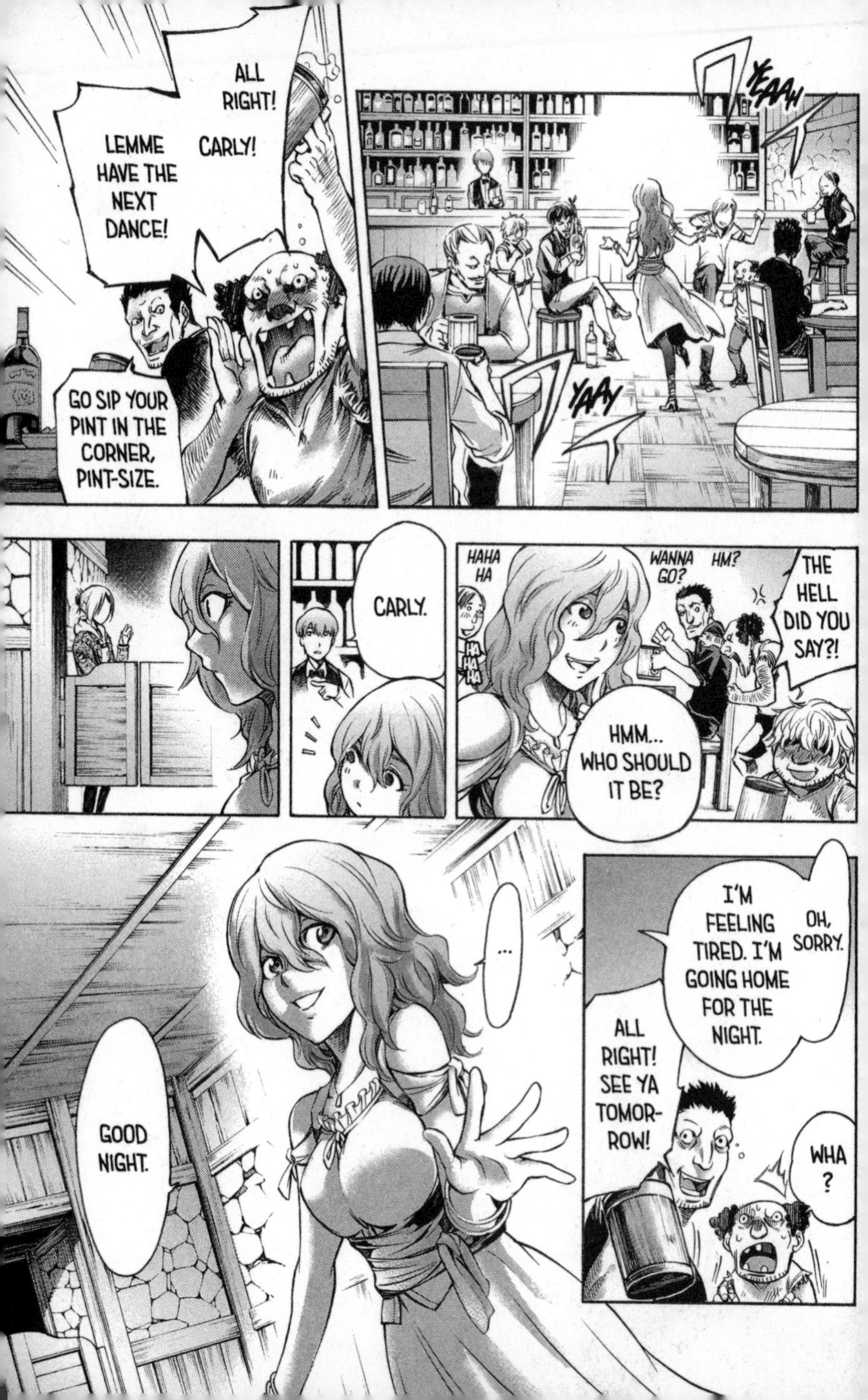
YEAAAH
YAAY
ALL RIGHT! CARLY!
LEMME HAVE THE NEXT DANCE!
GO SIP YOUR PINT IN THE CORNER, PINT-SIZE.
THE HELL DID YOU SAY?!
HM?
WANNA GO?
HAHA HA
HA HA HA
HMM... WHO SHOULD IT BE?
CARLY.
OH, SORRY.
I'M FEELING TIRED. I'M GOING HOME FOR THE NIGHT.
ALL RIGHT! SEE YA TOMOR-ROW!
WHA?
...
GOOD NIGHT.

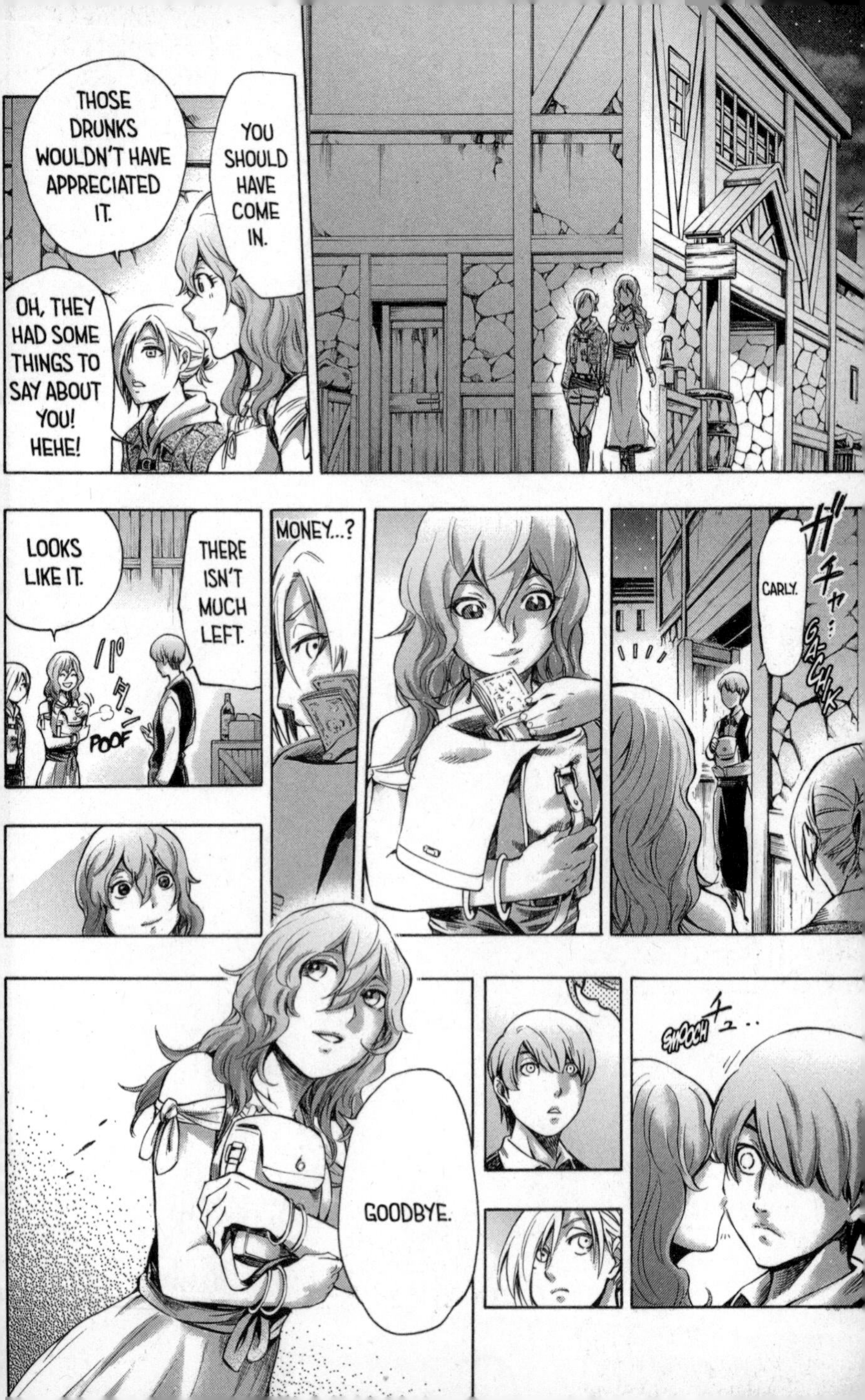
YOU SHOULD HAVE COME IN.
THOSE DRUNKS WOULDN'T HAVE APPRECIATED IT.
OH, THEY HAD SOME THINGS TO SAY ABOUT YOU! HEHE!
ガチャ
GACHAK
CARLY.
MONEY...?
THERE ISN'T MUCH LEFT.
LOOKS LIKE IT.
パタ
POOF
SMOOCH
チュ..
GOODBYE.

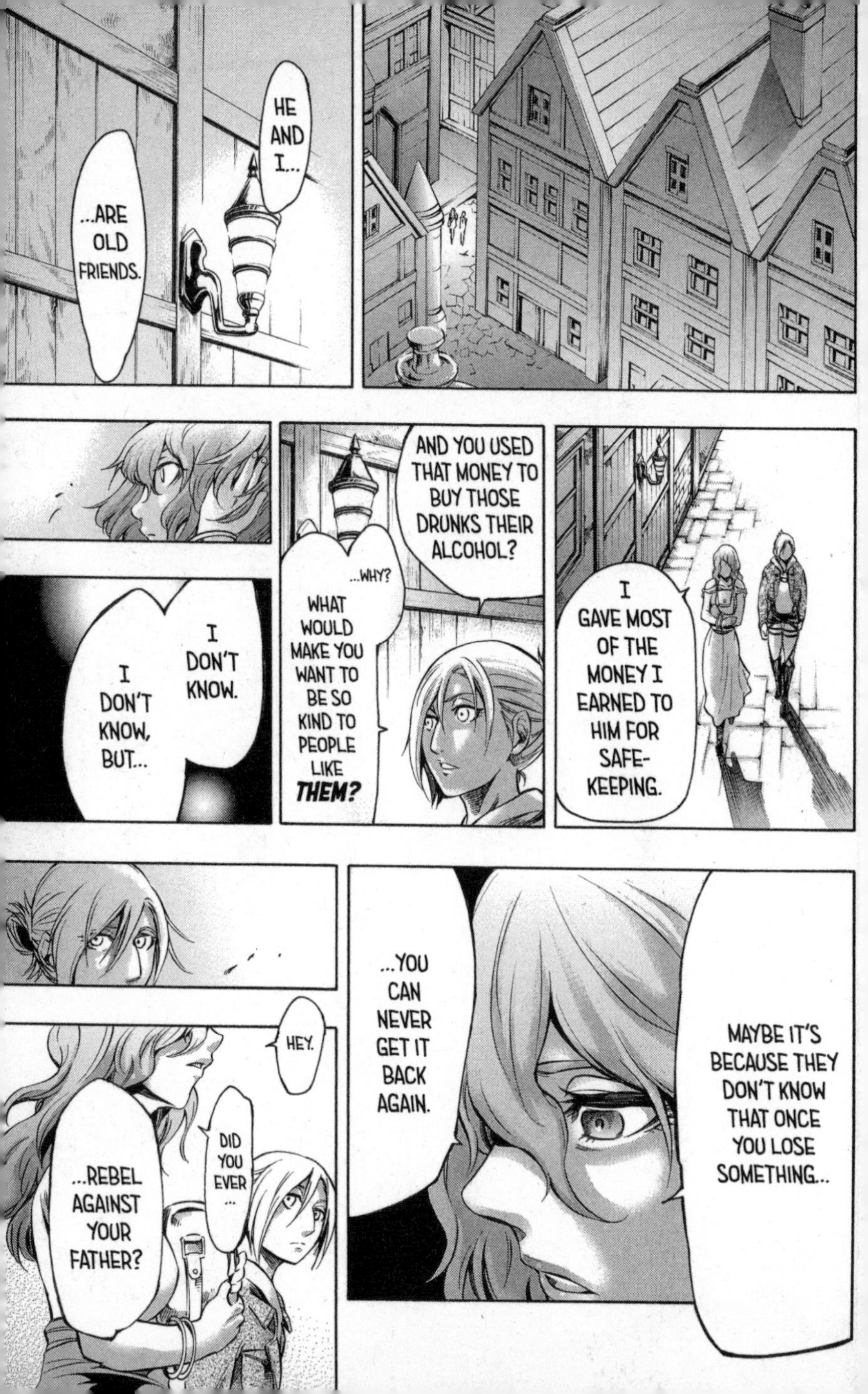
HE AND I...
...ARE OLD FRIENDS.
I GAVE MOST OF THE MONEY I EARNED TO HIM FOR SAFE-KEEPING.
AND YOU USED THAT MONEY TO BUY THOSE DRUNKS THEIR ALCOHOL?
...WHY?
WHAT WOULD MAKE YOU WANT TO BE SO KIND TO PEOPLE LIKE ***THEM?***
I DON'T KNOW.
I DON'T KNOW, BUT...
MAYBE IT'S BECAUSE THEY DON'T KNOW THAT ONCE YOU LOSE SOMETHING...
...YOU CAN NEVER GET IT BACK AGAIN.
HEY.
DID YOU EVER ...
...REBEL AGAINST YOUR FATHER?

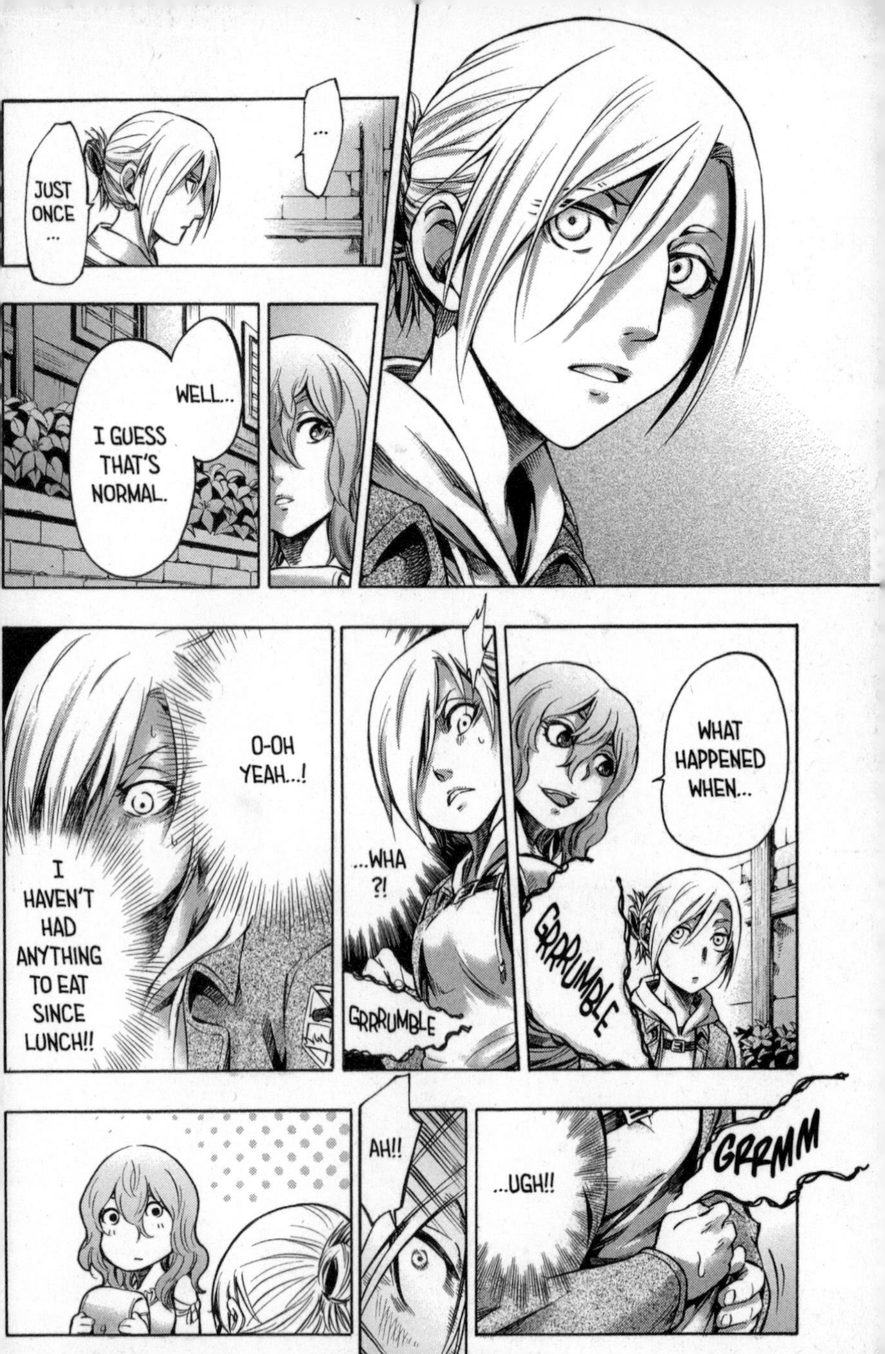
...
JUST ONCE ...
WELL...
I GUESS THAT'S NORMAL.
WHAT HAPPENED WHEN...
GRRRUMBLE
...WHA ?!
GRRRUMBLE
O-OH YEAH...!
I HAVEN'T HAD ANYTHING TO EAT SINCE LUNCH!!
GRRMM
...UGH!!
AH!!

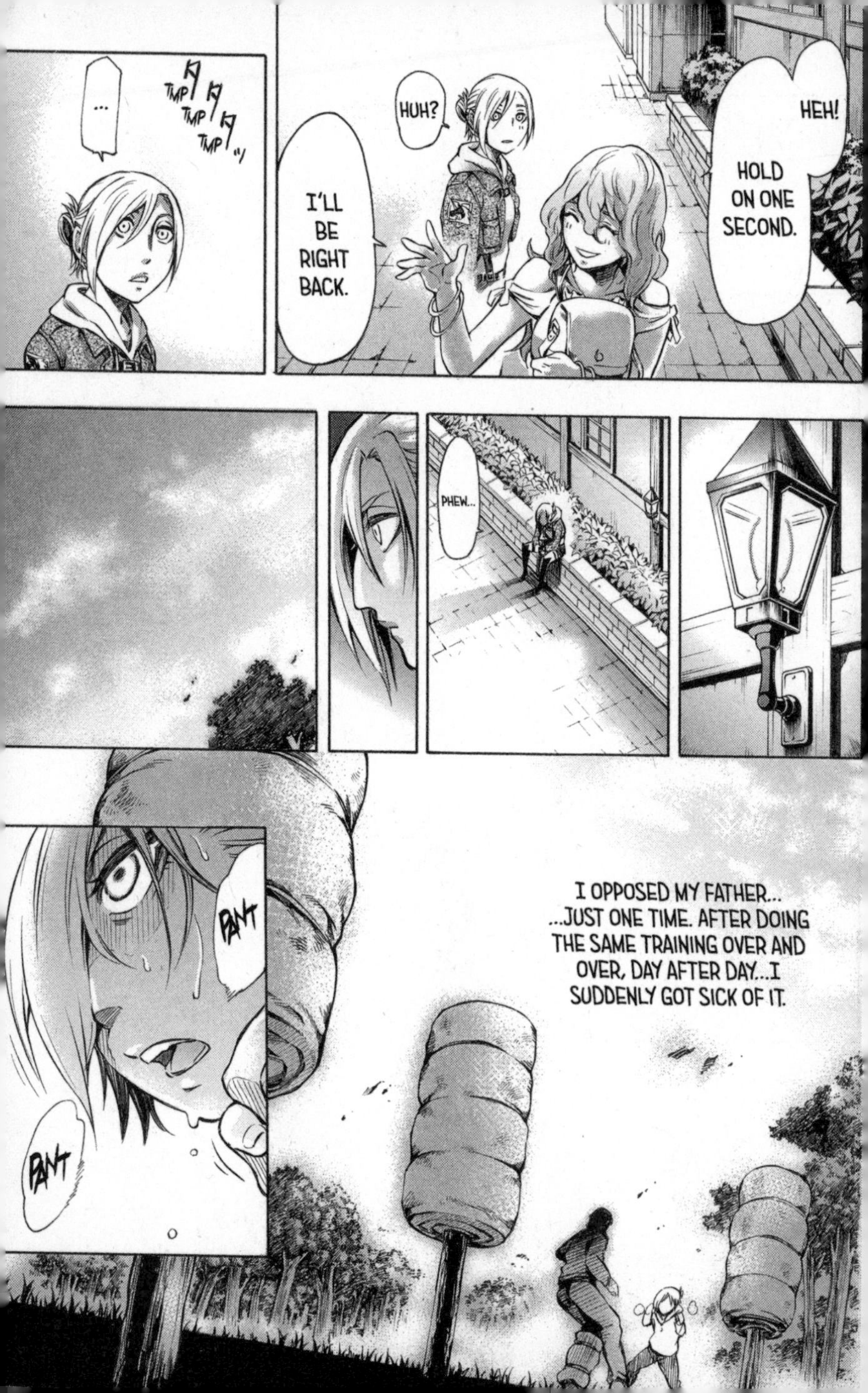
HEH!
HOLD ON ONE SECOND.
HUH?
I'LL BE RIGHT BACK.
...
TMP TMP TMP
PHEW...
I OPPOSED MY FATHER... ...JUST ONE TIME. AFTER DOING THE SAME TRAINING OVER AND OVER, DAY AFTER DAY...I SUDDENLY GOT SICK OF IT.
PANT
PANT

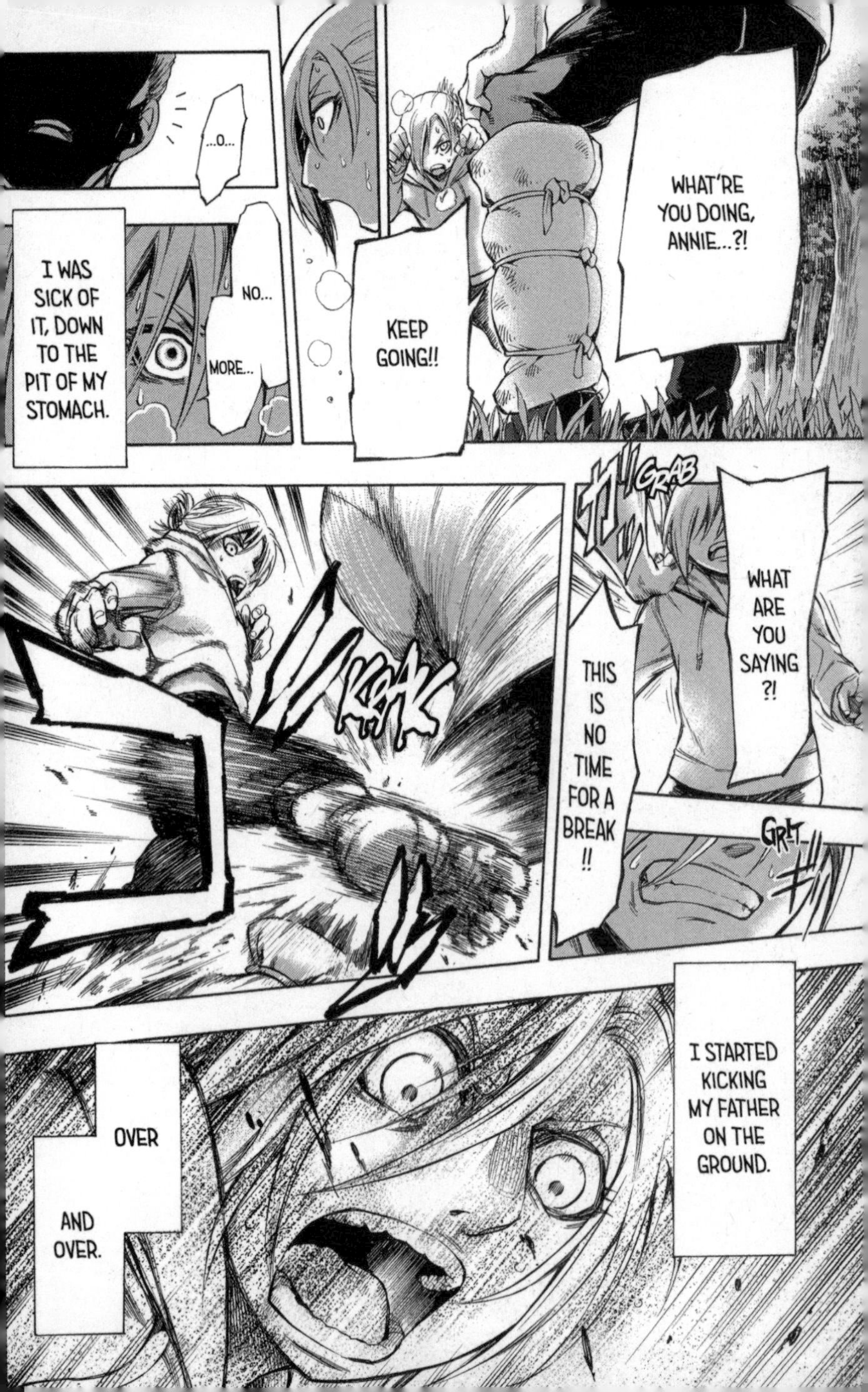
WHAT'RE YOU DOING, ANNIE...?!
KEEP GOING!!
...O...
I WAS SICK OF IT, DOWN TO THE PIT OF MY STOMACH.
NO...
MORE...
GRAB
WHAT ARE YOU SAYING?!
THIS IS NO TIME FOR A BREAK!!
GRIT
KRAK
I STARTED KICKING MY FATHER ON THE GROUND.
OVER
AND OVER.

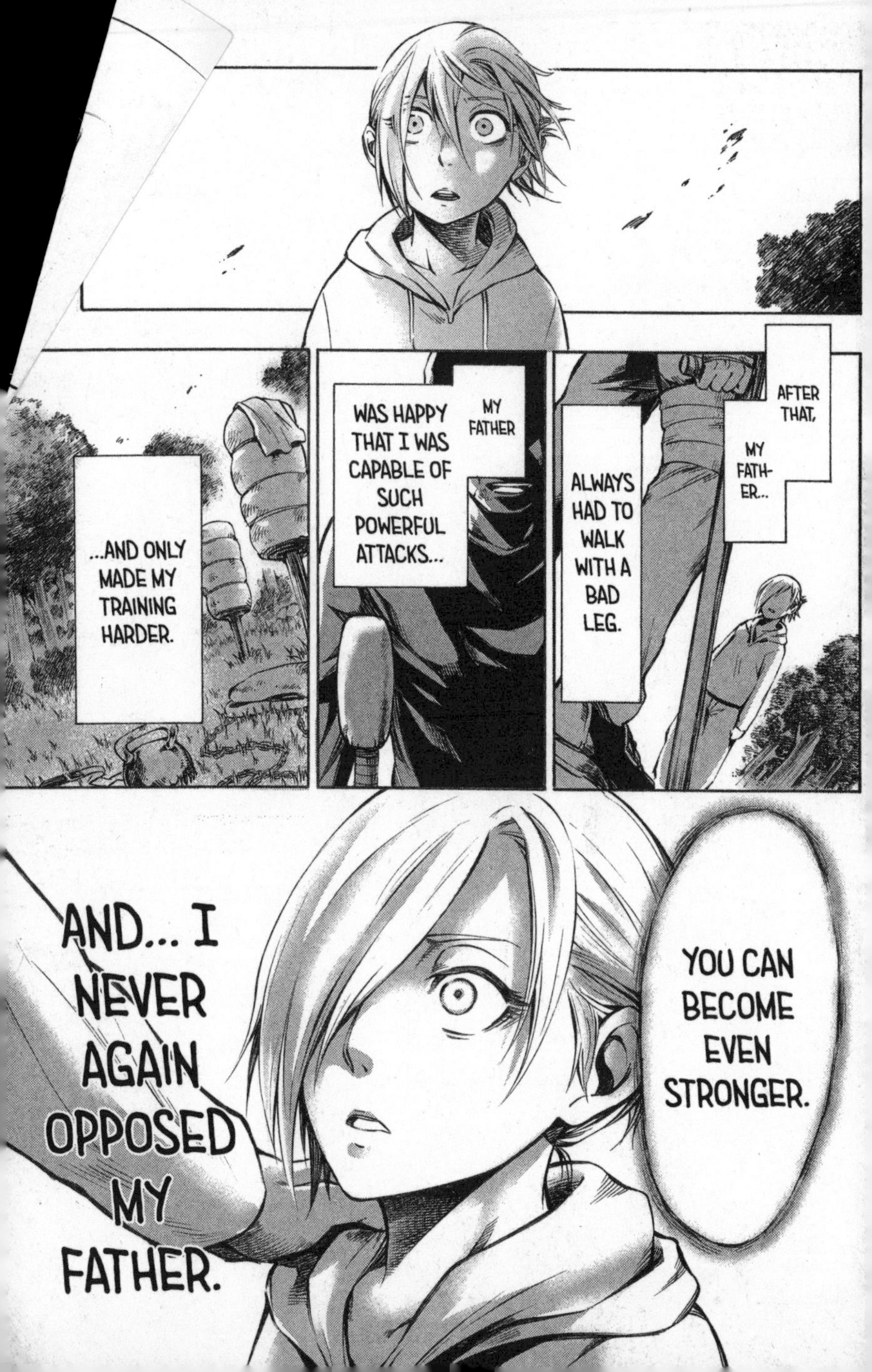
AFTER THAT,
MY FATH-ER...
ALWAYS HAD TO WALK WITH A BAD LEG.
MY FATHER
WAS HAPPY THAT I WAS CAPABLE OF SUCH POWERFUL ATTACKS...
...AND ONLY MADE MY TRAINING HARDER.
YOU CAN BECOME EVEN STRONGER.
AND... I NEVER AGAIN OPPOSED MY FATHER.

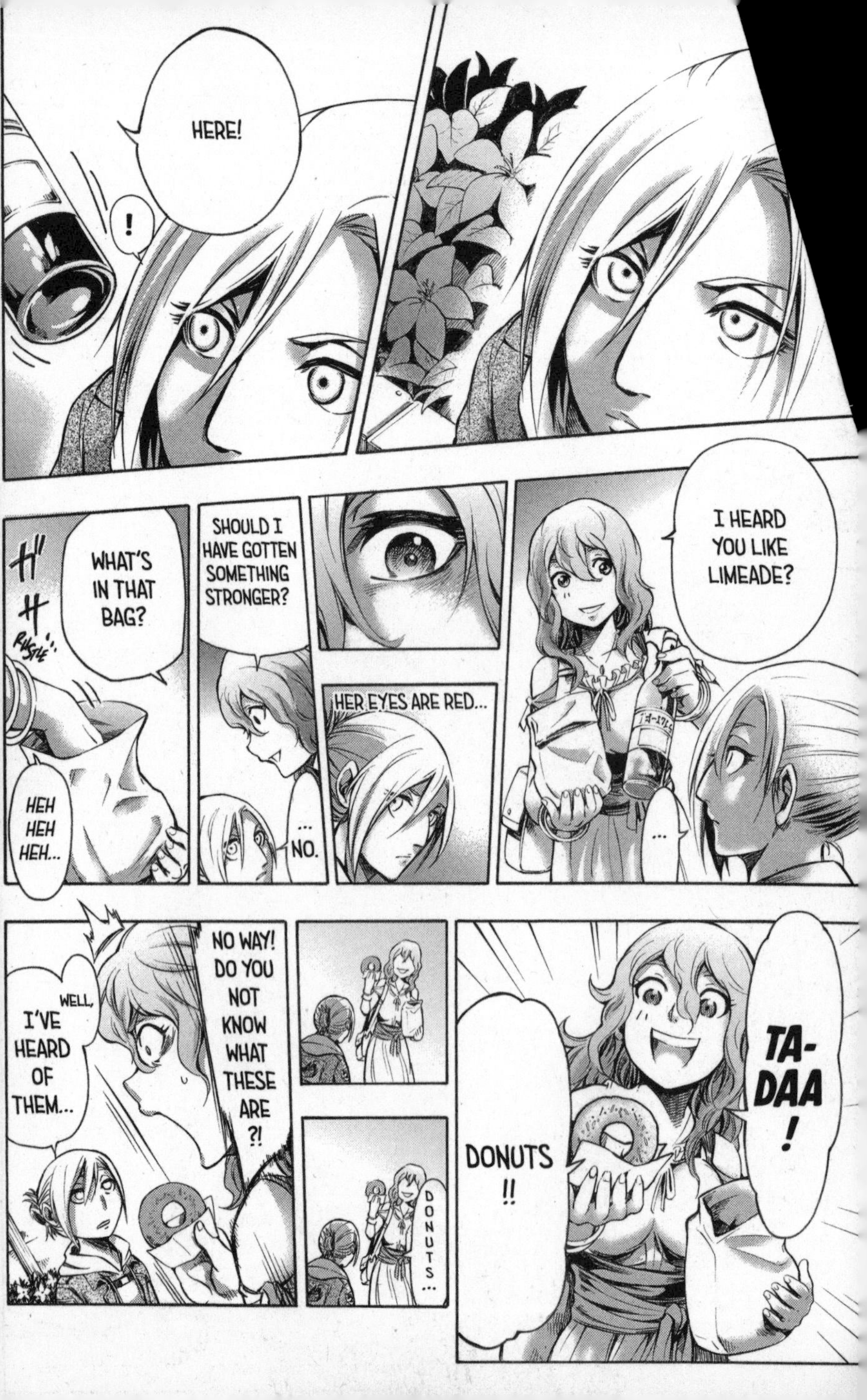
HERE!
!
I HEARD YOU LIKE LIMEADE?
...
HER EYES ARE RED...
... NO.
SHOULD I HAVE GOTTEN SOMETHING STRONGER?
WHAT'S IN THAT BAG?
RUSTLE
HEH HEH HEH...
TA-DAA!
DONUTS!!
DONUTS...
NO WAY! DO YOU NOT KNOW WHAT THESE ARE?!
WELL, I'VE HEARD OF THEM...

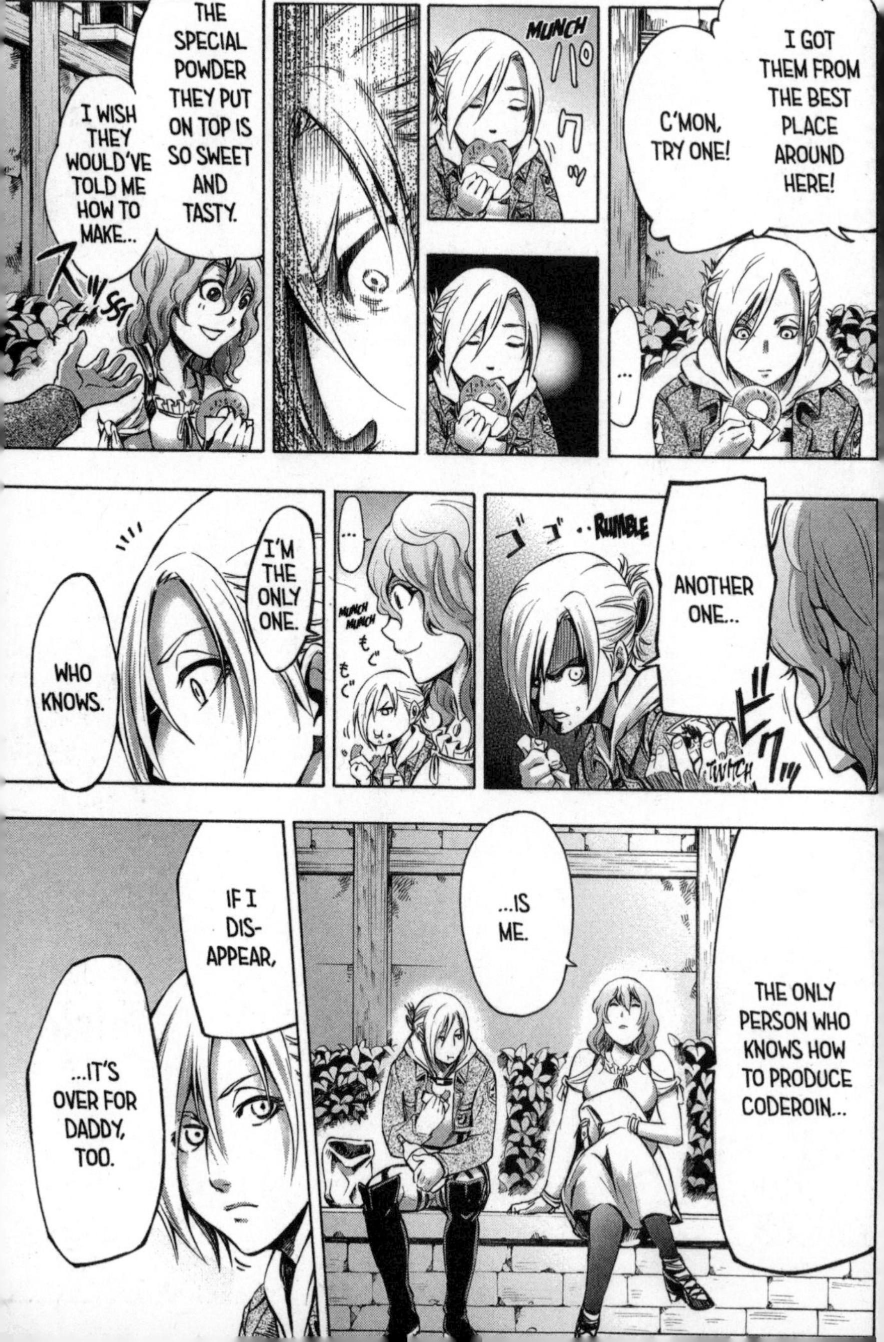
I GOT THEM FROM THE BEST PLACE AROUND HERE!
C'MON, TRY ONE!
...
MUNCH
THE SPECIAL POWDER THEY PUT ON TOP IS SO SWEET AND TASTY.
I WISH THEY WOULD'VE TOLD ME HOW TO MAKE...
SSS
RUMBLE
ANOTHER ONE...
TWITCH
...
I'M THE ONLY ONE.
MUNCH MUNCH
WHO KNOWS.
THE ONLY PERSON WHO KNOWS HOW TO PRODUCE CODEROIN...
...IS ME.
IF I DIS-APPEAR,
...IT'S OVER FOR DADDY, TOO.

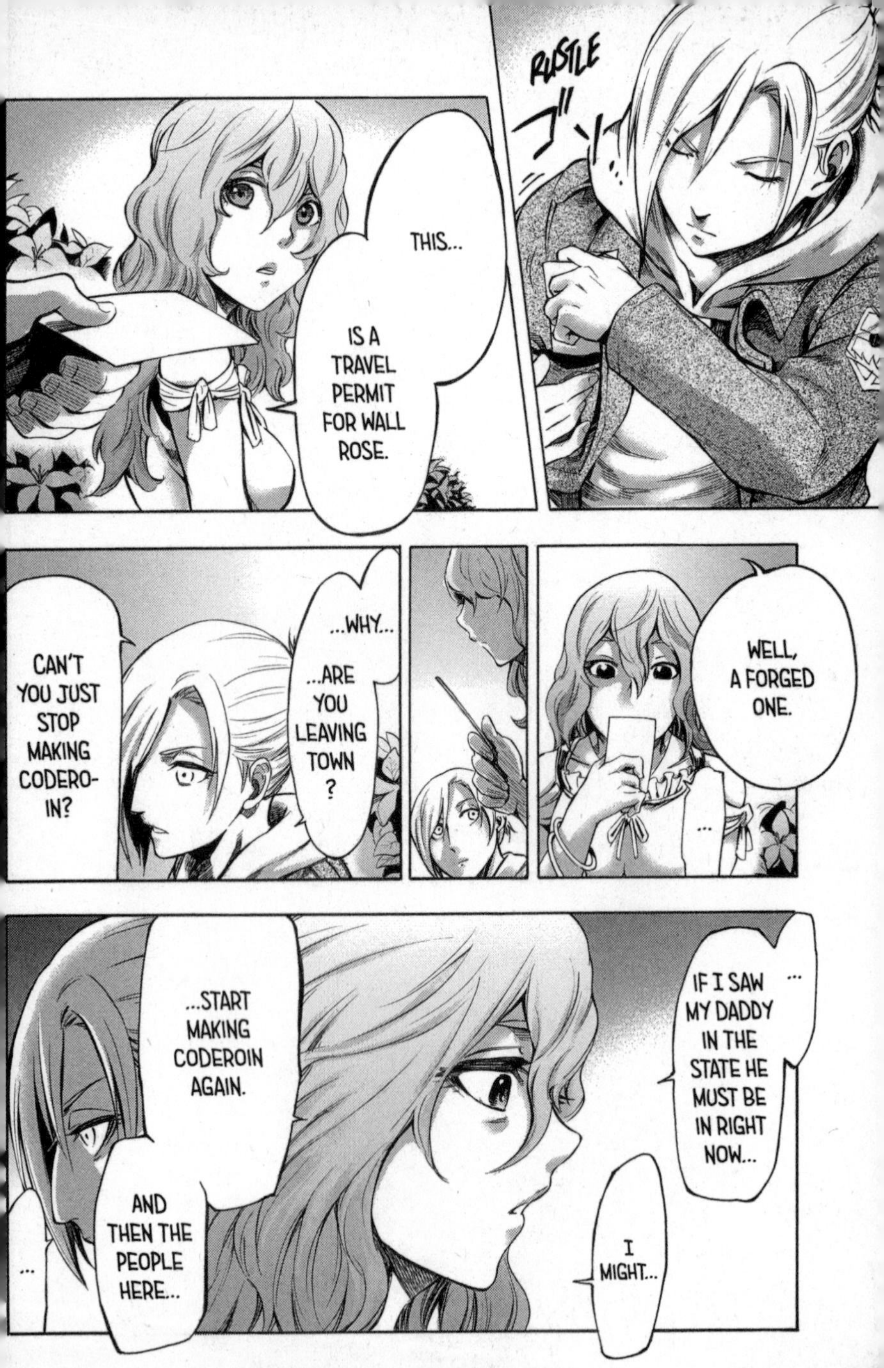
RUSTLE
THIS...
IS A TRAVEL PERMIT FOR WALL ROSE.
WELL, A FORGED ONE.
...
...WHY...
...ARE YOU LEAVING TOWN?
CAN'T YOU JUST STOP MAKING CODERO-IN?
...
IF I SAW MY DADDY IN THE STATE HE MUST BE IN RIGHT NOW...
I MIGHT...
...START MAKING CODEROIN AGAIN.
AND THEN THE PEOPLE HERE...
...

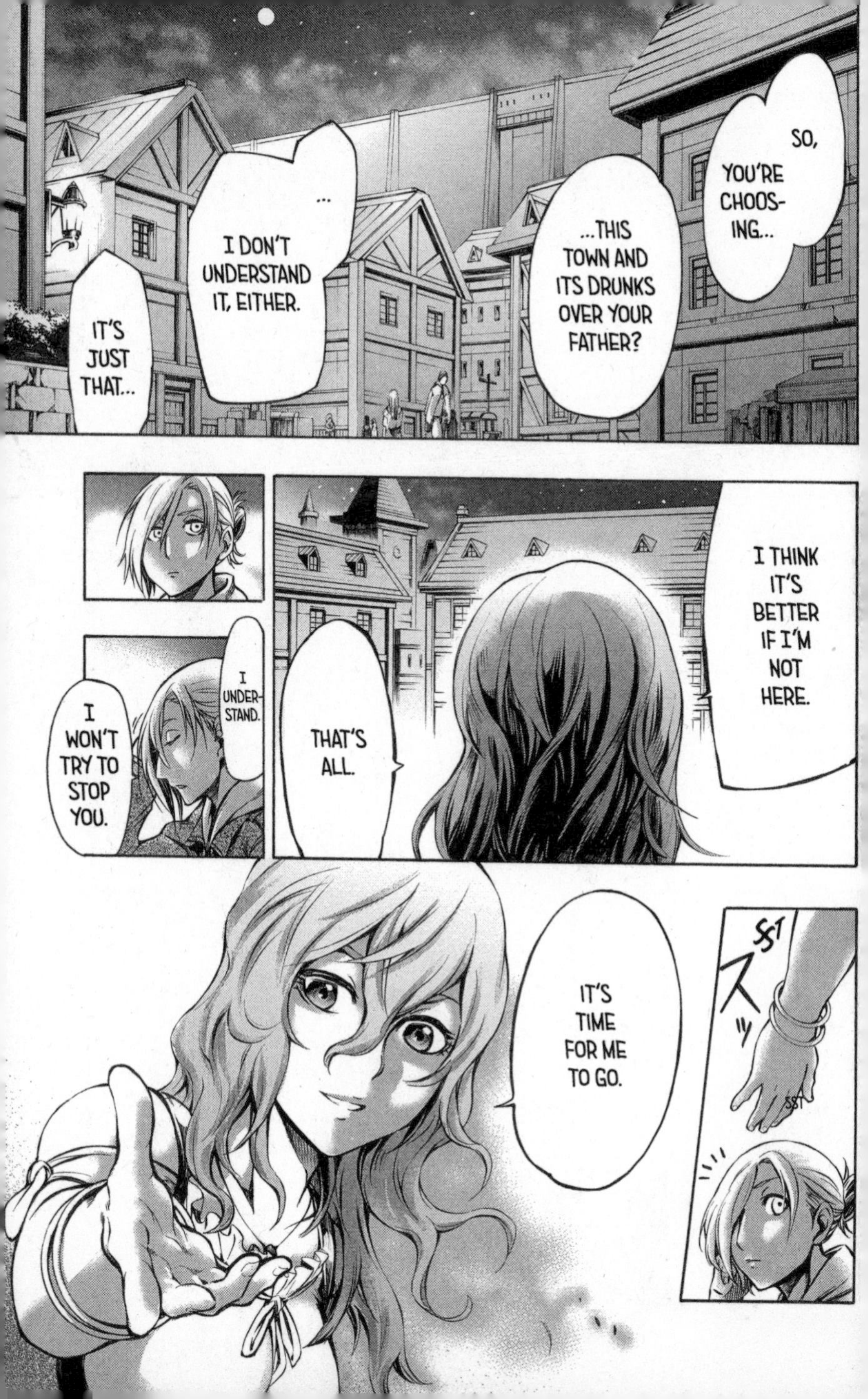
SO, YOU'RE CHOOSING...
...THIS TOWN AND ITS DRUNKS OVER YOUR FATHER?
... I DON'T UNDERSTAND IT, EITHER.
IT'S JUST THAT...
I THINK IT'S BETTER IF I'M NOT HERE.
THAT'S ALL.
I UNDERSTAND.
I WON'T TRY TO STOP YOU.
SST
SST
IT'S TIME FOR ME TO GO.

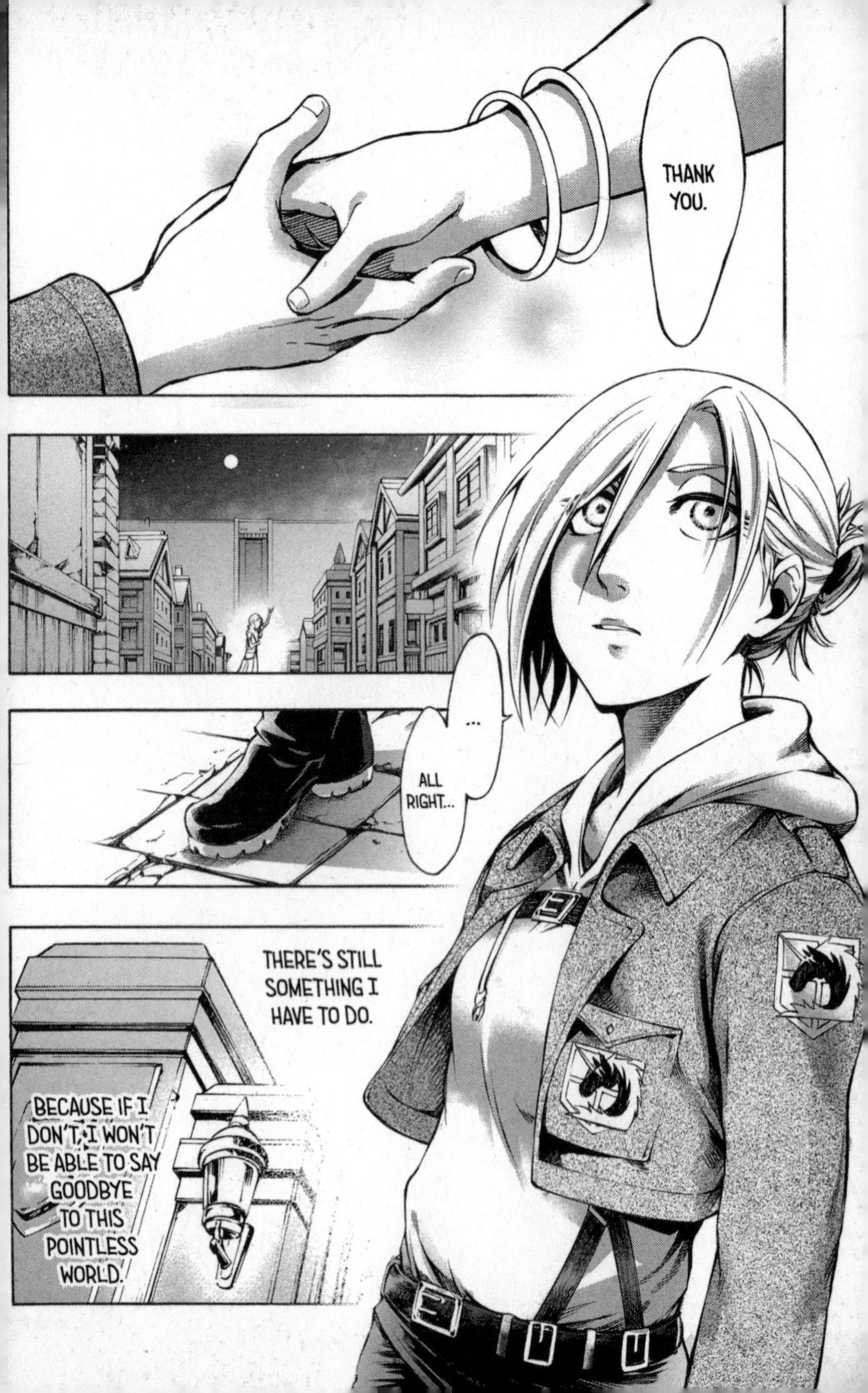
THANK YOU.
...
ALL RIGHT...
THERE'S STILL SOMETHING I HAVE TO DO.
BECAUSE IF I DON'T, I WON'T BE ABLE TO SAY GOODBYE TO THIS POINTLESS WORLD.

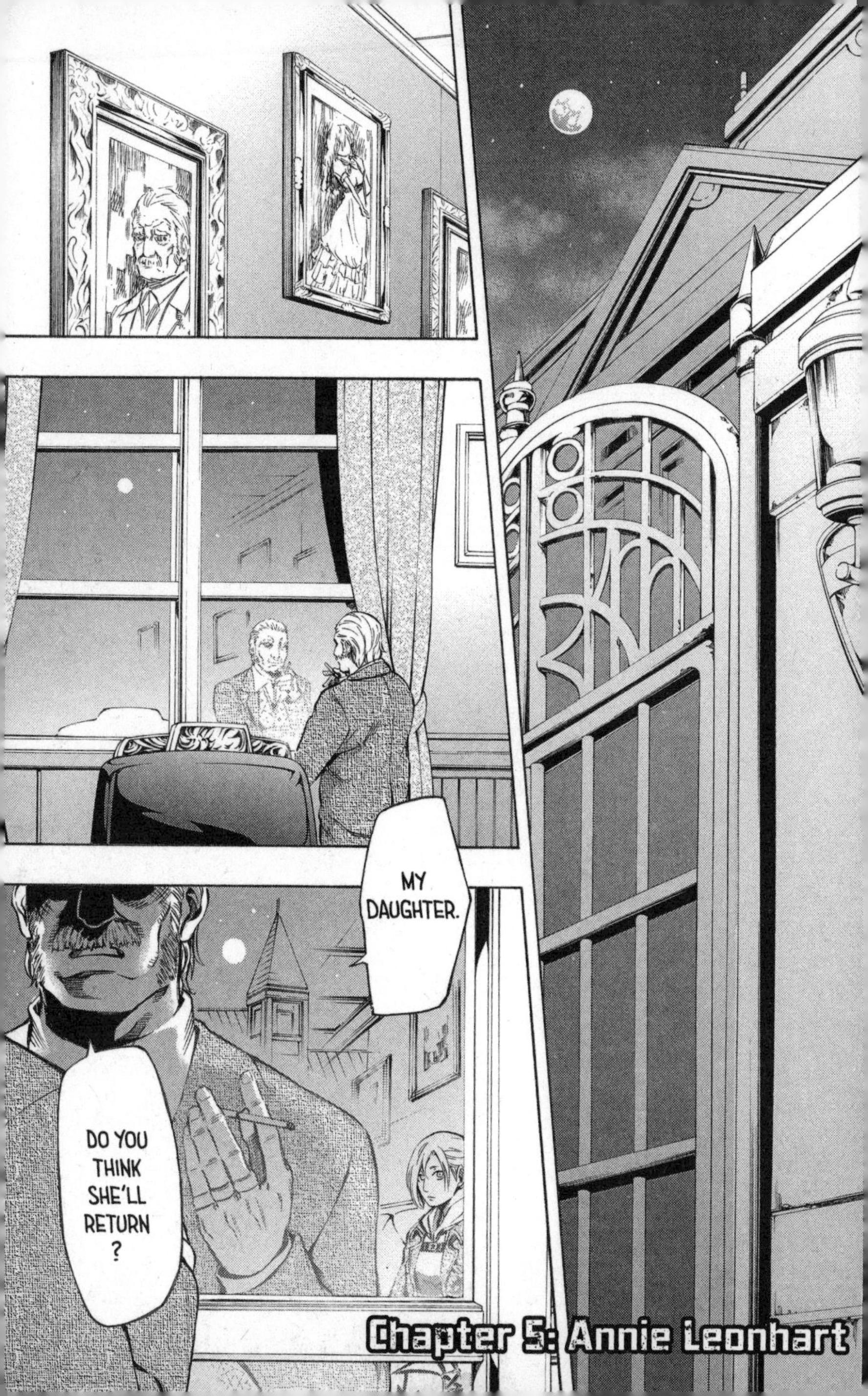
MY DAUGHTER.
DO YOU THINK SHE'LL RETURN?
Chapter 5: Annie Leonhart

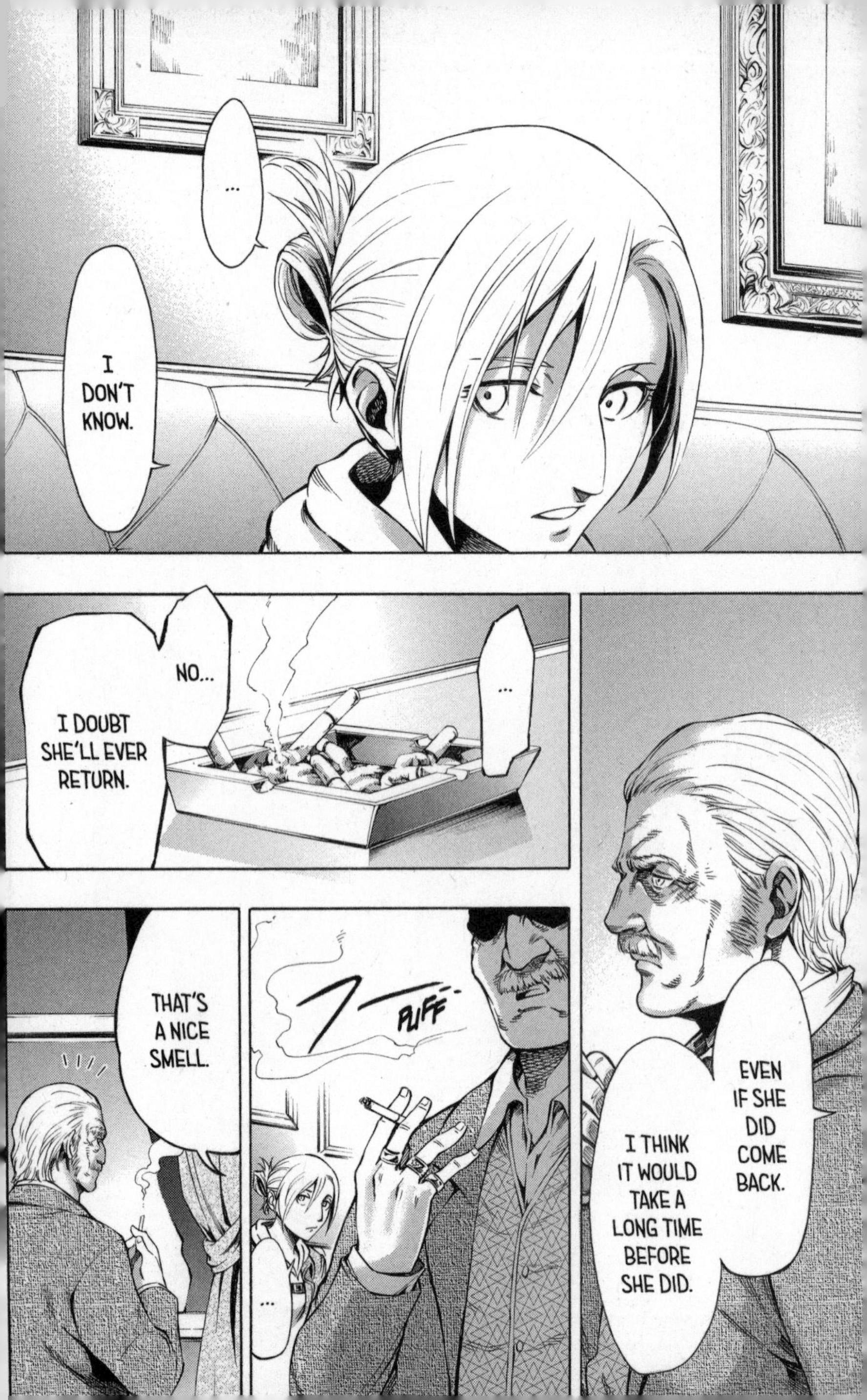
...
I DON'T KNOW.
EVEN IF SHE DID COME BACK.
I THINK IT WOULD TAKE A LONG TIME BEFORE SHE DID.
...
NO...
I DOUBT SHE'LL EVER RETURN.
PUFF
...
THAT'S A NICE SMELL.

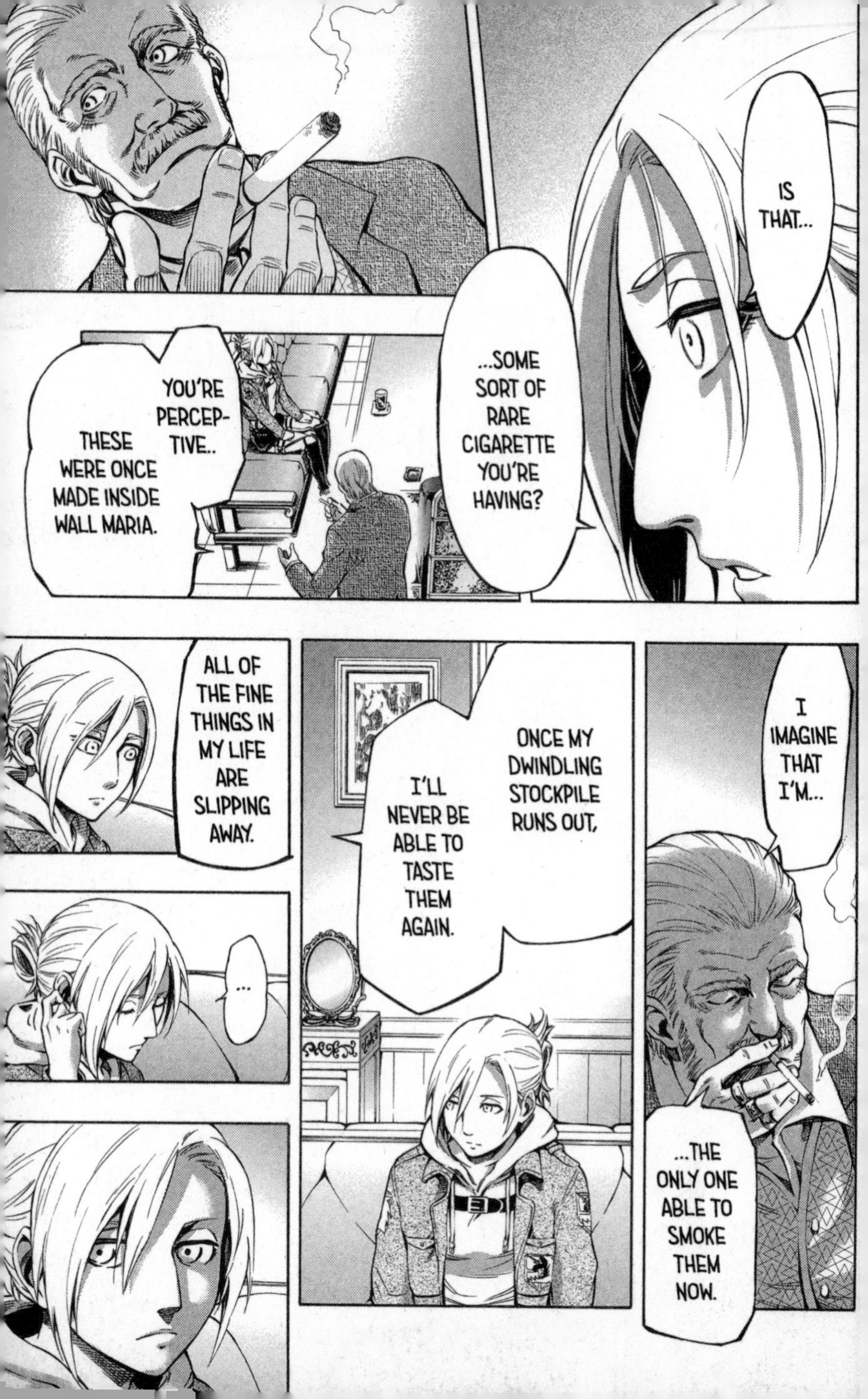
IS THAT...
...SOME SORT OF RARE CIGARETTE YOU'RE HAVING?
YOU'RE PERCEPTIVE..
THESE WERE ONCE MADE INSIDE WALL MARIA.
I IMAGINE THAT I'M...
...THE ONLY ONE ABLE TO SMOKE THEM NOW.
ONCE MY DWINDLING STOCKPILE RUNS OUT,
I'LL NEVER BE ABLE TO TASTE THEM AGAIN.
ALL OF THE FINE THINGS IN MY LIFE ARE SLIPPING AWAY.
...

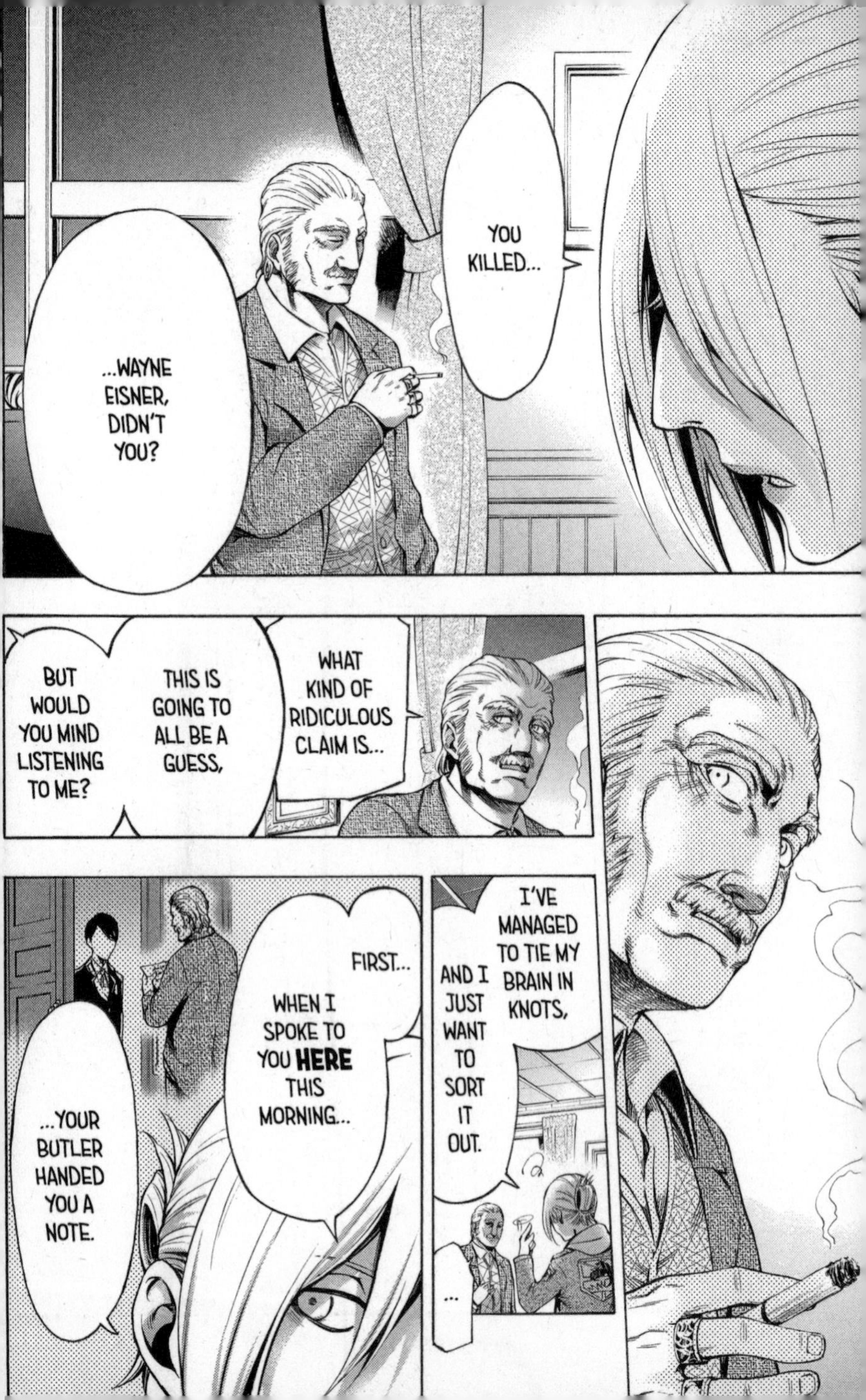

YOU KILLED...
...WAYNE EISNER, DIDN'T YOU?
WHAT KIND OF RIDICULOUS CLAIM IS...
THIS IS GOING TO ALL BE A GUESS,
BUT WOULD YOU MIND LISTENING TO ME?
I'VE MANAGED TO TIE MY BRAIN IN KNOTS,
AND I JUST WANT TO SORT IT OUT.
...
FIRST...
WHEN I SPOKE TO YOU **HERE** THIS MORNING...
...YOUR BUTLER HANDED YOU A NOTE.

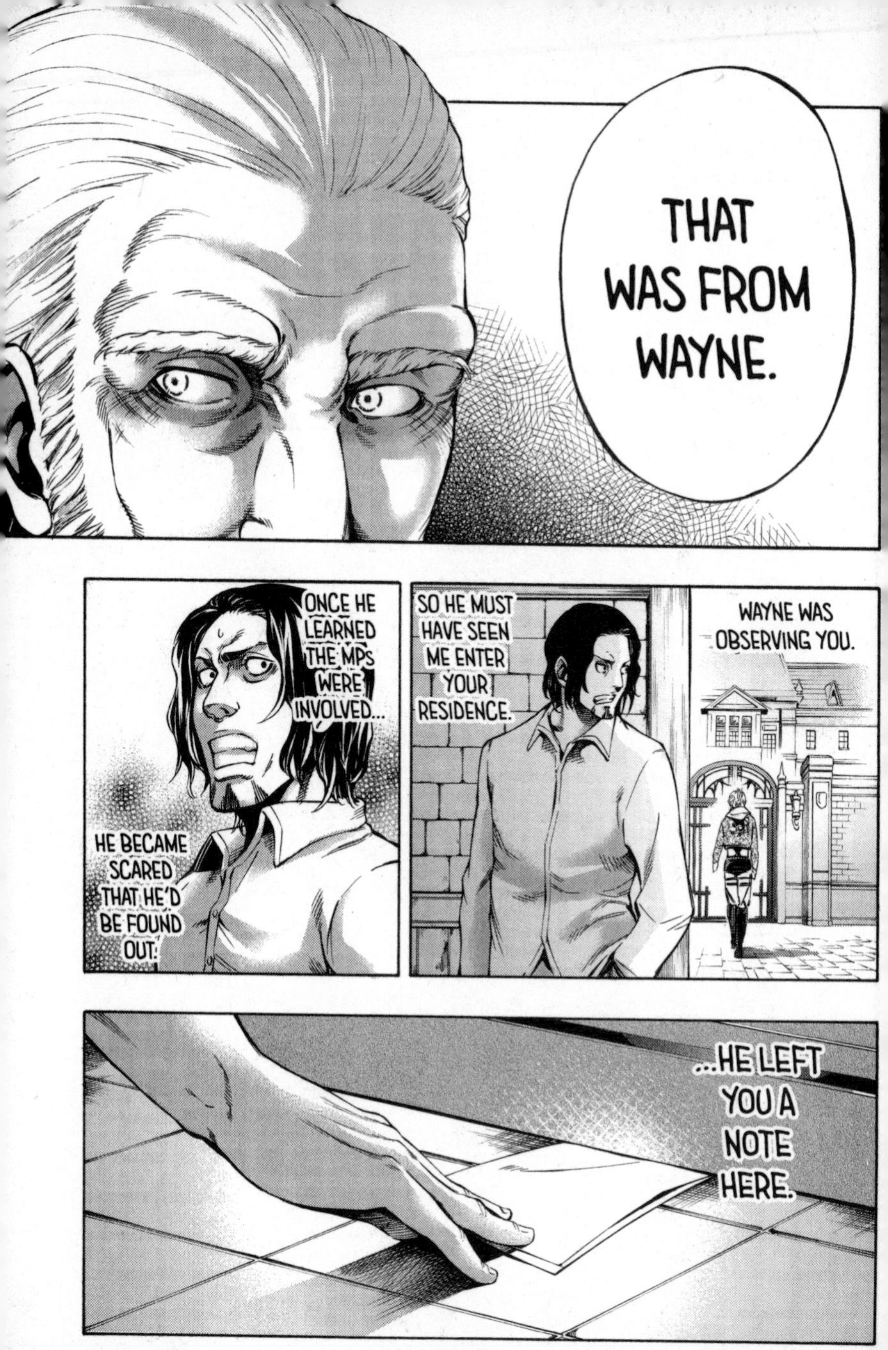
THAT WAS FROM WAYNE.
WAYNE WAS OBSERVING YOU.
SO HE MUST HAVE SEEN ME ENTER YOUR RESIDENCE.
ONCE HE LEARNED THE MPs WERE INVOLVED...
HE BECAME SCARED THAT HE'D BE FOUND OUT.
...HE LEFT YOU A NOTE HERE.

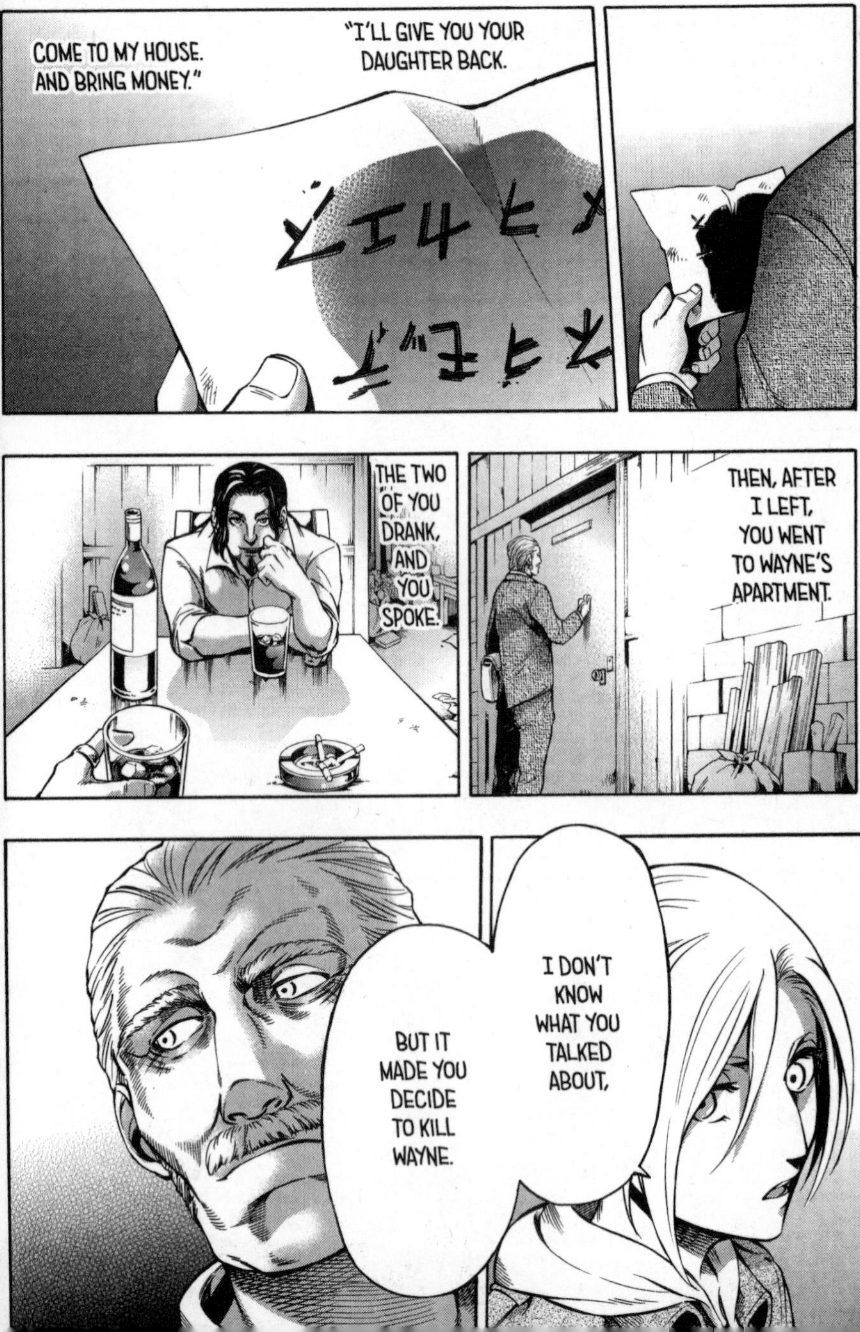
"I'LL GIVE YOU YOUR DAUGHTER BACK.
COME TO MY HOUSE. AND BRING MONEY."
THEN, AFTER I LEFT, YOU WENT TO WAYNE'S APARTMENT.
THE TWO OF YOU DRANK, AND YOU SPOKE.
I DON'T KNOW WHAT YOU TALKED ABOUT,
BUT IT MADE YOU DECIDE TO KILL WAYNE.

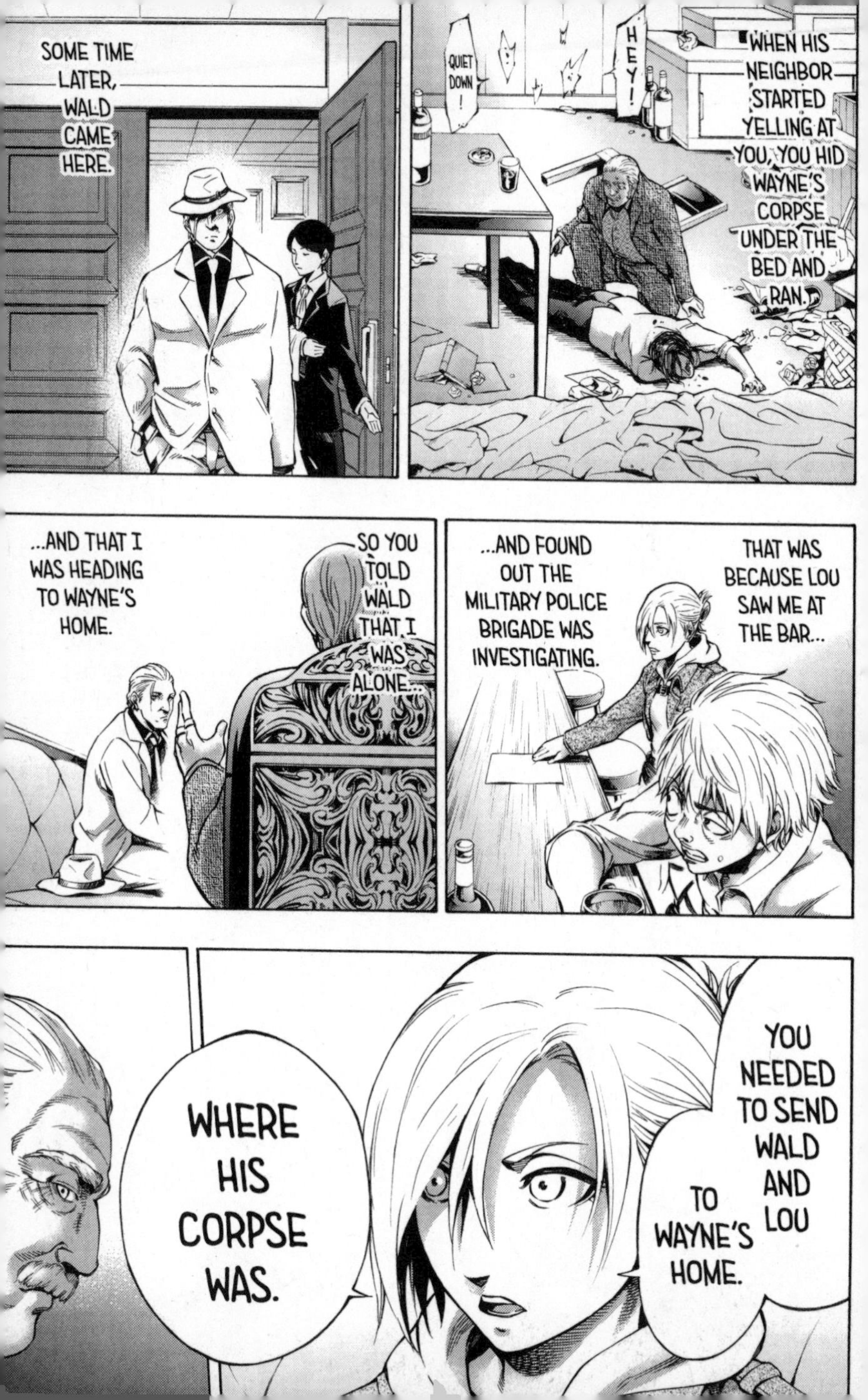
WHEN HIS NEIGHBOR STARTED YELLING AT YOU, YOU HID WAYNE'S CORPSE UNDER THE BED AND RAN.
HEY!
QUIET DOWN!
SOME TIME LATER, WALD CAME HERE.
THAT WAS BECAUSE LOU SAW ME AT THE BAR...
...AND FOUND OUT THE MILITARY POLICE BRIGADE WAS INVESTIGATING.
SO YOU TOLD WALD THAT I WAS ALONE...
...AND THAT I WAS HEADING TO WAYNE'S HOME.
YOU NEEDED TO SEND WALD AND LOU
TO WAYNE'S HOME.
WHERE HIS CORPSE WAS.

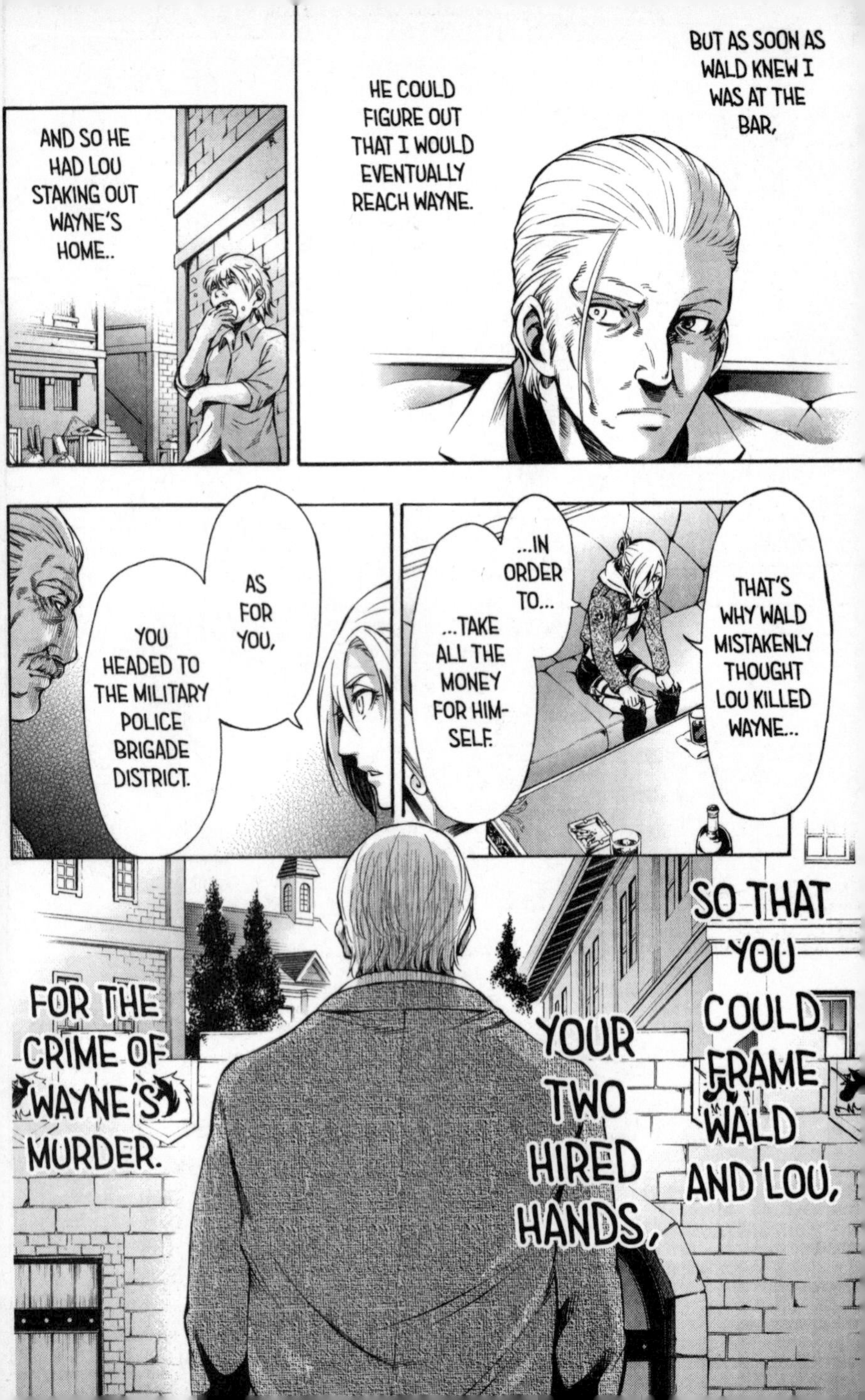
BUT AS SOON AS WALD KNEW I WAS AT THE BAR,
HE COULD FIGURE OUT THAT I WOULD EVENTUALLY REACH WAYNE.
AND SO HE HAD LOU STAKING OUT WAYNE'S HOME..
THAT'S WHY WALD MISTAKENLY THOUGHT LOU KILLED WAYNE...
...IN ORDER TO...
...TAKE ALL THE MONEY FOR HIM-SELF.
AS FOR YOU,
YOU HEADED TO THE MILITARY POLICE BRIGADE DISTRICT.
SO THAT YOU COULD FRAME WALD AND LOU,
YOUR TWO HIRED HANDS,
FOR THE CRIME OF WAYNE'S MURDER.

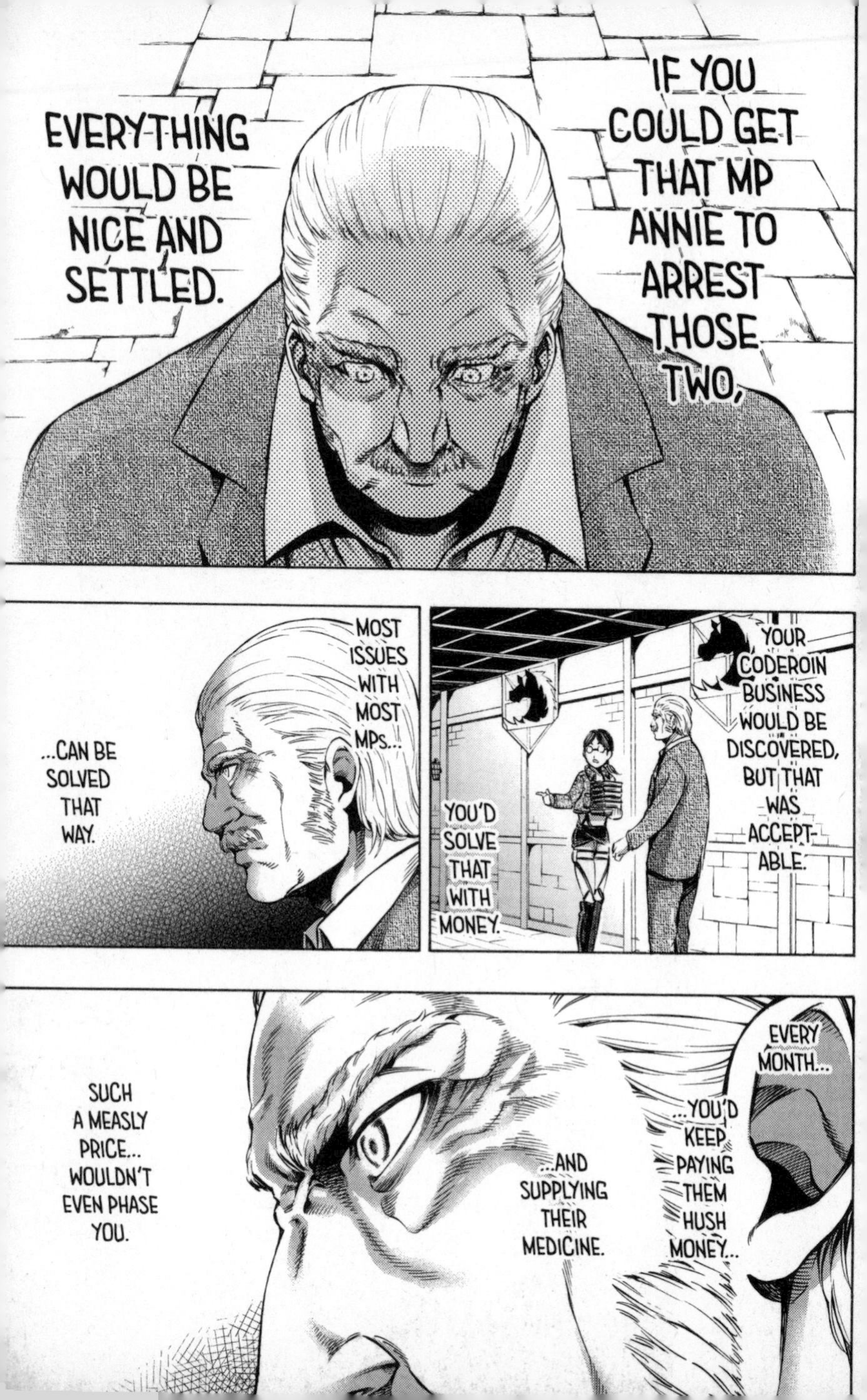
IF YOU COULD GET THAT MP ANNIE TO ARREST THOSE TWO,
EVERYTHING WOULD BE NICE AND SETTLED.
YOUR CODEROIN BUSINESS WOULD BE DISCOVERED, BUT THAT WAS ACCEPT-ABLE.
YOU'D SOLVE THAT WITH MONEY.
MOST ISSUES WITH MOST MPs...
...CAN BE SOLVED THAT WAY.
EVERY MONTH...
...YOU'D KEEP PAYING THEM HUSH MONEY...
...AND SUPPLYING THEIR MEDICINE.
SUCH A MEASLY PRICE... WOULDN'T EVEN PHASE YOU.

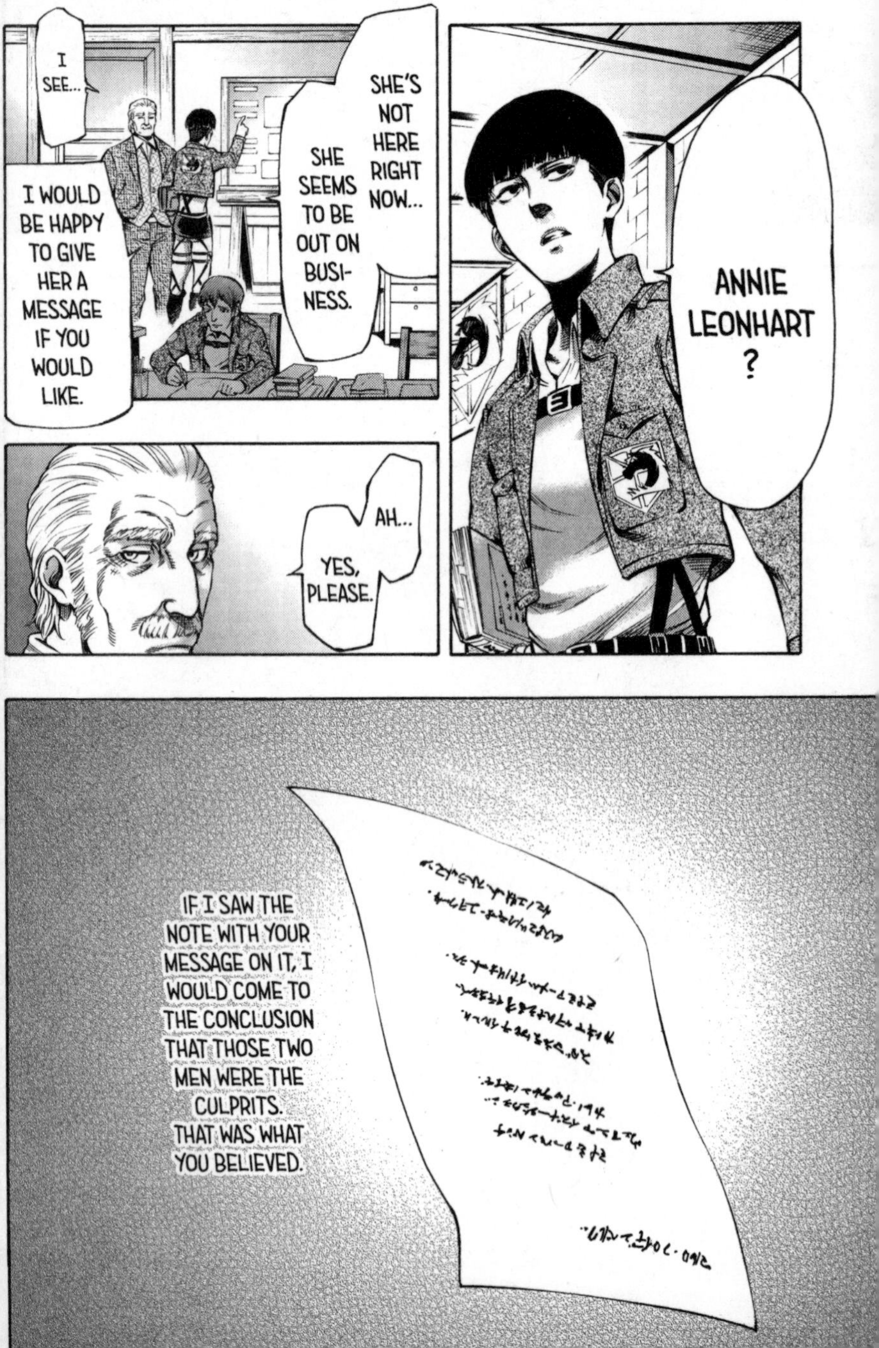
ANNIE LEONHART?
SHE'S NOT HERE RIGHT NOW...
SHE SEEMS TO BE OUT ON BUSINESS.
I SEE...
I WOULD BE HAPPY TO GIVE HER A MESSAGE IF YOU WOULD LIKE.
AH...
YES, PLEASE.
IF I SAW THE NOTE WITH YOUR MESSAGE ON IT, I WOULD COME TO THE CONCLUSION THAT THOSE TWO MEN WERE THE CULPRITS. THAT WAS WHAT YOU BELIEVED.

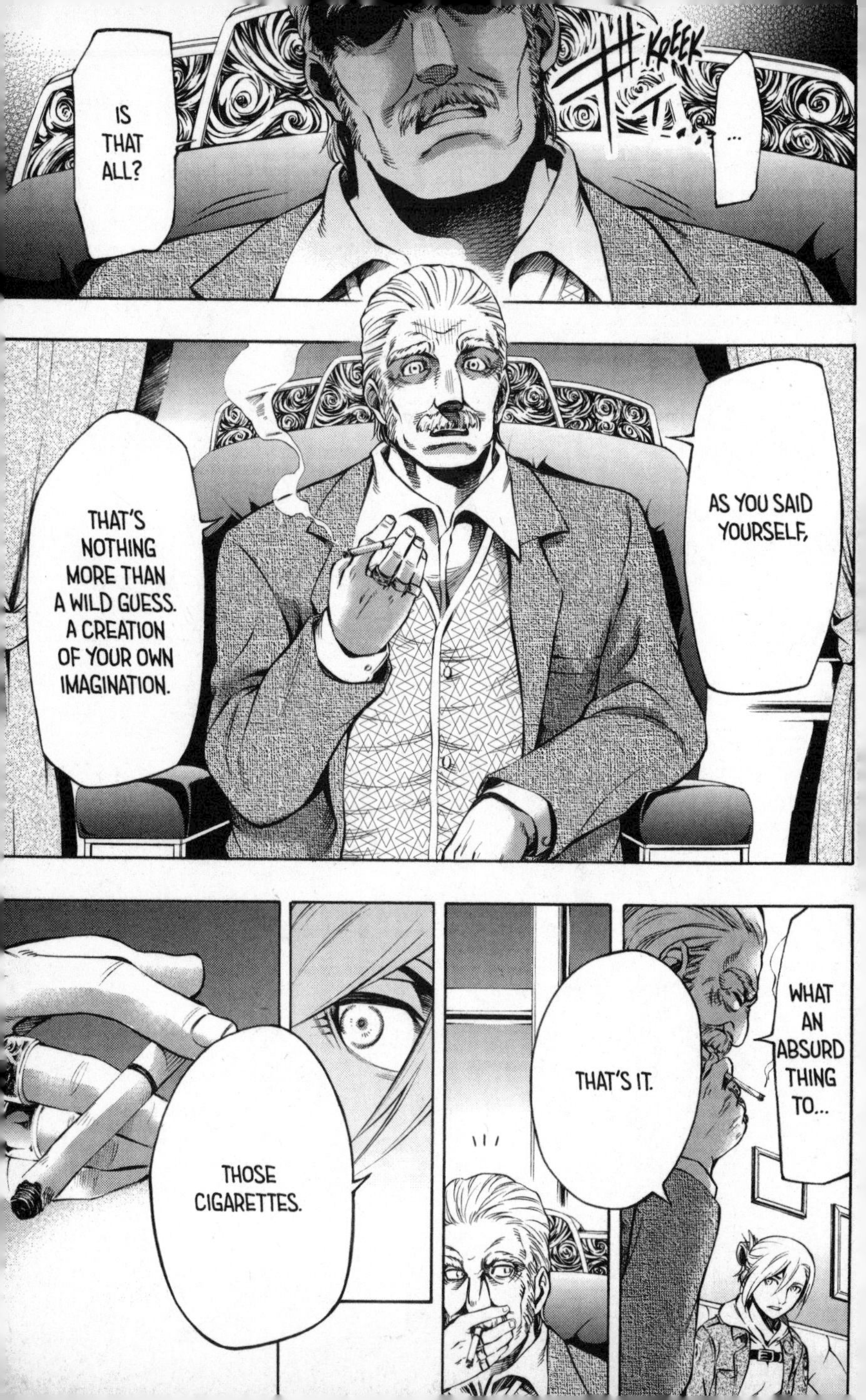
KREEK
...
IS THAT ALL?
AS YOU SAID YOURSELF,
THAT'S NOTHING MORE THAN A WILD GUESS. A CREATION OF YOUR OWN IMAGINATION.
WHAT AN ABSURD THING TO...
THAT'S IT.
THOSE CIGARETTES.

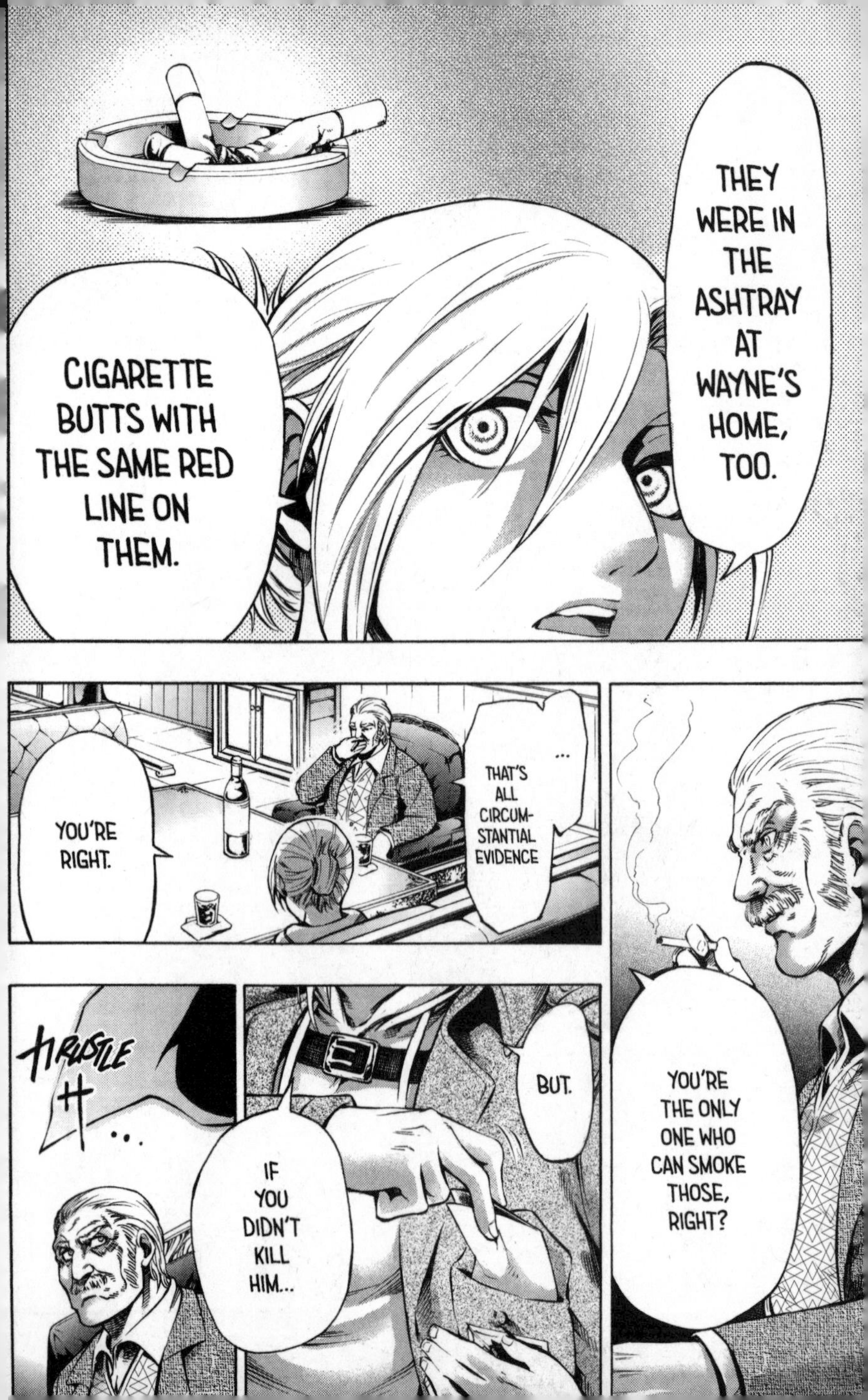
THEY WERE IN THE ASHTRAY AT WAYNE'S HOME, TOO.
CIGARETTE BUTTS WITH THE SAME RED LINE ON THEM.
YOU'RE THE ONLY ONE WHO CAN SMOKE THOSE, RIGHT?
...
THAT'S ALL CIRCUM-STANTIAL EVIDENCE
YOU'RE RIGHT.
BUT.
IF YOU DIDN'T KILL HIM...
RUSTLE
...

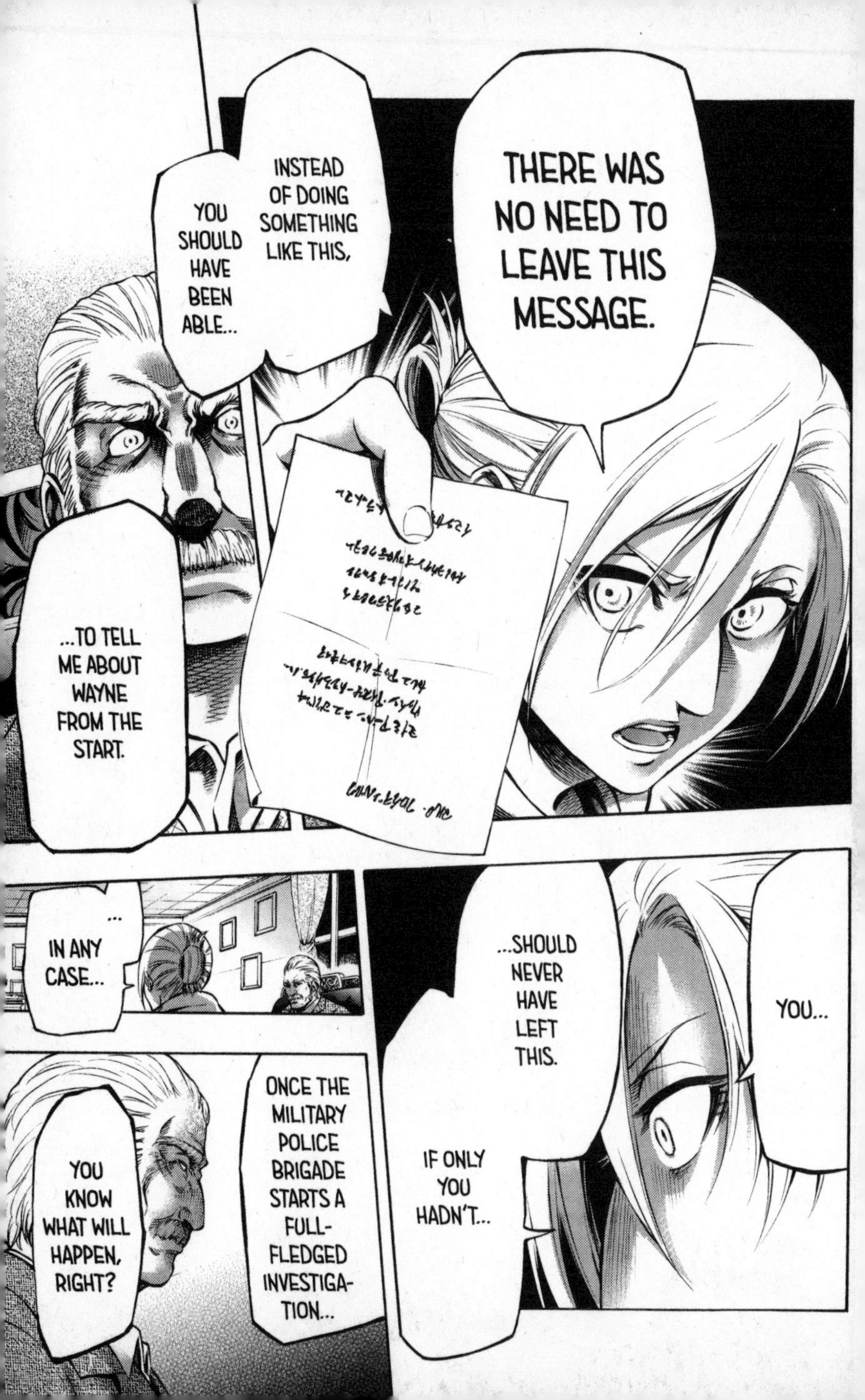
THERE WAS NO NEED TO LEAVE THIS MESSAGE.
INSTEAD OF DOING SOMETHING LIKE THIS,
YOU SHOULD HAVE BEEN ABLE...
...TO TELL ME ABOUT WAYNE FROM THE START.
YOU...
...SHOULD NEVER HAVE LEFT THIS.
IF ONLY YOU HADN'T...
... IN ANY CASE...
ONCE THE MILITARY POLICE BRIGADE STARTS A FULL-FLEDGED INVESTIGATION...
YOU KNOW WHAT WILL HAPPEN, RIGHT?

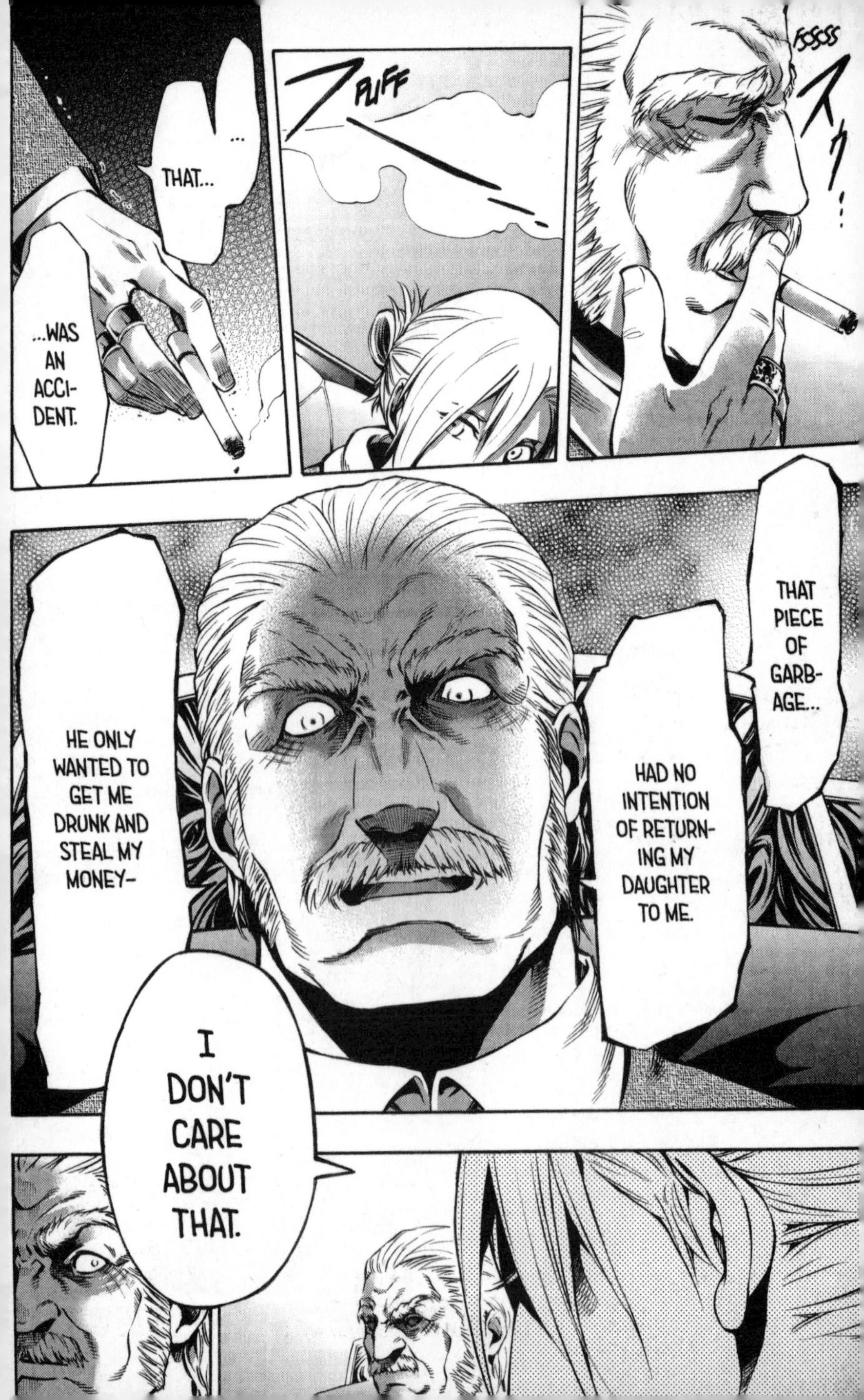
FSSSS
PUFF
...
THAT...
...WAS AN ACCI-DENT.
THAT PIECE OF GARB-AGE...
HAD NO INTENTION OF RETURN-ING MY DAUGHTER TO ME.
HE ONLY WANTED TO GET ME DRUNK AND STEAL MY MONEY-
I DON'T CARE ABOUT THAT.

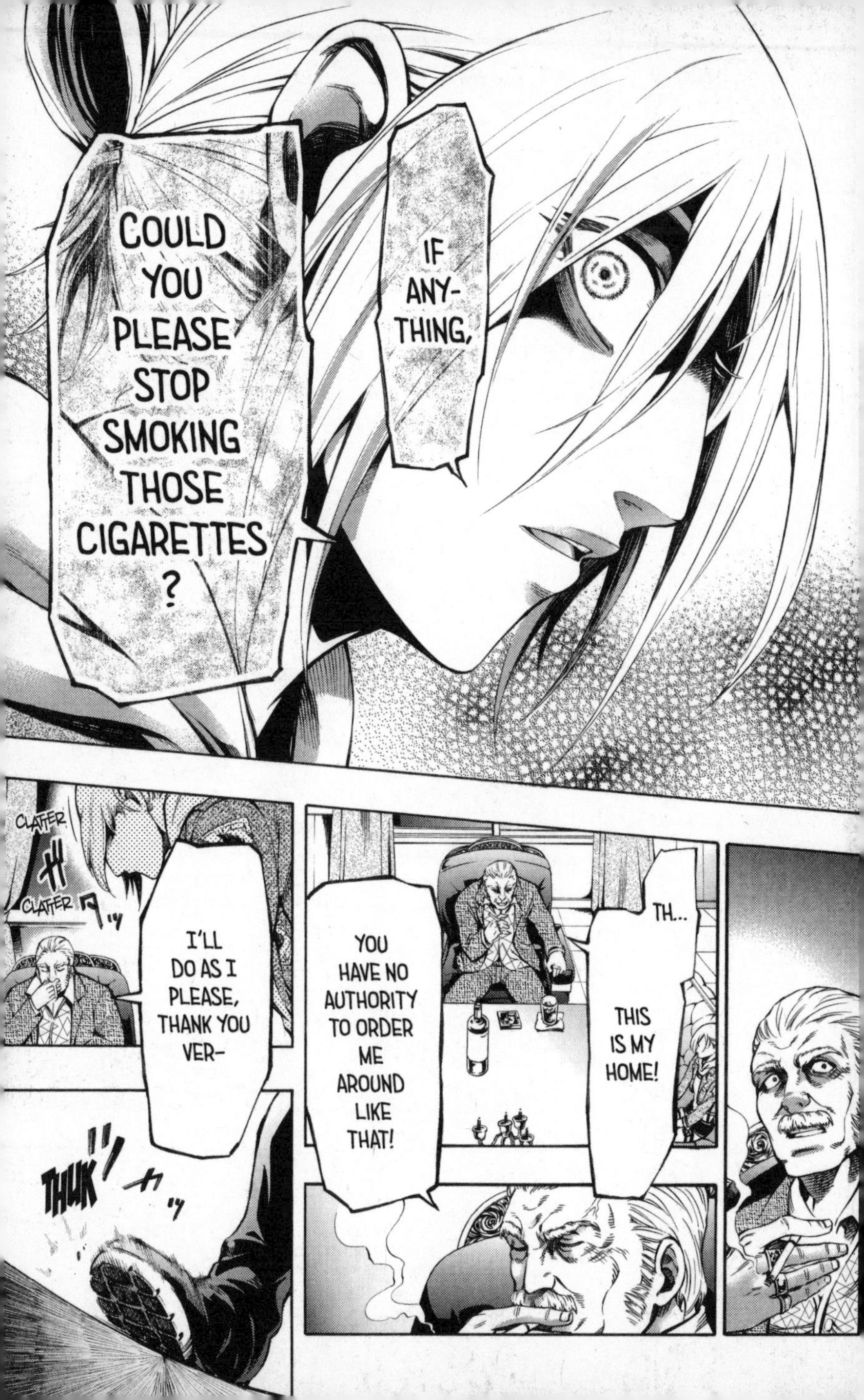
IF ANY-THING,
COULD YOU PLEASE STOP SMOKING THOSE CIGARETTES?
TH...
THIS IS MY HOME!
YOU HAVE NO AUTHORITY TO ORDER ME AROUND LIKE THAT!
CLATTER
CLATTER
I'LL DO AS I PLEASE, THANK YOU VER-
THUK

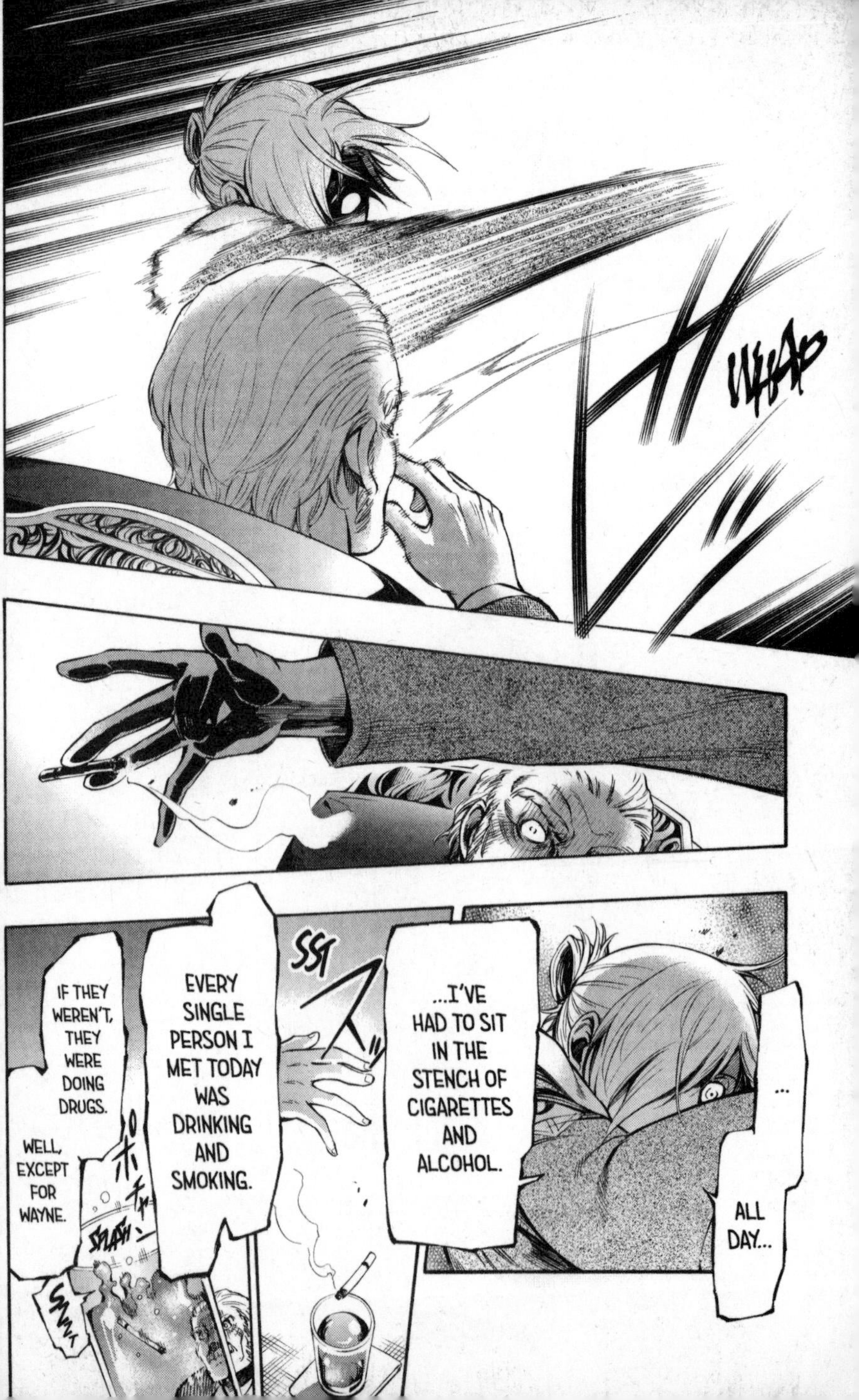
WHAP
...
ALL DAY...
...I'VE HAD TO SIT IN THE STENCH OF CIGARETTES AND ALCOHOL.
SST
EVERY SINGLE PERSON I MET TODAY WAS DRINKING AND SMOKING.
IF THEY WEREN'T, THEY WERE DOING DRUGS.
WELL, EXCEPT FOR WAYNE.
SPLASH

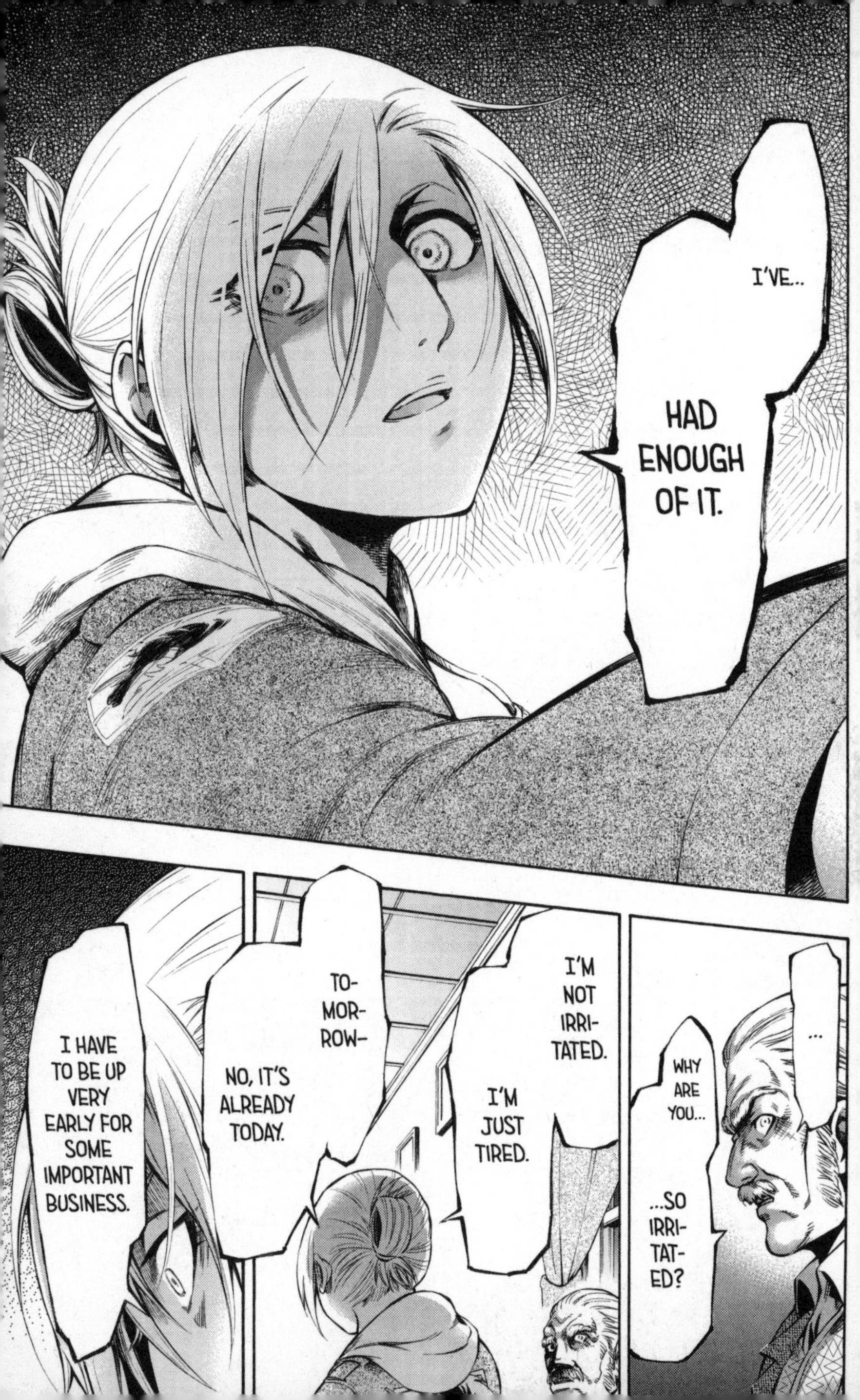
I'VE...
HAD ENOUGH OF IT.
...
WHY ARE YOU... ...SO IRRITATED?
I'M NOT IRRITATED.
I'M JUST TIRED.
TO-MORROW-
NO, IT'S ALREADY TODAY.
I HAVE TO BE UP VERY EARLY FOR SOME IMPORTANT BUSINESS.

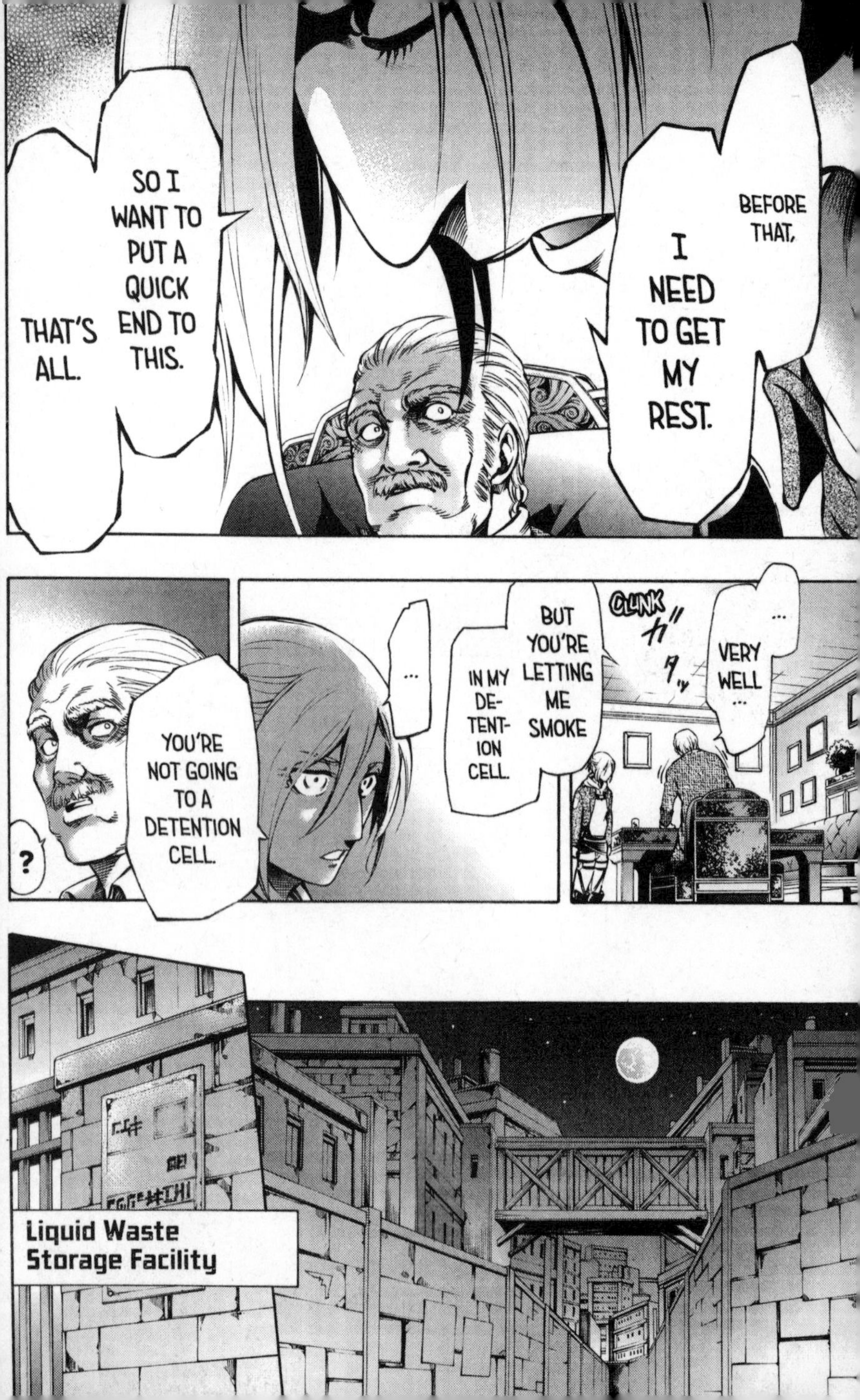
BEFORE THAT,
I NEED TO GET MY REST.
SO I WANT TO PUT A QUICK END TO THIS.
THAT'S ALL.
... VERY WELL ...
CLUNK
ガタッ
BUT YOU'RE LETTING ME SMOKE
IN MY DE-TENT-ION CELL.
...
YOU'RE NOT GOING TO A DETENTION CELL.
?
Liquid Waste Storage Facility

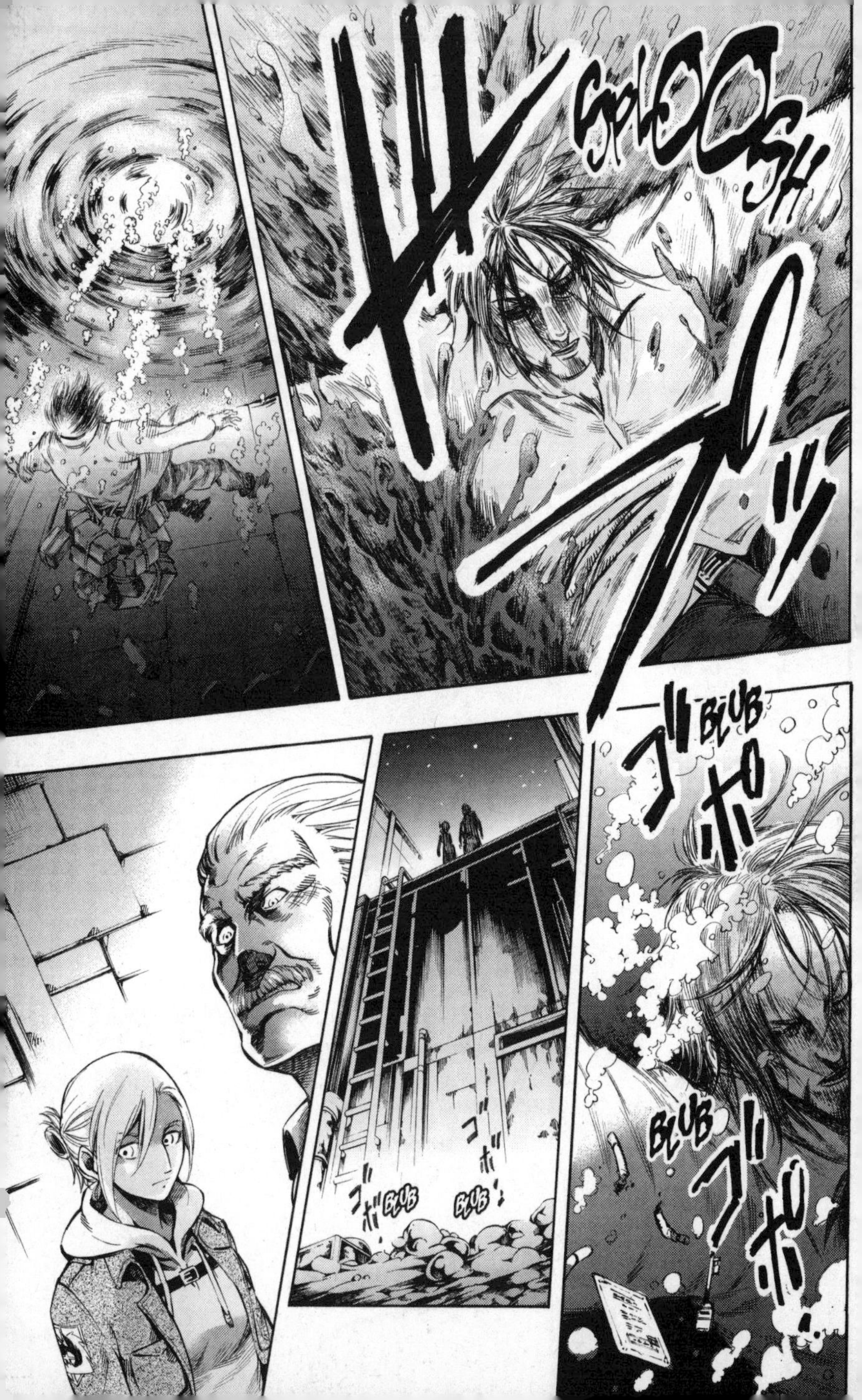
SPLOOSH!
BLUB
BLUB
BLUB
BLUB

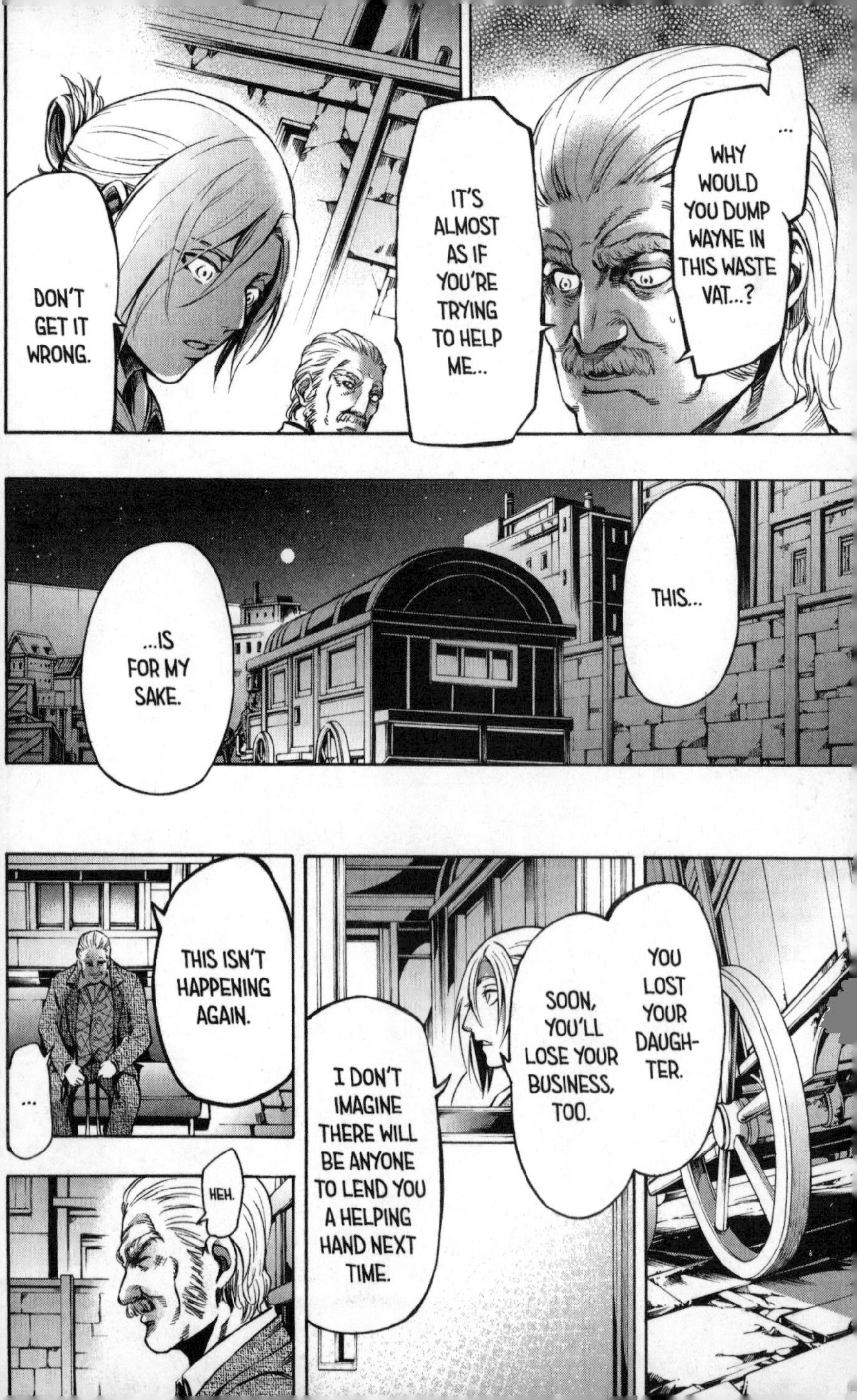
...
WHY WOULD YOU DUMP WAYNE IN THIS WASTE VAT...?
IT'S ALMOST AS IF YOU'RE TRYING TO HELP ME...
DON'T GET IT WRONG.
THIS...
...IS FOR MY SAKE.
YOU LOST YOUR DAUGHTER.
SOON, YOU'LL LOSE YOUR BUSINESS, TOO.
I DON'T IMAGINE THERE WILL BE ANYONE TO LEND YOU A HELPING HAND NEXT TIME.
THIS ISN'T HAPPENING AGAIN.
...
HEH.

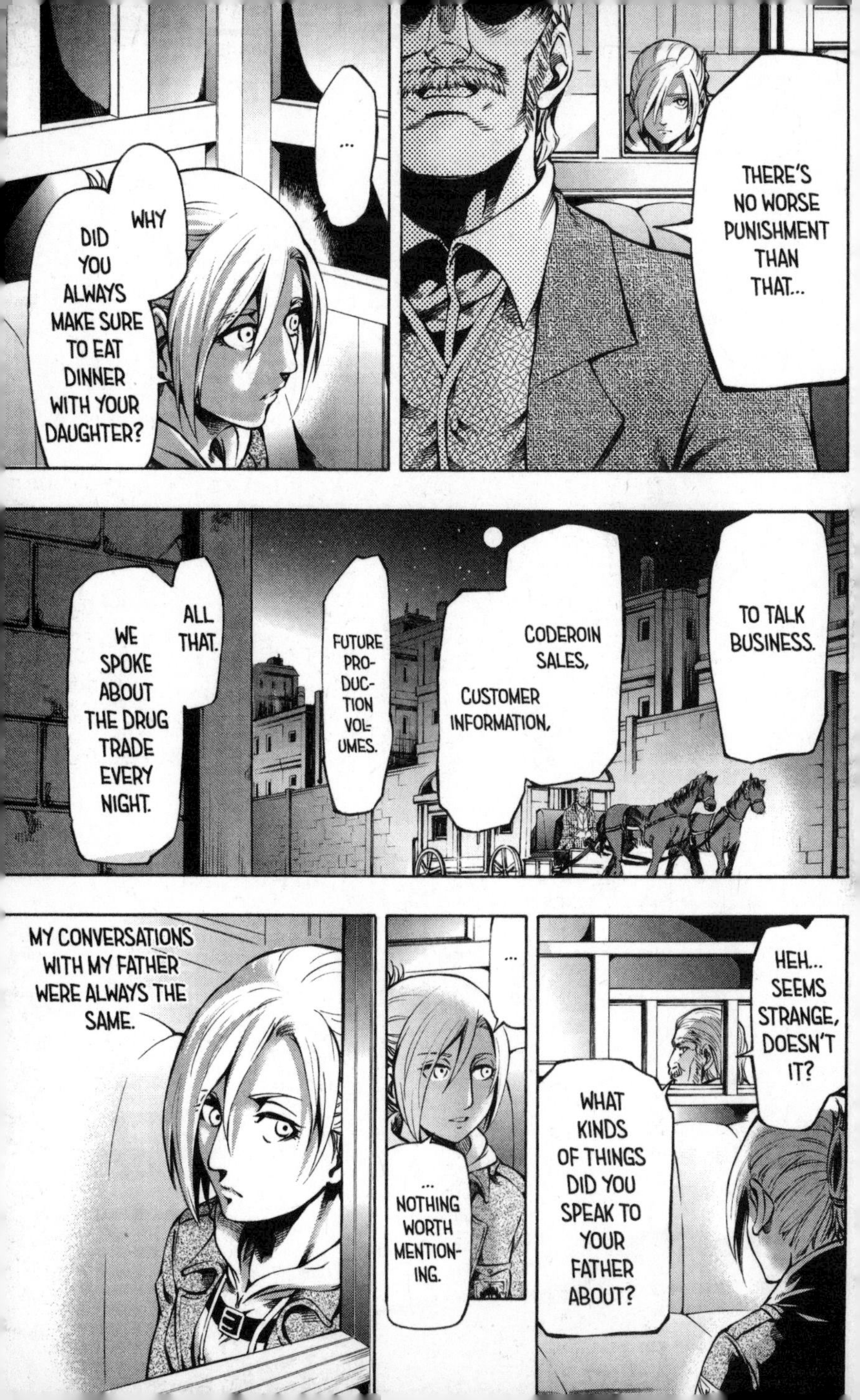

THERE'S NO WORSE PUNISHMENT THAN THAT...
...
WHY DID YOU ALWAYS MAKE SURE TO EAT DINNER WITH YOUR DAUGHTER?
TO TALK BUSINESS.
CODEROIN SALES, CUSTOMER INFORMATION,
FUTURE PRODUCTION VOLUMES.
ALL THAT. WE SPOKE ABOUT THE DRUG TRADE EVERY NIGHT.
HEH... SEEMS STRANGE, DOESN'T IT?
WHAT KINDS OF THINGS DID YOU SPEAK TO YOUR FATHER ABOUT?
...
... NOTHING WORTH MENTIONING.
MY CONVERSATIONS WITH MY FATHER WERE ALWAYS THE SAME.

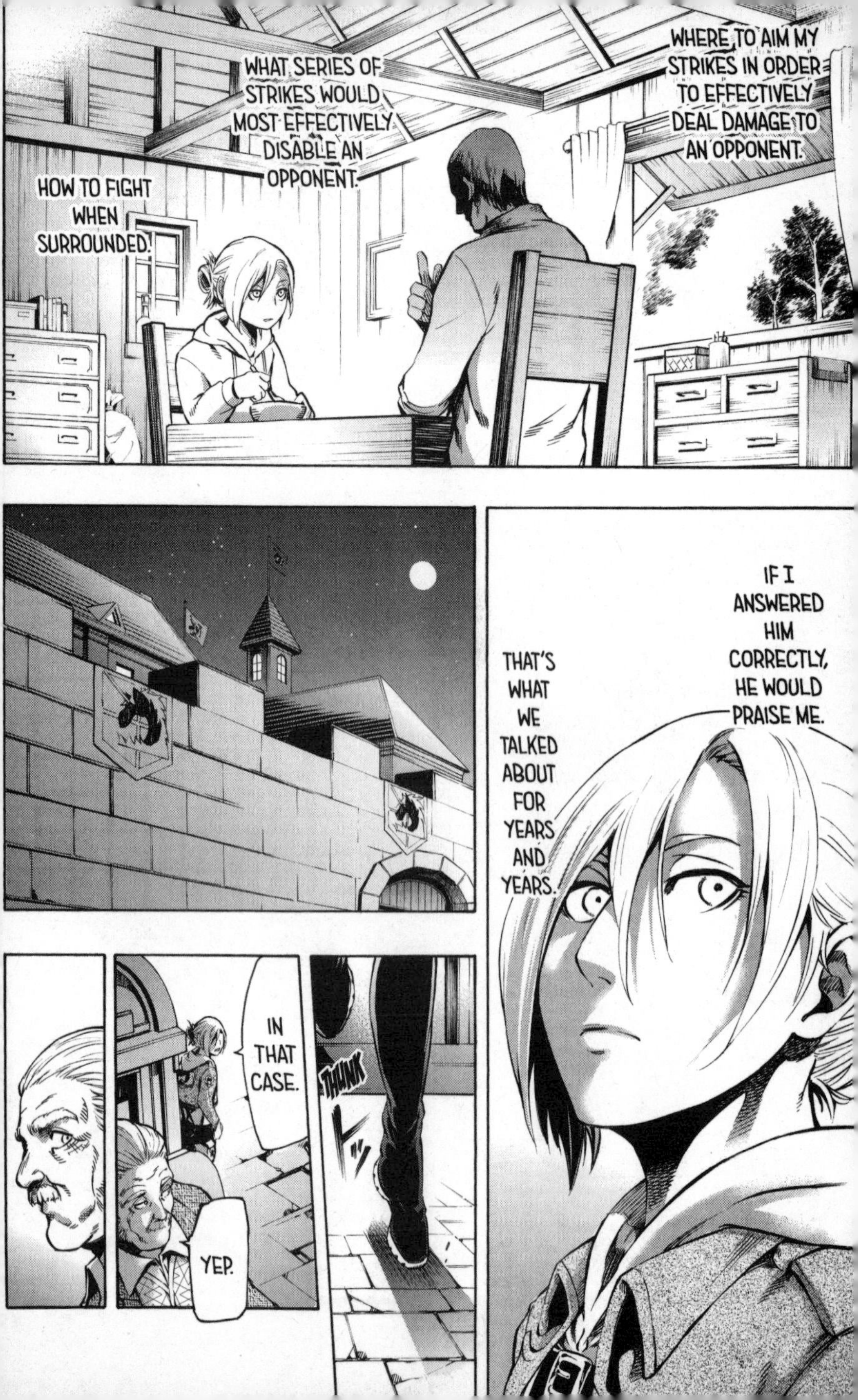
WHERE TO AIM MY STRIKES IN ORDER TO EFFECTIVELY DEAL DAMAGE TO AN OPPONENT.
WHAT SERIES OF STRIKES WOULD MOST EFFECTIVELY DISABLE AN OPPONENT.
HOW TO FIGHT WHEN SURROUNDED.
IF I ANSWERED HIM CORRECTLY, HE WOULD PRAISE ME.
THAT'S WHAT WE TALKED ABOUT FOR YEARS AND YEARS.
THUNK
IN THAT CASE.
YEP.

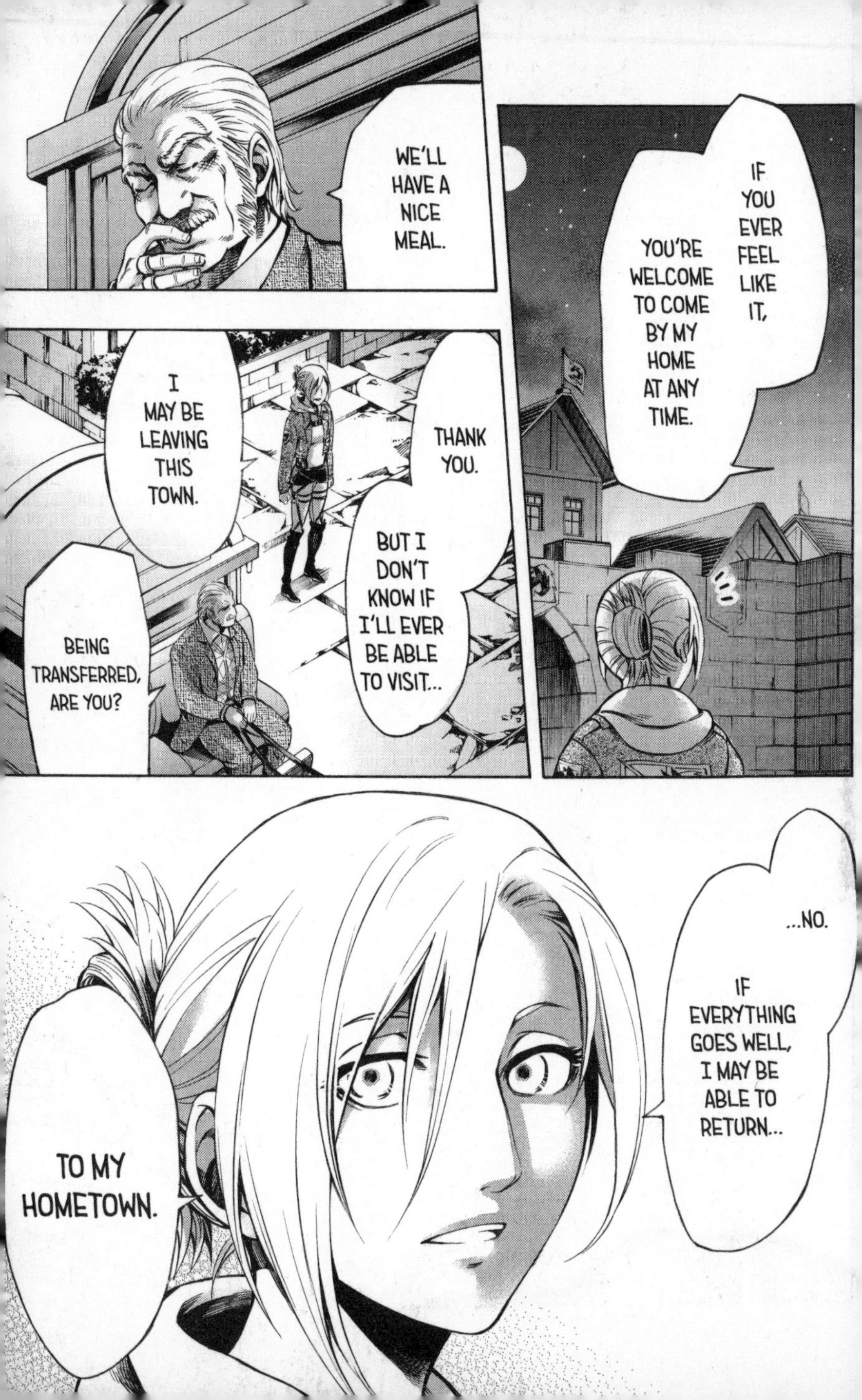

WE'LL HAVE A NICE MEAL.
IF YOU EVER FEEL LIKE IT,
YOU'RE WELCOME TO COME BY MY HOME AT ANY TIME.
THANK YOU.
BUT I DON'T KNOW IF I'LL EVER BE ABLE TO VISIT...
I MAY BE LEAVING THIS TOWN.
BEING TRANSFERRED, ARE YOU?
...NO.
IF EVERYTHING GOES WELL, I MAY BE ABLE TO RETURN...
TO MY HOMETOWN.

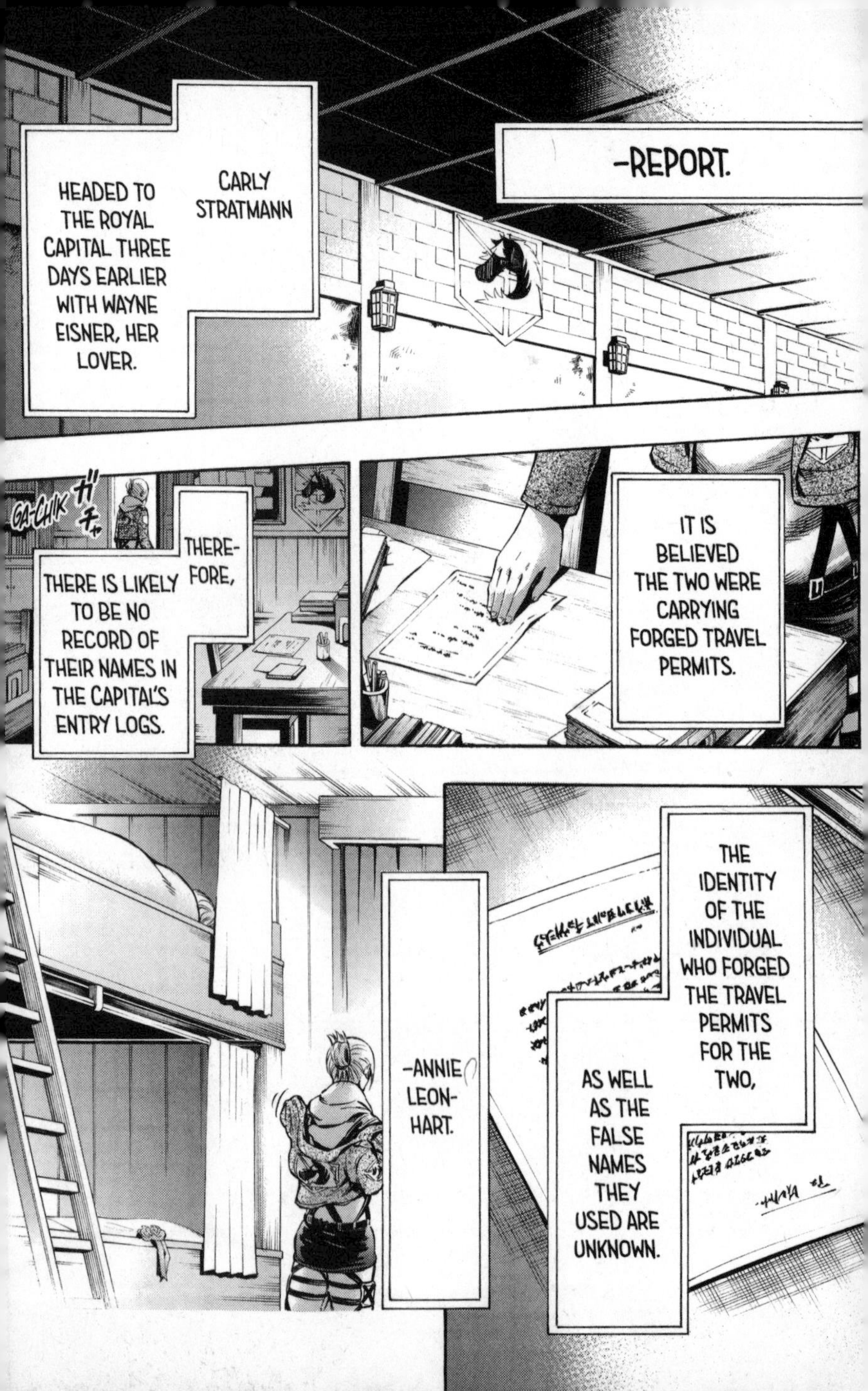

-REPORT.
CARLY STRATMANN
HEADED TO THE ROYAL CAPITAL THREE DAYS EARLIER WITH WAYNE EISNER, HER LOVER.
IT IS BELIEVED THE TWO WERE CARRYING FORGED TRAVEL PERMITS.
GA-CHIK ガチャ
THERE-FORE,
THERE IS LIKELY TO BE NO RECORD OF THEIR NAMES IN THE CAPITAL'S ENTRY LOGS.
THE IDENTITY OF THE INDIVIDUAL WHO FORGED THE TRAVEL PERMITS FOR THE TWO,
AS WELL AS THE FALSE NAMES THEY USED ARE UNKNOWN.
-ANNIE LEON-HART.

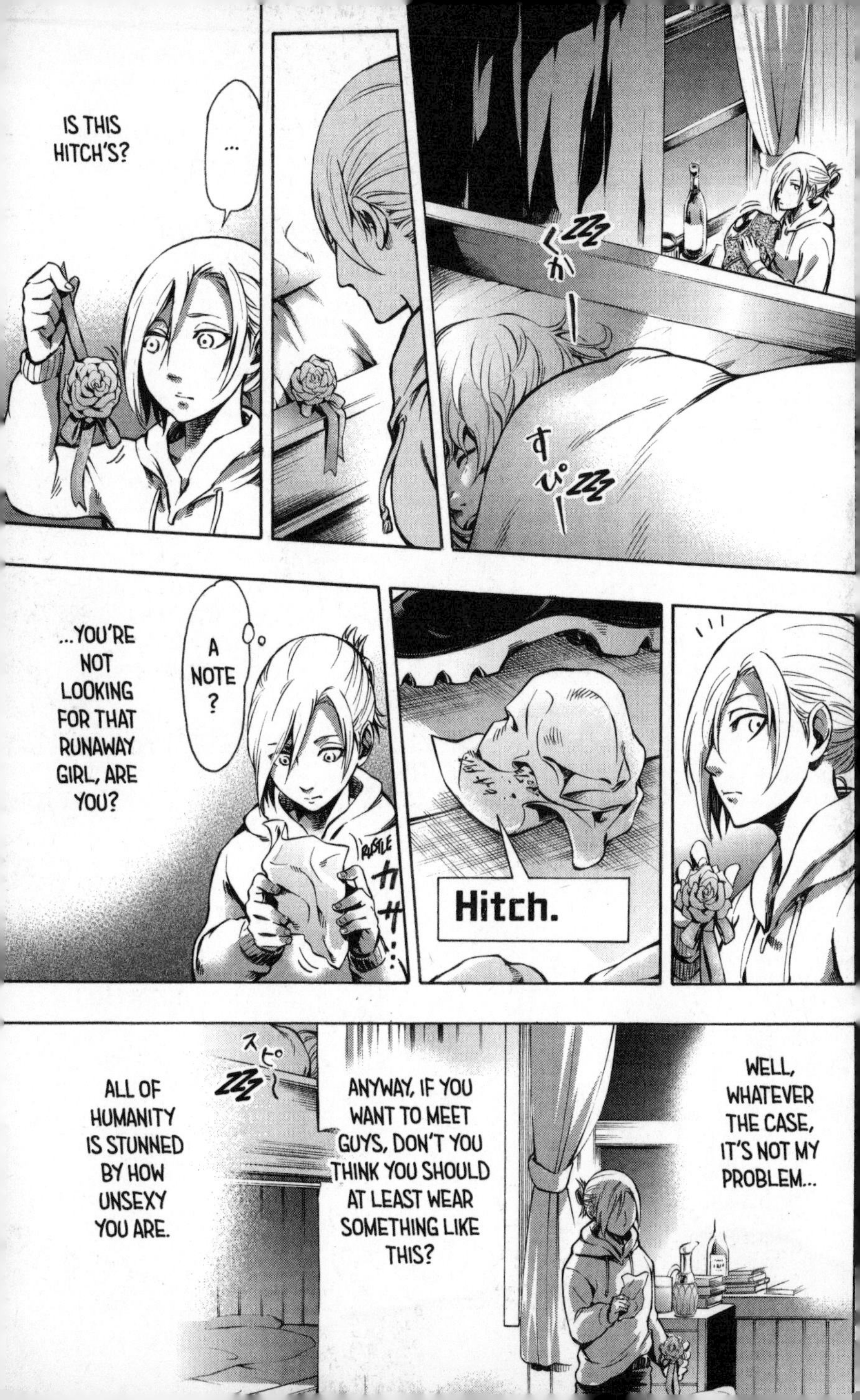ZZZ
くかー
すぴー
ZZZ
...
IS THIS HITCH'S?
Hitch.
A NOTE?
...YOU'RE NOT LOOKING FOR THAT RUNAWAY GIRL, ARE YOU?
RUSTLE
カサ
WELL, WHATEVER THE CASE, IT'S NOT MY PROBLEM...
ANYWAY, IF YOU WANT TO MEET GUYS, DON'T YOU THINK YOU SHOULD AT LEAST WEAR SOMETHING LIKE THIS?
スピー
ZZZ
ALL OF HUMANITY IS STUNNED BY HOW UNSEXY YOU ARE.

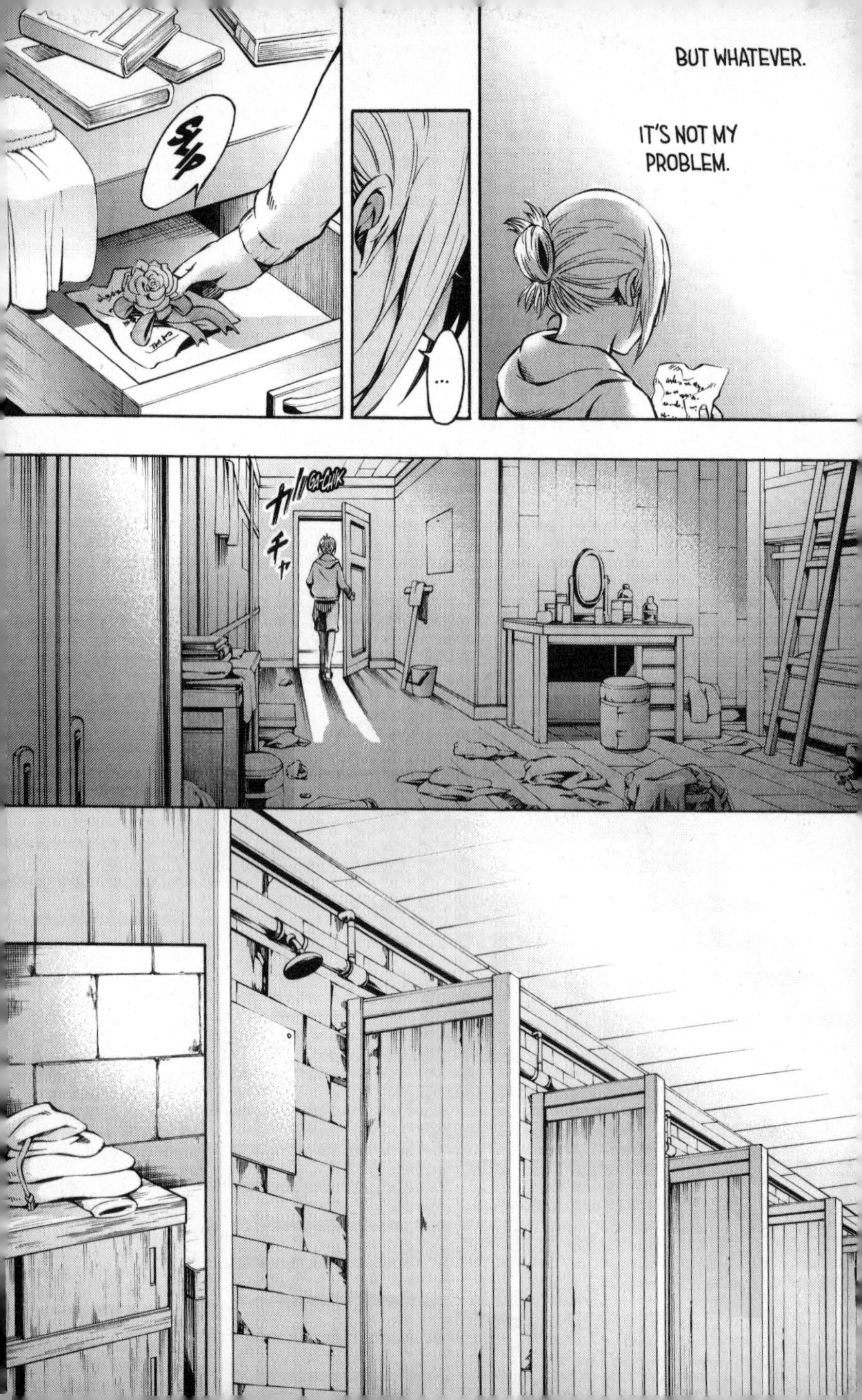
BUT WHATEVER.
IT'S NOT MY PROBLEM.
...
SLIP
GA-CHIK
カチャ

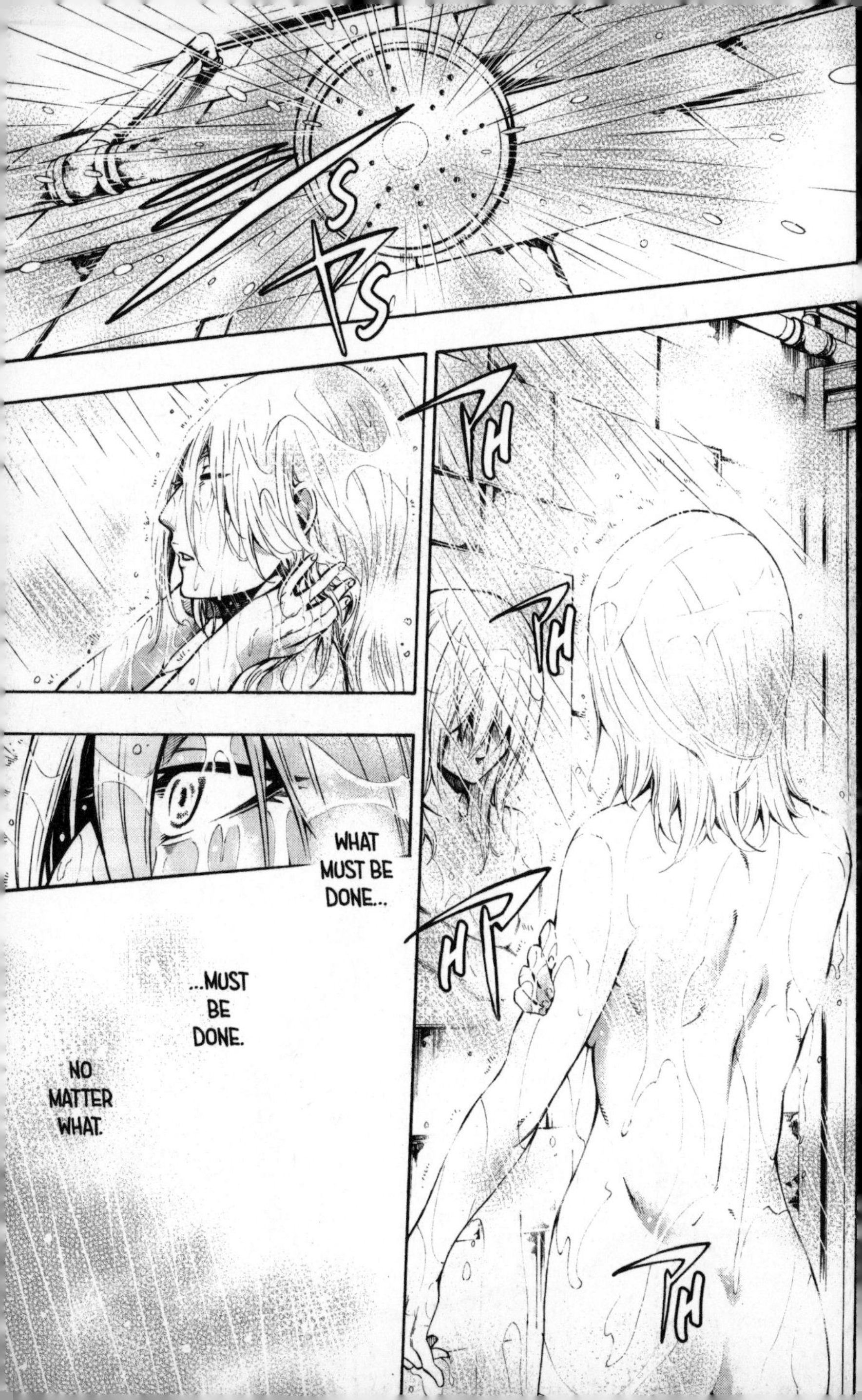
WHAT MUST BE DONE...
...MUST BE DONE.
NO MATTER WHAT.

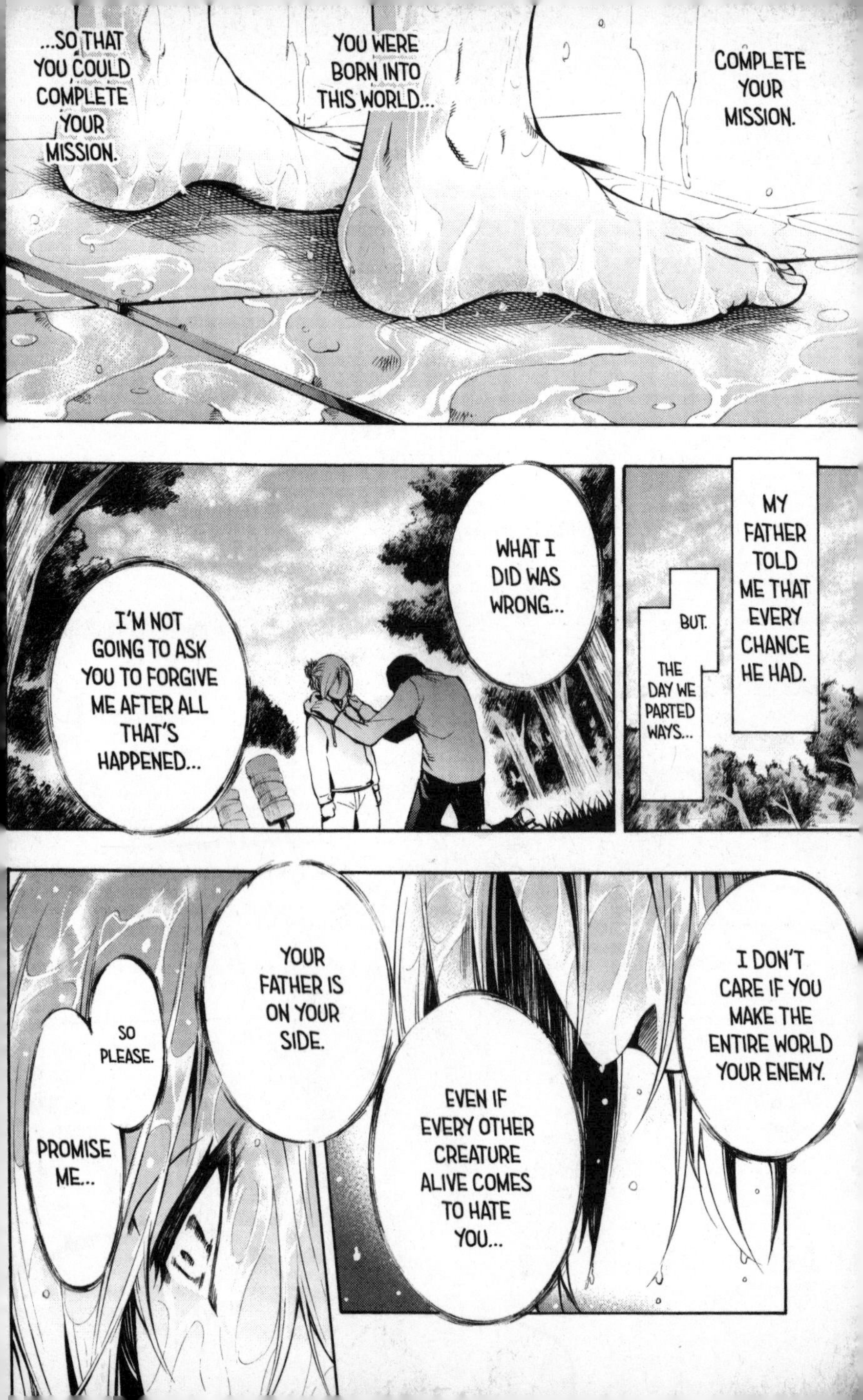
COMPLETE YOUR MISSION.
YOU WERE BORN INTO THIS WORLD...
...SO THAT YOU COULD COMPLETE YOUR MISSION.
MY FATHER TOLD ME THAT EVERY CHANCE HE HAD.
BUT.
THE DAY WE PARTED WAYS...
WHAT I DID WAS WRONG...
I'M NOT GOING TO ASK YOU TO FORGIVE ME AFTER ALL THAT'S HAPPENED...
I DON'T CARE IF YOU MAKE THE ENTIRE WORLD YOUR ENEMY.
EVEN IF EVERY OTHER CREATURE ALIVE COMES TO HATE YOU...
YOUR FATHER IS ON YOUR SIDE.
SO PLEASE.
PROMISE ME...

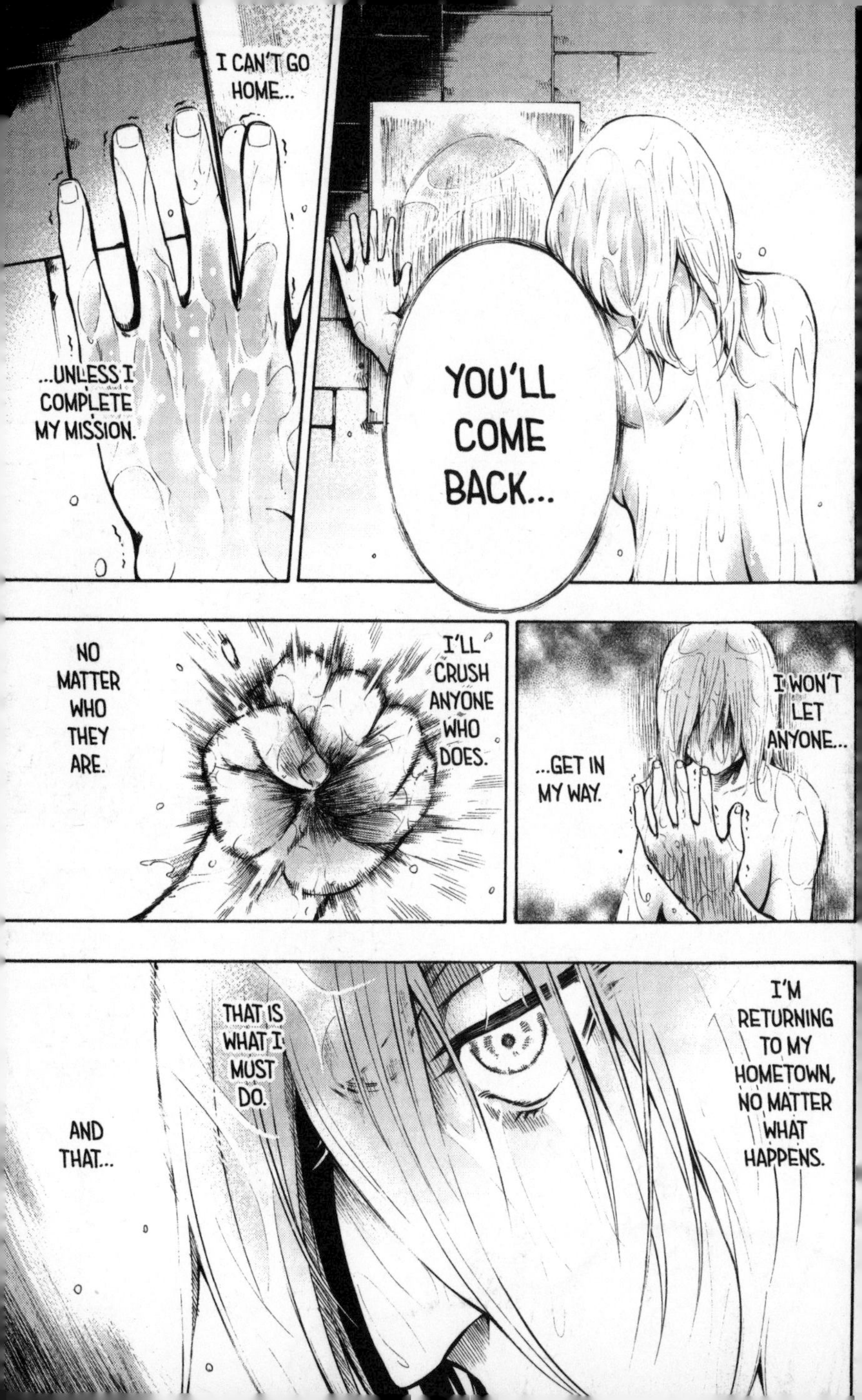
YOU'LL COME BACK...
I CAN'T GO HOME...
...UNLESS I COMPLETE MY MISSION.
I WON'T LET ANYONE...
...GET IN MY WAY.
I'LL CRUSH ANYONE WHO DOES.
NO MATTER WHO THEY ARE.
I'M RETURNING TO MY HOMETOWN, NO MATTER WHAT HAPPENS.
THAT IS WHAT I MUST DO.
AND THAT...

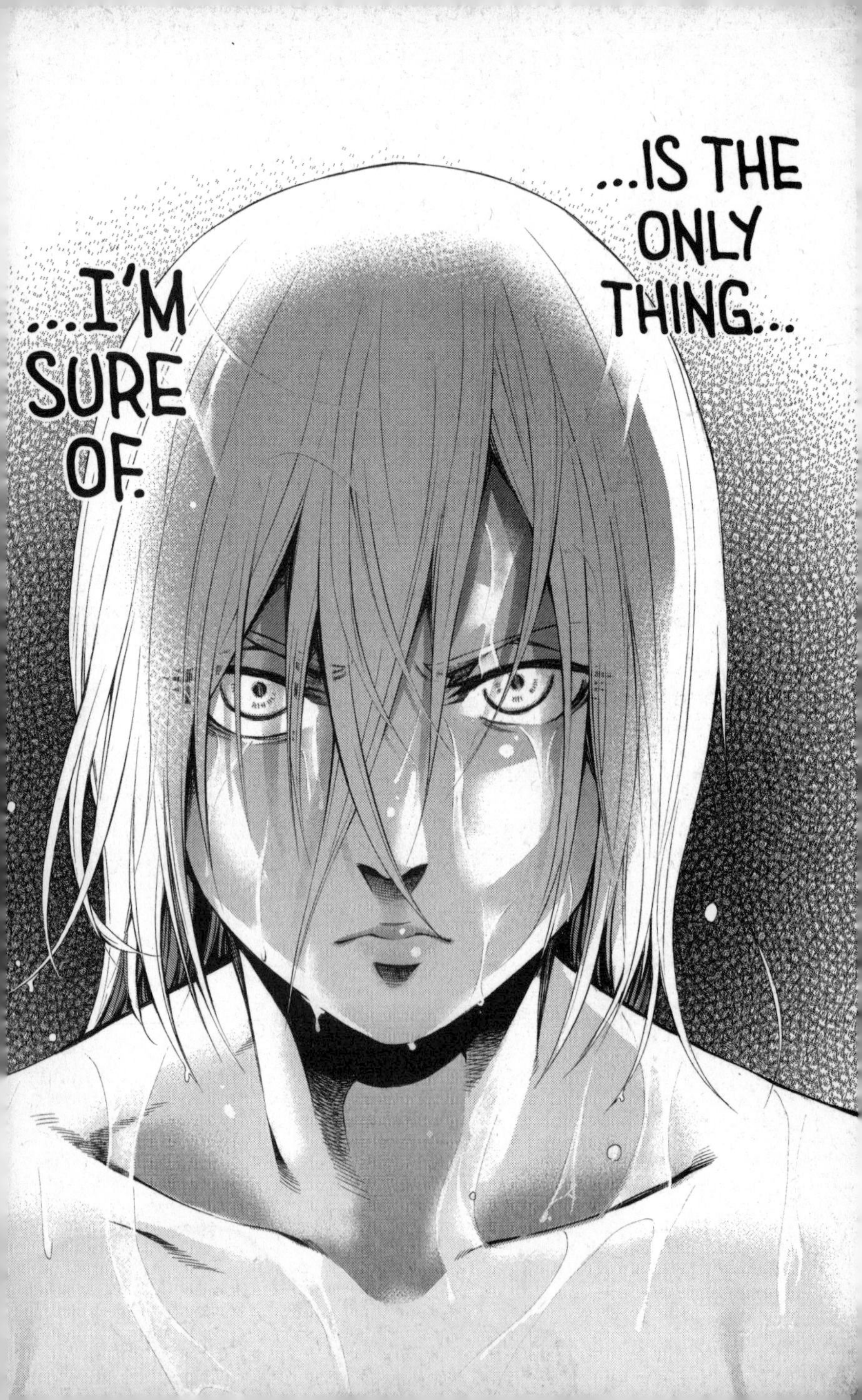
...IS THE ONLY THING...
...I'M SURE OF.

Staff

Shinichi Koseki
Kenichi Sato
Kanami Saito
Hitomi Takada
Yurie Murata
Hiroyuki Mitsui
Kazuki Nemoto
Takaaki Yamazaki

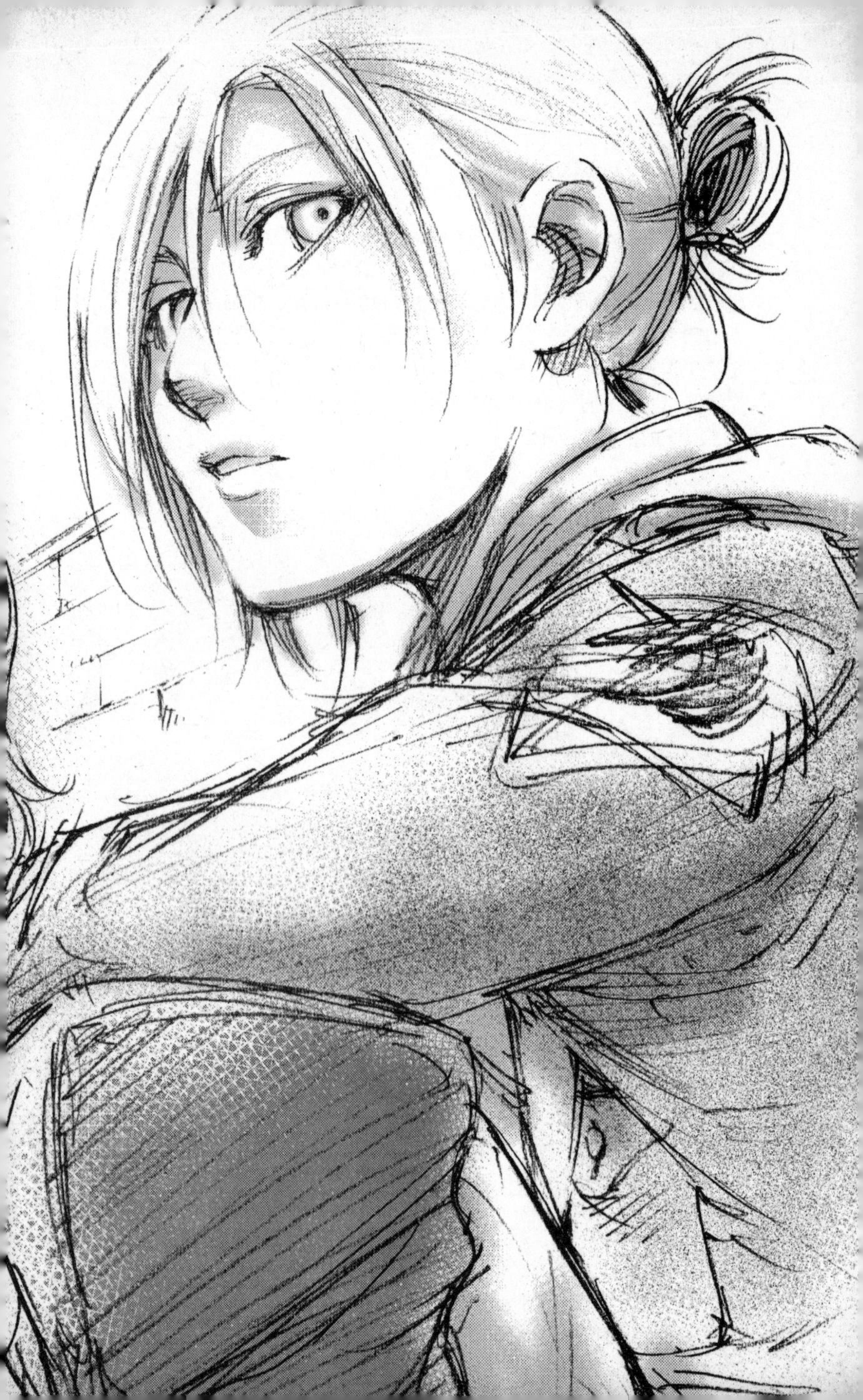

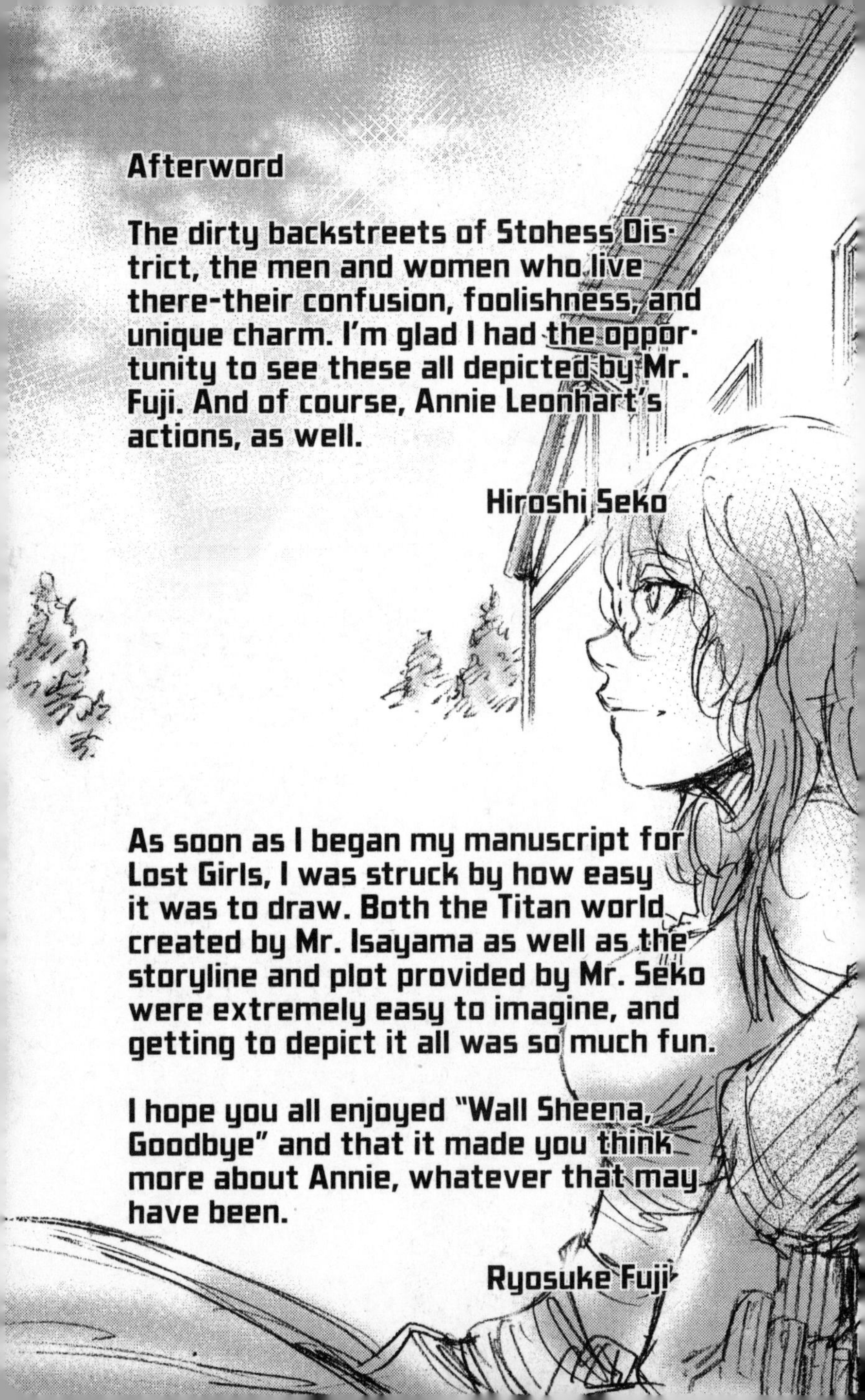

Afterword

The dirty backstreets of Stohess District, the men and women who live there-their confusion, foolishness, and unique charm. I'm glad I had the opportunity to see these all depicted by Mr. Fuji. And of course, Annie Leonhart's actions, as well.

Hiroshi Seko

As soon as I began my manuscript for Lost Girls, I was struck by how easy it was to draw. Both the Titan world created by Mr. Isayama as well as the storyline and plot provided by Mr. Seko were extremely easy to imagine, and getting to depict it all was so much fun.

I hope you all enjoyed "Wall Sheena, Goodbye" and that it made you think more about Annie, whatever that may have been.

Ryosuke Fuji

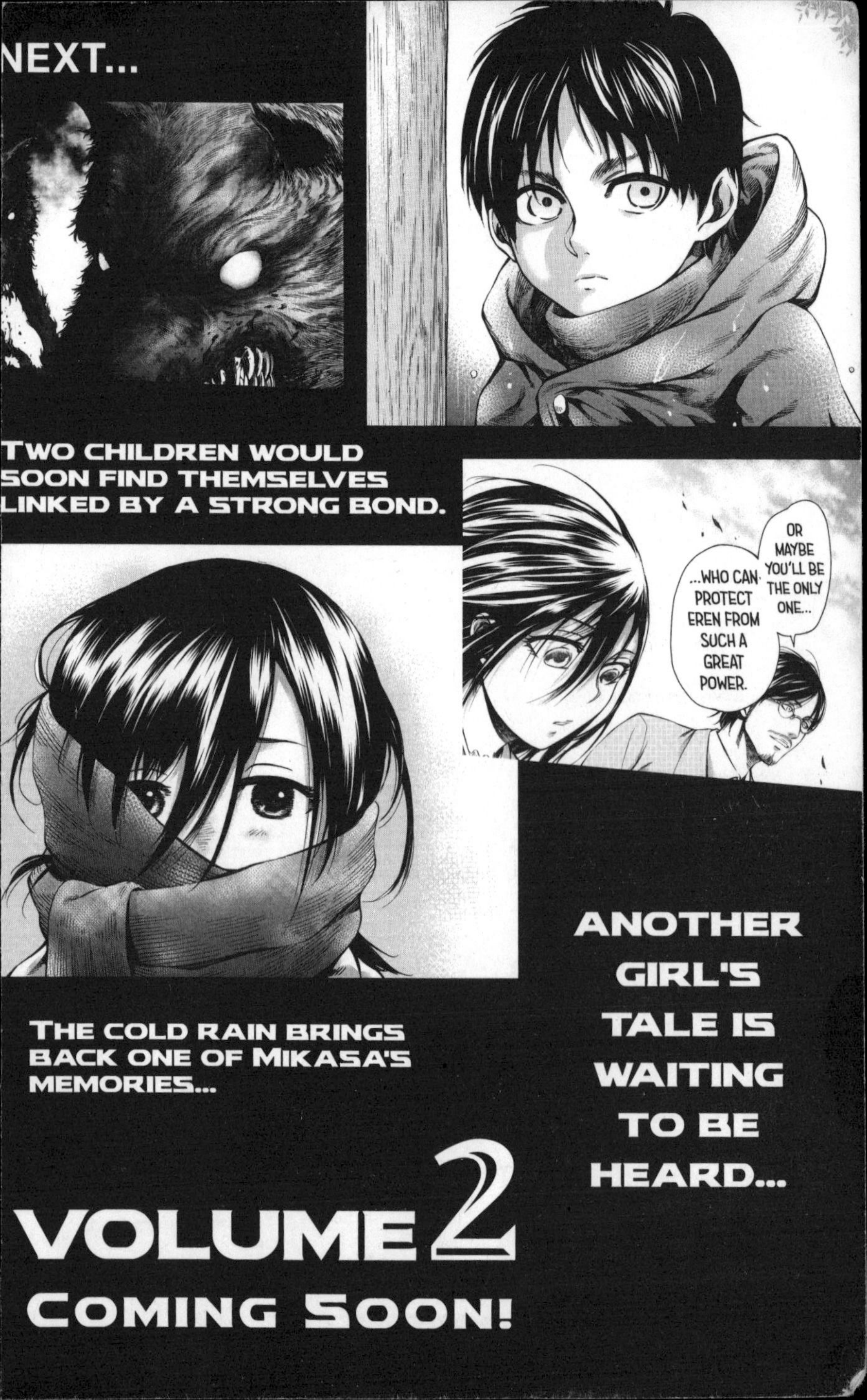
NEXT...
OR MAYBE YOU'LL BE THE ONLY ONE...
...WHO CAN PROTECT EREN FROM SUCH A GREAT POWER.
TWO CHILDREN WOULD SOON FIND THEMSELVES LINKED BY A STRONG BOND.
ANOTHER GIRL'S TALE IS WAITING TO BE HEARD...
THE COLD RAIN BRINGS BACK ONE OF MIKASA'S MEMORIES...
VOLUME 2
COMING SOON!

Attack on Titan: Lost Girls volume 1 is a work of fiction. Names, characters, places, and incidents are the products of the author's imagination or are used fictitiously. Any resemblance to actual events, locales, or persons, living or dead, is entirely coincidental.

A Kodansha Comics Trade Paperback Original

Published in the United States by Kodansha Comics, an imprint of Kodansha USA Publishing, LLC, New York.

Publication rights for this English edition arranged through Kodansha Ltd, Tokyo.

First published in Japan in 2016 by Kodansha Ltd., Tokyo as *Shingeki no kyojin LOST GIRLS*, volume 1.

ISBN 978-1-63236-385-5

Printed in the United States of America.

www.kodanshacomics.com

9 8 7 6 5 4 3 2 1
Translation: Ko Ransom
Lettering: Steve Wands
Editing: Haruko Hashimoto
Kodansha Comics edition cover design by Phil Balsman

STOP!

You are going the *wrong way!*

Manga is a *completely* different type of reading experience.

To start at the *BEGINNING,* go to the *END!*

That's right! Authentic manga is read the traditional Japanese way—from right to left, exactly the opposite of how American books are read. It's easy to follow: just go to the other end of the book, and read each page—and each panel—from the right side to the left side, starting at the top right. Now you're experiencing manga as it was meant to be.